Facing Empire

FACING EMPIRE

Indigenous Experiences in a Revolutionary Age

Edited by
Kate Fullagar and Michael A. McDonnell

FOREWORD BY Daniel K. Richter

Johns Hopkins University Press
Baltimore

Printed in the United States of America on acid-free paper
2 4 6 8 9 7 5 3 1

Johns Hopkins University Press
2715 North Charles Street
Baltimore, Maryland 21218-4363
www.press.jhu.edu

A catalog record for this book is available from the British Library.

ISBN-13: 978-1-4214-2656-3 (paperback : alk. paper)
ISBN-10: 1-4214-2656-0 (paperback : alk. paper)
ISBN-13: 978-1-4214-2657-0 (electronic)
ISBN-10: 1-4214-2657-9 (electronic)

Special discounts are available for bulk purchases of this book.
For more information, please contact Special Sales
at 410-516-6936 or specialsales@press.jhu.edu.

Johns Hopkins University Press uses environmentally friendly book materials, including recycled text paper that is composed of at least 30 percent post-consumer waste, whenever possible.

In recognition of the scholarship of
Tracey Banivanua Mar
(1974–2017)

CONTENTS

FOREWORD

"Now you are hearing the reasons of our paying so much attention to the British," the Seneca orator Sagoyewatha (Red Jacket) told a US commissioner in 1791. "[I]t is because they give us such good advice." They "always tell us we must be independent, and take advice from nobody, unless it pleases us."* Of course Sagoyewatha was speaking to the US enemies of the British and pulling their postcolonial beards. Still, it is hard to imagine a statement more opposite to the one that opens Kate Fullagar and Michael A. McDonnell's introduction to this fascinating volume: Woollarawarre Bennelong, visiting London from what colonizers called New South Wales, was so disgusted by what he heard—or rather did not hear—from British officials that, on his return home, he declared he would "go to England no more." No paying attention to British advice for him. There was no single way in which Indigenous peoples faced the British empire and heard its messages in the Age of Revolution.

Indeed, there were far more than thirteen ways, the number of chapters in this volume. As the following pages show, between about 1760 and 1840, empire revealed its many faces in places as diverse as the ones that Britons labeled Australia, North America, West Africa, the Pacific Islands, New Zealand, the Persian Gulf, and the Cape of Good Hope. Agents of the British empire used those labels as they looked out on peoples they ruled (or more often dreamed of ruling) around the world. To those peoples, however, the spaces had different names, and they belonged not to the British but to the Eora, Anishinaabeg, Fante, Māori, Wahhabis, Khoesan, and Macleods. The contributors to *Facing Empire* situate themselves in those contested

*Granville Ganter, ed., *The Collected Speeches of Sagoyewatha, or Red Jacket* (Syracuse, NY: Syracuse University Press, 2006), 27.

Indigenous spaces to help us understand the varied faces that the British empire displayed—or rather the varied faces that Indigenous peoples imposed on their would-be European rulers. For, as these chapters show, while there may have been one British empire, there was no single British imperial experience. Indigenous peoples saw to that.

So, too, did the varied ecological, human, and political landscapes where experiences of empire took shape. Indigenous Australians, Bill Gammage demonstrates, used "fire-stick farming" to divide their land into zones of "fire and no fire." Anishinaabeg, McDonnell explains, used dense but flexible bonds of kinship to structure a North American Great Lakes community that absorbed or rejected European empires on its own terms. Fante, Rebecca Shumway argues, used their connections to the British on the Gold Coast of West Africa to ward off a more threatening imperial foe, their Asante neighbors. And so it went in every locale, around the Pacific, around the Indian Ocean, around coastlines and continental interiors. What Fullagar and McDonnell call "Pathways," "Entanglements," and "Connections" all worked out largely on Indigenous terms, and, as the contributors to this volume show, it was often difficult to determine who was colonizing whom.

There was no single story, no unified British imperialism, no common experience of indigeneity. But comparisons, contrasts, and commonalities can emerge for readers who immerse themselves in the rich details these chapters provide. Familiar words take on new meanings. *Homeland security, class formation, commerce,* even *treaty* and *mission,* resonate differently after one hears from Colin G. Calloway, Nicole Ulrich, Tony Ballantyne, Robert Kenny, and Elspeth Martini. Meanwhile, unfamiliar juxtaposition—of Cherokees and Polynesians, Makahs and Māori, Asians and Scots—reveals unanticipated connections in the hands of Kate Fullagar, Joshua L. Reid, and Justin Brooks. The authors' approaches are as varied as the Indigenous spaces they explore.

To see how the British empire functioned from these varied perspectives is not just to face empire from its peripheries rather than its metropole. It is to appreciate that what those in the imperial metropole considered peripheries are better seen as empire's many centers, the dispersed sites of intense interactions with Indigenous peoples and, in many cases, settler colonists. To face empire from these dispersed centers, then, is to see imperialism at work, to glimpse anew its mechanisms, strengths, weaknesses, and violence. Most importantly, it is to escape a view of empire in which Europeans are active and Indigenous peoples passive, Europeans are aggressors and Indigenous peoples mere victims. When Sagoyewatha explained "the reasons of our paying so much attention to the British," he was also reminding us to shift our focus from the British themselves to Indigenous reasons and modes of attending to them. On the need for that shift in focus, Woollarawarre Bennelong surely would have agreed. The chapters in this volume bring us many steps closer to understanding why.

Daniel K. Richter

Facing Empire

Empire, Indigeneity, and Revolution

KATE FULLAGAR AND MICHAEL A. MCDONNELL

In the early spring of September 1795, an Indigenous Eora man arrived home on a ship from Britain. The man was Woollarawarre Bennelong. He had been gone for nearly three years, visiting the land of the people who had set up a penal colony in his native district back in 1788. Bennelong had been one of the first Aboriginal people to communicate with the leader of the New South Wales colony, Arthur Phillip. Accepting Phillip's invitation to accompany him to London in 1792, Bennelong became the first Indigenous person from today's Australia to step upon British shores.

Despite Phillip's high expectations, Bennelong did not elicit quite the level of attention in Britain that had accrued around earlier Indigenous envoys from other parts of the world. Few dignitaries were impressed enough to meet with him. Perhaps they were too distracted by the imminent prospect of war against their enemy, the French Revolutionary state. More significantly, though, Bennelong turned out to be rather "disappointed" with Britons, unmoved one way or another by their contemporary revolutionary challenges. In addition, the English weather and cramped naval living conditions made him ill and depressed.[1] Once back home, he was happy to dictate a letter to a British host confirming that "me go to England no more."[2]

Upon his return home, Bennelong forged a relationship with the incoming governor of New South Wales, John Hunter—despite his unpromising recent experience with the British. In turn, Hunter promised to maintain Phillip's open-door policy to Bennelong at Government House. Though generally unsympathetic to Aboriginal people, Hunter had learned from Phillip that the colony's success depended on good relations with Indigenous locals. For the next two years, Bennelong made occasional use of Hunter's invitation. Having seen firsthand the potential for conflict and violence between his people and the newcomers, as well as the impact of British diseases among the Eora, Bennelong wanted to keep up with all new developments around Sydney Cove. Bennelong may have been uninterested in the revolutionary politics of Europe, but he was concerned about the pathogenic and social revolutions that now threatened his community.

Still, by century's end, Bennelong was rarely seen among the white settlements. Most colonists at the time saw Bennelong's retreat from them as a form of backsliding. They shook their heads in resigned disappointment to see how he "preferred the rude and dangerous society of his own countrymen." They were sad that their own "effort was in vain," and that Bennelong was, after all, "beyond all hopes of amelioration by culture."[3] Subsequent historians have rightly cast a skeptical eye over such sentiments. But at the same time, these scholars have, on the whole, maintained the sense of decline implicit in the colonial narrative about Bennelong. They argue that Bennelong's retreat was the consequence not of his "savagery" but of his go-between status: caught between two worlds, he "rushed headlong to his dissolution"; driven by drink and despair, he "fumed his way to an outcast's grave."[4]

More recently, though, at least some historians have queried the idea that Bennelong's post-British life represented decline at all. Keith Smith, especially, has found that from the late 1790s Bennelong became a high-ranking elder among his Wangal people. He was beloved by his descendants and, later, even respected by many Indigenous rivals. His death occasioned a much grander ritual bloodletting among his kin than was typical. Bennelong's absence from the British colony turned out to indicate an important, and too-long ignored, presence elsewhere. His haggard looks later in life—so often taken to be a sign of drink—were instead perhaps the toll of responsibility in his own revolutionary age.[5]

Such a historiographical re-visioning is becoming more common in the disparate literatures on European-Indigenous relations across the globe. It has been made possible not simply by a richer and more sympathetic reading of older sources of cross-cultural encounters. It has also resulted from a total repositioning of the reader, from that of newcomers on foreign shores to that of Indigenous peoples on home shores. Drawing on innovatively researched accounts of the deep histories of Indigenous peoples—many of which have been written or recorded by Indigenous peoples themselves—historians of the colonial experience have begun to move beyond the standard encounter story to reconstruct a fuller picture of the early modern era.

This was the kind of move that both of us found ourselves undertaking, though separately, while colleagues at the University of Sydney (just a few miles south of Bennelong's country). McDonnell had published previously on conflicts between revolutionaries during the American War of Independence but was now moving toward a history of the Great Lakes Indians before and during the birth of the new republic.[6] Fullagar had worked earlier on popular British responses to "New World" Indigenous peoples visiting the eighteenth-century metropolis, but she was now turning the tables to investigate the experiences of the visitors themselves across the Age of Revolution.[7] Suddenly, our shared interest in Indigenous histories instigated serious conversations. In retrospect, it is odd that our initial research projects had not brought us together before—both dealt, after all, with the same empire in the same era. While this initial disconnect may be an indictment of the blinkering effect of national borders and historiographical trends in American and British history (and no doubt on ourselves), it was also revealing. Among the myriad promises of Indigenous history is the way it can raise questions about old historiographical boundaries and offer possibilities for new linkages and collaborations.[8]

One of our first conversations focused on the main models available for thinking about the Indigenous past in relation to European imperial edifices, especially in the critical period we now call the Age of Revolution. We had both benefited enormously from the finely grained studies of Indigenous societies that had flowered, in bursts, from the 1970s—especially, in our cases, of Native American and Pacific Islander societies. The depth of worlds recovered by scholars such as Theda Perdue on the Cherokee or Malama Meleisea on Samoans was a deafening rebuke to the idea that Indigenous peoples were "without history."[9] But these examples were not necessarily solutions to our problem of thinking about Indigenous relations with European empires from Indigenous perspectives. (Few Indigenous-focused historians, understandably, had much or any interest in diverting attention away from their recovery projects to go over what they considered to be more than well-worn historical tracks.) In other words, if we take the case of Bennelong, we valued the work done to recover his deeper Indigenous past, but we wanted eventually to return to the original question of his supposedly curious relationship with the British colony—only now with fresher eyes and more nuanced knowledge.

We also admired, and had even occasionally engaged in ourselves, the kind of "cross-cultural" history that tries to draw out "both sides" of a relationship between European and Indigenous. "Encounter histories" such as Richard White's influential work on the Great Lakes or Inga Clendinnen on Mexico have done much to destabilize old certainties of the imperial past. They have made us sensitive to seeing the means by which Indigenous peoples shaped relations, and ways of relating, with European newcomers in specific and often very local contexts. But including Indigenous voices is not the same as hearing the story from their perspective.[10] In Bennelong's case, again, it was because so many later historians maintained the centrality of the encounter in their investigations that they did not see alternative narratives for his behavior. We wanted to write histories of empire that did more than just include Indigenous people; we wanted to write histories of empire with Indigenous people as the *main* subjects.

Finally, we wanted to try to reenvision this history across a particularly crucial era in imperial and modern history. The deep histories of Indigenous peoples, together with the creative ways historians have begun to reimagine Indigenous-European relations in a variety of contexts, raised questions for us about the role of Indigenes in world history at a moment in which older ideas about politics, economics, and societies were coming undone. While for many Europeans the Age of Revolution ushered in new democratic possibilities, newly industrialized arrangements, and new public and private mores, it also reshaped and expanded the global imperial map. There was a profound acceleration in encounters and contacts between new peoples around the world. In the end, this may constitute the most significant revolution of all.

What did revolution look like to Indigenous peoples? What connections did they make between themselves, newcomers, and other Indigenous peoples, and what lessons were learned? In what ways did Indigenous people like Bennelong shape this critical moment in the global past?

Facing Empire

This collection is a first step in trying to answer these questions. Recognizing that much of the valuable insights from the new literature on Indigenous peoples still comes from those with a local or regional focus, we wanted to bring together emerging and senior scholars of often compartmentalized regions to put their work into conversation with one another in a more expansive, comparative framework. Our starting point was our shared appreciation of Daniel Richter's conceptually innovative work *Facing East from Indian*

Country: A Native History of Early America (2001). This book shows ways of narrating the foundational history of neo-imperial nations where Indigenous people were not just important but center stage throughout.[11]

Despite growing awareness of the place of Indigenous peoples in the history of an expanding British empire, and our increasingly sophisticated studies of Indigenous peoples themselves across the Revolutionary era, few scholars have tried to think comparatively about Indigenous experiences within and across expanding imperial borders. Historians of empire are now more attuned than ever to the interplay between the local and metropolitan, and have explored the myriad ways in which Indigenous people shaped European exploration, scientific expeditions, missionary efforts, and colonial settlement. Some scholars have also gone so far as to analyze the two-way processes at play—between colonizers and the colonized but also between periphery and metropole.[12] Yet comparative efforts across empire and between places have almost invariably taken a European perspective, as historians have followed on the shoulders of mobile British explorers, traders, missionaries, and settlers. In this seemingly European-driven imperial story, Indigenous peoples too often become distant and passive players—objects of European exploration, exchange, sexual relations, legalities, and academic consideration. This volume aims to switch that around, focusing instead on different Indigenous peoples and the various ways they found themselves "facing empire."[13]

Certainly, there are some good reasons for the scholarly neglect of such an enterprise, and to tread carefully in thinking comparatively about Indigenous experiences across empire. The great strength of recent, deep Indigenous histories, after all, has been the careful and very local excavations of cultures and knowledges that have emphasized complex pasts, dynamic and complicated relations with newcomers, as well as Indigenous resilience and persistence to the present. When we look at suprahistorical patterns, we run the danger of losing this depth. As Peter Wood noted some time ago, the multilayered stories of protracted, cumulative, and reciprocal associations—involving war and peace, weapons and diseases, sexuality and kinship, food and clothing, songs and stories, ideas and beliefs—that extended over many generations too often in large-scale surveys give way to summaries of "brief, decisive, and one-sided confrontations."[14] Given that many rich Indigenous histories are still not yet well integrated into larger national narratives, comparative work runs the risk of similar compression.

We need only look at the genealogy of Atlantic history, or even some settler colonial studies, to see just how much comparative-minded scholars can push Indigenous peoples even further into the background.[15] In addition, we recognize that some scholars might be reluctant to perpetuate the European framing that such a comparative effort must still entail: to place in historical relation Indigenous peoples from a scattered range of places on the globe who shared only a common experience of contact with European empires is to grant some special privilege to those very European empires.

Yet we argue that reluctance has come at a price. First, we miss opportunities to understand how Indigenous peoples shared some common means of repelling, accommodating, or appropriating the European encounter. Are there more similarities or more differences in the ways diverse peoples in the Americas, Africa, and the Antipodes treated gender relations, went to war, or conducted diplomacy with expectant Europeans? What common or opposing factors shaped Algonquian, Eora, and Xhosa responses to British trading and territorial claims in 1763, 1788, and 1795? Thanks to works that have "faced empire" in certain moments, we have more understanding of the complicated variables at play in European-Indigenous relations in specific settings from native, rather than newcomer, perspectives. But we now need to try to discover some larger patterns. Scholars sensitive to the nuances of these diverse histories must be able to answer some of these basic questions in order to inform the work of those already making comparisons across imperial sites—who too often rely on an older or more simplistic literature of Indigenous history. If historians trained and immersed in new approaches to Indigenous history do not ask or try to answer these questions, we lose the chance to enrich so-called transnational or global approaches.

Through comparison, we can also begin to map out possible networks of resistance, exchange, and communication among and between Indigenous communities during this period. We already know about at least some of the extensive networks of trade and communication among different Indigenous groups across rivers, lakes, and vast tracts of land in the Americas, Africa, and Australia, for example. Such networks helped prepare many Indigenous peoples for encounters with Europeans long before they ever saw them and shaped their response to the newcomers. As McDonnell points out in chapter 2, the networks also later provided the architecture for new imperial initiatives, as well as the nucleus for coordinated movements of resistance to, and exchanges with, Europeans. From time to time, too, we get tantalizing glimpses of disparate communities of Indigenous peoples laboring, exploring, sailing, fighting, marrying, and eventually communicating across far-flung imperial quarters. In growing numbers during the eighteenth century—like the subjects of Fullagar's and Martini's chapters, for instance—many Indigenous peoples traveled in formal groups to Europe. Others served informally in or with European armies and navies. Many more joined crews of merchant ships plying legal and illegal waters. Who did they talk to? What stories did they tell? Imperialism was a destructive force in the lives of many Indigenous communities, but it also created opportunities for meeting new allies and for the creation of ever-wider networks of resistance. We need more focus on these moments and some thought about their possible meanings and impact.

Once we have a deeper understanding of the differences, similarities, and connections between diverse Indigenous groups, and particularly their relations with Europeans, we can measure more effectively their overall influence on European theories, policies, and practices. A new generation of historians have written not just Indigenous-centered stories, but they have also demonstrated how profoundly native peoples have shaped European history, particularly at the specific, colonial level. We now have an opportunity to think about how Indigenous-shaped local exchanges, cultural relations, and intercultural warfare provoked discussion and policymaking in Whitehall as much as it did in Charleston, Cape Town, or Sydney. Even more than this, facing empire from Indigenous perspectives may push us to reform or transform the way we think about these processes. At the very least, facing empire will help move us closer to challenging our ideas of what is central in driving imperial history, from the "newcomers" to the "natives."

Indigenous Experiences

With some sense of a model, then, we set about inviting scholars to join us in a collective attempt to "face empire." Very quickly, we realized the necessity to impose some limits—for an initial publication anyway. First, we decided to deal only with Indigenous experiences of the British empire. This was the empire we knew best as historians, but it was also one of the most wide-ranging and longest-felt empires in modern times. And while we contemplated a more global approach—to encompass the extraordinary range of experiences elsewhere in this same era, such as in South and Central America—we concluded that focusing only on British expansion would help us better assess Indigenous influences on empire. Second, we narrowed the period to what has been variously termed the Age of Revolution, the "Imperial Meridian," or even the "birth of modernity"—again, familiar terrain for us but also, as discussed further later on, a turning point for both imperialism and Indigenous people.[16]

The most important limit to clarify, of course, was our definition of Indigeneity. Many historians struggle with the term. As C. A. Bayly long ago pointed out, it has always been "fractured and contested."[17] If it is always tied to land, how do we account for Indigenous mobility? If it is always tied to originality, how do we account for Indigenous people who colonize? How do we deal with mixed communities? And does there have to be a straight line of descent from Indigenous people in the past to Indigenous people in the present, and if so, how is that to be measured?

Bayly himself answered these queries by taking a metahistorical approach, pointing out that as an "epistemological" (or comparable) category at least, Indigenous people were the "creation" of empire—created, indeed, during the period investigated here.[18] While useful in reminding us of the artifices implied in the term, such an approach does not necessarily help us bridge the divide between its emergence in an imperial language and its currency in the global present. Contemporary international organizations such as the United Nations have preferred to define Indigenous as an identity both self-claimed and community endorsed.[19] Such an emphasis on identity must be absorbed for our histories to have any resonance or meaning today, but then so must a nod to why organizations like the United Nations should care about this identity in the first place. The peak international body for Indigenous studies, NAISA (Native American and Indigenous Studies Association), has offered a robust combination of each of these moves, stressing the need for self- and group inclusion as well as referencing the "hundreds of years of ongoing colonialism around the world" that led to the categorization.[20]

Similarly, our collective comparative Indigenous history of empire combines contemporary and historical valencies in understanding who counted as Indigenous in our given period. Indigenous people facing the British empire between 1760 and 1840, then, were those living in parts of three different oceanic regions—the Atlantic, the Pacific, and the Indian Oceans—who controlled the key resources desired by imperialists during this time *and* whose descendent communities still attest to the legacies of the British arrival. Our definition of "key resources" is necessarily broad. As the chapters by Gammage, Kenny, Shumway, and others here show, land was very often the resource most desired. Scholars Zoe Laidlaw and Alan Lester have recently commented on the "pervasive" and "close relationship" between "land-holding" and Indigeneity in both the colonial past and modern historiography.[21] This makes sense for readers interested solely in settler colonialism. But during the Age of Revolution, desired resources included more than just land. Reid's chapter in this volume details how marine space was often the first resource negotiated between Indigenous people and Britons. Sivasundaram and Ulrich point to the critical role of labor. Calloway's chapter reminds us of the role of arms and diplomatic skill; Newell's of food and sex; Ballantyne's, indeed, of no less than the convertible soul. The resources embedded in Indigenous identity for our period are vast.

Our definition of "descendent communities" is less clearly stated in the following chapters, which all make their claims on the present fairly implicit. What is certain is an eschewal of blood as the only means of measuring descent. All the Indigenous societies discussed in this volume have communities who recognize them as ancestors today, but each would trace the connection through a shared sense of social, cultural, religious, or historical practice rather than any unit of modern medicine. As many of the chapters in this volume are at pains to point out, Indigenous people were often already intensely cosmopolitan figures by the time Britons turned up. Indigenous intermixing with others during the imperial moment—like the Tahitians and Samoans of Newell's chapter or the Iroquois Confederacy of Calloway's chapter—only added to their mixed bloodlines. Recent scholarship elsewhere has argued with some passion how tracing descent through blood has a long history of perpetuating both the inclusions and exclusions that empires sought to embed.[22]

So, too, we might add, our volume eschews any hard line on descent through a steady understanding of place. While some of the Indigenous subjects here would see some descendants in recognizable places—the Eora of New South Wales and the Māori of Aotearoa, for instance—others, such as the lascars around the Indian Ocean or the slaves throughout the Cape, produced people who now locate their history of removal or mobility at the heart of their sense of Indigeneity.

To say all this another way, then, our volume does not limit the Indigenous only to those associated with now-dispossessed land. As Ravi de Costa has argued, if the term "Indigenous people" was first coined to signify those victimized by the particular structures of settler (land-focused) colonialism, it now includes those with other histories of other forms of imperial reach.[23] Our volume's definition of empire is much broader than merely settler colonialism.

As well, this collection does not wish to conjure the specter of authenticity when discussing Indigenous people. The proceeding chapters demonstrate that if the idea of a pure identity is a problematic notion for Indigenous people today, it was hardly less so two hundred years ago. "There was no authentic and 'pure' Indigenous identity" at the moment of contact, write Laidlaw and Lester, "just as there was no authentic and 'pure' British identity for colonial[s]."[24] The latter point is perhaps most aptly shown here in Brooks's chapter on differing British relations with various Indigenes, including the sometimes-inside, sometimes-outside Highland Scots.

A Revolutionary Age

As this volume was coming together, we were delighted to find two collections appear that answered some of our pleas for a comparative Indigenous history of empire. Jane Carey and Jane Lydon's *Indigenous Networks: Mobility, Connections and Exchange* (2014) and Zoe Laidlaw and Alan Lester's *Indigenous Communities and Settler Colonialism* (2015) make excellent starts on the benefits to accrue from placing deep histories of Indigenous peoples facing empire into a comparative frame.[25] They also challenge imperial and transnational historians to start taking seriously Indigenous peoples as dynamic and mobile historical actors. Both these volumes, however, concentrate on the nineteenth century and beyond (and Laidlaw and Lester focus, too, only on settler colonies). Neither tackles the critical period in which Britain both lost and gained an empire amid intensely global revolutionary struggles, and in which Indigenous peoples across the world faced similar challenges and opportunities in a range of different colonizing scenarios.

The Age of Revolution is currently enjoying something of a renaissance due to both the rebirth of Atlantic history and the surge of interest around the origins of the newly coined Anthropocene. Yet whether you take your cue from the Haitian radicals of C. L. R. James's *The Black Jacobins*, the liberal democrats of R. R. Palmer's *The Age of the Democratic Revolution*, the industrial workers and capitalists of Hobsbawm's *The Age of Revolution*, the motley crew of Rediker and Linebaugh's *The Many-Headed Hydra*, or the scientists and thinkers of Paul Dukes's *Minutes to Midnight*, one would struggle to find Indigenous peoples at all, let alone Indigenous peoples as the driving part of the story. They sometimes appear at the margins of liberationist stories, such as in North America, where they are typically depicted as being compelled by Europeans to make the best of a number of bad choices in choosing a side. In accounts of industrialization, they are usually accorded less agency than the commodities and textiles their bodies produced in order to foster commerce and manufacturing. And, of course, we know and sometimes acknowledge that dispossessed Indian lands were used to provide much of the fuel—in the form of new crops—driving the globally momentous turn to fossil fuels. In these studies, Indigenous peoples are victims, and objects of study, often hidden pawns in a game in which they could only lose.[26]

The omission is curious in part because overlaid across the same decades we typically think of as encompassing the Age of Revolution, from roughly 1760 to 1840, Europeans swarmed around the globe in a period of dramatic imperial expansion. At the heart of this movement was a "swing to the east" as European attention and interest turned from the Atlantic to new prizes and riches in the Pacific and Indian Oceans. Central to this swing were encounters with Indigenous peoples—in Africa, India, Australasia, and the Pacific. As Europeans expanded their reach, these meetings multiplied exponentially and were informed by the lessons learned or unlearned from imperial projects in the Atlantic. As Susan Thorne has noted, by 1820 the British empire alone had already "absorbed" almost one-quarter of the world's population. It is time to take account of the new relationships across this period when we discuss and define a "Revolutionary Age."[27]

In addition, when we do take into account Indigenous peoples in this Age of Revolution, we stand to gain a new perspective on the origins, nature, and consequences of Europe's so-called democratic and industrial revolutions. Contests with Indigenous peoples over land, resources, and new commodities sparked eighteenth-century imperial expansion, fueled economic innovations, and precipitated global conflict. For example, historians have now firmly established the role Native Americans played in precipitating and shaping both the Seven Years' War and the American Revolution—critical events that underpinned the Age of Revolution.[28] And as the essays by McDonnell and Calloway show, native peoples continued to influence and shape continental history in North America, but also as a consequence, conflicts in Europe and other colonial sites around the globe. As they did so, Indigenous peoples themselves were engaged in their own declarations of independence and enmeshed in vital contests over defining sovereignty that continue to reverberate today. The Age of Revolution was not merely a European construct.[29]

Indigenous peoples everywhere helped create and exploit the instabilities at the heart of the Age of Revolution. As Shumway's chapter on the West

African Fante demonstrates, they sometimes exploited European political conflicts, tensions, and uncertainties to enmesh them in local conflicts that were not always advantageous to empire. At other times, as Martini's chapter on the Anishinaabe Shawundais indicates, they made vital connections with newcomers that would both lay a foundation for future relations with European empires and form precedents for pan-Indigenous resistance movements. From playing a crucial role in the movement toward a more powerful centralized neo-imperial state in North America, to accelerating British territorial expansion in Africa, and more, Indigenous peoples helped create instabilities on the new frontiers that gave geographic shape and intellectual stimulus to nineteenth-century imperialism. They also contributed to the global interconnectedness of the economic and political turbulence of this period that C. A. Bayly has described as the "world crisis" that underpinned the Age of Revolution.[30]

Indeed, bringing Indigenous experiences into focus across this critical period might yet also give us a basis for a new kind of thinking about periodization per se. Such a reconsideration would firmly tie the roots of the newly reanalyzed "Settler Revolution" to the Age of Revolution—as both Reid and Kenny here remind us. Likewise, as Ballantyne's chapter signals, the origins of the globalization of Christianity might be traced to this period, too. In turn, we would be compelled to rethink ideas and concepts such as independence, sovereignty, and even the very notion of "European" and "Indigenous" peoples that arose in this era.[31]

Pathways, Entanglements, Connections

With these considerations and goals in mind, our contributors got to work. Some revisited and drew from recent research projects, and others saw this as an opportunity to pursue new leads. As the chapters came in, we urged engagement with each other's work, and encouraged each other to tease out the broader implications of our findings. It was no easy task. All of us found it harder than expected—not just to seek out the voices of Indigenous actors but also to keep in mind the general question about how they faced empire. And we also turned up darker stories than anticipated, too—ones where it was difficult to focus on Indigenous agency given the limited evidence available and the horrifically one-sided circumstances people suffered.

Moreover, when engaging with each other's chapters, we all found ourselves on some unfamiliar terrain, be it geographic, historic, or historiographic. But in confronting this unfamiliarity, we also found ourselves thinking creatively about how to frame it all. Indeed, as we read the essays together, some patterns emerged that suggested an alternate arrangement from the geographic or chronological plan initially envisaged. It was clear, for example, that in different places and at different times, Indigenous peoples experienced the coming of European empire in similar ways. Their own deep histories, rivalries with one another and with other Europeans, and their expectations and interests shaped first encounters, influenced the type and degree of enmeshment with the newcomers, and created the conditions for further associations and relationships with empire or each other. Separated by time and space, Indigenous experiences of empire cycled through phases that we have labeled pathways, entanglements, and connections.

Part I: Pathways

The chapters in this initial section remind us how much Indigenous peoples themselves defined the terms of new encounters in this era. It also introduces us to all five key areas canvased in the collection: North America, Australia, Africa, the Pacific Ocean, and the Indian Ocean. In each, everywhere they moved Britons traveled down distinctly Indigenous pathways. Indeed, all across the so-called old and new British empires, powerful groups of Indigenous peoples drew the British into new and uncertain environmental, diplomatic, and commercial worlds that rested on Indigenous foundations.

Bill Gammage opens the section with his bold thesis that Indigenous Australians not only practiced "fire-stick farming" in certain regions before and during Britain's earliest settlement but managed the entire continent through their complex understanding and use of "fire and no fire." Elsewhere, Gammage has argued that the extent of their control ("maintaining abundance" without traditional agricultural forms) is of world-historical significance. Australian Aboriginals rotated their efforts to suit conditions and to make resources "abundant, convenient, and predictable" across "the biggest estate on earth"; they encouraged a planned mobility that Europeans thought merely nomadic.[32] Europeans could often only make sense of the country because Aboriginal peoples had rendered it less "formidable" and more like the European "parks" that signified wealth and leisure to the invaders. It was a pathway that lured them to the most valuable land, even while they were oblivious to its managed state and importance in Aboriginal lives.

Gammage's work raises questions about the ecological histories of other places, particularly North America, and the unseen relations between land

and people that Europeans had trouble discerning but that profoundly shaped encounters throughout the early modern period and into the Age of Revolution. Yet even while the British wondered at the "estates" they found in Australia, they grappled with a different unseen pathway in North America. As Michael A. McDonnell notes in his chapter, when the British took possession of French settlements and territorial claims around the Great Lakes region in 1763, they also inherited a set of diverse and complex *relations* with Indigenous peoples. Native peoples soon made it clear that any territorial claims the British hoped to uphold would rest on a complicated Indian history that stretched well beyond the point of contact with Europeans, and with it a well-oiled practice of conducting trade and diplomacy hammered out on Indian terms. The British came to realize how dependent they were on this Indian world and were forced to adapt—with significant consequences for imperial relations more generally. As in Australia, the architecture of empire in the new British North American territories would be built on Indigenous pathways.

Deep and long inter-Indigenous relations, as well as shrewd diplomatic and trading practices, similarly shaped British ventures in West Africa in the Age of Revolution. As Rebecca Shumway shows, in what is now southern Ghana the Fante's relationship with the neighboring Asante compelled the British to retain and protect forts on the Gold Coast long after they wished to leave. With the abolition of the slave trade, there was little to formally hold the British in West Africa. But fear of European rivals and complicated prior commercial ties made them equivocate. Like the Anishinaabe Odawa of the Great Lakes, which McDonnell discusses, the Fante enmeshed the British in West African politics to their advantage at this very moment. Fante elites exploited British ambivalence, gaining arms and wealth in the process to help defend themselves against Asante rivals and to rebuild their economy after a drastic decline in their export trade. Though difficult to appreciate in retrospect, Indigenous peoples in West Africa thus dictated British imperial policy at a critical and uncertain moment in the Age of Revolution, even while these policies also tragically and paradoxically laid the groundwork for formal European colonization of the region later in the century.

In her exploration of British ventures in the Pacific, Jennifer Newell takes her cue from Islander scholars who have stressed Indigenous connections and knowledges across a unifying "sea of islands," in order to return us to the importance of Indigenous and environmental interactions in shaping European colonial projects. Newell's focus is Tahiti and Samoa. She also reminds us of some of the unequal exchanges that shaped colonization—life-giving food and cloth for deadly viruses and bacteria. Still, what the British could and could not do in the Pacific was often controlled by preexisting Indigenous relations to the land and animals upon which they relied and the cosmology that sustained those relations. Though British ecological and religious convictions eventually had a profound effect in the Pacific, it is notable, as Newell states, that by the end of our era "Britain had surrendered its interests in both Tahiti and Samoa"—in good measure because of its inability to overcome the difficulties posed by the preexisting pathways.

Sujit Sivasundaram's chapter on the Persian Gulf continues the maritime theme of Newell's to close this opening section. It also affirms the explicit claim of Newell that focusing on Indigenous peoples can illuminate new ways of viewing European imperialism and the Age of Revolution. Specifically, what Sivasundaram reveals is that in this case of an Indian Oceanic entrepôt, no one prior pathway dominated later encounters. The Revolutionary Gulf proved to be a far more "tangled" scene than any single empire could hope to comprehend. It included, after all, not just the competitions of multiple Arab states but also the effects of the Parsi from Bombay and of *lascar* sailors from around the region. The British never did "fill the whole picture" in the Gulf, as Sivasundaram notes, precisely because the "circles of historical memory" there during this critical era allowed for multiple groups to simultaneously "find their own paths."

Part II: Entanglements

Across the Age of Revolution, the initial pathways laid down by Indigenous peoples and encountered by British colonizers led to maturing relations and a variety of entanglements—political, economic, social, cultural, and religious. While we often note the ways in which Indigenous peoples were affected or changed in this process, we view native peoples less frequently as agents themselves. Yet, in the key areas of warfare and diplomacy, labor activism, missionary activity, and land settlement—all areas that help further define and refine an Age of Revolution—Indigenous peoples played pivotal roles. The chapters in this section demonstrate just how much the British found themselves entangled and enmeshed in a world that they had not envisioned at the start of the era, with diverse consequences for both Indigenous peoples and newcomers.

Colin Calloway's chapter shifts our North American focus from the Great Lakes to the Ohio Valley. Like the Anishinaabe of the Lakes, the Ohio Indians frustrated British imperial plans and were key in both the Seven Years' War and the American Revolution. They subsequently helped keep British-American animosity alive while protecting their own interests: British dependence on Native Americans in the Age of Revolution would help precipitate another North American conflict, the War of 1812. Like other essays in this collection, Calloway reminds us of the insights to be gained when focused on Indigenous histories and perspectives. In the case of the Ohio Indians, re-centering Indigenous history allows us to move past our retrospective and distorting views of revolutionary conquest. It makes us reconsider an era in which "Indian nations stalled the 'course of empire' in the Ohio country, when Indigenous foreign policies trumped imperial ambitions, and when Indigenous power shaped imperial outcomes and threatened the future of the United States."

Nicole Ulrich returns us to the African continent, this time to the southern Cape region. Her focus on the "popular classes" in this intensely diverse place reminds us of the ways in which Indigeneity could be multiple and changing all at once. By investigating the labor activism of slaves and ex-slaves, Asian servants, Khoesan laborers, and many others, she dramatizes the "historical juncture" of revolutionary proletarian consciousness with uneven imperial expansion. She shows her "motley crew" as being both shaped by and active agents against the resultant labor regime. Despite increasing discipline, they also prompted many real reforms from the British governors at the Cape—reforms and discussions that resonated across the expanding British empire.

If Indigenous peoples could and did affect British political ambitions, they also played a role in shaping global Christian evangelicalism. Tony Ballantyne charts this development by focusing on the interplay between the Church Missionary Society (CMS) and a small but influential group of rangatira (chiefs) from New Zealand's North Island. Sharpening "entanglement" as an analytical tool, Ballantyne focuses on "improvement" as a common goal of colonizers and the colonized, and the religious, economic, and political motives that gave rise to it on both sides. In part a reaction to Indigenous resistance to missionizing efforts in Tahiti, New South Wales, and elsewhere, the CMS linked "Christianity and Commerce" from an early stage. Ballantyne reminds us that while Indigenous sociopolitical formation and the cultural logics of Indigenous actions are crucial to understanding the nature and timing of missionary efforts, we also need to know how these interacted with imperial institutions and networks to understand how Māori and

Britons were increasingly drawn together and entangled in each other's histories.

As in New Zealand, previous British entanglements with Indigenous peoples in Australia also shaped new imperial efforts, and particularly what scholars have sometimes called the "settler revolution." The devastating tragedy of the Tasmanian Black Wars compelled British officials on the ground to turn back to the idea of treaty-making first tested in the North American context. Drawing on his previous groundbreaking work on Batman's Treaty of 1835, Robert Kenny explores the specific Indigenous worldview of one of the signatories to it.[33] He reminds us of the human and nonhuman relationships that shaped initial entanglements but also led to conflict. Indeed, if the more tragic consequences of Māori-British entanglements were opaque for some time in New Zealand, such was not the case for the western Taungurung people of present-day Victoria, Australia. Within a few years of the signing of the historic treaty, the "settler revolution" had a devastating deadly effect as British settlers killed and pushed Indigenous peoples from the land—testimony to the fact that entanglements, of course, could often be more destructive than productive.

Part III: Connections

Biography has rarely favored the Indigene, particularly in the early modern period when sources are scarce. But in her comparative history of two late eighteenth-century Indigenous visitors to Britain, Cherokee Ostenaco and Ra'iatean Mai, Kate Fullagar makes the argument that a biographical approach can make fruitful sense of the experiences of traveling Indigenous peoples. It can also, through its emphasis on whole lives, help bring the historical moment of imperial encounter for Indigenous people down to more modest size. As Fullagar shows, while visits to London did not figure as centrally in the lives of Indigenous travelers as we might have expected, their presence in the imperial metropole nonetheless often stirred contentious debates about the nature and meaning of empire at a critical moment. Moreover, the array of interests that brought Mai and Ostenaco to British shores connected their stories, as well as their histories, to that of empire.

Joshua L. Reid also employs a directly comparative approach in his study of Indigenous-Anglo interactions in the Pacific, specifically among the Makah of the Olympic Peninsula in northwest North America and the Māori of New Zealand's South Island. Reid pushes us to reconsider the centrality of contests over land at the start of the settler revolution and instead to see contests over marine space and its many resources as an important component of the early conflict over the Pacific British West. From Indigenous perspectives, such contests linked disparate regions and different peoples, and established long-running patterns that shaped relations between Indigenous peoples and settler-colonial governments. They also show us how much Indigenous peoples actively sought to engage with expanding settler-colonial economies even while they retained control over their marine spaces and resources. As Reid notes, these stories complicate binary narratives that are too focused on mobile settlers dispossessing Indigenous victims. They also help us understand the deep roots of contests over marine resources that continue today.

If marine space connected the experiences of Makah and Māori in the Pacific, imperial policy connected Indigenous peoples across North America, Scotland, and India. Indeed, by examining British imperial policy across its expanding empire in the mid-to-late eighteenth century, Justin Brooks pushes at the definition of Indigeneity and argues that we must not see it as necessarily fixed in any group but historically reconditioned over time. In this case, political changes in imperial administration—brought about themselves by Indigenous resistance to British reform efforts—helped redefine Indigeneity and connect diverse experiences across empire. Brooks argues that British political change and Indigenous political change have to be understood as intricately entwined and dialectically related in this era. While revealing the robust nature of Indigenous engagement with the eighteenth-century British empire, his chapter also shows that British reform efforts in North America and elsewhere were prefigured by British attempts to end similar types of decentered allied and negotiated forms of rule in India and Scotland.

The final chapter in the "Connections" section, Elspeth Martini's study of the Ojibwe chief and Methodist missionary Shawundais, shows that by the end of the Age of Revolution, Indigenous peoples themselves were making those connections across empire. Exemplifying again the strength of biography to tease out nuanced political positions, as well as the power of religion to serve Indigenous ends as much as European ones, Martini's work recalls the mutually constitutive process of Ballantyne's entangled empires. Drawing on the prestige he gained as a convert within the transatlantic Wesleyan-Methodist movement, Shawundais traveled to London at a critical moment—the convening of the Select Committee on Aborigines—to petition imperial officials to recognize his people's rights as original owners of their land. In doing so, Shawundais linked his arguments with those of his "Red Brothers" and other Indigenous peoples across empire, citing especially British restoration of Xhosa lands at the Cape as a precedent. As Martini reminds us, while not always successful in these efforts, the connections Indigenous peoples started to forge in this era need to be appreciated as part of a longer political negotiation and as part of an ongoing and global struggle to gain recognition of Indigenous sovereignty.

Conclusion

Taken together, the chapters in this collection can chart a new way forward for historians of empire, Indigenous studies, and the Age of Revolution. While we have not been able to answer all our original questions, the collection can mark the start of a new conversation and show why scholars can no longer continue to decenter Indigenous peoples from any comparative history of the Age of Revolution and modern imperialism.

Like Bennelong in the early colony of New South Wales, Indigenous people existed in almost every nook and cranny of the revolutionary effort to expand Europe from the late eighteenth century. Few experienced this invasion solely as an unprecedented onslaught. Some saw it as a manageable recurrence, others as a defeatable threat. Occasionally, Indigenous people saw European newcomers as a chance—to employ them in a longer-running feud with neighbors, to use them in the ousting of a more deadly invader, to enrich a cultural lacuna, or even to expand themselves.

That said, Bennelong was never a Pollyanna. He lived long enough to see as well some of the more devastating effects of European arrival. But he would also have known that these same effects had to contend always with his and other Aboriginal presences. Some lands and waters were less easily displaced than others because of Indigenous decisions and pressures. Some wars were not fought because their odds against the Indigenous appeared too long for Britons on the ground. Whatever modern edifices arose on Indigenous lands during the Age of Revolution—entrepôts, trade routes, missions, cities, democracies—each was significantly shaped by the people who were there first.

Bennelong stands in our collection, too, as an emblem of the many Indigenous subjects who came to know London and other centers of British imperialism as parts of *their* world, rather than simply as the places belonging to others. Imperial historians of our period are used to identifying an increasing British recognition of the globe, from Philadelphia to Hobart to Auckland to Durban, but they have been slower to see that from an Indigenous perspective, the reverse was also true. Like so many others, Bennelong did not experience his sojourn to London as an outsider to an insider's origin point; he saw it as an insider broadening his understanding of the outside world.

Bennelong may not have met other Indigenous people while away, but he surely heard of the many predecessors who traveled before him, forging a history of Indigenous mobility that he was active in continuing. Other native itinerants were in easier situations to become conscious of the links they were creating. Whenever the British moved across borders, countless additional capillaries of connection flowed also, in and between Indigenous societies.

Finally, Bennelong's story reminds us to rethink the very parameters of the periodization we assume when invoking an era like the Age of Revolution. As historian of Africa Joe Miller recently noted elsewhere, the Indigenous view often shows "longer and more complex rhythms of transformation" than current models of the field allow.[34] The stories told just in these pages alone—with their deep migratory patterns, their tales of disease, their revelations of ecological management—raise questions about the timing and nature of revolutionary change. The conflicts over space, labor and resources, and over hearts and minds that poured fuel over the fires that drove movements for the rights of man and industrialization have left a living legacy of contested relations that continue to resonate in contemporary politics and societies today.

Indigenous peoples were at the heart of the Age of Revolution. Acknowledging that history makes it clearer that we are all still living with, and are responsible for, its legacy.

Notes

1. Keith Vincent Smith, "Bennelong among His People," *Aboriginal History* 33 (2009): 36; Kate Fullagar, *The Savage Visit: New World Peoples and Popular Imperial Culture in Britain, 1710–1795* (Berkeley: University of California Press, 2012), 184.

2. Kate Fullagar, "Bennelong in Britain," *Aboriginal History* 33 (2009): 92.

3. David Collins, *Account of the English Colony at New South Wales* (London, 1798), 2:49, 96; *The Times*, 29 October 1805.

4. Manning Clark, *A History of Australia* (Melbourne: Melbourne University Press, 1962), 1:145; Inga Clendinnen, *Dancing with Strangers* (Melbourne: Text Publishing, 2003), 272.

5. Smith, "Bennelong among His People." Cf. K. V. Smith, *Bennelong: The Coming In of the Eora, Sydney Cove 1788–1792* (East Roseville: Kangaroo Press, 2001), and Grace Karskens, *The Colony: A History of Early Sydney* (Sydney: Allen and Unwin, 2009).

6. Michael A. McDonnell, *The Politics of War: Race, Class, and Conflict in Revolutionary Virginia* (Chapel Hill: University of North Carolina Press, 2007); McDonnell, *Masters of Empire: Great Lakes Indians and the Making of America* (New York: Hill and Wang, 2015).

7. Fullagar, *The Savage Visit*, and her forthcoming *Faces of Empire: Three Eighteenth-Century Lives.*

8. With the rise of the "new imperial history," the old historiographic divide between the so-called First and Second British empires has become more permeable, though it seems to persist when thinking about linkages between Indigenous peoples throughout the empire and across this era.

9. Theda Perdue, *Cherokee Women: Gender and Culture Change, 1700–1835* (Lincoln: University of Nebraska Press, 1998); Malama Meleisea, *The Making of Modern Samoa: Traditional Authority and Colonial Administration in the History of Western Samoa* (Suva: University of South Pacific Press, 1987). There are now many other examples, but for another pioneering effort, see J. B. Peires, *The House of Phalo: A History of the Xhosa People in the Days of Their Independence* (Johannesburg: Ravan Press, 1981).

10. Richard White, *The Middle Ground: Indians, Empires, and Republics in the Great Lakes Region, 1650–1815* (Cambridge: Cambridge University Press, 1991); Inga Clendinnen, *Aztecs: An Interpretation* (Cambridge: Cambridge University Press, 1991). Cf. Henry Reynolds, *Frontier: Aborigines, Settlers and Land* (Sydney: Allen and Unwin, 1987). For an extended discussion of the merits and ultimate limits of White's work at least, see Michael A. McDonnell, "Rethinking the Middle Ground: French Colonialism and Indigenous Identities in the *Pays d'en Haut*," in *Native Diasporas: Indigenous Identities and Settler Colonialism in North America*, ed. Gregory D. Smithers and Brooke N. Newman (Lincoln: University of Nebraska Press, 2014), 79–108, and McDonnell, *Masters of Empire*, esp. 5–19.

11. Daniel Richter, *Facing East from Indian Country: A Native History of Early America* (Cambridge, MA: Harvard University Press, 2001).

12. Again, there are many examples, but for notable works of comparative imperial history, see Marete Falck Borch, *Conciliation, Compulsion, Conversion: British Attitudes towards Indigenous Peoples, 1763–1814* (Amsterdam: Rodopi, 2004); Alan Lester, *Imperial Networks: Creating Identities in Nineteenth-Century South Africa and Britain* (London: Routledge, 2001); Elizabeth Elbourne, *Blood Ground: Colonialism, Missions, and the Contest for Christianity in the Cape Colony and Britain, 1799–1853* (Montreal: McGill-Queen's University Press, 2002); Richard Price, *Making Empire: Colonial Encounters and the Creation of Imperial Rule in Nineteenth-Century Africa* (Cambridge: Cambridge University Press, 2008); Lisa Ford, *Settler Sovereignty: Jurisdiction and Indigenous People in America and Australia, 1788–1836* (Cambridge, MA: Harvard University Press, 2010); Stuart Banner, *Possessing the Pacific: Land, Settlers, and Indigenous Peoples from Australia to Alaska* (Cambridge, MA: Harvard University Press, 2007); James Belich, *Replenishing the Earth: The Settler Revolution and the Rise of the Anglo-World, 1783–1939* (Oxford: Oxford University Press, 2011).

13. See Karen Fox, "Globalising Indigeneity? Writing Indigenous Histories in a Transnational World," *History Compass* 10, no. 6 (2012): 423–439, on the genealogy of comparative Indigenous history—that she claims began in the 1940s. In this respect,

the rise of settler colonial studies, too, is instructive. While generally a welcome turn in the field of Indigenous studies, settler colonial studies often focus on the colonial and imperial structures in which Indigenous people found themselves enmeshed. Starting with Patrick Wolfe's brilliant comparative analysis of the United States, Brazil, and Australia, settler colonial studies have widened our optics, given rise to new understandings of colonial-Indigenous relations, and emphasized a valuable political component to such work. But in its focus on imperial and colonial polities, legal systems, and their often genocidal policies, settler colonial studies tend to privilege the voice, and the subjectivity, of Europeans over Indigenes.

14. Peter H. Wood, "North America in the Era of Captain Cook: Three Glimpses of Indian-European Contact in the Age of the American Revolution," in *Implicit Understandings: Observing, Reporting, and Reflecting on the Encounters between Europeans and Other Peoples in the Early Modern Era*, ed. Stuart B. Schwartz (Cambridge: Cambridge University Press, 1994), 485–486, 500–501.

15. See Michael A. McDonnell, "Paths Not Yet Taken, Voices Not Yet Heard: Rethinking Atlantic History," in *Connected Worlds: History in Transnational Perspective*, ed. Ann Curthoys and Marilyn Lake (Canberra: Australian National University Press, 2005), 46–62; McDonnell, "Rethinking the Age of Revolution," *Atlantic Studies* 13, no. 3 (2016): 301–314. Compare, for example, the lack of Native American perspectives or topics in the pioneering collection by David Armitage and Michael J. Braddick, eds., *The British Atlantic World, 1500–1800* (Basingstoke: Palgrave Macmillan, 2002), and a more recent volume, Bernard Bailyn and Patricia L. Denault, eds., *Soundings in Atlantic History: Latent Structures and Intellectual Currents, 1500–1830* (Cambridge, MA: Harvard University Press, 2009). Jace Weaver, *The Red Atlantic: American Indigenes and the Making of the Modern World, 1000–1927* (Chapel Hill: University of North Carolina Press, 2014), has made some progress in this direction, but the literature on Atlantic history—particularly for the North Atlantic—continues to ignore Indigenous perspectives.

16. C. A. Bayly, *Imperial Meridian: The British Empire and the World, 1780–1830* (London: Longman, 1989).

17. C. A. Bayly, "British and Indigenous Peoples," in *Empire and Others: British Encounters with Indigenous Peoples, 1600–1850*, ed. M. J. Daunton and R. Halpern (Philadelphia: University of Pennsylvania Press, 1999), 20.

18. Bayly, "British and Indigenous Peoples," 21.

19. See the UN Permanent Forum on Indigenous Issues statement on Indigenous identity at https://www.un.org/development/desa/Indigenouspeoples/unpfii-sessions-2.html.

20. Home page for the Native American and Indigenous Studies Association (NAISA) website, http://www.naisa.org/.

21. Zoe Laidlaw and Alan Lester, "Indigenous Sites and Mobilities: Connected Struggles in the Long Nineteenth Century," in *Indigenous Communities and Settler Colonialism: Land Holding, Loss and Survival in an Interconnected World*, ed. Zoe Laidlaw and Alan Lester (London: Palgrave, 2015), 12.

22. See J. K. Kauanui, *Hawaiian Blood: Colonialism and the Politics of Sovereignty and Indigeneity* (Durham, NC: Duke University Press, 2008); P. D. Palmater, *Beyond Blood: Rethinking Indigenous Identity* (Saskatoon: Purich Publishing Limited, 2011);

and Kat Ellinghaus, *Blood Will Tell: Native Americans and Assimilation Policy* (Lincoln: University of Nebraska Press, 2017).

23. Ravi de Costa, "Fifty Years of Indigeneity: Legacies and Possibilities," in *Indigenous Networks: Mobility, Connections and Exchange*, ed. Jane Lydon and Jane Carey (London: Routledge, 2014), 273–285.

24. Laidlaw and Lester, "Indigenous Sites and Mobilities," 4.

25. Lydon and Carey, *Indigenous Networks*; Laidlaw and Lester, *Indigenous Communities*. Note also that we were much inspired by Tracey Banivanua Mar's even earlier comparative work, "Imperial Literacy and Indigenous Rights: Tracing Transoceanic Circuits of a Modern Discourse," *Aboriginal History* 37 (2013): 1–28.

26. C. L. R. James, *The Black Jacobins* (New York: Dial Press, 1938); R. R. Palmer, *The Age of the Democratic Revolution: A Political History of Europe and America, 1760–1800*, 3 vols. (Princeton, NJ: Princeton University Press, 1959–1964); E. J. Hobsbawm, *The Age of Revolution: Europe 1789–1848* (London: Weidenfeld and Nicholson, 1962); Peter Linebaugh and Marcus Rediker, *The Many-Headed Hydra: Sailors, Slaves, Commoners, and the Hidden History of the Revolutionary Atlantic* (Boston: Beacon Press, 2000); Paul Dukes, *Minutes to Midnight: History and the Anthropocene Era from 1763* (Cambridge: Cambridge University Press, 2012). Nor does a recent comparative collection make up for the neglect (see David Armitage and Sanjay Subrahmanyam, eds., *The Age of Revolutions in Global Context, c. 1760–1840* (Basingstoke: Palgrave Macmillan, 2009). For an extended discussion of this historiographic elision, see Michael A. McDonnell, ed., *Rethinking the Age of Revolution* (London: Taylor and Francis, 2017).

27. Susan Thorne, "'The Conversion of Englishmen and the Conversion of the World Inseparable': Missionary Imperialism and the Language of Class in Early Industrial Britain," in *Tensions of Empire: Colonial Cultures in a Bourgeois World*, ed. F. Cooper and A. L. Stoler (Berkeley: University of California Press, 1997), 254. In 2008, Jeremy Adelman renamed the Age of Revolution "An Age of Imperial Revolutions" (*American Historical Review* 113, no. 2 [April 2008], 319–340) but failed to note the role of Indigenous peoples in this process. On the other side of the discussion, Belich, in *Replenishing the Earth*, took note of the spread of colonial settlement with little reference to the Age of Revolution.

28. See Colin Calloway, *The Scratch of a Pen: 1763 and the Transformation of North America* (New York: Oxford University Press, 2006); McDonnell, *Masters of Empire*; Woody Holton, *Forced Founders: Indians, Debtors, Slaves, and the Making of the American Revolution in Virginia* (Chapel Hill: University of North Carolina Press, 1999); Kathleen Duval, *Independence Lost: Lives on the Edge of the American Revolution* (New York: Random House, 2016).

29. See, for example, Sinclair Thomson, "Sovereignty Disavowed: The Tupac Amaru Revolution in the Atlantic World," *Atlantic Studies: Global Currents* 13, no. 3 (2016): 407–431; Forrest Hylton, "'The Sole Owners of the Land': Empire, War, and Authority in the Guajira Peninsula, 1761–1779," *Atlantic Studies: Global Currents* 13, no. 3 (2016): 315–344.

30. Bayly, "Afterword," in *Age of Revolutions*. An older essay by John K. Galbraith, "The 'Turbulent Frontier' as a Factor in British Expansion," *Comparative Studies in Society and History* 2, no. 2 (January 1960), 150–168, is instructive.

31. Bayly, *Imperial Meridian*, 166.

32. Gammage, *The Biggest Estate on Earth: How Aborigines Made Australia* (Sydney: Allen and Unwin, 2011).

33. Robert Kenny, “Tricks or Treats? A Case for Kulin Knowing in Batman’s Treaty,” *History Australia* 5, no. 2 (2008): 38.1–38.14.

34. J. C. Miller, “The Dynamics of History in Africa and the Atlantic ‘Age of Revolutions,’ ” in *Age of Revolutions*.

PART ONE

PATHWAYS

CHAPTER ONE

The Future Makers

Managing Australia in 1788

BILL GAMMAGE

In January 1788 the Eora clans of Sydney Cove became the first Australians to face Empire when a British settlement was established in their country. I use the year Sydney Cove was occupied, 1788, as shorthand for the spread of British settlement across Australia during the next 140-odd years, and for the destruction of the distinctive and productive vegetation patterns that everywhere marked traditional Aboriginal land management. Similar patterns existed in North America: I ask what these imply, and briefly question some of the contrasts that farming peoples assume between themselves and what they call "hunter-gatherers."

One contrast is basic and obvious, but little puzzled over. No people were less urban than the people of 1788. They spread much more evenly over the land than do Australians today, and though some had villages, including of stone, they never occupied them permanently. But few people, perhaps no people, planned and maintained land, creatures, and resources with the fine-grained care they did. For them "conservation" meant maintaining abundance; for us it means repairing damage.

Aborigines made Australia in 1788, by using fire and no fire to distribute plants, and using plant distribution to locate animals, birds, reptiles, and insects (hereafter "animals"). People made a plant community a favorable habitat, associated communities to link feed to shelter, and used associations to lure animals. This put every species on ground it preferred, while people knew where resources were, and subject to Law could harvest them as they chose. They could make paddocks without fences, because in Australia, almost uniquely, the only large predators to disturb prey were people. They were not aimless "hunter-gatherers"; they planned and worked hard to make plants and animals abundant, convenient, and predictable. They depended not on chance, but on policy.

This is not how farmers think or act. Aborigines farmed, but never depended on farming.[1] The difference induces contrasting ways of seeing land. Anthropologist Peter Dwyer showed this brilliantly in comparing three Papua New Guinea Highlands groups, one gardeners, one largely "hunter-gatherers," one both. The more a group cultivated, Dwyer found, the more it drew mental and physical boundaries around its cultivation. Physically and mentally, only the gardeners fenced their world. The others had no words for center or periphery, no sense of being spiritually distinct from the rest of creation, no landform hierarchy. For the gardeners "wilderness" began just beyond their fences; for the "hunter-gatherers" it did not exist.[2] Fences on the ground made fences in the mind. Australia had no fences in 1788. Some places were managed more closely than others, but none were beyond the pale. To build a picture of this difference between "hunter-gatherers" and farmers, I start with a tree (fig. 1.1).

Figure 1.1. A Mountain Ash in Tasmania, January 2011. Reproduced with kind permission of Mike and Edwina Powell, Launceston, Tasmania.

Eucalypts chase light. In the open they spread, in forest they shoot straight up. Mountain Ash grows in dense forests of tall, straight trees—it is the world's tallest flowering plant. It is also the most flammable eucalypt, so when a fire rages the forest dies, in the rich ash thousands of seedlings race up to get light, and tall forest returns. But this Mountain Ash has spread because it has always stood in the open. How? A bushfire ("wildfire") would kill it and replace it with swathes of competing seedlings, whereas without fire this is rainforest land. Only centuries of controlled fire could burn back that rainforest without ever touching this fire sensitive tree.

Similarly, in Tasmania and along Australia's east coast, eucalypts are capturing ancient grassland, and under their cover rainforest is encroaching. In 1788, determined and repeated fire drove back those forests to make grass; now without fire, the trees return.

People favored grassland. It was a firebreak, carried many useful plants and most animals with most meat, made seeing and traveling easier, and confined forest, which made forest resources more predictable. In 1788 Australia almost certainly had more grass, more open forest, and less dense forest than now, and certainly less "underwood"—less scrub.

Colonial words, paintings, and survey plans show 1788 grassland where there is now eucalypt forest, or open woodland where there is now dense forest. Why only now? Why not then? Some researchers think bushfire converted pre-1788 forests to grass, but after a bushfire scrub comes back more, not less, and bushfire rarely clears big eucalypts: they soon resprout and recover their dominance. Only repeated fire, clearing seedling and sapling for centuries until the old trees die out, converts eucalypts to grass, and only people make such fire.

In short, for 230 years the land has been shouting that newcomers have got it wrong: it was not natural, but made.

In 1968 the great prehistorian Rhys Jones coined the term "fire-stick farming" to describe patch-burning grass to bring on fresh growth to lure grazing animals.[3] A few early newcomers recognized this. At Albany, Western Australia, George Vancouver observed in 1791:

> Fire is frequently resorted to by rude nations, either for the purpose of encouraging a sweeter growth of herbage in their hunting grounds, or as tools for taking the wild animals, of which they are in pursuit.[4]

In northwest Tasmania Henry Hellyer remarked in 1828:

> It is possible that the natives by burning only one set of plains are enabled to keep the kangaroos more concentrated for their use, and I can in no way account for their burning only in this place, unless it is to serve them as a hunting place.[5]

Aborigines themselves stated at Evans Bay, Queensland, in 1849,

> observing that the grass had been burnt on portions of the flats the Blacks said that the rain that was coming on would make the young grass spring up and that would bring down the kangaroos and the Blacks would spear them from the scrub.[6]

Evans Bay is on Cape York, next to Torres Strait, as far from Albany and Tasmania as you can get in Australia, yet all three peoples managed land similarly. Evans Bay is also next to islanders who gardened. People could compare their management with Torres Strait agriculture. Given the exotic edible plant species on Cape York, it is possible that its people did try gardening, but if so they abandoned it. Instead they matched the rest of the continent, choosing a course they thought more efficient and reliable. In 1845 explorer Ludwig Leichhardt called this choice "a systematic management" of country.[7]

The choice made large-scale gardening unlikely, because people allied with fire. About 70 percent of Australia's plant species tolerate or encourage fire. Trees and bushes reseed or resprout, while dominant fodder grasses are perennial, so, unlike Europe's fodder annuals, they reshoot. In other words they refuel. The first fire task of 1788 was to control fuel, by ceremony, and by constant, careful burning. This let people *prevent* the terrible killer fires that have recently immolated the fringes of every Australian capital except Darwin, fires that must have decimated people in 1788 had they occurred: no one could outrun them. Regular fires prevented irregular fires; instead of today's "Prevent bush fires," the Smokey Bear approach, the rule was "A fire a day keeps bushfires away." Taming fire was a great achievement.

It was also cause to manage every corner of the continent. There was no wilderness in 1788. Explorer Edward Eyre observed in 1841, "no part of the country is so utterly worthless, as not to have attractions sufficient occasionally to tempt the wandering savage into its recesses . . . the very regions, which, in the eyes of the European, are most barren and worthless, are to the native the most valuable and productive."[8] Of course people burnt the most useful land most, and sterile or sensitive land perhaps not for generations. But sooner or later they burnt everywhere, in "every part of the country, though the most inaccessible and rocky" surgeon John White observed in April 1788; on "the highest mountains, and in places the most remote and desolate . . . [in] every place," explorer Thomas Mitchell wrote in November 1836.[9] Except for specific purposes, if fuel built up, it was burnt.

This unleashed rich possibilities:

1. The more fuel is reduced, the more easily fire is controlled, so the more useful it is.
2. Even hot fires leave unburnt patches, but the cooler the fire, the bigger the patches.
3. Patches benefit animals by joining burnt land (feed) to unburnt land (shelter).
4. Patches form mosaics, which can be adjusted in extent by varying fire intensity.
5. Intensity can be regulated by fire frequency and fire timing.
6. Frequency and timing are local. They depend on local flora and local moderators like rain, wind, temperature, and aspect.
7. The better people understand these variables, the more they can burn with purpose. They can move from limiting fuel to shaping country.
8. This lets them selectively locate fire tolerant and fire sensitive plants, situate mosaics and resources conveniently and predictably, and arrange them so that one supplies what another does not. People could make the future.

How they managed fire and no fire varied. Local climate, terrain, and plant variety imposed this, and even locally people differ according to season and circumstance on what to burn or not burn. But everywhere the basic *purposes* of fire were the same: to limit fuel, to ensure diversity and abundance, to regulate plant and animal populations. The plant *patterns* people made with fire and no fire were the same too: grass on the best soil, forest split by grass, tree and scrub clumps in grassland, undergrowth uncommon. And the *benefits* were the same: plants and animals were made abundant, convenient and predictable.

Figure 1.2 shows dense forest rising from low ground between grassy hills. A strikingly sharp edge divides trees from grass. Fires drive grey kangaroos to waiting spears. So the hunters are not chancing on game, but predicting when and where it will come. They are also protecting the forest, firing its lee edge so that the wind takes the flames into the grass. If the wind lay the other

Figure 1.2. Joseph Lycett (c. 1775–1828), Aborigines Using Fire to Hunt Kangaroos, c. 1820 [PIC R5689, NLA]. Reproduced with kind permission of the National Library of Australia.

way they could burn the opposite edge. Skillful burning keeps the forest dense, the grass clear, and the game convenient.

Newcomers cursed dense forest, but some plants and animals prefer it, so in Law (explained on page 34-5) it must be provided. The value of dense eucalypt forest was strikingly demonstrated in January 1798, when John Wilson, an escaped convict who had lived with Blue Mountains people for almost ten years and undergone their basic initiations, was pardoned to lead an expedition from Sydney southwest into a maze of poor soil and tangles of scrub and timber. In one memorable week the party noted the first koala, the first lyrebird, the first gang-gang cockatoo, and the first mainland wombat recorded by a European. The gang-gang was new to Wilson, but he knew the wombat and the koala, giving them their Blue Mountains names, *wombat* and *cullawine*, from which no doubt "koala" derives. He knew the lyrebird but called it a pheasant, which is perhaps why today it has no familiar Aboriginal name. The point is that no one in a settlement thirsty to profit from new finds had reported these creatures. Their country was bad, formidable, seeming untouched. Wilson knew them because Aborigines valued them and made or left habitats for their benefit.[10]

People also sheet-burnt to clean country and back-burnt around fire sensitive plants to protect them. In central Australia, rainforest remnants in deep gorges seem curious anomalies, green oases ringed by aridity, but their survival shows that for generations people stopped fires breaking into them. On the Gulf of Carpentaria are stands of ancient cycads, and in Tasmania monopatches of mountain pepper, both reflecting long-term fire management.

Where a purpose is apparent, I call plant communities deliberately associated "templates." Water margins and dense forest could be as much templates as grass-open forest associations for fire-stick farming, but no matter which plant communities dominated locally, similar templates for similar purposes recurred across Australia. People everywhere associated food plants and shelter plants. By selecting optimum conditions on templates and not nearby, they made target plants and animals on them abundant, convenient, and predictable. They then activated the templates in planned rotation. Thus they knew where their resources would be, and when to harvest them. They could choose.

Joseph Lycett's painting depicts a template; here are others from opposite edges of the continent (figs. 1.3 and 1.4). You can stand where von Guerard stood and match this scene's features. Compare the plateau at center left, the "keyhole" at the top of the lake, and the boomerang-shaped rock face between them. The foreground rocks are still there, hidden in the scrub, and note the young foreground eucalypts, regenerating once 1788 fire was stopped.

But the plant pattern now is nothing like then. Those grass strips are forest. They were lanes made to lure wallabies by judicious patch burning, then,

Figure 1.3. Eugen von Guerard (1811–1901), Crater of Mt. Eccles, 1858 [PIC S1011, NLA]. Reproduced with kind permission of the National Library of Australia.

Figure 1.4. The Crater of Mt. Eccles, Southwest Victoria, 18 March 2007. Photograph by Bill Gammage.

once new grass came up, to trap them between hunters emerging from trees above and below.

Figure 1.5 is one of several similar plans along Cape York's east coast. Green is rainforest, white open eucalypt forest. Surveyor Cobon had to certify "on honour" that his plan was accurate, yet every vegetation type is on every terrain. Rainforest screens beach camps from hunting grounds. It follows creeks but not always, even on low ground where it grows best, while open eucalypts dominate hills but not always. Compare the swamp edges, obviously on the same level but supporting distinct plant communities. This template led early Europeans to think it good cropland, usually for tobacco,[11] which is why Cobon surveyed it, but without repeated fire this land becomes dense rainforest, as it is now.

Two factors blended to make templates, one ecological, the other religious. Ecologically, laying out country variably to suit and balance every species meant undeviating commitment to very intricate land management. Individual inclination and enterprise must be curbed, and ecological rules and knowledge must reach beyond living generations. The Law, a religious philosophy rooted in ecology, compelled this. To oversimplify a complex theol-

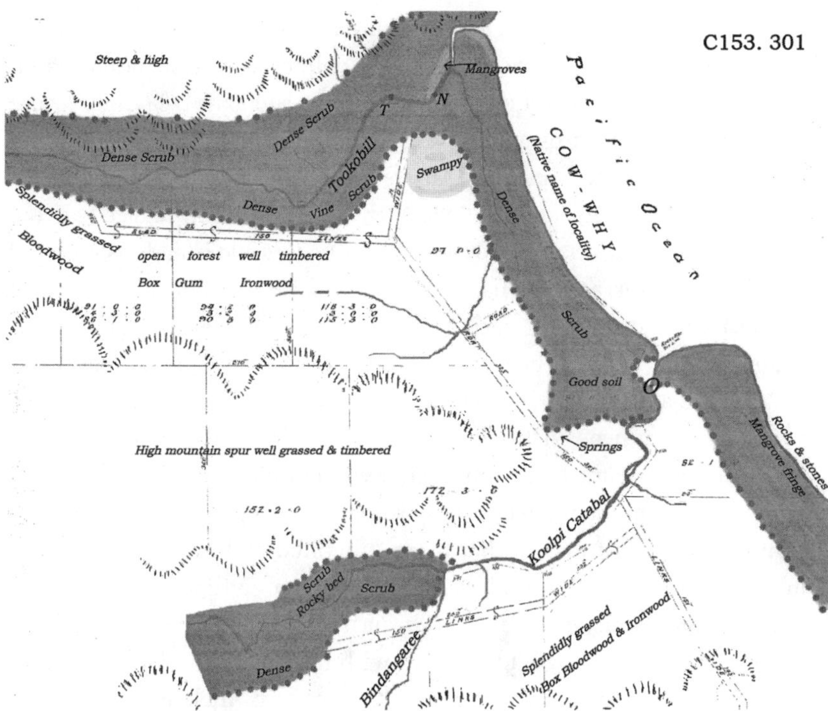

Figure 1.5. James J. Cobon, Survey Plan South of Cowie Point, Cape York, Queensland, 24 January 1891. C153.301, Lands Museum, Department of Environment and Resource Management, Brisbane.

ogy, it taught that everything with shape—people, plants, animals, earth, water, life-forms that Europeans introduced such as rabbits, camels, and house flies—has at least one totem derived from a creator ancestor, otherwise it cannot exist. Every totem has people who belong to it, and at the risk of their souls must care for it. Emu people must care for emus and emu habitat, and emus and emu habitat must care for them, and so on. Rules, myths, and ceremonies about the sanctity of totems warned and instructed, until the consequences of disobeying were too terrible to contemplate. Totems thus protected diversity and enforced conformity via religious sanction, powerful in any society. Evidence for this intricate fusion of Law and ecology exists in enough dispersed places to say that in this sense the whole continent was a single estate. "Think universal, act local" was habitual in 1788.

People went further. They made land beautiful. After "bush," in its Australian sense a word probably brought from South Africa, the most common word newcomers used to describe the landscape was "park." It is a striking choice. Europe's parks were made. They deliberately associated water, grass, and trees in picturesque array. Few were public in 1788—most were the preserve and mark of gentry. They signified wealth and leisure. Yet newcomers frequently compared Australia with just such places. In Port Jackson (Sydney) on 26 January 1788, Arthur Bowes Smyth rejoiced at "the beautiful and novel appearance of the different coves and islands as we sail'd up . . . the finest terras's, lawns, and grottos, with distinct plantations of the tallest and most stately trees I ever saw in any nobleman's grounds in England, cannot excel in beauty those w'h nature now presented to our view."[12] In November 1826 Robert Dawson thought the country inland from Port Stephens "truly beautiful: it was thinly studded with single trees, as if planted for ornament. . . . It is impossible therefore to pass through such a country . . . without being perpetually reminded of a gentleman's park and grounds. . . . The first idea is that of an inhabited and improved country, combined with the pleasurable associations of a civilized society."[13] In Tasmania John Hudspeth praised a "beautiful and rich valley . . . more like a gentleman's park in England, laid out with taste, than land in its natural state."[14] W. H. Leigh thought the country south of Adelaide "a wild but beautiful park, which reminded one of the domain of an English noble,"[15] and Alexander Buchanan considered semi-arid mallee "really most beautiful, like a gentleman's park all the way. Fine plains and thinly studded with trees."[16]

Parks were even in the far inland, that harsh country that horrified and sometimes killed newcomers. West of the Darling Charles Sturt came on "a beautiful park-like plain covered with grass, having groups of ornamental trees scattered over it. . . . I never saw a more beautiful spot. It was, however, limited in extent, being not more than eight miles in circumference . . . encircled by a line of gum-trees."[17]

This is the language of England. The plain is park-like because it reminds Sturt of English parks. Like a park it is limited in extent, but prettily bounded. It has scattered groups of trees, which in England could only be, as Sturt put it, "ornamental." And it has grass. Across the inland grass evoked parks. On Eyre Peninsula Edward Eyre "passed through a very pretty grassy and park-like country"; north of Glen Helen Egerton Warburton saw "country . . . beautiful, with park-like scenery and splendid grass"; in the west Petermanns Ernest Giles noted "a fine piece of open grassy country—a very park-like piece of scenery"; and in bleak country north of Lake Eyre, J. W. Lewis met "a plain thickly grassed and studded with fine green gum trees, most park-like in appearance."[18] There are hundreds of similar remarks, from every part of Australia.

Still most newcomers thought the land natural. They assumed that primitive "hunter-gatherers" lacked the skill and inclination to make parks. Yet a clue was there, in that observation that fire made fresh grass to lure kangaroos. The lure works on golf greens today, where kangaroos prefer to risk flying golf balls and angry greenkeepers to get at fresh growth, though safer but longer grass is just meters away.

To lure grey kangaroos such as Lycett depicted, you must ensure that they go where you have burnt. So you must (1) make sure the grass you burn is the sweetest and most nutritious available, (2) take care not to burn other grass too close, and (3) provide shelter nearby so kangaroos will not feel vulnerable.

To make sure the grass you burn is the sweetest and most nutritious available, you must put it on the best soil. Trees grow on such soil, so you must burn to keep it permanently clear of trees, or most trees. Yet grey kangaroos shelter among trees, so you must provide them, neither too open so the kangaroos feel exposed, nor too dense so they fear being slowed down. So next to grass you must have open forest, and perhaps beyond it dense forest, to shepherd the roos back toward the grass. In other words you must make not only the grass, but the land around, using at least three distinct fire regimes, probably more.

There is no point in doing all this just in one place, because after you hunt kangaroos they move. You must lure them to the next place you have prepared, then the next, and so on. In short you must pattern the whole country into places that will and will not shepherd grey kangaroos if you want to farm them successfully. This was so for every plant and animal that flourished when Europeans arrived—not all in the same area, of course, but each with habitat preferences. To accommodate such diversity an immense variety of templates, locally tuned, must be set up. Given how long some trees live, this might take centuries.

Templates for the same purpose could be close, but when activated had to be far enough apart not to disrupt each other, as this would make target animals unpredictable and the system pointless. Activating a template thus meant negotiating with neighbors and elders. The Law prescribed most of this, but still negotiation must have been constant, so the template system could not have had land boundaries. There could not *be* a place where it was practiced and next to it a place where it was not; a place where neighbors negotiated continuously next to a place where they behaved randomly. Australia was inexorably a single estate.

The system was much more than merely sustainable. Possibly even in hard times, it was so abundant that people may normally have harvested only resources made surplus by expanding off their templates. Such abundance was possible because people had plenty of land, so they could let plants and animals recover undisturbed. Farming peoples tend to think mobility primitive, but in Australia it was a great advantage. Whereas farming licensed population growth, mobility curbed it. Whereas farming drove people out of marginal land, mobility let them prosper there. People did not have to stay by their crops, and no livestock anchored them. Anthropologist Donald Thomson noted in 1939 that Arnhem Land clans spent several months mobile and several months sedentary each year, but each period was equally planned and predictable, "a regular and *orderly* annual cycle carried out systematically, and with a rhythm parallel to, and in step with, the seasonal changes . . . the nomadic movements of these people can be forecast with accuracy, and . . . their camps . . . foretold with reasonable certainty."[19] Anthropologist Phyllis Kaberry, also in 1939, thought mobility, abundance, and predictability let women in northwest Australia work less than any farmer's wife, yet get food more certainly: "the agriculturalist may be left destitute and almost starving if the [crops] fail or are destroyed. . . . I never saw an aboriginal woman come in empty-handed, though in 1935 there was a drought. . . . women's work . . . compares favourably with a European eight-hour day."[20] Historian Geoffrey Blainey pointed out that people worked many fewer hours a day to secure food and shelter than farmers anywhere.[21] Perhaps neither author counted fire or ritual as work, but only people untroubled about food could have held so many ceremonies. Of course there were hungry times, or people may not have managed their resources so carefully, but it was not the norm. People were not hinging on uncertainty or toil.

On the contrary, they could afford to host hundreds of guests, sometimes for months. This required setting aside big stretches of country years ahead to build up food, yet such occasions were common. Abundant resources are also seen in how much spare time people had. Some outsiders complain that Aborigines are lazy—that they sit for hours talking, dancing, or singing, even in broad daylight!—while many think the most distinctive features of Aboriginal society relate to art or corroboree: to what Europeans think of as leisure. In fact much of this is work, planning or performing to keep country and future alive, but only a well-ordered society could afford so much time away from the food quest.

How Aborigines made Australia—grass on good soil, forest split by grass, undergrowth uncommon—exactly suited invading Europeans. Eyre warned, “The localities selected by Europeans, as best adapted for the purpose of cultivation or grazing, are those that would usually be equally valued above others, by the natives themselves, as places of resort, or districts in which they could most easily procure food.”[22] At Albany John Wollaston noted, “*Warrung* [yam] . . . flourishes where the best feed for stock is found. Hence the usurpation of the ground and the secret destruction of the aborigines.”[23] “The very spots most valuable to the aborigines for their productiveness,” Protector of Aborigines Edward Parker declared in Victoria, “the creeks, water courses, and rivers—are the first to be occupied.”[24] Unseeing how carefully the land was made, the invaders displaced the people of 1788. The country richest in grass and game, in resource and story, passed to the white people, and a great tragedy began.

The parks vanished. Stopping fire let trees grow. Near Hahndorf in the Adelaide hills in midsummer 1839, Dirk Hahn saw people burning in the Onkaparinga valley: “They form a circle about twenty English miles in diameter, light fires around this area, and then direct the fire closer and closer in toward the centre of this circle. The long dry grass, bushes and young trees burn fiercely; all the animals living in this area flee toward the centre, where the savages then capture them.”[25] In the same valley Hahn saw the result of such fire: “beautifully-formed trees, which nature had planted there as if with the hands of a gardener. Every tree stood about 40 feet apart from the others. Some were perhaps an acre apart, so that the land could be cultivated without uprooting a single tree. . . . I found grass [a meter] high: they looked like our European cornfields.”[26]

Here is that valley thirty years later (see fig. 1.6). You see the scattered big trees Hahn admired. Like that Mountain Ash, their spread confirms that they grew in the open, but there are no cornfields now, no parks, only scrub. This ruin is what many assume Australia was like in 1788, but it is what it was like decades later, after 1788 fire was stopped, and on the eve of closer settlement.

To locate and rest resources, the template system needed big areas free of people, while allying with fire required a mobile population with few fixed assets. A scant and scattered population made 1788 Australia vulnerable to invasion, but this should not mask how impressive the Aboriginal

Figure 1.6. William Rodolph Thomas (1822–1889), Aboriginal Family Group on the Onkaparinga River Near Hahndorf, South Australia, 1870 [PIC/13591/13 NLA]. Reproduced with kind permission of the National Library of Australia.

achievement was. To balance land and people so richly for so long across so great an area ranks among humanity's great achievements. No other world civilization managed it. Almost all turned from "hunter-gathering" to agriculture, thence in time to a bad end or an uncertain future. Aborigines never joined the agrarian world's race to a complex technology. Fire gave too many advantages. It let people fuse the ecology and religion of an entire continent into the biggest estate on earth, and instead of dividing Aborigines into gentry and peasantry, it made them a free people.

Until 1788. Invaders assumed that what they found was natural, that "primitive" people lacked the intelligence and imagination to make country.[27] They displaced the people of 1788 with barely a whisper of regret.

Yet those people were truly future makers. What they did destroys an ancient European conceit that lands being colonized were virtually untouched. And what they did is the high-water mark in sustaining rather than consuming the resources of the earth. On present evidence no other continent practiced a single belief system, no other integrated Law and ecology so thoroughly, and no other depended nowhere on farming. On Earth's harshest inhabited continent, and anchored by a religious philosophy that ensured that it would continue forever unless invaders came, this was a momentous intellectual achievement.

What might it imply about nonfarmers and farmers elsewhere? Around the globe people in similar climates at similar times were sometimes farmers, sometimes not. Why? I ask, not answer. In puzzling over land management in pre-Columbus North America, I saw how crucial it is to know how fire and local plants interact. Near Pine Lake in northwest Ontario in 1624–25, missionary Gabriel Sagard wrote: "This spot was very pretty, sheltered by a very fine grove of big pine-trees very tall and straight and almost all of the same size and height, all pine-trees, without mixture of any other kind of tree, clean and bare of underbrush and thicket, so that it seemed to be the production and work of a first-rate gardener."[28] A Frenchman would hardly be ignorant of how pines grow, and by then Sagard had seen plenty of them in Canada, so I asked a local expert if the grove might have been man-made or maintained. No, she said, natural—happens all the time. Who am I to say if she is right or wrong? So I'm asking, but I do glimpse something like 1788 on other continents, and I hope that one day those continents might be researched and compared.

Several circumstances inhibit comparing Australian and North American "hunter- gatherers." First, in North America in 1491 farmers and nonfarmers were neighbors. This shreds the odds of a continent-wide, ecologically driven religious philosophy as in Australia, and thereby the odds of integrated continental land management. Second, Australians and North Americans had very different learning curves: Australia's 60,000-plus years versus North America's 25,000 (at Bluefish Cave in the Yukon, though South American dates imply an earlier North American arrival, unless the South Americans came by sea). Third, unlike Australia, North American predators would disrupt prey concentrated on a template, undermining its effectiveness. Nonetheless, on both continents bushfire/wildfire was an implacable presence, which sensible people were bound to confront. Early Europeans cited below indicate that North American "hunter-gatherers" managed fire well enough to avert the big fires periodically devastating the West Coast and elsewhere now. So I suggest, first, that a notion of them as mere transients over the land is a farmer prejudice, and second, that there is evidence that much of the North American landscape was not natural in 1491, but made. The question is, how much?

Hundreds of books or articles report on North American land before Columbus, many claiming that it was natural, many that it was made. The latter include Henry T. Lewis, Charles E. Kay, William Cronon, Charles C. Mann, and Stephen Pyne's later work.[29] Such writers quote early colonists describing Indian fire or its patterns that duplicate those in Australia. On the Massachusetts coast (where the West begins!) people used fire to " 'thin out and clear the woods of all dead substances and grass, which grow better in the ensuing spring. . . . Fire and flames are seen everywhere and on all sides.' " This kept open a mile-wide coastal belt (for crops Europeans assumed), and backing it a forest "open and park-like, the underbrush kept down by expert annual burning."[30] "Annual" may be too crude, but the template is familiar. Of Maryland, missionary Andrew White wrote in 1634: "Regular fall burning kept the . . . forest so open . . . that 'a coach and four horses may travel without molestation.' "[31] Charles Mann, who quotes this, found it hard to believe, but in Tasmania artist John Glover wrote of country now partly dense bush: "it is possible almost every where, to drive a Carriage as easily as in a Gentleman's Park in England,"[32] and colonial official Edward Lord declared under oath in 1812: "the forest land . . . is very open . . . from Hobart's Town to Launceston [150 miles/240 km], a loaded cart was drawn without the necessity of felling a tree."[33] Mann concludes of North America: "the great eastern forest was . . . an ecological kaleidoscope. . . . The first white settlers in Ohio found woodlands that resembled English parks—they could drive carriages through trees. Fifteen miles from shore in Rhode Island . . . trees [were] so widely spaced that the forest could be penetrated 'even by a large army.' "[34]

In Alberta about 1787 explorer Alexander Mackenzie wrote: "The Indians informed me, that, at a very small distance from either bank of the [Slave] river, are very extensive plains, frequented by large herds of buffaloes; while the moose and reindeer keep in the woods that border on it."[35] That is a basic 1788 template. In Alberta, too, surveyor Peter Fidler wrote in 1792: "Every fall & spring, & even in winter when there is no snow, these large plains either in one place or other is constantly on fire. . . . [This] makes excellent fine sweet feed for the Horses & Buffalo, &c,"[36] while as on the Onkaparinga people burnt to ring miles of country and steadily drive game into the center: this needs hot fire, and is quite a trick.

Again, as in Australia, when newcomers stopped Indigenous fire, trees and scrub spread. In "a frenzy of photosynthesis," as Mann memorably put it, forests thickened rapidly and their dominant species changed.[37] Appalachian balds—mountaintops of grass or heath from Virginia to Tennessee—are commonly taken to be natural, but now have trees invading their edges. A stock question: if trees grow there now, why not then?

Yet there seem to be striking differences from Australia in what I detect in North America. First, North American land patterns need more explaining. When Mann takes that grassy belt along the Massachusetts coast as being for farms, he does not then explain the next belt inland, the open forest. Why was that there? It makes little farming sense, but in Australia and in Mackenzie's Alberta grass / open forest sequences were frequent. Others too have noted man-made open parkland and edge habitats in North America, the Amazon Basin, and among the Jomon in Japan, but not how or conclusively why they were made.[38]

Second, North American patterns seem less diverse and precise. For example some say that the Great Plains are man-made. Meriwether Lewis noted in March 1805: "This want of timber is by no means attributeable to deficiency in the soil to produce it, but ows it's orrigine to the ravages of the fires, which the natives kindle in these plains at all seasons of the year."[39] This makes sense as trees grow on the plains now, but why were they made so open? For buffalo? Open land suits their migrations, but hunting them there suits horses, which arrived only recently. Were the plains made after horses arrived but before 1805? Unlikely, but pollen analysis could say. And why burn only for buffalo? Those vast spaces seem clumsy echoes of 1788 burning for diversity.

Third, beyond making grass and open forest, I've found virtually nothing on fire and no fire as a technique, though of course you need to appreciate fire as a management tool before the use of no fire can be detected. Skillful fire managers though North American "hunter-gatherers" were in 1491, fire to reduce fuel, hunt, or even make grass is not evidence of fire to manage country.

Fourth, and most striking, I've found nothing on fire and no fire to conserve animal, bird, reptile, and insect habitats, nor beyond grass in general, plant habitats. Given the animist beliefs of people in 1491, and their concern for country today, this borders on unbelievable. The primary purposes of 1788 fire were to reduce fuel and to make and maintain habitats. So far as I can tell,

North American ecologists and historians see simply what is useful to humans. That may be a difference, and a blindness, farming makes.

For there are fundamental differences in mindset between farmers and others. More than industrialization much later, farming may have been humanity's most significant shift from nature. The shift deserves to be understood, if only because environmental movements today may be seen as seeking in some way to repair an ancient breakdown. "Hunter-gatherer" societies may illuminate their search. Recall Peter Dwyer on how in Papua New Guinea fences on the ground make fences in the mind. In the Congo, nonfarming Pygmies and their farmer neighbors occupied similar country, but "there was a complete opposition of the forest to the village. The Pygmies in the forest consciously and energetically reject all village values. That is why they never sing their sacred songs in the village. . . . There is an unbridgeable gulf between the two worlds of the two peoples."[40] This parallels a north Australian woman who remarked, "rather patronizingly, as she watched a Fijian missionary working in his mission garden, anxiously concerned because a few plants had died: 'You people go to all that trouble, working and planting seeds, but we don't have to do that. All these things are there for us, the Ancestral Beings left them for us. In the end, you depend on the sun and the rain just as we do, but the difference is that we just have to go and collect the food when it is ripe. We don't have all this other trouble.'"[41] She thought that she was better off than any farmer, that managing country was better than putting fences across it.

She was not alone. Here a farmer describes "hunter-gatherers": "[They] have no proper weapons, no horses, no homes . . . a makeshift covering of interlaced branches . . . is the shelter to which the young come back and in which the old must lie. Yet they count their lot happier than that of others who groan over field labour, sweat over house building, or hazard their own and other men's fortunes in the hope of profit and the fear of loss. . . . they have reached a state that few human beings can attain."[42] This is the Roman author Tacitus on the Fenni somewhere east of Germany, about 98 AD. He anticipates James Cook's much-quoted summary of Australia's east coast people in 1770: "in reality they are far more happier than we Europeans. . . . They live in a Tranquillity which is not disturbed by the Inequality of Condition";[43] Elizabeth Macarthur's 1807 remark: "[They] certainly maintain their independence, and have hitherto resisted any infringement on their rights. Nor will they become servants . . . whatever temptation may be offered them";[44] and Gabriel Lalemont's observation on Canada's Nipissing in 1640: "they are a rich people and live in comfort. They cultivate a little land near their summer dwelling; but it is more for pleasure, and that they may have fresh food to eat, than for their support."[45]

What pressure might have persuaded the first farmers to abandon such freedom? No doubt the transition was gradual, but why make it at all? Not by choice, Australia suggests, but from necessity. Was it inevitable or irreversible? Historian Elliott Coues observed of Great Plains people: "nomadism was a more recently adopted lifestyle . . . agriculture was older. . . . [Early Europeans] explained the shift in lifestyle as a 'degeneration' of Indian society."[46] Yet at least in some circumstances a farmer or nonfarmer option remained open, so farming as an inevitable progression is suspect.

1788 thus raises world-historical questions. Were 1788 templates only in Australia? Or did nonfarmers have a common land management philosophy, albeit locally derived? If "hunter-gatherers" made their future as argued here, why did some abandon such systems? We assume too much about how or why farming and its consequences took hold. We think so little of "hunter-gatherer" societies that we cannot even label them accurately. We should see them not as a mere prelude to us, outfaced by empire, but as alternatives in understanding, managing, and sustaining the earth. We should explore more carefully the transitions from them to us, and why so great a mindset change followed. This is central to one of history's big tasks, to say how we came to be as we are.

Notes

The author thanks Ian Campbell, Fred Damon, Kyle Edwards, Norm Etherington, Jake Gillen, Shirley Lindenbaum, and Roger Rosewarn for help with non-Australian sources.

1. B. Gammage, *The Biggest Estate on Earth* (Sydney: Allen and Unwin, 2011), 281–99; R. Gerritsen, *Australia and the Origins of Agriculture* (Oxford: Oxford University Press, 2008); B. Pascoe, *Dark Emu* (Broome: Magabala Books, 2014).

2. P. Dwyer, "The Invention of Nature," in *Redefining Nature*, ed. R. Ellen and K. Fukui (Oxford: Oxford University Press, 1996), 157–86.

3. R. Jones, "Fire-Stick Farming," *Australian Natural History* 16 (1969): 224–48.

4. G. Vancouver, *A Voyage of Discovery to the North Pacific Ocean and Round the World, 1791–1795* [1801] (London: Hakluyt, 1984), 1:355.

5. 7–23 November 1828. Hellyer Report, Van Diemen's Land Co. Papers, MM71/5/20, 238, AO Tasmania.

6. Oswald Brierly, 1 December 1849, in D. R. Moore, *Islanders and Aborigines at Cape York* (Canberra: AIATSIS Press, 1979), 127.

7. L. Leichhardt, *Journal of an Overland Expedition in Australia* [1847] (Adelaide: LBSA, 1964), 354–55.

8. E. J. Eyre, *Journals of Expeditions of Discovery into Central Australia and Overland from Adelaide to King George's Sound* [1845] (Adelaide: LBSA, 1964), 1:351.

9. J. White, *Journal of a Voyage to NSW* [1790] (Sydney: Angus and Robertson, 1962), 129; T. L. Mitchell, *Three Expeditions into the Interior of Eastern Australia* [1839] (Adelaide: LBSA, 1965), 2:328.

10. 27 April 1891. J. J. Cobon letter, SUR/A 91/5517, Cape York survey C153.301-2, Qld State Archives, Brisbane.

11. *Australian Dictionary of Biography* (Canberra: ANU Press), 2:610; F. M. Bladen, ed., *Historical Records of NSW* (Sydney: Government Press, 1892–1901), 3:820–23; R. H. Cambage, "Exploration beyond the Upper Nepean in 1798," *Journal of the Royal Australian Royal Historical Society* 6 (1920): 1–35; A. H. Chisholm, "How and When the Lyrebird Was Discovered," *Emu* 55 (1955): 1–13.

12. Bladen, *Historical Records*, 2:392.

13. R. Dawson, *The Present State of Australia* [1830] (Alburgh: Archival Facsimiles, 1987), 108–9.

14. R. W. Giblin, *The Early History of Tasmania* (Melbourne: Melbourne University Press, 1939), 2:306.

15. K. Moon, "Perception and Appraisal of the South Australian Landscape 1836–1850," *Journal of the Royal Geographical Society of Australia (SA)* 70 (1969): 45.

16. A. Buchanan, "Diary of a Journey Overland," *Proceedings of the Royal Geographical Society of Australia (SA)* 24 (1922): 76.

17. 18 February 1845. C. Sturt, *Narrative of an Expedition into Central Australia* [1849] (Adelaide: LBSA, 1965), 1:286–87.

18. Eyre, *Journals*, 1:190; P. E. Warburton, *Journey across the Western Interior of Australia* [1875] (Adelaide: LBSA, 1968), 148; E. Giles, *Australia Twice Traversed* [1889] (Perth: Hesperian Press, 1995), 176; "Journal of Mr Lewis's Lake Eyre Expedition, 17 Feb 1875," *SA Parliamentary Paper* 19 (1876): 1–42.

19. D. F. Thomson, "The Seasonal Factor in Human Culture," *Proceedings of the Prehistorical Society* 5 (1939): 209, 211–12; emphasis original.

20. P. M. Kaberry, *Aboriginal Women: Sacred and Profane* (London: Routledge, 1939), 20, 23.

21. G. Blainey, *Triumph of the Nomads* (Melbourne: Macmillan, 1975), 162–63, 167.

22. J. Waterhouse, ed., *Edward Eyre's Autobiographical Narrative 1832–1839* (London: Caliban Books, 1984), 168.

23. S. J. Hallam, *Fire and Hearth* (Canberra: AIATSIS, 1975), 72.

24. E. Parker report 1839–40, Vic PRS 4410, unit 2, 52.

25. January 1839. M. Buchhorn, ed., *Emigrants to Hahndorf* (Adelaide: Lutheran Publishing House, 1989), 117.

26. 24 January 1839. D. M. Hahn, "Extracts from Reminiscences . . ." *South Australiana* 3 (1964): 120–21.

27. See Gammage, *Biggest Estate*, 307–13.

28. M. Leatherdale, *Nipissing from Brule to Booth* (Victoria, BC: Trafford, 2010), 103.

29. See, for example, H. T. Lewis, "Patterns of Indian Burning in California: Ecology and Ethnohistory," in *Before the Wilderness: Environmental Management by Native Californians*, ed. T. C. Blackburn and K. Anderson (Menlo Park: Ballena Press,

1993), 55–116; H. T. Lewis, "Why Indians Burned: Specific versus General Reasons," in *Proceedings—Symposium and Workshop on Wilderness Fire: Missoula, Montana, November 15–18, 1983*, ed. J. E. Lotan et al. (Missoula: US Forest Service, 1985), 75–80; B. Harrison and R. W. Judd, eds., *A Landscape History of New England* (Cambridge, MA: MIT Press, 2012); W. Cronon, *Changes in the Land: Indians, Colonists, and the Ecology of New England* (New York: Hill and Wang, 2003); C. E. Kay and R. T. Simmons, eds., *Wilderness and Political Ecology: Aboriginal Influences and the Original State of Nature* (Salt Lake City: University of Utah Press, 2002); C. C. Mann, *1491: New Revelations of the Americas before Columbus* (New York: Vintage, 2006); C. C. Mann, *1493: How Europe's Discovery of the Americas Revolutionized Trade, Ecology and Life on Earth* (London: Granta, 2011); S. J. Pyne, *The Still-Burning Bush* (Melbourne: Scribe, 2006). See also P. A. and H. R. Delcourt, *Prehistoric Native Americans and Ecological Change: Human Ecosystems in Eastern North America since the Pleistocene* (Cambridge: Cambridge University Press, 2004); C. Grier, J. Kim, and J. Uchiyama, *Beyond Affluent Foragers: Rethinking Hunter-Gatherer Complexity* (Oxford: Oxbow Books, 2006); E. S. Morgan, *American Slavery, American Freedom* (New York: W. W. Norton, 1975).

30. Mann, *1491*, 249.

31. Mann, *1493*, 49, 421.

32. J. Glover, *Catalogue of 68 Pictures Descriptive of the Scenery, and Customs of the Inhabitants of Van Diemen's Land* (London, 1836), 9.

33. House of Commons 1812/341, appendix 78–79.

34. Mann, *1491*, 251; Mann, *1493*, 48–49.

35. D. Egan and E. A. Howell, *The Historical Ecology Handbook* (Washington, DC: Island Press, 2005), 79.

36. Mann, *1491*, 251–52.

37. Mann, *1491*, 252; Mann, *1493*, 31–49.

38. B. Bryson, ed., *Seeing Further* (London: William Morrow, 2010), 286; G. W. Crawford, "The Jomon in Early Agriculture Discourse: Issues Arising from Matsui, Kanehara and Pearson," *World Archaeology* 40, no. 4 (2008): 459; Mann, *1491*, 285, 303.

39. C. Gilman, *Lewis and Clark: Across the Divide* (Washington, DC: Smithsonian, 2003), 30.

40. C. Turnbull, *The Forest People* (London: Simon and Schuster, 2001), 227.

41. R. M. and C. H. Berndt, ed., *The World of the First Australians* (Canberra: AIATSIS, 1996), 108.

42. Tacitus, *Germania*, chapter 46.

43. 23 August 1770. R. Parkin, *HM Bark Endeavour* (Melbourne: Melbourne University Publishing, 1997), 453.

44. S. M. Onslow, *Some Early Records of the Macarthurs of Camden* (Sydney: Angus and Robertson, 1914), 137.

45. Leatherdale, *Nipissing from Brule to Booth*, 7. See also S. Champlain, 26 July 1615: "they are a race who cultivate the soil very little," cited in Leatherdale, *Nipissing from Brule to Booth*, 93.

46. Gilman, *Lewis and Clark*, 303.

CHAPTER TWO

The Indigenous Architecture of Empire

The Anishinaabe Odawa in North America

MICHAEL A. MCDONNELL

In July 1764, at least a dozen ogimaag from Waganawkezee traveled to Niagara to meet with British Indian superintendent William Johnson. Waganawkezee (or, as the French called it, "L'Arbre Croche") was an Anishinaabe Odawa town near the strategic crossroads of the straits of Michilimackinac that joined Lakes Michigan and Huron. Johnson had invited the Odawa, along with more than two thousand other Indians from the *pays d'en haut*, ostensibly to put an end to the disastrous Anglo-Indian War that has come to be called Pontiac's War—a conflict that had seen the British attacked and thrown out of their newly established post at Michilimackinac. But if Johnson was pleased with the unprecedented numbers that gathered at Niagara, he was disappointed with the result. Most, like the Odawa, had come not to end the war but to negotiate the reopening of trade in the region. As a precursor to those negotiations, they expected the British to grease the wheels of a good trading relationship with presents and provisions as the previous Europeans in the region, the French, had always done.

Johnson had little choice but to comply, since the British were reeling from the staggering costs of the Anglo-Indian War, which had come hot on the heels of the global Seven Years' War. He gave out more than £38,000 in presents at Niagara. He also spent more than £20,000 on provisions for the assembled delegates. To put this into perspective, at this single council, the British spent almost as much as they initially hoped to raise from the colonies when they passed the Stamp Act the following year.[1]

Yet in return for this enormous outlay, the superintendent later admitted that all he could secure from the Odawa in particular was an agreement to *let* the British reestablish the post at Michilimackinac—and a promise that they would protect it "as far as they are able." He also got a lecture on the geopolitics of the pays d'en haut, and the Odawa place in it. Ultimately, Johnson was forced to acknowledge the central role of the Odawa in the region with a large wampum belt, twenty-three rows wide, depicting Johnson holding the hands of all nations between Fort Johnson in New York and the Ojibwe at St Mary's, near the Sault. The Anishinaabe delegation insisted that the "great Belt" be kept at Waganawkezee—"as it is the Centre, where all our People may see it."[2] For the Odawa, the conference at Niagara was a diplomatic success. No wonder that at the end of the meetings, Odawa speaker Mechskima declared they would now be happy to see the British at Michilimackinac. "We always loved them," he announced, "but we now like them better than ever, as they come for our Good."[3]

Johnson's concessions and Mechskima's announcement point to the reality behind the so-called British conquest of North America during the Seven Years' War. In 1763, the British formally took possession of French settlements and territorial claims in North America after the fierce and international conflict that had, in fact, as Colin Calloway notes in his chapter in this volume, started in Indian country. Imperial officials who inherited lands stretching from the St. Lawrence to the Mississippi looked forward to lasting peace across the continent and a monopoly on the still lucrative fur trade while their colonial counterparts eyed up western lands now that the French no longer stood in their way.

But in taking possession of former French posts and garrisons in the interior, the British quickly realized that they had also inherited a set of diverse and complex relations with Indigenous peoples across the territory who contested their victory and new claims, and made it clear that "although you have conquered the French, you have not yet conquered us."[4] The story of the Anishinaabe Odawa of Michilimackinac during this tumultuous period shows just how much and how quickly British officials in the Great Lakes had to reshape their imperial approach in North America—and at what cost. This chapter argues that the architecture of empire in the new British North American territories was very much built upon Indigenous foundations, and on Indigenous terms.

Anishinaabewaki

Composed of what we now call Ojibwe and Odawa settlements, the Anishinaabeg around Michilimackinac had some centuries prior to the arrival of Europeans drifted west and north up the Ottawa River Valley and across into the Great Lakes. Through incorporation and competition, they came by about

1600 to dominate the lakes and riverine systems of the central pays d'en haut. But they did not dominate in a way that made immediate sense to European newcomers. As historians have recently uncovered, Anishinaabewaki was made up of webs of communities connected by kinship. As Michael Witgen has written, the Anishinaabeg were held together by "strands of real and fictive kinship" that had been established through trade, language, and intermarriage. These strands intersected and crisscrossed over a vast space, knitting together disparate peoples and places across the pays d'en haut. They connected winter bands and village communities in far-flung places. And they shifted across time, as trading and kinship relations changed.[5]

While many Europeans struggled to understand the kinship-based political-social geography of the pays d'en haut, Native peoples themselves did not. The Odawa at the straits of Michilimackinac saw themselves simultaneously as members of particular lineages, doodemag (or totems), towns, and a greater Anishinaabe world. They shared close relations with the other Anishinaabe doodemag nearest to them, including those who made up the Ojibwe and the Potawatomi. Together, these three groups would come to be known—at least later—as the "Three Fires Confederacy." But the Odawa also had relations with other Anishinaabeg nations further afield, including the Nipissing, Algonquin, and Mississauga on their eastern and southeastern flanks. Indeed, by the time Europeans arrived on the scene, Anishinaabemowin speakers could be found from the upper stretches of the Gulf of the St. Lawrence River as far west as the Mississippi River. Across this great territory, the Anishinaabeg shared a mutually intelligible language, many cultural characteristics, and kinship relations. And while Anishinaabewaki was not as clearly defined as the French or English colonies, or even some of the larger confederacies of Indian nations farther to the south, it was no less powerful.[6]

While this kinship system often confused Europeans, its inherent flexibility was the great genius of Anishinaabe social organization and expansion. Indeed, while this decentralized system led to disagreements among the Anishinaabeg, it almost never led to outright conflict. As one ogimaa told British officials in 1760: "All the Indians in this Country are Allies to each other and as one People." Marriages outside the community allowed for an ever-thickening network of relations across great spaces. They also facilitated the establishment of new villages and communities and the peaceful sharing of resources across the region. In turn, because of kinship obligations, these new communities ensured an expansive and powerful network of alliances throughout the Great Lakes. This network helped the Anishinaabeg consolidate their hold on the Great Lakes and underpinned their expansion—even amid European imperialism. Ultimately, these relations defined Anishinaabewaki—their territory, or homeland.[7]

Situated at the heart of Anishinaabewaki, the Odawa families at Waganawkezee were well positioned to benefit from this formidable array of relationships. They enjoyed extensive trade and alliance relations with thousands of kin across the Lakes and were well respected for their mediation skills by both Indians and Europeans. But the Odawa at the straits also came to play a central part in the history of colonial America because they stood at the heart of the continent, too. For centuries, Michilimackinac was one of the few strategic entry points into and out of continental North America. Any nation, European or Native, wishing to pass back and forth from east to west, or, indeed, even from north to south, would have to come through either Michilimackinac or the Sault sixty miles to the north. If Michilimackinac was the door to North America, the Odawa, backed up by a powerful array of relations across the Lakes, held the key.[8]

Significantly, there is no real evidence throughout this long era to suggest that the Odawa viewed either the French or the English as a threat to their existence. Instead, they created alliances or provoked wars with others that often conflicted with European interests. They threatened Europeans themselves and at several critical moments did not hesitate to turn on them when it was in their interests to do so, paying little regard to the possible consequences. The Odawa were able to exploit European imperialism when it came, and they did so mostly for their own purposes. The collective strength of the Anishinaabeg across the pays d'en haut meant they were too important to be ignored, and too powerful to be cowed.

The hold that different Anishinaabe communities had on key strategic and resource-rich points throughout the Lakes meant that they dominated the newcomers at the local level, too. At Michilimackinac, the Odawa allowed the French to maintain a post at the straits in return for generous provisions, presents, and offers of alliance. Yet European posts did not mean European dominance. Quite the contrary. For most of the colonial period, Europeans at Michilimackinac were dependent on the Odawa for their very subsistence. The French could only maintain a tiny post at the strategic crossroads of Michilimackinac at the invitation of and as a result of the encouragement of thousands of Anishinaabeg who lived along the shores of the Lakes nearby. For this reason, the Odawa were able to hold their own and insist on their own terms when it came to dealing with French missionaries, traders, and colonial officials. The French were there because the Anishinaabeg wanted them there. The British were yet to learn this.

Nor were Anishinaabe relations with the French ever as settled or as harmonious as the British—and many subsequent historians, too—believed them to be. To be sure, they were helped a bit by intermarriages between natives and newcomers. Since at least the early years of the eighteenth century, some Anishinaabe doodemag had also expanded their kinship relations with select French traders. But these marriages were relatively few and far between and always need to be placed into the context of other and more extensive Indigenous kinship relations throughout Anishinaabewaki. Moreover, French officials constantly complained that métis traders confounded efforts to impose imperial policies at places like Michilimackinac—because they acted too much in the interests of their Indian kin. While historians have tended to view métis traders as go-betweens, or mediators, and often as French agents, their Indian kin were, of course, just as likely to see them as Anishinaabeg. As one French official complained as early as 1709, the children born of mixed marriages "try to create as many difficulties as possible for the French."[9]

Bringing the British to Heel

In the aftermath of the Seven Years' War—a conflict that the Anishinaabeg had helped trigger—the British inherited French claims to the pays d'en haut. But they also fell heir to these uncertain relations with the Indian nations of the region. Though they had plenty of warnings, they quickly blundered their way into another war—this time with Native Americans in a conflict we often now call Pontiac's War. At the end of the Seven Years' War, Native Americans insisted the British had only conquered the French, and not them. But British military officers, with their confidence brimming from their previous successes, acted imperiously and ignored native claims to sovereignty and their land. After hearing a British officer boast to a delegation of Native Americans that the English could crush them "whenever they pleased," one wary British agent responsible for Indian relations complained that military officers were "so intoxicated with providential Success that we will presently stumple over the whole Universe, if no Block should happen to lay in our way."[10]

But the British were about to be blocked. As if on a signal, Native Americans all across the Great Lakes rose up together in 1763 and attacked British forts in one of the largest pan-Indian wars in North America. Dozens of forts were overrun. Within months, attacking Indians captured or killed an estimated two thousand British soldiers and colonial settlers, rolling back the frontier hundreds of miles. The British were powerless to stop the onslaught. They struggled to bring a military end to the war. Every step they took turned into a quagmire. When a supply convoy attempted to reach Fort Niagara in September 1763, for example, some three hundred Seneca Iroquois, together with Odawa and Ojibwe from Detroit and the Ohio River Valley, attacked and managed to overwhelm a relief force as well. More than seventy soldiers and wagoners were killed at what became known as the Devil's Hole Massacre—one of the deadliest skirmishes of the war for the British.[11]

At Michilimackinac, events took what seemed to be a surprising turn. In the first place, Anishinaabe Ojibwe Indians took the lead and gained access to the British fort by playing a game of lacrosse. They flipped the ball into the fort and rushed after it. Once inside, they overwhelmed the garrison, killed at least sixteen soldiers, and took the rest—along with their officers—prisoner. In taking the fort, they surprised everyone, including their kin the Odawa, who were thirty miles away at the time. In turn, the Odawa traveled to the post and mediated between the British and the Ojibwe, reestablishing their control over the situation. Eventually, the Odawa managed to ransom back most of the remaining captives and return them to Montreal, to great acclaim from grateful British officers.

Though historians have long been at a loss to explain these events, the Odawa's long history of mastering empires helps shed light. The Odawa were simply not interested in exterminating the British, which they could have done at any time. Instead, as Mechskima suggested the following year at Niagara, they were happy to have a British post at Michilimackinac—to sell surplus provisions to and help facilitate the fur trade—but on their own, very specific terms, including giving generous presents and supplies. This is what they had long demanded, and received, from the French. Though Indian "presents" are today often seen as handouts, they were effectively the "rent" the British had to pay to use Indian lands.

The ultimate aim of the Odawa was not to keep the British out of the Anishinabewaki but to force them to recognize the politics of the pays d'en haut and the central place of the Anishinaabeg of Michilimackinac in that geopolitical arrangement. They were remarkably successful. The British did not forget the role played by the Odawa in supposedly saving the surviving officers and soldiers of the garrison. As importantly, they acknowledged their importance in the region, and never again sidelined Michilimackinac as a commercial and diplomatic strategic center. In Montreal in 1763, General Gage promised that the British would consider them "the largest tree that could be found in all the woods."[12]

The Politics of Trade

Following the Anglo-Indian War, the Odawa continued to employ the same strategies they had used since the arrival of Europeans in North America. Whereas before the Seven Years' War the Odawa had played off the French and English to get what they needed, afterward they played off the English against the French who remained in their midst and the French and Spanish on their borders along the Mississippi—an option that was not available to nations farther east, such as the Iroquois. They reported rumors of war, threatened to trade with the French, and simultaneously reminded the British of their role in the Anglo-Indian War and as peacemakers in the region. As one Odawa ogimaa put it to a new British commander, he and his troops could always "Sleep in Safety" because the Odawa would "watch over you." But good relations with the Odawa were vital to British security because, as he noted in what was effectively a thinly veiled warning, the Odawa were "a check to all the Nations, whose harts are not True to the English."[13]

The leverage the Anishinaabe Odawa enjoyed at Michilimackinac can best be seen in their relations with successive British commanders at the post, and particularly in their fight to reestablish the crucial—and very particular—trade practices that had allowed the Odawa to flourish during the French regime. While they were pleased with the rearrival of the British in late 1764 and cheered by seemingly new attitudes and policies, Odawa celebrations were short-lived. The new post commander, Captain William Howard, made it clear that the reopening of trade came with two important and related provisions: no longer would traders be allowed to winter over with the Indians, nor could they supply the Indians with goods on credit. William Johnson, mindful of the problems that unlicensed and unregulated traders posed in his own backyard, wanted to keep trade under strict regulations and to oversee it at the major posts. He believed the only way to maintain a lasting peace with the Indians was to ensure that trade was conducted fairly. The giving of credit, he thought, had precipitated too much conflict. Unscrupulous traders would ply the Indians with alcohol on credit and then give low prices for the pelts and skins they brought in return in the spring. There was too much room for abuse, Johnson thought.[14]

Johnson's thinking did arise from Indian complaints about traders, but mainly from those farther to the south who had to deal with the British. But these regulations were ill-suited to the customs and conditions of the trade at Michilimackinac that had evolved over many decades of exchange with the French. While Johnson was beginning to understand the politics of the pays d'en haut, he still seemed in the dark about the nuances of northern trade practices. In the first place, the extension of credit was part of a developed and sophisticated set of practices that arose because of the need to winter away from summer residences. At the start of the long winter, hunters and trappers needed an ample source of provisions to sustain themselves and their families through the coming season. Some may have been happy to accept alcohol, but the large majority took mostly clothing, blankets, and hunting tools. They had come to expect these provisions on credit, to be paid back on their return from their hunts in furs and hides. There were clear advantages for the Anishinaabeg. Having been given credit for their goods in the autumn, Indians returned from their winter hunts in debt to traders, a debt that they usually settled through the exchange of furs. But it also meant they had a guaranteed buyer for their goods. Though Johnson worried this meant the Indians were liable to be swindled, Anishinaabeg and others trading at Michilimackinac well knew where the balance of power lay. Many traders had married into Indian families and so were less likely to try to deceive them. Yet even if they were not so intimately related, in the fluid, connected, and Indian-dominated world of the straits, a trader offered poor prices at his peril.[15]

Yet the issue of credit was also a political one, particularly when it came to admitting incoming British traders into the region. Credit was intimately tied to any new relationship the northern nations might forge with the British. The extension of credit was a sign of great trust and thus a starting point for good relations with newcomers. The Anishinaabeg also saw unpaid debt as an anchor for a continuing reciprocal relationship. In starker terms, everyone knew that a creditor would protect the interests of those in debt to him—especially when there were no real powers to enforce the payment of debts. While in debt to traders and merchants at Michilimackinac, Indians out on their winter hunts would be assured of a safe reception upon their return and would know that their creditors would protect their interests in their absence. The English trader Alexander Henry had to learn this lesson when the Odawa had confronted him on his arrival at Michilimackinac in 1761. Their main demand was that he issue his goods to them on credit.

They were testing him. Though Henry failed this first challenge, he soon learned what was expected. A couple years later, when he set out for the unfamiliar waters of Lake Superior, he repeatedly encountered Indians who promised to hunt for him, but only on condition that he advance credit for their necessities to them. Henry extended credit.[16]

The practice of traders wintering over with the Anishinaabeg was a critical issue for the Odawa at Michilimackinac. It, too, had its basis in the reality of the northern winter hunts. Anishinaabeg at places like Waganawkezee traditionally traveled far to undertake their winter hunts, usually away from French or British posts and into more remote regions. Wintering with a trader meant immediate access to replacement goods if the necessity arose. Without these replacements, a damaged weapon or lost knife could mean the difference between life and death. It would certainly make the difference between a good and a bad hunt. Moreover, as post commander Robert Rogers noted, accompanying traders acted as a spur to those out on the hunt. Given their still limited need of European goods, Rogers thought on average Indians would bring in to the posts only about two-thirds of the pelts and skins they now traded to the British if no traders accompanied them.[17]

Other traders agreed with him. Though today we often assume Native nations were dependent on Europeans by the middle of the eighteenth century, traders and merchants at the time believed that without a steady supply of consumer goods, the Indians would "not kill a quarter part of the beaver etc. but only hunt for sustenance and a few skins to make themselves cloathing." The Odawa from Waganawkezee got most of their needs supplied through gifts and the provisioning trade at Michilimackinac, so there was little incentive to keep hunting for trade purposes through the winter. Still others far distant from the post would also not bother to amass large quantities of pelts if they did not have accompanying traders. Rogers knew that some Indians complained that they had no conveyances with which to bring their furs and pelts to the posts, and many were reluctant in times of war to leave their families behind in the springtime to travel to the posts. Having a trader nearby would not only encourage them to hunt or trap through the winter, but it would also obviate the need for Indians to haul their goods to a post in the spring.[18]

What we often forget is that traders were almost always dependent on the Indians. Food and provisions were scarce at posts such as Michilimackinac over the long winter. And it was expensive to bring up enough goods from Montreal to last the winter or purchase them in advance. British traders quickly learned that the key to staying in the pays d'en haut over the harsh months was to winter with an Indian family. Even French post commanders had sometimes taken to wintering over with the Indians because they had a better chance of surviving the winter. In return for their trade goods, their Native family would ensure the trader had enough to eat and enough pelts to stay warm. As many a French trader had learned, the best way to secure a winter refuge was to marry into Native families.[19]

Partly because of this dependence of traders on their Indian connections, Johnson, Rogers, and others came to realize there was more than just economics or even survival involved. Under the French regime, traders, and especially those wintering over with Indians, often mediated relations between the Odawa and French officials. French or Métis traders such as Charles Michel Mouet de Langlade—who had an Odawa mother and a French father—often spent the long winter months among their kin, or their trading partners. The closer the relationship, the more mutually beneficial it was. Traders were privy to discussions among members of different doodemag over the winter. They acted as vital conduits of information.[20]

In theory, at least, traders could also represent official European interests far from the outposts of empire; certainly, that is how historians have often interpreted their presence. More often, wintering traders acted in the interest of the relationship they had with the family, or families, with whom they lived or into which they had married. As the British Indian agent George Croghan noted in 1765, the French and Indians had been "bred up together like Children in that Country, & the French have always adopted the Indians Customs & manners, Treated them Civily & supplyed their wants generously." Sometimes, as in the case of Langlade and others like him, General Thomas Gage's observation that the French had become "almost one People with them" was literally true. Yet even traders who were not related by blood had a vested interest in protecting and nurturing the interests of the Indians.[21]

Though the British tended to idealize the relationship between French and Indians and to think these kinds of relationships suited imperial interests, French officials themselves, of course, had constantly complained about the "interior French." Rarely could these traders be counted on to carry out orders from French officials. Most often, they acted in the interests of their Indian families. Traders were loath to jeopardize a trust that may have taken years to build for the sake of orders emanating from Versailles or Quebec. The long history of rocky relations between the Anishinaabeg and French officials is testimony to the fact that traders in their midst rarely worked on behalf of imperial interests. It was more accurate to say that the Anishinaabeg and other Algonquians in the pays d'en haut maintained relations with French traders and not with the French empire.

The politics behind these crucial trading relationships formed at least part of the reason for Johnson's objection to the practice of wintering over. He believed that those most likely to be invited out to winter over with the Indians were the traders least likely to keep British imperial interests at heart—whether they be French or English. Johnson knew that only those with close connections and ties to the Indians could survive a winter with them. While there were a few new English traders who appeared to adapt quickly to Indian ways of trading and secure their trust, by and large the majority of those who wintered over with Indians were long-established French or Métis traders, such as Langlade. They either kept trading themselves or worked for English merchants who knew the French were key to the trade. For merchants, this made good economic sense and made their lives easier even if they sometimes could not trust their agents. But Johnson and Gage believed the practice was bad for the business of empire. They assumed that even those French employed by the English simply represented their own interests with the Indians. Invariably, the British would be blamed for any trouble.[22]

Thus the finer details of northern trade practices were about much more than trade itself. The practices were a vital part of the diplomatic and political process. Though Johnson and other British officials were often concerned about traders having undue influence over the Indians, the Indians themselves saw traders as crucial in gaining influence over Europeans. As a later British officer complained about Langlade: "[H]e can refuse the Indians nothing they can ask, and they will loose nothing for want of asking." The closer their relations with traders, the more reliable was Indian information about the posts, official policy, and British strategic interests. Winter traders with close relations to the Indians would more likely act in their best interest when dealing with Indian agents or post commanders. At the very least, many Anishinaabeg could and did use these relationships to pass along news—and rumors—to the British, whether welcome or unwelcome, in order to gain political and diplomatic leverage. Indeed, this was precisely how the Anishinaabeg and others manipulated their relations with the French.[23]

Restoring Empire

Anishinaabe strategies to reinstate credit and wintering over help illuminate how much British imperial efforts in the Great Lakes were shaped by Indigenous politics and trade practices. William Johnson simply assumed that European traders provided the main impetus behind efforts to undermine his new trade policies. Subsequent historians have reproduced his faulty assumption. In their eyes, it was another example of the undue influence that traders had over the Indians. But it was the Anishinaabeg and other Indians trading at the post who called the shots. Traders, French or English, could not and would not have gone out to winter among the Indians if they were not welcome and encouraged. William Leslye, one of the first British post commanders at Michilimackinac, had learned this lesson before the outbreak of the Anglo-Indian War. In a council with Leslye, the Odawa demanded winter traders and told him it was "always Custommary for the french to send traders to Winter With them." Leslye, amid swirling rumors of an imminent attack on the post, conceded.[24]

On the arrival of Captain Howard in 1764, the Anishinaabeg and other visiting parties of Indians again besieged the new post commander with requests to allow traders among them. Howard quietly allowed at least one English trader, Edward Chinn, to go out with the Odawa. He may have secretly allowed other French and English traders to go as well. The following year, the flood of cheap goods from Albany and Montreal that accompanied the official reopening of the trade brought hundreds of northern Indians down to Michilimackinac. They, too, added to the demands of the Indians at the straits to allow traders to go back home with them. Howard had to decide whether to follow official British policy.[25]

The Anishinaabe Odawa gave Howard plenty of reasons to disobey his orders. As he settled into Michilimackinac, the Odawa alarmed him with rumors of possible conspiracies. While wintering over with the Odawa, Edward Chinn, too, had heard many wild stories: the St. Joseph's Potawatomi were reportedly in touch with the French via the Mississippi, fifty canoes of Ojibwe had gone to the Illinois and found plenty of rum at Chicago, and fifty thousand livres' worth of goods had gone out to the nations in and around Green Bay from French traders now in Spanish territory across the Mississippi. The Odawa ogimaa Manétewabe even told Howard that while wintering over at the Grand River, he heard talk that the French had retaken Quebec and Trois-Rivières, and would soon come up the Mississippi.[26]

In order to manipulate Howard to their advantage, the Waganawkezee Odawa alternately spread rumors of war and assured him of their peaceful intentions. The continued uncertainty of British relations with the nearby Ojibwe and the more distant Potawatomi helped increase the importance of the Odawa to post commanders such as Howard. He felt isolated at Michilimackinac, and uneasy about the sincerity of the Ojibwe. Throughout 1765, he talked to them, but he did not trust them. Howard's main informant, a Frenchman named Marsac, kept him on his toes with reports that Indians from the Grand River planned to attack English traders on Lake Erie, and that the Odawa who made peace at Detroit the previous year were plotting another pan-Indian uprising. War belts were in motion again, and the "great Chief of the Chippaweighs [Ojibwe]" intended to strike somewhere as "soon as the *Strawberries are ripe*." The Odawa also told an English trader wintering over with them that the French from Illinois supplied the Indians as far north as Green Bay with everything they wanted. Amid these troubling reports, Howard sighed with some relief that the "Odawas near me, seem inclinable for Peace," and he loaded them with presents to keep them that way.[27]

Odawa strategy paid dividends during a series of Indian councils throughout June 1765. Eighty canoes of Indians from Lake Superior and its tributaries came in, and thirty more were rumored to be on their way. For many of them, it was their very first meeting with the British. They reached the straits just as the Menominee and Winnebago from Green Bay along with all the Odawa and Ojibwe of the Michilimackinac region got there. John Porteous, a trader who had just arrived at the post, thought there were upward of eleven hundred to twelve hundred Indians at Michilimackinac in mid-June. The Odawa used the opportunity to show their influence and power in the region. During the councils, they brought out the covenant belt that Johnson had presented at Niagara for the first time, exhibiting it to the other nations. With the Odawa supporting reconciliation, Howard managed to persuade most nations present to swear their fidelity to the British and criticize the Ojibwe who had attacked them in 1765. In return, though, the Odawa took the opportunity to push Howard to send traders out with them over the winter. With his nerves already stretched, Howard consented so as not to "offend them, and perhaps make them change their way of thinking." Without waiting for official sanction, he promised to send a select few traders out (mostly French), distributed a large number of presents, and clung to the hope that with these measures the "Indians will remain in our Interest." Howard told his superiors it was a strategic move: the traders would gather intelligence about the temper of all the Indian nations. Later, though, Howard confessed that he thought if he had not allowed the traders to winter with the Indians, "they would then have declared Warr."[28]

Stuck between the politics of the pays d'en haut and the dictates of empire, Howard had to improvise. It would cost him his job as post commander. As early as July 1765, one British Indian agent told Superintendent Johnson that it was whispered about Montreal that Howard had allowed some traders to go, and that he had shown great "partiality" in selecting them. The response from the rest of the trading community was fast and furious, and they effectively accused Howard of accepting bribes in choosing who would go out. But it is most likely that the Anishinaabeg had chosen who would accompany them. Both Johnson and General Gage believed that Howard acted only with the "prudence" needed in such a delicate situation, and that the complaints arose purely from the "Resentment & Jealousy" of other traders. Still, Howard was eventually forced to return to Montreal to face charges. Though acquitted, he was reprimanded, and he never returned to Michilimackinac.[29]

Howard's successor at Michilimackinac, Robert Rogers, fared even worse. Within days of his arrival at the post in the summer of 1766, Rogers recorded in a detailed journal that the Odawa summoned him to a council at Waganawkezee. Once there, the Odawa reminded Rogers of their previous fidelity to the British but put him on notice. There were plenty of "bad birds flying from the West side of the Missisipi to this part of the World," they told him. Some were already among the Potawatomi at St. Joseph's. This was a none-too-subtle reminder of the murder of two English traders near the Rouge River thought to be killed by the Potawatomi. Nissowaquet, one of the Odawa ogimaag (and Charles Langlade's uncle), made sure to repeat rumors that the French were assembling a force to come up the Mississippi, through the Great Lakes, and down to Niagara until they met another army landing in New York. He also showed an astute awareness of the colonial crisis sparked by the Stamp Act, which had been passed in Parliament in March 1765. The legislation precipitated public demonstrations, violence, and threats of violence all along the eastern seaboard, as groups calling themselves Sons of Liberty burned court records and attacked the homes of prominent British officials. The Odawa took note of the divisions in the colonies—perhaps presciently—argued that the French could invade "with great ease" because the "English people are divided in America, & more than one half of them will join the French."[30]

Having set the context in an unsubtle manner, Nissowaquet proceeded to business. He pressed Rogers to expand the practice of sending out traders. If he refused, the Odawa reminded Rogers they had alternatives. The French had sent strings of wampum from the Mississippi "inviting all the Indians to go there with thier [*sic*] furs & Peltry to trade with thier [*sic*] old fathers." Though Rogers scoffed at the Odawa for believing lies about a French invasion, he knew that the threat to trade with the French was only too real. So he listened. From the start, he was careful to meet with the Odawa regularly, and he always brought a good supply of presents. Despite the fate of his predecessor and his instructions, Rogers also consented to allowing a limited number of traders out on winter hunts.[31]

The following spring, in May 1767, Nissowaquet and other Odawa ogimaag continued to press their case. After returning from the winter hunt, Nissowaquet again demanded an audience with Rogers. The ogimaa took pains to note how the Odawa had kept the traders with them safe and well fed through the winter and had paid back all their credits. He even brought the traders to Michilimackinac himself to confirm this claim. Then, throughout the summer, Nissowaquet and others from Waganawkezee kept up pressure on Rogers by warning of great unrest in the west. That autumn, Rogers caved in once again on winter traders and effectively opened up the winter trade to all. He granted a total of seventy-seven wintering permits between July and August 1767, and two more in the following month, allowing 121 canoes out on the Lakes. Almost all the men who went out and wintered around Lake Michigan and Green Bay and points farther west were Frenchmen, though at least some were there on behalf of English merchants or traders.[32]

Rogers was convinced that allowing traders to winter over with the Indians would be the key to peace. Justifying his actions, he wrote that the Michilimackinac nations were unanimous on this front: "[T]heir principal Request of the Commandant is that Traders may come into their respective Countries, That their Wives, Children, Old Men Friends and Countrymen may be Supplied with such things as / having long been accustomed to the use of / they cannot comfortably and patiently Subsist without." By the time he wrote his defense, Rogers was preaching to the converted. As early as February 1767, while the Board of Trade in London was again busily trying to work out a formal policy, General Gage also joined the chorus of arguments in favor of permitting traders from the northern districts to winter over with the Indians, admitting that Johnson's policy was not working. When General Guy Carleton took over later in the year, he also argued for winter traders. By

1768, just as colonists on the eastern seaboard were coming to terms with a new round of onerous revenue-raising taxes passed by the British, the Odawa at Michilimackinac formally wrested key concessions from the Board of Trade. The Townshend Acts, which placed taxes on a number of essential goods including glass, paper, and tea, were in part designed to control and channel trade within the empire. Yet in that same year, imperial officials also loosened restrictions on the Indian trade. They formally recognized the wintering of traders and the giving of credit as a necessary part of the political economy of the pays d'en haut.[33]

The Anishinaabeg even managed to protect their French and Métis trading partners, who were often their kin, despite British frustration with them. As one official noted about French traders, their "Influence over & Connection with the Indians will make it a Work of much difficulty to remove them." The Indians would "hardly consent," and it would likely be "productive of a Quarrel."[34] By 1768, the new British governor of Quebec, Guy Carleton, was forced to admit that the British should follow the "system pursued by the French government" and believed British success in the pays d'en haut and beyond would depend on the help of the French, "who are well acquainted with the country [and] the language and manners of the natives."[35] French and Métis traders such as Langlade were thus able to hold their own in the early years of the British regime in the pays d'en haut. Not only did they compete with the British traders who flocked to Michilimackinac, but they also kept traders from the middle colonies at bay in the region south of the Lakes. One British official believed that because of their "long connections with those Indians and their better knowledge of their languages and customs," the Canadians had an "advantage over the English, which it is not improbable they will endeavour to improve, and use every artifice to keep the trade in their hands as long as they can." They did. One historian has argued that French merchants and French and Métis voyageurs, guides, interpreters, and traders dominated the northern fur-carrying trade through Michilimackinac for the next sixty years at least.[36]

Having secured their diplomatic and economic interests, the Anishinaabe Odawa at Michilimackinac throve amid the new imperial arrangements. While enjoying the lavish presents and provisions of the British post commanders, the Odawa made a living, as they had done for many years, feeding the Europeans at the post. The imperial garrison at Michilimackinac struggled to grow enough on the dry, sandy, and barren soil—"a Mear Sand bank"—that surrounded the post. Indians from around the straits thus made a tidy profit on keeping them alive. Anyone wanting to stay at the post was dependent on fish, corn, and dried and fresh meats that the Michilimackinac Indians brought to them. That included the many Indian traders who came into the post in the early summer laden with furs. The Odawa would greet both natives and newcomers with furs, skins, maple sugar, grease, and dried meats that they had trapped or prepared over the winter. They would trade these essentials with the growing number of traders returning from winter hunts or coming up from Montreal. They kept on trading throughout the summer. Anishinaabe women at Waganawkezee especially took advantage of the "Verey Good Ground" they cultivated thirty miles from the post and grew "Corn Beens and meney articles which thay youse in Part themselves and Bring the Remander to Market." Meanwhile, Anishinaabe men continued to fish and hunt throughout the summer, since the woods were still full of partridges, hares, venison, foxes, raccoons, and wild pigeons, while the lakes and straits still yielded a massive bounty in fish. Traders and soldiers alike complained that the Anishinaabeg charged high prices for their goods. As Michilimackinac renewed its role as the center of a vast trading network—by 1766 even General Gage acknowledged that it was "the greatest Mart of Trade"—the Waganawkezee Odawa were still positioned to take continued advantage.[37]

With their base once again secure and prospering, the Anishinaabe Odawa also continued to grow in numbers during this period. A later account of the settlement at Waganawkezee in 1779 referred to three distinct and well-established villages stretching for miles along the shoreline. It also named as many as nineteen different ogimaag in the settlement, including three Ojibwe and one Odawa of mixed French and Anishinaabe parentage. But Odawa growth went beyond the confines of Waganawkezee. Population growth and the resources available meant that settlements continued to proliferate in this era. Unlike the growth of new towns and cities in Europe, population growth in Anishinaabewaki was dispersed. New Odawa villages continued to spring up all along the eastern shore of Lake Michigan, at least as far south as the mouth of the Grand River. Both Odawa from northern Lake Michigan and Ojibwe from the Bay de Noc region (at the north end of Green Bay) also filtered southward along the Wisconsin shore of the lake, mixing with the Indians already there. Most of the evidence points to continued growth of Native populations in the central, western, and northern Great Lakes regions, and the Odawa were in the middle of that growth. The leading historical geographer of the region, Helen Hornbeck Tanner, concluded that the Indian population of the Great Lakes had reached about sixty thousand by 1768, plus another twenty thousand or so who were peripheral to the Lakes but active in them. Tanner argues that across the central and northern Lakes regions, the Native nations had achieved, or were in the process of achieving, long-term stability even while the nations of the southern Lakes were on the verge of rapid and violent alterations.[38]

Conclusion: Masters of Empire

Within a few years, then, the Anishinaabeg at Michilimackinac had brought the British to heel by force and persuasion. Not only had they restored a favorable trade at the straits, but the Odawa also made Michilimackinac a central strategic and commercial site for the British. Thus they made themselves key players within the British empire. Despite themselves, the British ended up as presiding over an imperfect imperial system very similar to the one they defeated in 1760. And as they quickly learned, this was not an easy relationship. The Anishinaabeg were more than happy to use any leverage they had to manipulate the relationship in their favor. Of course, this was what the Odawa and others had done to the French for years before—they used the threat of trade or alliance with the English (or, indeed, other Indian nations) to get what they wanted from the French. Now the situation was reversed. A continental perspective helps us appreciate that when the British came to Michilimackinac, they, like the French, found themselves enmeshed in and dependent on an Indian world of diplomacy and trade that stretched both east and west from the straits.[39]

William Johnson was one of those who seemed to have learned some hard lessons since the English had inherited French claims in the pays d'en haut. The Indians were, Johnson wrote, a "free people who had independent Lands, which were their ancient possessions." They insisted the French only occupied their posts "by favour" and not by conquest, and by ceding Canada had "granted what was not in their power to give." If the Indians conceded any rights to the English, it was to the occupation of those forts only, and on the same terms as the French. They scoffed at English offers of "protection" and replied by saying they feared only each other, not Europeans. And they paid little heed to any terms of "submission"—they called themselves "no more than our friends and Allies." If the British wanted more than these tentative promises from the nations of the pays d'en haut, Johnson concluded—as many French officials had previously—they must have a "good army at his back, to protect them from their resentment."[40]

Yet Johnson concluded that most of the nations of the pays d'en haut had little interest in seeing any group of Europeans defeated entirely and one victorious power seizing total control, for as they often said, "the White people were for reducing them to nothing," and both the French and English had the same aim. In that light, most Native nations instead "were desirous to preserve a kind of equilibrium between us, and inclined occasionally to throw their weight into the lightest scale." When the French occupied the posts, the Indians flirted with the English and used threats of going over to them to pursue their interests. Now that the British occupied the posts, Native Americans were happy to practice the same manipulative flirtations with the French and Spanish on their flanks and in their midst. Some among them were heartier for one side or another, as Johnson noted, but most wanted to maintain a balance of power. This was little different from what Europeans did, Johnson noted. It was, he concluded, a way of thinking "so exactly correspondent with that of the most Civilized Nations."[41]

Yet while William Johnson fretted that the nations of the pays d'en haut wanted to maintain a balance of power, other British officials, already enmeshed in a seemingly intractable colonial crisis along the eastern seaboard, worried that the Indians were up to something much more sinister. General Gage noted that the Indians of the Lakes happily circulated rumors of invitations they had received encouraging them to join the French and Spanish against the English. They spread these rumors not only to gain leverage with the British, he thought, but also to provoke the British into another war: "I believe the Indians would be glad to embroil us," he noted, "as our Quarrells are generaly the Indian Harvests."[42]

Though ostensibly at peace with the British from 1764 onward, the Anishinaabe Odawa and others showed a great awareness of the tensions between Europeans. They were quick to report all news of Spanish and French intrigues and take advantage of any rumors of war in Europe or America. They were also quick to point out and exploit the divisions between British officials and their colonists. Ultimately, continued Indian agitation helped convince British officials to maintain the western posts to try to keep the Spanish and French from gaining too much influence in the region. They did so even as they abandoned Fort Duquesne and other posts in the Ohio Valley to cut costs.[43]

Of course, the ultimate irony is that just as the British imposed a new round of trade restrictions on its own colonists on the eastern seaboard in the 1760s, the Anishinaabeg at Michilimackinac managed to wrest crucial trade concessions from William Johnson and the Board of Trade. The two issues were not unrelated. The spiraling expenses of maintaining the western posts helped keep the pressure on the British to reform their North American empire. Thus the Odawa helped set the fuse that would eventually ignite the American Revolution.

In turn, as Colin Calloway's chapter in this volume goes on to show, the shaky and Indigenous-based foundations of the newly expanded British empire in North America meant that Indian nations across the continent continued to play an important role in the political and military history of the period. And for the Odawa at Michilimackinac in particular, the American Revolution and the ensuing tensions between Britain and the new republic ensured they maintained leverage, and their place, in the pays d'en haut, well into the nineteenth century. Long after many of the major nations to their south had suffered the worst effects of dispossession and removal, the Anishinaabeg continued to negotiate their way in the new republic, shape the new nations that arose, and remain where they were. Many remain there still.

Notes

1. Johnson to the Lords of Trade, August 30, 1764, E. B. O'Callaghan, ed., *Documents Relating to the Colonial History of the State of New-York*, 15 vols. (Albany: Weed, Parsons, 1853–1857) [hereafter *NYCD*], 7:648. The British hoped to raise somewhere between £60,000 and £100,000 from the Stamp Act; see P. D. G. Thomas, *British Politics and the Stamp Act Crisis: The First Phase of the American Revolution, 1763–1767* (Oxford: Clarendon Press, 1975), 69–90.

2. General Meeting with All the Western Indians in Their Camp, July 31, 1764, James Sullivan et al., eds., *The Papers of Sir William Johnson*, 14 vols. (Albany: University of the State of New York, 1921–1962) [hereafter *JP*], 11:309–312; Bradstreet to Gage, August 4, 1764, Thomas Gage Papers, Clements Library [hereafter Gage Papers]; Michilimackinac, August 19, 1766, The Odawas Answer to the Speech Made to Them the Day Before, MS/Rogers, Robert, 1:1 Correspondence, 1760–1771, Burton Historical Collection, Detroit Public Library; Keith R. Widder, *Beyond Pontiac's Shadow: Michilimackinac and the Anglo-Indian War of 1763* (East Lansing: Michigan State University Press, 2013), 200–201.

3. Nations at Indian Congress at Niagara, July 1764, *JP* 11:276; Johnson to the Lords of Trade, August 30, 1764, *NYCD* 7:648; Bradstreet to Gage, August 4, 1764, Gage Papers; Gage to Halifax, September 21, 1764, Clarence Edwin Carter, ed., *The Correspondence of Thomas Gage*, 2 vols. (Hamden, CT: Archon Books, 1969–) [hereafter *CTG*], 1:57; Fred Anderson, *The Crucible of War: The Seven Years' War and the Fate of Empire in British North America, 1754–1766* (New York: Alfred A. Knopf, 2000), 620; Jon Parmenter, "Forging New Links in the Anglo-Iroquois Covenant Chain, 1758–1766," *Ethnohistory* 44, no. 4 (Autumn 1997): 631–632; Colin G. Calloway,

The Scratch of a Pen: 1763 and the Transformation of North America (New York: Oxford University Press, 2006), 96–98.

4. Milo Milton Quaife, ed., *Alexander Henry's Travels and Adventures in the Years 1760–1776* (Chicago: Lakeside Press, 1921), 44; Henry Balfour's Conference with Indians, September 29, 1761, *JP* 3:537–545; Amherst to Johnson, March 13, 1762, *JP* 3:645.

5. Richard White, *The Middle Ground: Indians, Empires, and Republics in the Great Lakes Region, 1650–1815* (New York: Cambridge University Press, 1991), 1–9; Michael J. Witgen, "The Rituals of Possession: Native Identity and the Invention of Empire in Seventeenth-Century Western North America," *Ethnohistory* 54, no. 4 (2007): 648; Michael J. Witgen, *An Infinity of Nations: How the Native New World Shaped Early North America* (Philadelphia: University of Pennsylvania Press, 2012), 29–115; Heidi Bohaker, "*Nindoodemag:* The Significance of Algonquian Kinship Networks in the Eastern Great Lakes Region, 1600–1701," *William and Mary Quarterly* 63, no. 1 (January 2006): 23–52.

6. Witgen, "Rituals of Possession," 645–647; Witgen, *Infinity*, 69–107.

7. Proceedings of an Indian Conference, December 3–5, 1760, *JP* 10:202; Bohaker, "*Nindoodemag*," 47–48; Witgen, *Infinity*, 31–34, 42, 372.

8. Reuben Gold Thwaites, ed., *The Jesuit Relations and Allied Documents*, 73 vols. (Cleveland: The Burrows Brothers Company, 1896–1901) [hereafter *JR*], 55:155–159.

9. Vaudreuil and Raudot to the Ministry, November 14, 1709, *Michigan Pioneer and Historical Collections*, 40 vols. (Lansing: Michigan Pioneer and Historical Society, 1874–1929) [hereafter *MPHC*], 33:453–454. On the importance and endurance of French and Métis influence at places like Michilimackinac, see especially Susan Sleeper-Smith, "Women, Kin, and Catholicism: New Perspectives on the Fur Trade," *Ethnohistory* 47, no. 2 (Spring 2000): 423–452, and Sleeper-Smith, *Indian Women and French Men: Rethinking Cultural Encounter in the Western Great Lakes* (Amherst: University of Massachusetts Press, 2001); Jacqueline L. Peterson, "The People in Between: Indian-White Marriage and the Genesis of a Métis Society and Culture in the Great Lakes Region, 1680–1830" (PhD diss., University of Illinois-Chicago, 1981); Keith R. Widder, "After the Conquest: Michilimackinac, a Borderland in Transition, 1760–1763," *Michigan Historical Review* 34, no. 1 (Spring 2008): 43–61; Jay Gitlin, "On the Boundaries of Empire: Connecting the West to Its Imperial Past," in *Under an Open Sky: Rethinking America's Western Past*, ed. William Cronon, George Miles, and Jay Gitlin (New York: Norton, 1992). Cf. Widder, *Beyond Pontiac's Shadow*, for a more detailed view of these relations and a different interpretation of their import during Pontiac's War. Chapter 4 in Michael A. McDonnell, *Masters of Empire: Great Lakes Indians and the Making of America* (New York: Hill and Wang, 2015), deals with the issue at length. I'm indebted to Eric Hemenway of the Little Traverse Bay Band of Odawa for illuminating conversations about the ways Langlade might have understood his Anishinaabe identity.

10. Johnson Diary, September 4, 1761, in Reuben Gold Thwaites, ed., *Collections of the State Historical Society of Wisconsin*, 20 vols. (Madison: State Historical Society of Wisconsin, 1855–1911) [hereafter *WHC*], 18:231; Andrew Sturtevant, "Jealous Neighbors: Rivalry and Alliance among the Native Communities of Detroit, 1701–1766" (PhD diss., College of William and Mary, 2011), 253; Claus to Johnson, December 3, 1761, Johnson to Claus, February 9, 1762, *JP* 3:576, 629.

11. Lords of Trade to William Johnson, September 29, 1763, *NYCD* 7:567; Gregory Evans Dowd, *War under Heaven: Pontiac, the Indian Nations, and the British Empire* (Baltimore: Johns Hopkins University Press, 2002), 137–138, 142, 145–146, 274–275.

12. Claus to Johnson, August 29, 1763, *JP* 10:806–807; An Indian Conference, *JP* 10:779–780; Major Rogers's Speech to the Several Chiefs of Ottawas at Michilimackinac, August 18, 1766, National Library of Canada, MG 19, F 35—Superintendent of Indian Affairs in the Northern District of North America, Original, n.d. 1762–1829, Photocopy, n.d. 1753–1795, series 1, lot 646, pp. 1–7, 11.

13. Gage to Hillsborough, January 5, 1769, *CTG* 1:209–210; B. Glasier, "Speech of La Force, and All the Ottaway Chiefs Delivered at Michimackina, Aug. 30, 1768," *JP* 6:348–349; John Vattas to Thomas Gage, May 16, 1773, *MPHC* 19:299.

14. Kent, *Rendezvous*, 2:434; Marjorie G. Jackson, "The Beginning of British Trade at Michilimackinac," *Minnesota History* 2, no. 3 (September 1930): 244; Johnson to the Lords of Trade, October 8, 1766, *NYCD* 7:871–872; Johnson to Gage, August 28, 1765, Gage to Johnson, September 8, 1765, *JP* 4:833–835, 5:838–840.

15. White, "Skilled Game of Exchange," 236–240; Anderson, "Flow of European Goods," 385–410.

16. Parmenter, "Anglo-Iroquois Covenant Chain," 622; White, "Skilled Game of Exchange," 236–240; Henry, *Travels*, 39–52, 183–188.

17. Clements, ed., *Journal of Rogers*, 42–43.

18. Timothy J. Kent, *Rendezvous at the Straits: The Trade and Military Activities at Fort de Buade and Fort Michilimackinac, 1669–1781*, 2 vols. (Ossineke, MI: Silver Fox Enterprises, 2004), 2:434; Marjorie G. Jackson, "The Beginning of British Trade at Michilimackinac," *Minnesota History* 2, no. 3 (September 1930): 249–252; William L. Clements, ed., *Journal of Major Robert Rogers* (Worcester, MA, 1918), 42–43. On dependence, see White, *Middle Ground*, 479–485. But see also Kent, *Rendezvous*, for a detailed sense of the trade goods exchange at Michilimackinac and the operation of the trade.

19. Kent, *Rendezvous*, 2:410–411, 434; Jackson, "Trade at Michilimackinac," 249–252; Robert Rogers, *Concise Account of North America* (London, 1765), 250–251.

20. Johnson to Gage, August 28, 1765, *JP* 11:915–917.

21. Croghan to Johnson, November 1765, *Collections of the Illinois State Historical Library* 38 vols. (Springfield: Illinois State Historical Library, 1903–1978) [hereafter *IHC*], 11:53–54; Gage to Hillsborough, November 10, 1770, *CTG* 1:275; White, *Middle Ground*, 316–317.

22. Johnson to the Lords of Trade, October 8, 1766, *NYCD* 7:871–872; John Lottridge to Johnson, December 12, 1762, Johnson to Gage, August 28, 1765, Gage to Johnson, September 8, 1765, *JP* 3:969, 4:833–835, 5:838–840; *JP* 11:879–880, 902–904, 915–917, 926–927; Jackson, "Trade at Michilimackinac," 240–241. Kent, *Rendezvous*, 2:408–409, maintains that the French and Métis remained central to the trade at the straits for another sixty years at least, until about 1820.

23. De Peyster to Carleton, June 6, 1777, *MPHC* 10:275–276.

24. William Leslye to Amherst, September 16, 1762, Amherst Papers, W.O. 34/49, pp. 116–117, microfilm copy, Reel 40 (September 1760–October 1763), Public Record Office, UK.

25. Journal of William Howard, [November 3, 1764–April 16, 1765], *JP* 11:698; Daniel Claus wrote to Johnson, July 11, 1765, *JP* 4:789–790; Johnson to Gage,

August 9, 1765, *JP* 4:815; Kent, *Rendezvous*, 2:434–435; Johnson to Howard, July 2, 1765, *JP* 4:781.

26. Journal of William Howard, [November 3, 1764–April 16, 1765], *JP* 11:696–698.

27. Howard to Johnson, May 17, 1765, and Campbell to Johnson, June 3, 1765, both in *JP* 11:739–740, 764–765.

28. John Porteous, "Schenectady to Michilimackinac, 1765 & 1766," *Ontario Historical Society Papers and Records* 33 (1939): 91; William Howard to William Johnson, June 24, 1765, *JP* 11:804–809, 816–817; Howard to Burton, September 24, 1765, Howard to Eyre Massey, June 16, 1766, enclosed in Massey to Gage, July 10, 1766, Gage Papers.

29. Daniel Claus to Johnson, July 11, 1765, *JP* 4:789–790; Jackson, "Trade at Michilimackinac," 244–245, 247–249; *JP* 4:870–872, 883; Gage to Conway, June 24, 1766, *CTG* 1:96–97.

30. Clements, ed., *Journal of Rogers*, 11–12, 27; Johnson to Gage, December 12, 1766, *JP* 12:227–229; Sleeper-Smith, *Indian Women and French Men*, 62–63.

31. Clements, ed., *Journal of Rogers*, 28, 48.

32. Clements, ed., *Journal of Rogers*, 27–37, 48; Kent, *Rendezvous*, 457–461; Charles E. Lart, ed., "Fur-Trade Returns, 1767," *Canadian Historical Review* 3, no. 4 (December 1922): 351–358.

33. Clements, ed., *Journal of Rogers*, 28, 48; Jackson, "Trade at Michilimackinac," 253–254, 256–257; Sleeper-Smith, *Indian Women and French Men*, 62–64; Lart, "Fur-Trade Returns," 351–358; "Orders and Regulations," [1767], *JP* 12:246–247; "Regulations for the Indian Trade," January 15, 1768, *JP* 12:409–413.

34. Clements, ed., *Journal of Rogers*, 19, 49–50; Johnson to Gage, July 25, 1765, *JP* 11:869; Croghan to Johnson, November 1765, *NYCD* 7:788; Jackson, "Trade at Michilimackinac," 247–249; Gage to Halifax, August 10, 1765, *CTG* 1:65; *JP* 5:331, 339; Johnson to the Lords of Trade, January 20, 1764, *NYCD* 7:600; Johnson to the Earl of Shelburne, December 3, 1767, *NYCD* 7:1002; Bouquet to Gage, November 30, 1764, *MPHC* 19:284–285; Robert Rogers to Thomas Gage, February 12, 1767, Clements Library; Gage to Carleton, October 5, 1767, Gage Papers; Peter Marshall, "Imperial Policy and the Government of Detroit: Projects and Problems, 1760–1774," *Journal of Imperial and Commonwealth History* 2, no. 2 (1974): 170–171; Guy Johnson to Thomas Gage, May 20, 1768, *JP* 7:509.

35. Carleton to Shelburne, March 2, 1768, *WHC* 18:288–292; Carleton to John Caldwell, October 6, 1776, 270.

36. Marjorie G. Reid, "The Quebec Fur-Traders and Western Policy, 1763–1774," *Canadian Historical Review* 6, no. 1 (March 1925): 26–27; Sleeper-Smith, *Indian Women and French Men*, 62–64; Kent, *Rendezvous*, 2:408–409.

37. Gage to Johnson, March 23, 1766, *JP* 5:95; "Journal of Peter Pond, 1740–1775," *WHC* 18:327–328, 329, 341; Rogers, *Concise Account*, 250–252; Daniel Ingram, *Indians and British Outposts in Eighteenth-Century America* (Gainesville, FL: University Press of Florida, 2012), chap. 3; Kent, *Rendezvous* at the Straits, 2:429, 446, 448; Henry, *Travels*, 47, 54–56; William Leslye to Amherst, September 16, 1762, Amherst Papers, W.O. 34/49, pp. 116–117, microfilm copy, Reel 40 (September 1760–October 1763), Public Record Office, UK.

38. At least as many as four thousand Odawa ringed the shores Lake Michigan, along with another three thousand Potawatomi, while up to another fifteen thousand Ojibwe-Mississauga provided a buffer of sorts between the Odawa and their rivals to the south and northwest. De Peyster's Speech at Arbre Croche, July 4, 1779, *WHC* 18:377–390; Arendt Schuyler De Peyster, *Miscellanies by an Officer* (Dumfries, Scotland: C. Munro, 1813), 5–15; Helen Hornbeck Tanner, ed., *Atlas of Great Lakes Indian History* (Norman: University of Oklahoma Press, 1987), 62–63, 65–66; Jeanne Kay, "The Fur Trade and Native American Population Growth," *Ethnohistory* 31 (1984): 265–287; Jeanne Kay, "The Land of La Baye: The Ecological Impact of the Green Bay Fur Trade, 1634–1836 (PhD diss., University of Wisconsin, Madison, 1977), 166–167.

39. Parmenter, "Anglo-Iroquois Covenant Chain," 639; Gitlin, "Connecting the West," 81–82; Jackson, "Trade at Michilimackinac," 258–267, 269–270; White, *Middle Ground*, 311–312.

40. Johnson, "Review of the Trade," 1767, *NYCD* 7:958–959; Carleton to Shelburne, March 2, 1768, *WHC* 18:288–292.

41. Johnson, "Review of the Trade," 1767, *NYCD* 7:958–959.

42. Gage to Hillsborough, January 5, 1769, *CTG* 1:210.

43. Anderson, *Crucible of War*, 633–637; Patrick Griffin, *American Leviathan: Empire, Nation, and Revolutionary Frontier* (New York: Hill and Wang, 2007), 92–94.

CHAPTER THREE

Exploiting British Ambivalence in West Africa

Fante Sovereignty in the Early Nineteenth Century

REBECCA SHUMWAY

West African societies were deeply connected to European empires across the Atlantic—and around the globe—in the Revolutionary Age. From the beginnings of European maritime trade on the West African coast in the fifteenth century, Africans shaped and were shaped by the growth of European empires.[1] This was particularly true of European nations that participated heavily in the transatlantic slave trade from Africa: the Portuguese and British. But the Age of Revolution did not usher in European imperialism in West Africa. The vast majority of sub-Saharan Africa did not become a target of European colonization or settlement until the 1880s. The influence of Europeans was greatest in places where trading settlements had been established for transatlantic trade, especially at the mouths of the Senegal and Gambia Rivers and the Gold Coast (Ghana) and the Slave Coast (Benin and Nigeria), but these settlements were entirely commercial in nature and made no formal claims to control over African territory or people.[2] The British abandoned most of them after the Abolition Act of 1807, which made 90 percent of their trade illegal. Britain's abolitionist movement articulated an Africa policy that demanded the end of the trade of enslaved Africans and the development of other forms of commerce and, eventually, the spread of Christianity in Africa. Prior to the 1870s, there were few European advocates for colonizing African territory except to have a place to settle slaves freed from slave ships.

Several other important distinctions further set Africa apart from other world regions during the Age of Revolution. While slavery was slowly being eradicated in many parts of the world, it expanded significantly across the African continent during the eighteenth and nineteenth centuries. Abolition of the transatlantic slave trade caused the price of slaves to plummet within

African economies and thus enabled the accumulation of slaves by African elites.[3] Joseph Miller has argued that African social values continued to favor a communal ethos during this time, even while individualism was on the rise in much of the rest of the world.[4] Be that as it may, West African forms of political organization were trending toward more monarchical systems during this period, in contrast to the wave of democratic revolutions elsewhere. Key examples include the Sokoto Caliphate, the Oyo Empire, and the kingdoms of Dahomey and Asante. Culturally, the most significant development in West Africa was the continued spread of Islamic religious and political institutions, particularly in the Western Sudan.[5]

Overall, the most significant European activity in Africa between 1760 and 1840 was the continuation of the transatlantic slave trade, which peaked in volume in the 1780s, when roughly 87,000 enslaved Africans were shipped across the Atlantic every year.[6] In the years following British abolition of the slave trade, slave ship voyages to British colonies (and former British colonies) declined significantly, but the opposite was true for Spanish and Portuguese America.[7] Brazil alone received more than two million enslaved Africans after 1807. In those regions of Africa supplying the transatlantic slave trade with captives in the nineteenth century—particularly modern-day Nigeria, Cameroon, Democratic Republic of Congo, and Angola—the chronic violence spurred by the slave trade permeated African political, economic, and social institutions.

On the coast of modern-day Ghana, the Age of Revolution coincided with significant new patterns in African life, some of which reflected the broader ideological, economic, and political changes that characterize the era, others of which were entirely local in nature. The coastal Fante society was integrally connected with Britain's imperial and commercial operations as a result of hosting the headquarters of the British slave trade in the town of Cape Coast since the 1660s, as well as several other British trading posts.[8] Over the course of the eighteenth century, Fante elites formed a coalition government across the central Gold Coast, using wealth and weapons acquired mainly from the British to secure their middleman position in the slave trade and to defend themselves against the imperialistic Asante kingdom to the north. Following the passage of the Abolition of the Slave Trade Act in 1807, however, British trade on the Gold Coast and British strategic interests in Fante affairs diminished drastically.

While British abolition of the slave trade certainly affected the course of Fante history in the nineteenth century, the Fante's relationship with neighboring Asante played a far greater role in shaping Fante life in the first half of the nineteenth century. Fante history took a dramatic turn in 1806, when Asante troops invaded Fanteland and defeated the Fante at one of their most important towns, Abura. This loss was followed by a yearlong occupation of the coast by Asante's army and the even more devastating attack on the Fante town of Anomabo, including the large British fort there, in June 1807.[9] In contrast to what Miller describes as a pattern of African warlords succumbing to the power of African merchants during this period, the region of southern Ghana was succumbing to the ongoing expansion of one of Africa's most militarily powerful precolonial kingdoms. Asante forces finally retreated from the coast in October 1807 due to an outbreak of smallpox and dysentery, but the invasion set in motion a period of chronic warfare. In 1816, Asante forces returned to the coast and decisively defeated Fante forces, this time setting up Asante officials to collect taxes and ensure the loyalty of the conquered coastal territories. The British fort administrators noted in 1809 that the effects of the abolition of the slave trade were not visible because all of the African communities along the Gold Coast were engaged in wars.[10]

From 1806 until the latter part of the nineteenth century, the Fante struggled repeatedly to protect and regain their sovereignty and to rebuild their economy from the dual impacts of war and the withering Atlantic market for export slaves. The presence of British merchants, military personnel, and civil servants, while greatly diminished since 1807, proved an essential source of wealth and military supplies for the Fante in achieving their objectives. In particular, the presence of several British fortified outposts on the Gold Coast, funded by an annual grant from Parliament, made essential military support and diplomatic leverage available to the Fante during a crucial period when their political sovereignty was threatened by the expansion of Asante.

The history of the Gold Coast during this period has mainly been analyzed with a focus on the evolving conflict between Britain and the Asante kingdom, which escalated in the latter part of the nineteenth century in several famous "Anglo-Asante wars."[11] To consider instead the Fante's ultimately successful struggle for sovereignty in the early decades of the nineteenth century offers new perspectives on the complex ways in which the history of the Gold Coast remained intertwined with changes taking place around the Atlantic World during the crucial period after British abolition of the slave trade and before the formal declaration of British colonial rule in 1874.[12]

The ways in which the Fante manipulated the British government's ambivalence toward Africa during this period toward their own local pursuits also offer new perspectives on the Age of Revolution, particularly how it related to Indigenous people on the periphery—but not entirely off the radar—of the British empire. The Fante case reveals the instability in British foreign/imperial policy, the multiplicity of European interests involved in British affairs in West Africa, and the impact of changing British ideas about slavery and the roles of Africa and Africans in the evolving British empire. British concerns with preventing other European or American powers from surpassing their influence in Africa, combined with the abolitionists' pressure to stop the slave trade and develop so-called legitimate commerce, forced Britain to retain and protect the forts on the Gold Coast even though the cost in money and men was consistently far greater than the benefit to the metropole.[13] All of the aforementioned circumstances created opportunities for Fante elites to exploit Britain's commercial and military presence in West Africa as the Fante combated the imperialist threat from their Asante neighbors.

A Note on Indigenous Africans

For most societies in West Africa, the matter of an "Indigenous" identity was an entirely African issue in this period, since the presence of non-African invaders and settlers was virtually nil. The question: "Who was the original founder of a particular settlement?" was and is central to African societies' own historical records, in the form of oral traditions, and being the first to settle has long constituted both political authority and group identity. In many ways, it was only in the 1890s that formal European colonialism and settler colonialism (in eastern and southern Africa) created the notion of Africans, in general, as "natives."

Like many port towns around the Atlantic basin in the late eighteenth century, the Gold Coast commercial centers were cosmopolitan communities rich in the cultural, linguistic, and ethnic/racial markers of the entire Atlantic basin.[14] During the last quarter of the eighteenth century, the seaside towns of the Gold Coast were bustling with European, African, and mixed-race traders and workers of all kinds. The commercial life of these towns was centered around the exchange of African captives for the products of European countries and European colonies—textiles, alcohol, firearms, tobacco. The resident African population of the coastal towns was a mixture of people speaking several different African languages as well as English, Dutch, and pidgin Portuguese. Their ancestors may have inhabited other parts of West

Africa only a generation or two prior. The Fante language became the common language of the central Gold Coast over the course of the eighteenth century, as a variety of ethnolinguistic influences converged within the newly formed Fante Coalition. It could be said, therefore, that Fante identity itself was still in the process of becoming one of many "Indigenous" identities on the Gold Coast in the eighteenth century.[15] Another notable aspect of African identity on the Gold Coast during the early nineteenth century is how some members of the population began to recognize a shared identity with people of African descent in the diaspora. The notion that the Fante had something in common with other "African" or "Black" people, or in the parlance of the times, "Negroes," would become a powerful basis for Pan-African political movements in subsequent decades.

In many ways, the Fante experience can be usefully compared to that of other "Indigenous" people during the Age of Revolution. Fante lands were targeted for commercial (and eventually territorial) expansion by European foreigners. And of course, like other people colonized by Europeans, their racial identity was not that of the "white man," which made them the victims of Europe's pseudoscientific racism. Moreover, the majority of the Fante—those whose livelihoods were based in farming or fishing rather than long-distance trade—were non-Christian and nonliterate, which fit the mold of other Indigenous people who Europeans classified as inferior and in need of "civilizing." At the same time, however, most Fante merchant families in the early nineteenth century were the product of several generations of intimate personal and commercial partnerships between Africans and Europeans. Their Dutch, English, Irish, and Danish surnames testify to multiple generations of intermarriage between Europeans and Africans. And their family records reveal that Christianity and Western-style education were well founded among the Fante elite by this time. Influences on Fante culture from around the Atlantic ran so deep that it is often impossible to determine from the nineteenth-century records who is "African" and who is "European," much less who are the "Indigenous" people.

The Fante Struggle for Sovereignty in the Early Nineteenth Century

At the dawn of the nineteenth century, the Fante polity was a powerful military and commercial presence on the West African coast, founded on the wealth and military capability accumulated through the sale of African captives from several coastal towns over the course of the previous century.

Fante merchants had for centuries acted as middlemen in the trade, which channeled first gold, then enslaved people, from interior markets to the coast. Throughout the era of the slave trade on the Gold Coast, the Fante purchased enslaved people primarily from their northern neighbors, including the Asante kingdom, and sold them on the coast to both passing slave ships and to the resident agents of European trading companies, who resided in large stone forts all along the coast. The most important of these were the British Royal Africa Company, reorganized as the Company of Merchants Trading to Africa in 1750, and the Dutch West Indies Company. These bodies supervised a large portion of the transatlantic slave trade from their headquarters at Cape Coast and Elmina, respectively. European observers remarked on the Fante polity's importance in the region's commercial and diplomatic affairs and the fact that the English language was spoken all along the coast, evidence of the Fante's long-term ties to British traders.[16] Fanteland was governed by a coalition of powerful *ahenfuo* (chiefs / traditional rulers in modern parlance), each of whom was the premier political and military leader in one of several prominent Fante towns on the coast or in the hinterland.

Like many other coastal West African societies, the Fante experienced the ending of Britain's transatlantic slave trade as a commercial loss.[17] The number of captives embarked from the Gold Coast peaked during the last quarter of the eighteenth century at roughly eleven thousand annually.[18] By the 1830s, that number had fallen to less than two hundred annually. But while the abolition of the transatlantic slave trade had an undeniable impact on the Fante economy, a much more dramatic and enduring change came in the form of military invasion and occupation by the Asante kingdom. With uncanny timing, the Asante army completed its first successful invasion into Fante territory—the only area in the region that was still independent of Asante rule—in the same year that Britain abolished the trade upon which the Fante economy had been built. In three major invasions between 1807 and 1816, Asante seized control of the coast, deposed or killed the Fante ahenfuo, and made the Fante people tribute-paying subjects of the *Asantehene*. Rebelling against their Asante colonizers was the primary concern of Fante leaders throughout the period from 1807 until 1826, when an Asante withdrawal was finally negotiated. Protecting their fragile independence from renewed Asante conquest was the Fante's primary concern for the remainder of the nineteenth century, as Asante's military power continued to grow.[19]

In some ways, the Fante struggle against Asante in the early nineteenth century was merely a continuation of the rivalry between these two African states that originated in the 1750s, when Asante first threatened to invade the coastal region.[20] The kings of Asante tried repeatedly to destroy the Fante middleman and gain direct access to coastal markets in the era of the slave trade. Asante and European merchants both recognized that Fante merchants inflated prices and adulterated goods to their own benefit. The fact that Fanteland remained sovereign throughout the eighteenth century owed much to the Fante's lucrative commercial and diplomatic partnerships with British traders and fort administrators, most of whom resided along the Fante stretch of the Gold Coast. The Company of Merchants paid rent, stipends, gifts; facilitated negotiations and oath-swearing; and sold guns, gunpowder, and trade goods with which weapons and men could be acquired. The difference in the Asante-Fante rivalry after 1806 was that Asante not only invaded but occupied several Fante towns, at a time when the British forts were scarcely occupied, much less stocked with trade goods, guns, and gunpowder. Nevertheless, in the Fante's struggle to regain their independence from Asante, the British forts and personnel still provided crucial support.

The financial records associated with British forts on the Gold Coast reveal that even after abolition, the British government continued to provide financial support to the personnel in the forts, and that a portion of this wealth went directly to Fante elites. From 1750 to 1821, and again from 1828 to 1843, the maintenance of the forts was entrusted by the British government to an association of British merchants known as the Company of Merchants trading to Africa, who received an annual grant from Parliament to cover the costs of maintaining the forts and facilitating British trade.[21] The company was represented in Britain by a committee consisting of nine merchants who made annual reports to the Commissioners for Trade regarding their proceedings. On the Gold Coast, Company business was administered by a council of salaried men, the highest ranking of whom were the so-called governors of the largest forts.

From the beginning, the operation of British trading posts on the Gold Coast (and those of the Dutch and Portuguese before them) had required the permission of local African rulers and the payment of "ground rent" for the right to live and trade within their jurisdiction.[22] These practices continued after the abolition of the slave trade. In addition to ground rent, the Company of Merchants fed the local African economy through several other forms of direct payment to Africans, including "dashes" or stipends to prominent political and religious figures; wages paid to hired laborers, interpreters, soldiers, and canoemen; and the "allowances" given to unfree workers who performed various domestic, medicinal, and military tasks. These payments to Africans easily accounted for anywhere from 25 percent to 50 percent of the annual budget (parliamentary grant) of the Company. For example, the cost of maintaining the settlements on the Gold Coast for the twelve months ending in March 1823 totaled £10,049 and included the following charges (34 percent of total):

—Allowance to kings and cabboceers: £810
—Pay and pensions to artificers, laborers, etc.: £1,648
—Contingencies (canoe hire, presents to kings in the interior, incidentals): £1,000

Most of the remainder of the annual budget (58 percent) went toward the salaries of (European) officers, with an additional allowance to officers in command of forts.[23]

Payments to African political elites and laborers strained the Company's budget, and Fante chiefs ensured that they and their subjects received the highest possible payments that could be extracted from their European "guests." When the British offered sums in payment for chiefs' stipends or laborers' wages that were considered inadequate, the forts would be cut off from supplies and laborers until a satisfactory adjustment was made. These frequent "palavers" over payments, gifts, and wages constantly drained the revenue of the forts. The British government regularly assessed the costs and benefits of the Gold Coast forts, and records of these inquiries show clearly and repeatedly that the forts were costing Britain more than they were worth in purely financial terms. In 1811, a report by the commissioners appointed to investigate the state of the settlements and forts on the coast of Africa recommended that five of the forts on the Gold Coast either be dismantled or disposed of to individuals.[24]

Another area of Company spending that benefited the Fante was the maintenance and regular deployment of the Company's military force. The British government was clear and consistent in its orders to the Company of Merchants to avoid getting involved in wars between Africans on the Gold Coast. Experience had shown that these wars were costly to the British both in terms of men killed or injured and in terms of expensive gift-giving required to settle disagreements or secure allies. Particularly in the context of the abolition of the slave trade, when profits were scarce, participation in African wars was well beyond the Company's budgetary constraints. Yet the agents of the Company found it impossible to remain neutral in many of the conflicts occurring in the Fante region in the early nineteenth century, and the Fante benefited in various ways from British support during the ongoing wars of the period.[25]

Most of the time, the Company of Merchants participated in Gold Coast wars as protectors of the Fante townspeople—thousands of whom took refuge in the forts when fighting broke out—or as allies providing troops to fight alongside Fante soldiers in the field. The need for British assistance became acute amid the Asante invasions and wars between coastal polities in the period 1806 to 1817. As the Asante king claimed authority over the lands on which the English forts stood, the Company was forced to give up entirely on their policy of nonintervention in Asante-Fante conflicts.[26]

The most striking example of British military support for the Fante in their struggle against Asante took place from 1823 to 1826, when British and Fante troops fought together and finally defeated Asante forces, ending a decade of Asante occupation of the central Gold Coast. The Fante elite never accepted Asante rule as a permanent condition, and in the early 1820s they seized the chance to revolt. In September 1822, a sergeant employed by the British at Anomabo Fort was arrested and taken captive in the inland town of Abura.[27] British agents on the coast demanded the man's release, on the basis that he was a soldier and subject of King George. But Asante officials refused to return the man because, as a citizen of Anomabo, he was technically an Asante subject. The conflict deepened when the sergeant was executed in captivity. These events came to the attention of Sir Charles MacCarthy, then governor of Sierra Leone and, by extension, the forts on the Gold Coast. As a Crown official, MacCarthy took the matter of sovereignty over British subjects very seriously. He immediately sent a punitive expedition to the scene of the execution, and while this expedition was ultimately judged a failure, it signaled to the Fante and their coastal neighbors that the time was right for rebellion against Asante. Late in 1823, MacCarthy met with Fante and other coastal chiefs to form an alliance and proceeded to launch what has become known in British historiography as the First Asante War. Within a month, MacCarthy's skull had become a trophy of the Asante king, but the fighting continued until August 1826, when the rebels finally achieved a decisive victory over Asante at Dodowa.[28] While peace negotiations continued for the next five years, the Fante had clearly achieved their main objective: independence from Asante, including the withdrawal of Asante tax collectors.

British Ambivalence in a Critical Era

The fact that the Fante were able to regain their autonomy from Asante, largely by relying on wealth, arms, and military alliance with the British, is remarkable considering that the British government had no intention of engaging in diplomatic or military affairs in West Africa during this period. The following analysis points out a number of contradictions within Britain's policy toward Africa in the first half of the nineteenth century. These contradictions reveal an essentially confused or at best ambivalent attitude toward Africa in general and the Gold Coast in particular. Fante elites played no small part in perpetuating Britain's confusion by demanding regular payments from the British for their occupation of the forts and for the recruitment of labor from local communities. They also taxed and regulated the export trade in palm oil.

It is worth remembering that at the beginning of the nineteenth century and for several decades thereafter, the British empire in Africa was more ideology than tangible fact. The antislavery and abolitionist ideas that began circulating in Britain in the 1770s gradually redefined British ideas about and policies toward Africa and condemned the slave trade, if not the enslavement of Africans itself. The stated goal of the abolitionist movement was to "improve Africa" by stopping the transatlantic slave trade, developing other forms of trade, and spreading Christianity and "civilization" or "modernity" among African people.[29] Prior to the 1850s, these goals were meant to be pursued as an extension of the existing commercial contacts British merchants maintained in Africa. It was understood that Africans still governed themselves and their territories, and that European traders, missionaries, and military personnel in Africa operated at the sufferance of African authorities. This dynamic changed over the course of the nineteenth century, as Europeans stopped *asking* for trade, diplomatic relations, and converts, and began instead to *demand* and then *command* these things.[30]

Developments around the Atlantic World during the Age of Revolution—especially abolitionism and antislavery—created conditions in which Britain really had no further use for its fortified trading posts in West Africa. The belief that Africa should be "improved" through the spread of Christianity and commerce was at odds with the fact that there was not yet an alternative commodity trade in which Britain could profitably develop commerce in West Africa.[31] Most British merchants either abandoned West African markets altogether or found ways to participate in the now illegal trade in enslaved people.

The creation of the Sierra Leone colony best demonstrates how British policy was out of touch with West African realities in the Age of Revolution. The settlement of free blacks from the Americas and, later, captives liberated from slave ships was intended, among other things, as a foundation for the grand scheme of "improving" Africa by encouraging the formation of a population of free, Christian African farmers who would produce and sell crops formerly produced in the New World colonies for the benefit of the British economy. Not surprisingly, this experiment failed to meet expectations. Black settlers and recaptives pursued urban lifestyles rather than becoming farmers and remained largely separate from the Indigenous population of the region, who did not embrace the settlers' Christian message. Sierra Leone also quickly produced its own class of African-descended political authorities, missionaries, and teachers whose loyalty to Britain was, naturally, secondary to their goals for their own autonomous state governed by black people.

Like Freetown, Fante towns such as Anomabo and Cape Coast were run by an African elite that was receptive to some of the ideologies and cultural practices of British abolitionists but primarily concerned with improving local conditions according to their own vision of sovereignty and prosperity. The struggle against Asante imperialism was far more important than trade or diplomacy with the British, but the latter proved an important resource for the former.

The Gold Coast was a persistent dilemma for the British government because their ownership of several massive stone fortresses there made the Gold Coast the site of the strongest British presence in tropical Africa. From a global imperial perspective, the possibility that another European power might occupy the forts in the event that Britain abandoned them was reason enough to maintain them, even at a financial loss.[32] Moreover, the British merchants who continued to trade on the Gold Coast were heavily invested in the trade and effectively lobbied the government to maintain support for the forts. They also provided convenient, relatively inexpensive personnel to inhabit and maintain the forts. Britain's maintenance of an administrative presence in the Gold Coast forts, in spite of its own repeated assessments showing that it was unprofitable to do so, is perhaps the penultimate example of the confusion and internal contradictions within Britain's policy toward Africa in the early nineteenth century. The Fante elite took advantage of that confusion in numerous ways.

It is easy to see in retrospect how the continuation of a commercial and military presence—however small—gave Britain a foot in the door on the

Gold Coast once the scramble for Africa heated up in the 1880s. But as T. C. McCaskie has warned, the temptation to view British activities in Africa during the nineteenth century as part of an inevitable British ascendancy only obscures the complex, ambiguous, and unstable nature of the encounter between Africans and the British.[33] Rather than laying the foundations for future West African colonies, as colonial-era historians would claim, what the British government's actions in and policies toward West Africa were really doing is experimenting and largely floundering.[34]

This floundering is demonstrated by two key questions facing the British on the Gold Coast throughout most of the nineteenth century. Neither were ever resolved. First, should the forts be administered by merchants, as they had been throughout the previous century and a half, or by the Crown itself? And second, was it better to pursue a treaty with Asante—the juggernaut of African trade and military power in the region—or to check Asante's power on the coast, where the British flag flew over several large forts?

Between 1807 and 1850, the British government entirely reorganized the administrative apparatus for its possessions on the Gold Coast no less than four times, twice placing them under the government of the Sierra Leone colony and finally managing them directly through the colonial government by appointing the governor of Cape Coast head of a new legislative council. In each instance, the reorganization was prompted by a particular event or assessment indicating a problem with the existing administrative system. The overall pattern of fluctuation reveals an underlying confusion about the purpose of maintaining the forts at all. The Company of Merchants remained in place as the administrators of the forts after abolition of the slave trade, in spite of the sharp decline in merchants' interest in the African trade overall and a thinly veiled continuation of slave trading by those who remained on the Gold Coast.

In 1821, after two failed British diplomatic missions to the Asantehene and in an era of very little trade apart from the illegal slave trade, the British government abolished the Company of Merchants. The forts and settlements previously occupied by the African company were vested in His Majesty and annexed by the king to the government of Sierra Leone.[35] This change marked the first time in nearly two hundred years of operating forts on the Gold Coast that the British government had direct dealings with these trading communities, rather than leaving matters in the hands of merchants. This arrangement created numerous immediate problems, the most obvious being that slavery was illegal according to the laws of Sierra Leone but was a widespread phenomenon and key to the economy of the Gold Coast. The more critical incongruity, however, was in putting the British military in charge of communities that had always been governed by the logic of commerce and diplomacy. Because of the new arrangement, the governor of Sierra Leone, Sir Charles MacCarthy, became involved in the aforementioned dispute surrounding a sergeant from Anomabo Fort who was seized and ultimately executed by Asante forces.[36]

Politicians in London viewed these developments as a failure, rather than a victory, given the widespread view that Britain should avoid engagement in African wars. Lord Bathurst, secretary of state for the colonies, ordered a complete abandonment of British settlements on the Gold Coast in 1827, and this idea was endorsed by the Privy Council for Trade and Plantations.[37] But British merchants invested in the trade recognized that peace between Asante and Fante would facilitate the growth of the increasingly profitable palm oil trade. They lobbied for and achieved a reincarnation of the Company of Merchants with control over the British forts. As an early Gold Coast historian has explained: "A middle course was adopted, which relieved the government from the troublesome affairs of the Gold Coast, and, at the same time, gave its countenance and a slight pecuniary assistance to the merchants for their protection."[38] The Company of Merchants resumed the administration of British forts and settlements in 1828.

Under the new Company of Merchants, the British witnessed "a key period of transition in trade and economic change" on the Gold Coast, amounting to "spectacular economic growth" that continued into the 1860s.[39] The company's president was commended for an excellent job managing the forts and suppressing transatlantic slave trading.[40] But a renewed interest in antislavery exemplified by the Slavery Abolition Act (1833) and new policies aimed at shutting down the supply of captives within Africa itself led the British government to appoint a special commission and then a select committee to investigate the state of affairs in West Africa.[41] Finding evidence of collaboration between the Company of Merchants and non-British slave ships, these bodies advised the British government to resume responsibility for the Gold Coast forts. In 1843, the forts were placed under the jurisdiction of the governor of Sierra Leone for a second time. Whether under the administration of the merchants of the Company or military officers appointed through the colonial administration at Sierra Leone, the British personnel on the ground always found that their interests coincided with those of the

Fante elite when it came to conducting trade and retaining ownership of the Gold Coast forts.

Treaty or War with Asante?

Britain's inconsistent policy regarding the Asante kingdom, which wavered from courting Asante as a trade partner to forcibly challenging Asante power on the coast, reveals extensive contradictions within British policy toward Africa during this period. Since the rise of Asante's first king, Osei Tutu, in 1701, English traders and those of all other European nations recognized Asante's vast power in the region and sought commercial and diplomatic partnership with its leader. Throughout the eighteenth century, it was the Dutch West Indies Company that established the strongest alliance with Asante, and the flow of trade to Dutch forts—especially Elmina and Accra—was the constant envy of the English.[42] Events in the early nineteenth century renewed Britain's interest in establishing a treaty with Asante. They particularly sought the Asantehene's consent to stop the slave trade but also recognized the dominant role Asante would play in the development of other forms of trade, including gold and ivory.

When Asante first invaded Fanteland in 1806–1807, the commander in chief of the British forts and settlements, Colonel George Torrane, wasted no time in siding with the victor and went to great measures to show his loyalty to the Asante king, Osei Bonsu.[43] "Assure the king," he advised his subordinate at Anomabo, "that notwithstanding the steps I have taken to give protection to the Fantees, I have ever held him in the highest respect, from the many reports I have heard of him."[44] He met with the Asante king in an elaborate ceremony in Anomabo and accepted the king's invitation to establish a permanent British residency in Kumasi. Once Asante had completed a decisive conquest of the Fante polity and established an administrative structure for taxing and governing the subordinate territories in 1816, British policy again flirted with an Anglo-Asante alliance. Two British embassies were sent to Kumasi in 1817 and 1820, respectively, to establish the terms of peace between Asante and the coast in the interest of improving and reestablishing trade.

The policy makers' vision for an alliance with Asante to promote the abolition of the slave trade and the development of new forms of commerce proved incompatible with the commercial and political realities on the Gold Coast. The Asantehene who met the British ambassadors is now well known for candidly pointing out that the slave trade had always been lucrative for both Asante and Britain, and asking "why should they change now?" More importantly, the success of British commercial activity on the Gold Coast still depended on generations-old relationships between resident British merchants and Fante families. The merchants understood clearly that the complete subjugation of Fanteland to Asante rule would give the Asantehene complete control over the trade—as was the case for the king of Dahomey just down the coast—and destroy what few lucrative commercial relationships British merchants had maintained. In response to the government's abolition of the Company of Merchants, they drafted a "Memorial of the Cape Coast Merchants of 30 September, 1822," in which they argued that Asante were extortioners and monopolists who prevented His Majesty's government from establishing a footing in the country that was "safe and respectable," and that Asante would impede the leading object of His Majesty's government in "the increase of our knowledge respecting the unknown countries in the interior of this vast continent, the extension of our intercourse with the natives, the promoting their improvement and civilization, and eventually the gradual diffusion of Christian knowledge."[45] They further recommended that the government incur the "considerable expense" and "much time" required to overthrow the king of "Ashantee," and argued that unless this was done or "his power greatly reduced," the British might as well withdraw completely from the Gold Coast.

Governor MacCarthy's aggressive response to the seizure of the Anomabo sergeant in 1822, discussed earlier in the chapter, fulfilled the merchants' request, though for entirely separate reasons. At the end of the day, the national pride that British officers like MacCarthy carried with them to Africa, and the embodiment of that pride in the massive forts flying the British flag along the Gold Coast ensured that the Asantehene's domination of coastal affairs would require the British government either to defend the forts with force or to withdraw altogether. In the context of the abolitionist movement, the budding industrial revolution and the continued threat (real or perceived) of another European power taking over the forts in Britain's absence, withdrawal from the Gold Coast proved impossible, in spite of repeated recommendations from within the British government to do so.

Conclusion

Fante society faced tremendous challenges in the early nineteenth century, including conquest by a foreign power (Asante) and a drastic decline in the export trade upon which the economy was founded. They successfully regained their sovereignty and rebuilt their economy in the 1820s and 1830s by recognizing and exploiting Britain's reluctance to abandon her massive trading forts on the Gold Coast. The joint Fante-British defeat of Asante forces in 1826 marks the pinnacle of the Fante's successful exploitation of British military resources. But perhaps the Fante's greatest success was in exposing the contradictions inherent in Britain's continued occupation of Gold Coast forts and exploiting them to their own advantage. As long as Britain—and indeed most of Europe—remained ambivalent about investing in actual colonies in West Africa, savvy Fante elites found ways to take advantage.

Notes

1. This view was popularized by John Kelly Thornton, *Africa and Africans in the Making of the Atlantic World, 1400–1680* (New York: Cambridge University Press, 1992).

2. The formal occupation of African territories (south of the Sahara) by European nations prior to the 1880s was limited to South Africa and Luanda (Angola). On the nature of relations between African rulers and European traders, see Robin Law, "'Here Is No Resisting the Country': The Realities of Power in Afro-European Relations on the West African 'Slave Coast,'" *Itinerario* 18, no. 2 (1994): 50–64.

3. Paul E. Lovejoy, *Transformations in Slavery: A History of Slavery in Africa* (Cambridge: Cambridge University Press, 1983); Patrick Manning, *Slavery and African Life: Occidental, Oriental, and African Slave Trades* (Cambridge: Cambridge University Press, 1990).

4. Joseph C. Miller, "The Dynamics of History in Africa and the Atlantic 'Age of Revolutions,'" in *The Age of Revolutions in Global Context c. 1760–1840*, ed. David Armitage and Sanjay Subrahmanyam (New York: Palgrave Macmillan, 2010), 101–124.

5. See, for example, Boubacar Barry, *Senegambia and the Atlantic Slave Trade* (Cambridge: Cambridge University Press, 1998); David Robinson, *The Holy War of Umar Tal: The Western Sudan in the Mid-Nineteenth Century* (Oxford: Clarendon Press, 1985); James F. Searing, *West African Slavery and Atlantic Commerce: The Senegal River Valley, 1700–1860* (Cambridge: Cambridge University Press, 1993).

6. www.slavevoyages.org.

7. www.slavevoyages.org.

8. Rebecca Shumway, *The Fante and the Transatlantic Slave Trade* (Rochester, NY: University of Rochester Press, 2011).

9. John Kofi Fynn, *Asante and Its Neighbors* (Evanston, IL: Northwestern University Press, 1971), 139–151.

10. George E. Metcalfe, *Great Britain and Ghana: Documents of Ghana History 1807–1957* (Accra: University of Ghana, 1964), 15.

11. The classic text is W. Walton Claridge, *A History of the Gold Coast and Ashanti* (London: John Murray, 1915). See also Ivor Wilks, *Asante in the Nineteenth Century: The Structure and Evolution of a Political Order* (Cambridge: Cambridge University Press, 1975).

12. This view of Ghana's precolonial history was previously articulated by Margaret Priestley and Mary McCarthy, to whom I am indebted. Margaret Priestley, *West African Trade and Coast Society: A Family Study* (London: Oxford University Press, 1969), and Mary McCarthy, *Social Change and the Growth of British Power in the Gold Coast: The Fante States, 1807–1874* (New York: University Press of America, 1983).

13. In the early nineteenth century, the possession of trading forts in Africa offered little commercial advantage because of the costs of their upkeep, relative to coastal trade as a whole. Newbury wrote, "The merchants' case for the retention of the African posts which was still based on the eighteenth-century promise that a fort offered protection of the principal national interest in the African market was, by the 1830s, an extremely weak one" (C. W. Newbury, *British Policy towards West Africa: Select Documents, 1786–1874* [Oxford: Clarendon Press, 1965], 5).

14. Ira Berlin identified the Gold Coast as one of the first sites of the development of "Atlantic creole" culture (Ira Berlin, *Many Thousands Gone: The First Two Centuries of Slavery in North America* [Cambridge, MA: Belknap Press, 1998], 18–25).

15. Fante is one of several languages, including Asante Twi, that comprise a language family called "Akan." According to oral tradition, the ancestors of the Fante migrated southward from the Akan forest in the interior of Ghana to settle the coast and live among non-Akan people who were already settled there. For a discussion of the crystallization of Fante culture in the eighteenth century, see Shumway, *Fante and the Transatlantic Slave Trade,* chap. 4.

16. Alfred Burdon Ellis, *A History of the Gold Coast of West Africa* (New York: Negro University Press, 1893); P. Labarthe, *Voyage a la cote de guinee* (Paris: Chez Debray, 1803) as cited in McCarthy, *Social Change and the Growth of British Power,* 34.

17. The economic impact of the ending of the slave trade for West Africa has been described as a "crisis of adaptation," a heavily debated concept. See Robin Law, "The Historiography of the Commercial Transition in Nineteenth-Century West Africa," in *African Historiography: Essays in Honour of Jacob Ade Ajayi,* ed. Toyin Falola and J. F. Ade Ajayi (Harlow: Longman, 1993), 91–115. Some of the main arguments in the debate about this interpretation are presented in A. G. Hopkins, "Economic Imperialism in West Africa," *Economic History Review* 21 (1968): 580–606; Robin Law, ed., *From Slave Trade to 'Legitimate' Commerce: The Commercial Transition in Nineteenth-Century West Africa* (Cambridge: Cambridge University Press, 1995).

18. As estimated in www.slavevoyages.org (accessed 4 May 2018).

19. The classic work on Asante history is Wilks, *Asante in the Nineteenth Century.*

20. Fynn, *Asante and Its Neighbors,* 84–98.

21. The Company of Merchants' predecessor was the Royal African Company, which maintained the forts in exchange for a monopoly of the British trade with the coast.

22. This practice dates back to the earliest Portuguese settlement at Elmina in the fifteenth century. See also Metcalfe, *Great Britain and Ghana,* 13.

23. John Joseph Crooks, *Records Relating to the Gold Coast Settlements from 1750 to 1874* (London: Cass, 1973), 145–146.

24. Crooks, *Records Relating to the Gold Coast,* 109–110.

25. An example of the inevitability of violent conflict occurred in 1812: the Fante accused one of the employees of the British fort at Winneba of stealing a quantity of

gold that had been stored in the fort for safekeeping during an Asante invasion of the previous year. The governor of Winneba Fort, Mr. James Meredith, was subsequently seized and beaten to death by the Winneba people. While the Committee in London instructed the Council to seek justice in this affair "without resorting to measures of rigour," the other officers met at Cape Coast Castle and decided to obtain the help of the senior officer of the British West Africa Squadron, who happened to be in the vicinity, to invade and burn the town of Winneba, and to bombard the fort. This action was condemned by the committee "in the most pointed manner," but the damage was done and Winneba became a haven for Brazilian slave ships for several years thereafter (Crooks, *Records Relating to the Gold Coast*, 110–112).

26. Eveline C. Martin, *The British West African Settlements, 1750–1821* (Westport, CT: Negro Universities Press, 1970), 158.

27. These events are described in Crooks, *Records Relating to the Gold Coast*, 161–166; Metcalfe, *Great Britain and Ghana*, 71–72; Newbury, *British Policy towards West Africa*, 291.

28. There are many accounts of this war. See, for example, Claridge, *A History of the Gold Coast*; Ward, *A History of Ghana*; and Wilks, *Asante in the Nineteenth Century*.

29. Zachary Macaulay to Lord Castlereagh, 8 May 1807, reprinted in Metcalfe, *Great Britain and Ghana*, 4–6.

30. T. C. McCaskie, "Cultural Encounters: Britain and Africa in the Nineteenth Century," in *Black Experience and the Empire*, ed. Philip D. Morgan and Sean Hawkins (Oxford: Oxford University Press, 2004), 193.

31. As the industrial revolution changed the British economy, several such African commodities did become valuable, especially palm oil.

32. Metcalfe, *Great Britain and Ghana*, 13.

33. McCaskie, "Cultural Encounters," 166.

34. It is noteworthy that historian David Kimble characterized the period 1807–1852 as the "Age of Experiment" (David Kimble, *A Political History of Ghana: The Rise of Gold Coast Nationalism, 1850–1928* [Oxford: Clarendon Press, 1963]).

35. Metcalfe, *Great Britain and Ghana*, 65–66.

36. For details on this incident, see Crooks, *Records Relating to the Gold Coast*, 161–166. The arrested man represented both British and Asante pride, as a subject of King George as a soldier and as a subject of the Asantehene because he was a native of Anomabo.

37. Newbury, *British Policy towards West Africa*, 5.

38. Brodie Cruickshank, *Eighteen Years on the Gold Coast of Africa: Including an Account of the Native Tribes, and Their Intercourse with Europeans* (London: Cass, 1966), 1:166.

39. Edward Reynolds, *Trade and Economic Change on the Gold Coast, 1807–1874* (London: Longman, 1974), 78.

40. Metcalfe, *Great Britain and Ghana*, 147, 156.

41. Reynolds, *Trade and Economic Change on the Gold Coast*, 95–96; Metcalfe, *Great Britain and Ghana*, 147–159. Robin Law has written about the new campaign to end the supply of slaves from Africa. Robin Law, ed., *Dahomey and the Ending of the Transatlantic Slave Trade: The Journals and Correspondence of Vice-Consul Louis Fraser, 1851–1852* (Oxford: Oxford University Press, 2012).

42. The main work on this topic is Larry W. Yarak, *Asante and the Dutch 1744–1873* (New York: Oxford University Press, 1990).

43. Henry Meredith, *An Account of the Gold Coast of Africa, with a Brief History of the African Company* (London: Cass, 1967), 132–162; Fynn, *Asante and Its Neighbors,* 139–151.

44. Meredith, *Account of the Gold Coast,* 153–154.

45. Metcalfe, *Great Britain and Ghana,* 80–82.

CHAPTER FOUR

New Ecologies

Pathways in the Pacific, 1760s–1840s

JENNIFER NEWELL

Histories written from Indigenous perspectives are inherently powerful for overturning assumptions about agents and authority. In the Pacific, historians and philosophers such as Katerina Teaiwa, Epeli Hau'ofa, and Joshua Reid, among others,[1] along with non-Indigenous scholars writing on exchanges from positions informed by Indigenous ontologies,[2] have been opening up new understandings of mutually constitutive interactions within this "sea of islands." These scholars understand the Pacific as a living, spirited, dynamically intermingled space, deeply inflected with signs and stories. In this understanding, the Pacific's people, living biota, the rivers and ocean, are entities with power. Their works are enabling a rethinking of the stretches of time in which outsiders arrived and endeavored to bring islands under control; they are opening up ways to see such times as periods of negotiation not only imposition. In these accounts, the human and nonhuman inhabitants of the Pacific maintain considerable agency, meeting the newcomers with welcome or resistance, as situations demanded.

An important foundation within these approaches is captured by anthropologist Tim Ingold's construction of understanding humans, plants, and animals as "components of each other's environments."[3] Rather than imagining humans "inhabiting a social world on their own," Ingold sees, more effectively, "both humans and the animals and plants on which they depend for a livelihood . . . as fellow participants in the *same* world, a world that is both social and natural."[4] In this view, humans "do not so much transform the material world as play their part, along with other creatures, in the world's transformation of itself." Thus "nature is not a surface of materiality upon which human history is inscribed; rather history is the process wherein both people and their environments are continually bringing each other into being."[5]

This "mutually constitutive relationship"[6] is the key engine within this chapter, as it is in Bill Gammage's chapter in this volume. Here, I uncover the mutually constituted ecologies and cultures of Samoa and Tahiti (more concisely, their social-ecological systems). The history I tell here shows how each of these Pacific systems worked to attract or repel elements of the social-ecological systems of Britain.[7] The chapter is an exploration of the complexities of encounter between these several systems. As in Gammage's history, these interactions demonstrate the agency of Indigenous people in the face of an influx of agents of the British empire as well as the agency of the Indigenous and introduced plant and animal species that were part of these encounters. How human and nonhuman actors interacted in Tahiti and Samoa over the course of the "revolutionary age" did much to shape the ways in which the British colonial project proceeded. These early interactions impacted the ecological and social constitution of the two islands over time. Specific observations in the Central Pacific can usefully inform broader investigations of the ways in which relationships across cultural and species boundaries have shaped the course of colonial encounters in Indigenously managed spaces.

The story here starts with the ancient pathways forged between Samoa and Tahiti. It then tracks British routes to Tahiti, secured in the 1760s. The route from Britain broadened in the decades that followed and brought a flow of exchanges of plants and animals. Finally, the story moves with British and Tahitian missionaries as they reached Samoa in the 1830s and worked to establish converts and commodities. This final part of the story explores growing commercial relationships in Samoa, the intermingling of ecologies, and the surrendering of Samoan forests to plantations.

Considering both Samoa and Tahiti in this study opens up useful comparisons and enacts the method called for by Hau'ofa and more recently by Teaiwa to explore connections across a unifying sea, rather than supporting assumptions of isolation by focusing on a single island. Additionally, studies linking francophone and English-speaking parts of the Pacific are not common, and it is useful to breach these colonially imposed barriers and recover the vibrant, connected histories these two places share.

SAMOA and TAHITI

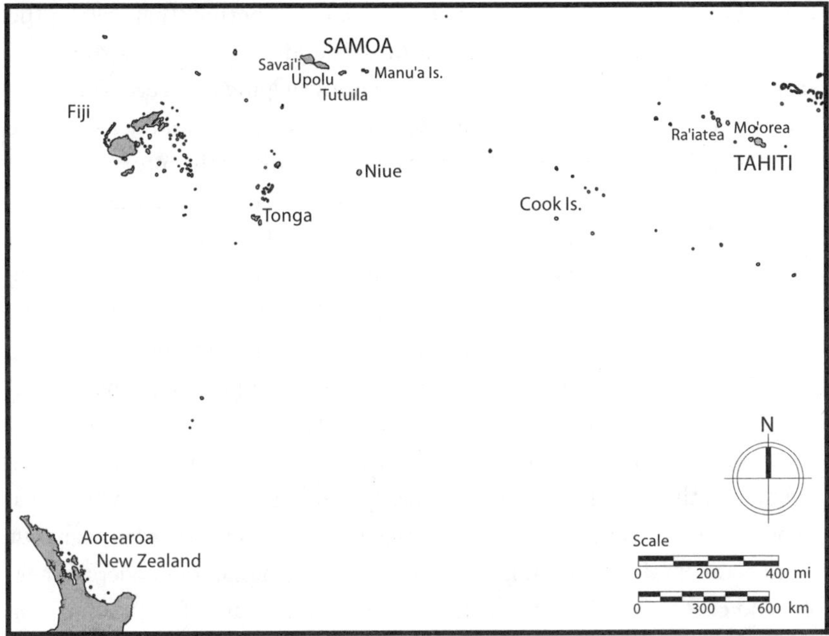

Figure 4.1. Map of the Samoan and Society Island Groups, Central Pacific. © Mark Gunning, Gunningdesign.com.

Island Beginnings

The islands and their living things had always been shifting, fluid, and changing in substance. In the beginning, Tagaloa, Samoa's creator god (named Ta'aroa in Tahiti), cavorted and wrestled with lesser gods in sky and sea, pulling up islands out of the great ocean with giant fishhooks, creating rocks, birds, plants, then humans and other animals, unfurling them out of each other.[8] In the Society Islands—the group that includes Tahiti—the staple fruit *uru* (breadfruit, *Artocarpus altilis*) was created when a father in Ra'iātea wanted to feed his starving family during a long drought. He turned himself into a tree and his head became the first breadfruit, sustaining his family.[9] An *ari'i* (chief) then took a cutting, propagated it, and sent it out to other chiefs. The tree soon sustained all families of the island group.[10] The mutually constitutive relationships within these understandings of the creation of the world remain at the foundation of Tahitian and Samoan ontologies.

Another account begins from around 950 BC, when canoes with double hulls and sails of finely woven leaf strips arrived in the Samoan archipelago.[11]

The people on board were of the culture named Lapita, from Fiji or Tonga, bringing food plants and animals and the decorated pottery that enables the culture to be traced across a wide swathe of islands.[12] The ocean's great currents had provided pathways for the navigators, helping them cross vast distances. The navigators would have selected paths along and across these currents, guided by stars, reading the wave patterns for the intersections of currents, and reading the signs of the proximity of islands in the wave echoes, the presence of clouds, and a scent of vegetation in the wind. Finding a chain of islands, the navigators settled down on several, naming them Upolu, Savai'i, Tutuila, and Manu'a. It was not until some 1,500 years had passed that subsets of these people made a new set of journeys eastward, on voyaging canoes stocked with a living survival kit—breadfruit and other plant seedlings, chickens, pigs, dogs—finding islands in the central Pacific, including Tahiti.[13]

A further 1,700 years strode by. In both Samoa and Tahiti, village groups now dotted the island, with governance systems specific to the two places, but both centered on groups of lineages led by an *ari'i* selected by descent but reliant on maintaining a clear fitness to rule.[14] *Ari'i,* priests, commoners, fisherfolk, and other specialists all maintained particular ways of communicating with gods and spirits. The means were different in the two sets of islands, but in common was the use of sacred sites and the ability to read messages from gods, spirits, and ancestors in signs given by particular birds, animals, clouds, lightning, and waves. Managing the potentially dangerous spirit beings who could move between the dark realm of the nonliving (the *Pō* in Tahitian) and the realm of the living and light (the *Ao*) was a key component of how Islanders lived within their environments.[15] Each family had its own close association with a spirit, embodied within a particular kind of animal (*aitu* in Samoan, *ata* in Tahitian), with which they held a relationship of mutual care.[16]

In both Samoa and Tahiti, an extended family lived together on the family's strip of land, which typically ran from the coast to the interior, giving access to the spectrum of ecological niches the island offered. A family maintained a cluster of *fale* (houses) with gardens of food plants, domesticated pigs, chickens, and dogs, plus access to the reef and sea for shellfish and fish.[17] In both Samoa and Tahiti, when chiefs went to war with each other their attacks were made not only on opponents but also on life support systems, destroying trees and gardens and carrying away their animals.[18]

In the 1750s, a priest called Vaita, at Taputapuatea, the great *marae* on the island of Ra'iātea (near Tahiti in the Society Islands), went into a trance when some invaders from another nearby island, Porapora, cut down a sacred tree. He spoke a prophecy of a new people and a new force coming to their world:

The glorious offspring of Te Tumu
Will come and see this forest at Taputapuatea.
Their body is different, our body is different
We are one species only from Te Tumu.

And this land will be taken by them
The old rules will be destroyed
And sacred birds of the land and sea
Will also arrive here, will come and lament
Over that which this lopped tree has to teach
They are coming up on a canoe without an outrigger.[19]

A similar prophecy, that also foretold the arrival of an outriggerless canoe (*"va'a-ama-ore"*), was reportedly made in Samoa. This occurred early, well before it was described to a British missionary in 1830. An old *taulaitu* (spirit medium) apparently announced the arrival of an "outriggerless canoe from foreign lands," which, according to the missionary's record, was prophesied to bring a time of peace.[20]

Pathways from Britain

Europeans started threading pathways across the Pacific Ocean from the late 1500s.[21] During the 1600s and early 1700s, European privateers went in search of new lands and new commodities. From the mid-1700s, acquisitive and competitive impulses prompted the rival nations of France and Britain to send out expeditions to find, document, and claim new territories, resources, and knowledge.[22]

In 1767, within the island of Britain, two tall ships without outriggers were being readied for a journey, with a crew of people whose skin was protected from the cold with thick woolen fabric, and whose visions and cosmologies were vastly different to those of the islands they would be sailing toward. They held in their imaginations a Great Southern Land, which philosophers had reasoned must lie within the Pacific Ocean, to balance the weight of the northern continents. They knew their journey would be long, and they loaded potatoes and pumpkins into the hold, with barrels of water and boxes of hard bread, and embarked a noisy collection of animals: goats, sheep, chickens, ducks, and geese. They tucked away wax paper–wrapped packets of seeds into the cramped quarters, ready for whatever useful soil might be found.[23] The first British pathway to Tahiti was under way.

The ship, the HMS *Dolphin*, made its way through the Atlantic, through the terrifying storms of Cape Horn, losing contact with its consort, the *Assistant*, and continuing on alone across huge expanses of Pacific Ocean.[24] By the time it approached the Tuamotus, the barrels and boxes were empty, many of the animals had died, and stomach complaints and scurvy gripped the captain and crew.[25] Finding food and water had become the highest priority, above scouting, mapping, or staking claim to territory. An island was desperately needed.[26]

The ship crested Tahiti's horizon on 19 June 1767. As they came to anchor on the south side of the island on 21 June, crowds gathered. The well-known prophecy would have leapt to the mind of many there.[27] Several men climbed into canoes, pushed off from the shore, and went to meet the outriggerless ship. The Islanders had fruit and pork in their canoes, and held up large plantain leaves, calling out in an effort to placate and to discover the nature of this arrival.[28] Men on the ship, looking over the edge, called back and made the sound of grunting pigs and crowing roosters—resorting to a language of animals and food.[29]

The exchanges that followed involved miscommunication, the testing of boundaries, and great violence. The ship, with its strange inhabitants, had stayed days on end with no sign that they might move on. On 24 June 1767, hundreds of canoes approached the ship, and crowds swarmed the beaches and cliffs.[30] The canoes carried things to trade and young women who stood up and beckoned to the sailors. There were stones hidden under leaves under their feet. When a man with a headdress on a large double canoe gave a signal, the occupants of the canoes pelted a storm of stones on the ship and the sailors. The captain, Samuel Wallis, knowing how thoroughly he and his crew were outnumbered, responded by firing on the crowds with cannon, round shot, and grapeshot. Officer George Robertson, writing of it, said this "struck such terror amongst the poor unhappy crowd that it would require the pen of Milton to describe."[31] Many were killed and wounded. A silence fell, the people gathered themselves onto what was left of the canoes, and they retreated. The next day, through tentative offerings of symbolic plantain leaves, food, and *tapa* (bark cloth), the Tahitians brokered peace.[32] Trade of fruit, taro, coconuts, pigs, and chickens resumed. These plants and animals, offered up in gifts and in trade, established and reestablished relationships of mutual gain.

Figure 4.2. "The Natives of Otaheite attacking Captn. Wallis" and "The Interview between Captn. Wallis and Oberea [Purea] after Peace being established with the Natives." Engraved by W. Grainger for Bankes's *New System of Geography* (London, c. 1790), National Library of Australia.

The abundance of the island's plant and animal foods brought Wallis and his crew back to health.[33] Before leaving, Wallis gave their main host, the chiefly woman Purea, a gift of thanks. In a continuation of the centrality of the nonhuman actors within the course of events, the gift included the several animals and seeds that had survived from the journey from England. Wallis kept the ship's goat (for the milk she would continue to provide), but presented Purea with "two turkies, two geese, three Guinea hens, a cat big with kitten, . . . peas, some small white kidney beans . . . and about sixteen different sorts of garden seeds, and a shovel."[34] The British, along with the French and Spanish voyagers who stopped there soon afterward, also left ashore microbes: viruses and bacteria that transferred themselves to the Tahitian's bodies, causing epidemics of plague, gonorrhea, and syphilis.[35]

The *Dolphin*'s pathway looped back to Britain. The surveys and maps and stories of the warm welcome from the Tahitian people and their bountiful ecology prompted the Admiralty to send another expedition, headed by James Cook, along the same path.[36] Members of the Royal Society and Admiralty, shaping the expedition's program of exploration for new territories and new knowledge, discussed the best way to establish Tahiti as a useful port of call for provisioning future British journeys and made selections of animals, plants, and seeds to install on the island.

The British establishment at this stage was also motivated by the desire to beneficently assist (or at least to be *seen* assisting) the Islanders, especially "helping" them to "advance toward civilization." Bringing them useful material goods was seen to help, but doubly useful would be bringing them farm animals and healthy fruits and vegetables from Britain, to cultivate in an orderly manner.[37] As George Forster, naturalist on Cook's second Pacific voyage, said: "I cannot help thinking that our late voyage would reflect immortal honour on our employers, if it had no other merit than stocking Taheitee with goats . . . and New Zeeland and New Caledonia with hogs."[38] Such gifts would give a helping hand to Tahitians and others who were already deemed by Britons to possess a certain degree of "natural civility" and a preexisting capacity to cultivate the land.[39] When Cook and his crew came ashore in May 1769 after nine months at sea, they landed cattle, horses, goats, and a wide range of exotic seeds and cuttings.[40] These were expected to be of use to the Islanders and to future British crews, providing familiar and accessible provisions.[41]

Things did not quite go to plan. Certainly, from the Tahitians' point of view, many of the new arrivals were intriguing additions to the corpus of chiefly possessions.[42] Whenever the opportunity arose, Tahitians chose gifts of European woven red fabric, exactly the color required to catch a god's attention, red feathers the ships brought from other Pacific islands, and metal tools that retained their point in a way that shell, shark tooth, and stone did not.[43] Whether exotic new animals or exotic new tools and materials, possessing them bolstered the capacity of chiefs and their families to demonstrate their *mana*—their sacred ancestral power—and their capacity to manage the newcomers.

However, some species were rooted out. Cook noted in 1776 that when a grapevine that had been planted three years earlier fruited, the locals tried the grapes and found them very bitter. "It was unanimously declared," Cook wrote, "that if it was suffered to grow it would poison every person in the island and was immediately trodden underfoot."[44] Other bitter fruits such as grapefruit were not tended to or left to burn when a tree caught fire.[45] William Bligh wrote crossly in 1792, after several attempts to establish gardens of British plants on his repeated stops at the island: "No Value is set upon any of our Garden productions, it is really taking trouble to no purpose to bring them any thing that requires care to get it to perfection."[46] Other challenges to introducing exotic plants lay in the mismatch of ecologies: the high humidity, heat, and range of local predators were too much for some northern-hemisphere species.

Efforts to establish cattle, sheep, and other useful animals also disappointed British expectations, as local complexes of use and the challenges of competition from other chiefs and other large animals got in the way. Local dogs often killed the sheep,[47] and breeding pairs of cattle, horses, and other imported animals were often broken up when chiefs redistributed livestock between them, to cement their alliances, or seized them during battles. This meant many of these larger animals never established a secure footing on the island.[48] Smaller, unintentional introductions tended to be more successful. European rats (*Rattus rattus*), larger than the local Polynesian rat (*Rattus exulans*), added themselves with vigor to the Tahitian ecology. *Rattus rattus* bred well and contributed to the eating of several of the island's species into nonexistence.[49] Purea's goose and turkeys lived under her care, and while she lost Wallis's cat to her political rivals, Captain Cook brought in twenty more and gave Purea one, which she kept as a favored pet.[50] These various cats started to hunt in the forest around the chiefly residences. They found the flightless Tahiti rails were an especially easy catch, and they soon became extinct. Introduced animals altered each other's domains. The ecological composition of Tahiti was entering a new phase of rapid change.

As the decades passed, the island's plants and animals continued to bring British visitors and Tahitians together. This occurred not only because Britons were bringing new species onto the island but also because islanders were giving or trading them out in large numbers as provisions and as trade goods. British interests developed several projects of ecological imperialism—transplanting breadfruit plants from Tahiti to British sugar plantations in the Caribbean[51] and, from 1801, turning Tahitian pigs into salt pork to feed the struggling penal colony in New South Wales.[52]

In 1801, one of the early leaders of the invasion of Australia, Philip Gidley King, governor of New South Wales, sent a ship with a letter for Tu, the *ari'i* of the Matavai Bay region.[53] He requested that Tu supply pigs for processing into salt pork. The colony had been established on the basis of profound misreadings of the land and its people, misreadings that have held tragic implications for First Nations people, who cared for their country for more than 65,000 years. The trauma of frontier violence and colonial governance, taking land and kin and disrupting ways of living with country, continues.[54] Another, more prosaic implication of the imperial enterprise failing to understand the land was colonial officials being unable to produce sufficient food, particularly protein, to sustain the convicts. The colony was spending more than it could afford importing salted meat from Britain. Tu agreed to trade with King, and over the following twenty-five-year period, Tu and his son were able to transform pigs from being sacred animals into a food commodity that paid great political dividends.[55] Pigs had once been the embodiments of the war god, the means to attract a god's attention during a crucial ceremony, one of a priest's mediums to discern the best time to go to battle, and the precious gift a family needed to enact a marriage. Under Tu, the animals became something to be cut up, salted, and packed into barrels and sent to Sydney Town in return for muskets and ammunition.[56] The conceptual changes that were required to make such shifts were substantial and significant. By 1815, Tu's son, known by the British as Pomare II, had sufficient concentration of firepower, and additional support from some of the pork traders willing to join his army, to defeat other chiefly lineages in the Battle of Fe'i Pi.[57] It was the first time an *ari'i* had destabilized the balance of power between the lineages to the extent that he won control of the entire island.[58] Pigs had arguably always been deployed in the chiefly management of sacred and political power, but turning them into a commodity equivalent to muskets endowed them with a more brutal form of political potency and excised the animal from most of their former roles in the life of the island.[59] The long-term transport of pork over more than three thousand miles between Tahiti and New South Wales sustained the penal colony through its shaky beginnings. As was often the case with early colonial ventures, it was Indigenously managed food sources and a willingness to share them that saved the colonists' bacon. This, the first truly commercial enterprise Europeans established in the Society Islands, was the colony's first successful trading venture. It is indicative of the extensive, but generally unacknowledged, intermingling of Australian and Pacific Island histories.

Pigs constitute one of the earliest examples of the deep-rooted meanings of an animal or plant being dug up and repositioned that was to occur repeatedly as British imperial interests continued to play in the Pacific world. By the time the century closed, the Maohi of Tahiti, especially those who lived near Matavai Bay, walked, swam, and canoed within a coastline and seascape that was still very familiar, surrounded by almost all the same marine creatures, coastal plants, and reef that they and their grandparents had known. But in their terrestrial lands—in their gardens, groves, mountain sides and valley floors, forests, river banks, and swamps—ecologies and ways of living with them had altered distinctly.

In 1797, Tahiti's first British settlers arrived, sent by the London Missionary Society. As soon as they settled into a house that Tu granted them at Matavai Bay, they started to try to support themselves by establishing gardens and encouraging the rather sickly livestock that had survived the journey to the island.[60] Journal keepers for the mission kept a daily record of their attempts to garden and establish flocks of converts as well as sheep. The Maohi were not inclined to pay much heed to the missionaries, who had brought in almost no goods or weapons to trade, and were forever cajoling people to sit still for long preaching sessions.[61] Some would sit but asked for payment, talked among themselves, or laughingly parroted the preachers' words back at them.[62] The families who owned the land at Matavai Bay made no secret that they disliked the interlopers. The missionaries also raised ire by failing to participate in the broad system of sharing garden produce. The local method for dealing with such lack of cooperation was to forcibly take the offender's possessions.[63] Over the years, the missionaries recorded frequent losses from their gardens and pens. John Davies wrote on 26 December 1807:

"Within these few days and nights the natives have repeatedly robbed our gardens of a great number of pine apples, they continue their old custom of committing their depredations generally at the time the brethren are assembled for worship."[64] Davies also recorded the theft of nearly two hundred pigs over a period of eighteen months.[65] He wrote in his journal at the end of 1807: "[I]f we view ourselves in our principal work as Christian missionaries, we see little but discouragements on every hand; if we look upon the pains we have taken for a number of years in the cultivation of the ground, gardening, &c., we can see nothing but disappointments."[66]

As ever, trying to introduce new components into someone else's social-ecological system proved more challenging than the British expected. Moving to the communities on the nearby islands of Huahine and Mo'orea eased some of the friction. With no support or supplies arriving from London, the missionaries worked to become as independent as possible. They galvanized their few followers to assist with supplying local produce and tending plantations, built themselves a ship, and set up as commodity traders.[67] From December 1817, their ship *Haweis* took cargoes of salt pork, coconut oil, coconut fiber, copra, sugarcane, and arrowroot to sell at the colony in New South Wales.[68] This commercial turn was to have ongoing and growing impacts on the Tahitian ecology, expanding plantations for income and connecting the island to the increasingly global economy that was reaching out across the Pacific.

In 1814, a series of events, including some missionary "rescues" of people in difficulty, lent weight to the claim that the Christian God was a powerful one.[69] More locals decided to convert. Tu's heir, Pomare II, was weighing up the various political and practical utilities of conversion. He was baptized in 1819, formally bringing the entire island into the Christian faith.[70] The LMS directors and their brethren in the Society Islands started to feel sufficiently sure of their roots to resolve to try to branch out their mission to other islands. In 1830, they decided to try Samoa.[71]

The Reverend John Williams, at the LMS mission in Ra'iātea, oversaw the project of building a twenty-meter schooner, *The Olive Branch*, with the assistance of local workers.[72] A number of the missions' "teachers" (men who had converted to Christianity, worked at the mission, and helped with proselytizing) embarked on the journey to Samoa. Three were from the Ra'iātean mission, two from Huahine, and three from Mo'orea, some bringing their wives and children.[73]

New Pathways

The Olive Branch arrived into an archipelago that had experienced few engagements with Europeans. Samoans had been interested in interacting with the first European voyagers who stopped by: Roggeveen in 1722, Bougainville in 1768, and La Pérouse and de Langle in 1787. Quite likely encouraged by the positive prophecy surrounding these visitors, Samoans were willing to provide food animals and fruits in return for glass beads and iron.[74] The people of Tutuila, for instance, provided La Pérouse with "500 pigs, many chickens, pigeons and fruits" in exchange for beads.[75] When a scuffle broke out over some property on La Pérouse's ship, a local man was either roughly handled or shot (accounts vary).[76] The next day, a group of Islanders attacked a party from the *Astrolabe*. The commander, Fleuriot de Langle, and eleven of his crew were killed, as were thirty-nine Samoans.[77] Another attack was launched in 1791 on the HMS *Pandora*, when it stopped at Tutuila in search of the *Bounty* mutineers.[78] News of Samoan hostility spread rapidly. This meant British and other European colonial enterprises kept well away from the islands for more than forty years.[79] This important factor kept the Samoan islands relatively isolated throughout the eighteenth century from the importations of material goods, exotic species, and cosmologies that were making inroads in other island groups.

It was teachers from Tahiti and other Society Islands, with a few British representatives of the London Missionary Society, who created a new bridge to Samoa. After leaving Tahiti, *The Olive Branch* had stopped in Tonga and provided passage for a Samoan chief, Faueā, who wished to return home.[80] On reaching Savai'i (in the west of the archipelago), Faueā endorsed the mission—thereby adding critical support to the British enterprise.[81] He pointed out to his people that the missionaries, with their large ship, elaborate clothes, and many possessions, were obviously well cared for by their God.[82] When John Williams returned two years later, in 1832, the teachers had made rapid headway. The general interest in adopting Christianity in Samoa compared to Tahiti has many likely causes, including the effective translations provided by the Tahitian teachers, which supported smoother incorporation of Christian cosmology into existing Samoan cosmology. Also, in Samoa it was the missionaries rather than the mariners who brought in material goods, plants, and animals from Europe—things that held a range of efficacy and carried, as Nicholas Thomas writes, an "aura of prestige."[83]

An intermingling of imported and local ecologies and approaches to the human and nonhuman world got under way, managed very much by the Samoans and their desire to encompass Christianity. Captain Charles Wilkes of the United States Exploring Expedition in Tutuila in 1838 observed that a chief had a family *aitu* (spirit being) that "had been a freshwater eel which he fed at a nearby stream," but he had "long ago made it his meal."[84] This was not the only report of Islanders making a demonstration of their conversion by symbolically breaking existing relationships with the spirit realm by eating the animals that had previously been their special guardians.[85] To what extent this was an actual break is probably not possible to know. On the whole, however, the foundations of the *fa'a Samoa* (Samoan way) remained in place. Historian Malama Meleisea writes that "Christianity became part of *fa'a Samoa,* and was used, like the old religion, to validate its institutions."[86] R. P. Gibson writes of the "selectivity of the Samoan reaction to European contact" and notes that Samoans adopted Christianity with "resilience, experiencing scarcely any disintegration of their traditional social structure and way of life."[87]

On John Williams's final visit to Samoa in 1839, he summed up the overall benefits he and many of his countrymen saw in these islands: "Whether we view this group as a mart for commercial enterprise, a field for scientific research or a sphere for the exercise of Christian benevolence, we must regard it with feelings of the liveliest interest."[88] Commerce was the cornerstone of Britain's involvement with Samoa, managed by the missionaries and the traders and whalers who, from the early 1830s, rapidly gained confidence about stopping for trade and provisions.[89] By 1847, the British and American governments had sent consuls and a trading store was set up in Apia, the village developing alongside a comfortable harbor on the northern coast of Upolu (fig. 4.3).[90]

Unlike the initial "scientific" visitors to Tahiti, those arriving on the later pathway between Britain and Samoa were interested in "improving" the local ecology for their own commercial gain. The Duke of Devonshire supplied Reverend Williams with plants "for introduction to the islands of Polynesia," including the "Chinese banana" (*Musi cavendishii*). It proved popular and resilient to storms. Samoan mission teachers took cuttings with them as they proselytized in nearby islands, and they were soon flourishing around the region.[91] Some less helpful species, such as cats, jumped ship in Samoa. Their numbers grew steadily. Missionary John Stair, in Samoa between 1838 and 1845, and writing in 1897, noted: "The cat, *Ngosi*, or *Ngeli*, was also known as

Figure 4.3. [Artist unknown], Town and Harbour of Apia on the Island of Upolu, Navigator Group, South Pacific (c. 1867). Ref: C-036-005. Alexander Turnbull Library, Wellington, New Zealand. http://natlib.govt.nz/records/22917583.

pusi, and largely domesticated, being found in most houses. These animals have also become wild in great numbers, and prove most destructive to many kinds of birds, especially those roosting in stumps and low bushes. One or two species of great interest have been almost exterminated by them of late years, especially the *Manu Mea* and Apteryx, both of scientific value."[92]

The manumea ("Red Bird"), known in English as the tooth-billed pigeon, *Didunculus strigirostris*, is Samoa's only endemic bird. [93] Flightless like the Tahitian red-billed rail (or "Tahiti Rail"), *Gallirallus pacificus*, the manumea was similarly vulnerable to cats, but it seems they dealt with a gradual buildup of predators, rather than the sudden and substantial attack force the Tahitian rails faced.[94]

The two islands experienced very different cat histories: by the time a few cats jumped ship in Samoa, Tahiti had already experienced forty years of purposeful and intensive introductions from Britain. As Cook wrote, he "furnished" the islanders with "a Stock of Catts, no less than twenty" in 1774, and the chiefly families he gave them to valued them and cared for them as pets. Bligh noted in 1789 that several other voyagers had also been leaving cats on the island.[95] The early voyagers' deliberate, repeated, and numerous introductions, with a focus on gifts to establish chiefly relations, intersected with local priorities and ecologies in ways that held different outcomes for local species. The Tahitian rail survived only long enough for George Forster, naturalist on the voyage that had brought twenty cats, to make a single illustration. The species went extinct soon after.[96] The manumea, on the other hand, managed to survive. There is no evidence that cats were given out as diplomatic gifts within the Samoan islands. They may only have been numerous around the port in Upolu. Though the manumea has long been endangered, it survives in small numbers in the remote forests of Savai'i.[97] It is now Samoa's national bird and features on twenty *tala* notes.[98]

Trading Samoa

In the early years of the Samoan missionary stations, Williams wrote: "At present, the Samoa islanders have nothing to dispose of but a little cinet, and small quantities of tortoise-shell. In a very few years, however, should our labours be successful, they will be taught to prepare hundreds of tons of coconut oil annually; to manufacture sugar; to cultivate their land; and to supply our shipping with provisions. Thus, wherever the Missionary goes, new channels are cut for the stream of commerce."[99] For this to happen, however, the mission needed the cooperation of its congregations. LMS records from Tutuila (in the east of the Samoan archipelago) are revealing of these dynamics.[100] In May 1840, the mission at Pagopago collected material support from the congregation during their annual mission service. The people, Archibald Murray reported, "had no money, but they gave liberally of such things as they had."[101] This included about two thousand pounds of arrowroot, fifty-two lengths of *siapo* (bark cloth), and twelve fine mats. "These, the mats, are the most valuable property, in their estimation, that they possess."[102] Thus began the process, already established in Tahiti, of the congregation demonstrating its support of the mission through gifts of valuables and foods suitable for sale as commodities. Only four years later, production and gift-giving had stepped up. In 1844, a report of a sermon in Taū, Manu'a, notes: "Every man, woman and child gives a present after the sermon = about 2400 lbs of arrowroot, 50 gals of coconut oil (worth £25)."[103]

The general willingness to support the mission in Tutuila continued: the number of gallons of coconut oil increased, bringing in 835 gallons in 1854 (to ship out on the missionary vessel *John Williams*).[104] But the "stream of commerce" did not always run as smoothly as the missionaries hoped. The following year, contributions were lower, and missionary Thomas Powell attributed this grumpily to the "establishment of several stores in the district, for the exchange of property for cocoa-nut oil; a great desire for boats, which are paid for in oil." He also put it down to the locals' "general indifference to divine things."[105] The error of the last point aside, Powell was correctly registering the Samoans' autonomy in managing the expenditure of the oil they produced. The congregation was also diversifying their productions and contributions by 1866, adding cotton to the gifts of oil and arrowroot.[106]

Civil war broke out repeatedly from midcentury over the power scuffles between the main chiefly lineages, and the dizzying complexes of alliances made, broken, and remade between local and foreign interests kept the Samoan archipelago in a "chronic state of unrest."[107] The various factions signed "friendship" treaties in quick succession, assigning "Favored Nation" status to first the United States, then Germany, then Britain.[108] Skirmishes between these foreign powers seeking control of the archipelago's resources and harbors added to tensions.[109] In the rush to buy firearms, many Samoans sold their lands to companies such as Godeffroy & Sohn (Germany) and the Central Polynesian Land and Commercial Company (USA), who were vying to gain Samoan land and labor to produce cotton, copra, and cocoa.[110]

One of the distinctive features of the spread of a capitalist economy in the Samoan islands, however, was the considerable degree to which Samoans maintained control of their lands. While an *'āgia*'s (decent group's) land was at its heart and people were "most adverse to selling their land,"[111] there were profitable ways forward. A single piece of land could be sold to many buyers, or land that belonged to an estranged member of the family, or to a rival's *'āgia*, could be sold surreptitiously.[112]

By the end of the century, Britain had surrendered its interests in both Tahiti and Samoa. Forced out of Tahiti by the 1840s, Britain withdrew from Samoa at the conclusion of the Samoan civil war in 1899. Through the twentieth century, the British focused instead on other Pacific regions.

Conclusion

Outsiders have long seen islands as isolated and vulnerable.[113] There is a common assumption—especially in landlocked places—that islands are fragile, precarious environments, that one small imposition of newness will unsettle its balance.[114] Looking to the actual histories of specific attempts that outsiders made to change island environments, it quickly becomes clear that it can take substantial effort to try to shift an established ecology in a new direction. British imperial authorities strove, in the early phase of their engagement in the Pacific, to create provisioning stations for their ships as they traversed this new field of potential wealth and political advantage. They also wanted to "improve" the productive capacities of the islands, for the inhabitants and themselves. From the islanders' perspective, the new pathways brought a new range of human and nonhuman entities that provided opportunities and challenges, all of which they managed to suit their own needs. Both sides endeavored to maintain and reclaim positive relationships when things went wrong. The material and commercial gains from their exchanges were extensive but carried losses within them: of forests, of species, of relationships to animals and plants that were once kin. Today, in Tahiti and Samoa, conservation efforts attempt to protect the islands' remaining endemic and Indigenous species. The later history of the rendering of many Samoan forests into capital is a painful one for many Samoans to think through now. Mata'afa Autagavaia, a *tulafale*, said recently to a group of environmental science students in a workshop at the Museum of Samoa that when former generations sold trees to timber-getters, it was like they were selling their brothers and sisters.[115]

There are many imperial legacies within the social-ecological systems of Tahiti and Samoa. But the deep-seated relationships with enlivened landscapes have continued to inform ways of being in Samoa and Tahiti, even interwoven as they often are with Christian worldviews.[116] Many practices still continue in both places, such as protecting homes from menacing forest spirits by planting protective *ti* plants around the fence line.[117] Professor Leasiolagi Malama Meleisea of the National University of Samoa told me recently of a still-active proverb: "We love the forest, but we fear the spirits."[118]

Throughout the era of pathways meeting each other in the central Pacific, it was the combined agency of the locals—the people of the land and the nonhuman entities of the land, sea, and air—that created the potent, ongoing relationships with the broader world. These active engagements between Tahitian, Samoan, and British social-ecological systems, creating new ecologies between them, forged pathways that Islanders pushed forward into an increasingly interlinked and challenging world.

Notes

1. Katerina Teaiwa, *Consuming Ocean Island: Stories of People and Phosphate from Banaba* (Bloomington: Indiana University Press, 2015); Epeli Hau'ofa, "Our Sea of

Islands," *Contemporary Pacific* 6 (1994): 146–161; Joshua Reid, *The Sea Is My Country: The Maritime World of the Makahs* (New Haven, CT: Yale University Press, 2015).

2. Anne Salmond, Nicholas Thomas, and Paul D'Arcy, among others.

3. Tim Ingold, *The Perception of the Environment: Essays on Livelihood, Dwelling, and Skill* (London: Routledge, 2011), 87.

4. Ingold, *The Perception of the Environment*, 87.

5. Ingold, *The Perception of the Environment*, 87.

6. Tim Ingold and Terhi Kurtilla, "Perceiving the Environment in Finnish Lapland," *Body and Society* 6, nos. 3–4 (2000): 183–196.

7. Which, with only slight shifts in emphasis, can alternatively be referred to as "biocultural" or "coupled human environment" systems.

8. Corey Muse and Shirley Muse, *The Birds and Birdlore of Samoa: O Manu ma tala'aga o Manu o Samoa* (Walla Walla, WA: Pioneer Press, 1982), 55; Oliver, *Ancient Tahitian Society*, 3 vols. (Canberra: Australian National University Press, 1974) 1:48–56.

9. Teuira Henry, "Ancient Tahiti: By Teuira Henry Based on Material Recorded by J. M. Orsmond," *Bernice P. Bishop Museum Bulletin* 48 (1928): 423–426.

10. Henry, "Ancient Tahiti," 423–426.

11. Peter Bellwood, *The Polynesians: Prehistory of an Island People* (London: Thames and Hudson, 1987), 50–54; Nicholas Thomas, *Islanders: The Pacific in the Age of Empire* (New Haven, CT: Yale University Press, 2012), 8.

12. K. R. Howe, *Where the Waves Fall: A New South Sea Islands History from First Settlement to Colonial Rule* (Sydney: George Allen and Unwin, 1984), 13; G. Lay, T. Murrow, and M. Meleisea, *Samoa* (Auckland: Pasifika Press, 2000), 42.

13. Bellwood, *The Polynesians*, 50–56; David Burley, Marshall I. Weisler, and Jian-xin Zhao, "High Precision U/Th Dating of First Polynesian Settlement," *PLOS ONE* 7, no. 11 (2012): e48769; T. C. Rick, P. V. Kirch, J. M. Erlandson, and S. M. Fitzpatrick, "Archaeology, Deep History, and the Human Transformation of Island Ecosystems," *Anthropocene* 4 (2013): http://dx.doi.org/10.1016/j.ancene.2013.08.002.

14. Bellwood, *The Polynesians*, 78–84; Oliver, *Ancient Tahitian Society*, 2:759–765, 783–796.

15. Hank Driessen, "From Ta'aroa to Oro: An Exploration of Themes in the Traditional Culture and History of the Leeward Society Islands (PhD diss., Australian National University, 1991), 41, 44.

16. John B. Stair, *Old Samoa, or Flotsam and Jetsam from the Pacific Ocean* (London: Macmillan, 1897), 216–217; Oliver, *Ancient Tahitian Society*, 1:59–62.

17. Lay et al., *Samoa*, 43–45.

18. See, for instance, Owen Rutter, ed., *The Log of the Bounty* (London: Golden Cockerel Press, 1935), 1:378. This remained the case during the civil wars of the mid-to-late 1800s in Samoa: see, for example, commentary by Reverend Powell, Tutuila (Samoa), 19 July 1854, LMS/CWM archives, SOAS, Box 25, folder 8.

19. Hank Driessen, "Outriggerless Canoes and Glorious Beings: Pre-contact Prophecies in the Society Islands," *Journal of Pacific History* 17 (1982): 8–9.

20. Stair, *Old Samoa*, 291, 292.

21. Jean-Louise Saquet, *Le Livre de Tahiti: Te Fenua* (Papeete: Editions avant et après, 2001), 72–74.

22. Howe, *Where the Waves Fall*.

23. Jennifer Newell, *Trading Nature: Tahitians, Europeans and Ecological Exchange* (Honolulu: University of Hawai'i Press), 27.

24. Oliver Warner, ed., *An Account of the Discovery of Tahiti: From the Journal of George Robertson, Master of HMS* Dolphin (London: Folio Press, 1973).

25. John Hawkesworth, *An Account of the Voyages Undertaken by the Order of His Present Majesty, for Making Discoveries in the Southern Hemisphere* (London: W. Strahan and T. Cadell, 1773), 422; Anne Salmond, *Aphrodite's Island: The European Discovery of Tahiti* (Berkley: University of California Press, 2009), 45.

26. Warner, *An Account of the Discovery of Tahiti*, 14, 19, 27.

27. Salmond, *Aphrodite's Island*, 40.

28. Hawkesworth, *An Account*, 363.

29. Salmond, *Aphrodite's Island*, 46.

30. Robertson reported that three hundred canoes had gathered by 8 a.m., carrying about four thousand people. Warner, *An Account of the Discovery of Tahiti*, 40–41.

31. Warner, *An Account of the Discovery of Tahiti*, 41.

32. Warner, *An Account of the Discovery of Tahiti*, 46–51.

33. Warner, *An Account of the Discovery of Tahiti*, 61, 74, 120.

34. Hawkesworth, *An Account*, 469. An account of this gift, which included a variety of tools, cloth, and other goods, was also recorded by Francis Wilkinson, Log of Francis Wilkinson on HMS *Dolphin*, 1767, Public Record Office, Kew (ADM 51/4541/96), book 2, 553.

35. Anne Salmond, *Trial of the Cannibal Dog: Captain Cook in the South Seas* (London: Penguin, 2004), 53.

36. N. Thomas, *Discoveries: The Voyages of Captain Cook* (London: Allen Lane / Penguin Books, 2003), 22–23; Salmond, *Trial of the Cannibal Dog*, 30–32; Joseph Banks, in J. C. Beaglehole, ed., *The Endeavour Journal of Joseph Banks 1768–1771*, 2 vols. (Sydney: Public Library of New South Wales, 1963), 1:247–248.

37. Peter Borsay, "The Culture of Improvement," in *The Enlightenment Century, 1688–1815*, ed. Paul Langford, 183–210 (Oxford: Oxford University Press, 2002); Nigel Rigby, "The Politics and Pragmatics of Seaborne Plant Transportation, 1769–1805," in *Science and Exploration of the Pacific European Voyages to the Southern Oceans in the Eighteenth Century*, ed. Marguerite Lincoln (Woodbridge: Boydell Press with the National Maritime Museum, 1998), 81–100.

38. George Forster in N. Thomas and O. Berghof, eds., *A Voyage around the World by George Forster* (Honolulu: University of Hawai'i Press, 2000), 12.

39. Newell, *Trading Nature*, 94–98; Thomas, *Discoveries*, xxii–xxiii.

40. See Newell, *Trading Nature*, 91–114.

41. See, for instance, comments by James Cook and George Forster in J. C. Beaglehole, ed., *The Journals of Captain James Cook*, 4 vols. (Cambridge: Cambridge University Press, 1955–1967), 23, and Thomas and Berghof, eds., *Voyage*, 12. See also Newell, *Trading Nature*, 94–98.

42. Anne D'Alleva, "Framing the 'Ahu Fara: Clothing, Gift-Giving and Painting in Tahiti," paper presented on 23 June 2003 at the "Translating Things: Clothing and Innovation in the Pacific" conference, University College London, 23–25 June 2003.

43. Jennifer Newell, "Exotic Possessions: Polynesians and Their Eighteenth-Century Collecting," *Journal of Museum Ethnography* 17 (2005): 75–88.

44. Beaglehole, ed., *Cook Journals*, 3:195.

45. William Bligh, *The Log of HMS* Providence *1791–1793*, facsimile edition (Guilford, Surrey: Genesis Publications, 1976), "A fine Shaddock Tree I saw Yesterday, very nearly destroyed by Fire, and the Fruit of it they told me was good for nothing," 19 April 1792 (n.p.).

46. Bligh, *The Log of HMS* Providence *1791–1793*, 19 April 1792 (n.p.).

47. The missionary journals recount the repeated losses of their sheep to dog attacks. Reverend John Jefferson wrote in 1804: "The society has now no more than 7 sheep though we have been upwards of 8 years in endeavouring to rear them on the island." J. Jefferson, Journal of the Missionaries Proceedings on Otaheite, 1799–1804, South Seas Journal MS series, London Missionary Society Church World Mission Archives, School of Oriental and African Studies, Journal 1804, 28.

48. See especially Newell, *Trading Nature*, 115–137.

49. David W. Steadman, *Extinction and Biodiversity in Tropical Island Birds* (Chicago: University of Chicago Press, 2006), 273, 296, 381, 405, 406.

50. Beverley Hooper, ed., *With Captain James Cook in the Antarctic and the Pacific: The Private Journal of James Burney Second Lieutenant of the* Adventure *on Cook's Second Voyage, 1772–1773* (Canberra: National Library of Australia, 1975), 69.

51. See Newell, in *Trading Nature*, 141–170.

52. See Newell, in *Trading Nature*, 171–193.

53. Formally Tu-nui-e-a'a-i-te-Atua. See Oliver, *Ancient Tahitian Society*, 3:1179–1193, and passim, for a history of the Pomare lineage.

54. For more on this, see chapter 1, this volume.

55. See H. E. Maude's chapter, "The Tahitian Pork Trade, 1800–1830: An Episode in Australia's Commercial History," in his book *Of Islands and Men: Studies in Pacific History* (Melbourne: Oxford University Press, 1968), 178–232; and Newell, *Trading Nature*, 171–193.

56. Newell, *Trading Nature*, 175–184.

57. Oliver, *Ancient Tahitian Society*, 3:1346–1350.

58. J.-A. Moerenhout, *Voyages aux îles du Grand Océan: contenant des documens nouveaux sue la géographie physique et politique, la langue, la literature, la religion, les moeurs, les usages et les coutumes de leurs habitans; et des considerations générales sur leurs commerce, leur histoire et leur gouvernement, depuis les temps les plus reculés jusqu'a nos jours*, 2 vols. (Paris: A. Bertrand, 1837), 2:464–468.

59. Newell, *Trading Nature*, 191–193.

60. London Missionary Society, *Transactions of the Missionary Society to the End of the Year 1812* (London: J. Dennett, 1813), 3:39.

61. The missionaries' complaints about these issues appear frequently in the Tahitian Mission's daily journals. South Sea Journals, LMS/CWM Archives, SOAS, London. See also Newell, *Trading Nature*, 85–86.

62. See the daily journals of the Tahitian mission, South Sea Journals, LMS/CWM Archives.

63. Vanessa Smith and Nicholas Thomas, eds., *Mutiny and Aftermath: James Morrison's Account of the Mutiny on the Bounty and the Island of Tahiti* (Honolulu: University of Hawai'i Press, 2013), 213–214.

64. J. Davies, "A Journal of Missionary Proceedings on Tahiti, 1807–1808," unpublished manuscript, South Seas Journals, LMS/CWM Archive, SOAS (box 3 folio 31), 26 December 1807.

65. J. Jefferson, "Journal of the Missionaries Proceedings, 1802–1803," unpublished manuscript, South Seas Journals, LMS/CWM Archive, SOAS (box 1 folio 13), 17.

66. J. Davies, "A Journal of Missionary Proceedings on Tahiti, 1807–1808," unpublished manuscript, South Seas Journals, LMS/CWM Archive, SOAS (box 3 folio 31), 25 December 1807 (n.p.).

67. Maude, "The Tahitian Pork Trade," 200; *Sydney Gazette*, 9 November 1819.

68. Maude, "The Tahitian Pork Trade," 201–202.

69. London Missionary Society, *Transactions of the Missionary Society to the End of the Year 1817* (London: Directors of the Missionary Society, 1818), 148.

70. For this phase of Tahitian history, see Niel Gunson, *Messengers of Grace: Evangelical Missionaries in the South Seas* (Melbourne: Oxford University Press, 1978), and Newell, *Trading Nature*, 186–187.

71. Richard Moyle, ed., *The Samoan Journals of John Williams 1830 and 1832* (Canberra: Australian National University Press, 1984), 3.

72. Moyle, ed., *The Samoan Journals of John Williams 1830 and 1832*, 7.

73. John Williams, "A Journal of a Voyage Undertaken Chiefly for the Purpose of Introducing Christianity among the Fegees [Fiji] and Haamoas [Samoa] by Messers Williams and Barff in 1830," in Moyle, *The Samoan Journals of John Williams 1830 and 1832*, 23.

74. The journals of the voyages record these enthusiastic exchanges. See, for instance, "The islanders were very eager to have iron; they exchanged coconuts for some rusty nails" (from *Dagverhaal der Ontdekkings-Reis van Mr. Jacob Roggeveen, met de Schepen Den Arend, Thienhoven en De Afrikaansche Galei, in de jaren 1721 en 1722* [Middelburg: Abraham, 1838], 14 June 1722, 2:195, quoted and translated in Augustin Kramer, *The Samoa Islands: An Outline of a Monograph with Particular Consideration of German Samoa* [Honolulu: University of Hawai'i Press, 1995]), 2:5.

75. Quoted in Kramer, *The Samoa Islands*, 2:11.

76. Accounts from La Pérouse's *Voyage* (also recounted in Kramer, *The Samoa Islands*, 2:11–12); George Turner, *Samoa: A Hundred Years Ago and Long Before* (London: London Missionary Society, 1884), 196; and Stair, *Old Samoa*, 27.

77. Lay et al., *Samoa*, 49.

78. Many Samoans were killed in this incident. Lay et al., *Samoa*, 49.

79. Howe, *Where the Waves Fall*, 235.

80. See the first part of Williams's "Journal of a Voyage," in Moyle, *The Samoan Journals of John Williams 1830 and 1832*, 24–70.

81. Moyle, *The Samoan Journals of John Williams 1830 and 1832*, 67–70.

82. Moyle, *The Samoan Journals of John Williams 1830 and 1832*, 68.

83. Thomas, *Islanders*, 115.

84. Quoted in Kramer, *The Samoa Islands*, 2:30.

85. See Felix Keesing, *Modern Samoa: Its Government and Changing Life* (London: Allen and Unwin, 1934), 401.

86. M. Meleisea, *Change and Adaptations in Western Samoa* (Christchurch: University of Canterbury, 1992), 23.

87. R. P. Gilson, *Samoa 1830–1900: The Politics of a Multi-cultural Community* (Melbourne: Oxford University Press, 1970), quoted in Sean Mallon, *Samoan Art and Artists* (Nelson, NZ: Craig Potton Publishing, 2002), 18.

88. John Williams, *A Narrative of Missionary Enterprises in the South Pacific: Remarks upon the Natural History, Origins, Languages, Traditions and Usages of the Inhabitants* (London: John Snow, 1842), 127.

89. N. A. Rowe, *Samoa under the Sailing Gods* (London: Putnam, 1930), 68.

90. Keesing, *Modern Samoa*, 296.

91. A. W. Murray, *Forty Years Mission Work in Polynesia and New Guinea, from 1835 to 1875*, original edition, 1876 (London: Forgotten Books, 2013; reprint), 270–271.

92. Stair, *Old Samoa*, 187–188.

93. Stair, *Old Samoa*, 195–199.

94. Beaglehole, ed., *Cook Journals*, 2:412.

95. William Bligh, *The Log of the Bounty 1787–1789*, facsimile edition (Guildford, Surrey: Genesis Publications, 1975), 121.

96. The illustration by George Forster is the type specimen for the species. J. Hulme and M. Waters, *Extinct Birds* (London: Bloomsbury Publishing, 2010), 93; Beaglehole, ed., *Cook Journals*, 2:412.

97. J. R. Platt, "Manumea Found," *Scientific American*, 11 February 2014.

98. By contrast, the manumea was first described in 1845, by Sir William Jardine. Scientists in Australia and Britain acquired several specimens, and a living manumea was sent to the Zoological Society in Britain in 1864. Stair, *Old Samoa*, 198.

99. Quoted in Rowe, *Sailing Gods*, 46.

100. I am grateful to Karen Armstrong for her useful archival work: "The London Missionary Society Tutuila Mission: A Timeline of Missionaries, Events and Buildings on Tutuila, Samoa, 1830–1910," http://ashpo.com/downloads/TutuilaMission1910.pdf.

101. Archibald Murray, *Forty Years' Mission Work in Polynesia and New Guinea, from 1835 to 1875* (York: Robert Carter and Brothers, 1876), 154.

102. Murray, *Forty Years' Mission Work*, 154.

103. Letter, South Sea CWM/LMS/02 incoming correspondence, Box 17, Folder 7, 6 August 1844.

104. Mr. Sunderland, 4 July 1854, Pagopago, Tutuila. South Sea Reports, SOAS/CWM Archives, Box 25, folder 7.

105. Thomas Powell, 4 July 1855, Pagopago, Tutuila. South Sea Reports, SOAS/CWM Archives, Box 26, folder 4.

106. Archibald Murray, South Sea Reports, Box 1, 1866, South Seas CWM/LMS/02 1798–1970 Annual Reports (1866–1970).

107. J. B. Thurston, colonial secretary of Fiji, 1886, quoted in Thomas, *Islanders*, 275, and see also 270–274; Howe, *Where the Waves Fall*, 248–249.

108. Thomas, *Islanders*, 272.

109. Malama Meleisea, *The Making of Modern Samoa: Traditional Authority and Colonial Administration in the History of Western Samoa* (Suva: University of the South Pacific, 1987), chapter 2.

110. Howe, *Where the Waves Fall*, 248–249; Thomas, *Islanders*, 270.

111. Lay et al., *Samoa*, 45.

112. Thomas, *Islanders*, 270–271.

113. Alfred Crosby, *Ecological Imperialism: The Biological Expansion of Europe 900–1900* (Cambridge: Canto, 1986).

114. For one example, see Andrew Mitchell, *The Fragile South Pacific: An Ecological Odyssey* (Austin: University of Texas Press, 1989).

115. Autagavaia, "Rethinking Home" workshop.

116. Lay et al., *Samoa*; Newell, *Trading Nature*, 86–87.

117. Robert Levy, *Tahitians: Mind and Experience in the Society Islands* (Chicago: University of Chicago Press, 1973); conversation between J. Newell and an informant [name withheld], an active Catholic, Papeete, Tahiti, 5 July 2001.

118. Interview with J. Newell at the Center for Samoan Studies, National University of Samoa, Apia, 9 July 2013.

CHAPTER FIVE

Closed Sea or Contested Waters?

The Persian Gulf in the Age of Revolution

SUJIT SIVASUNDARAM

In geographical terms, the Persian Gulf is one of the world's most closed stretches of sea. It opens to the Indian Ocean through the tortured course of the Strait of Hormuz and the Gulf of Oman. Given the difficulty of access, it is perhaps understandable that it is forgotten in recent global histories.[1] The oceanic turn of present historiography is only now arriving in the Gulf. The area studies approaches of the Middle East, South Asia, and Central Asia still divide up the story that this chapter weaves together. In the general literature on the Age of Revolution, there is little reference to it as worthy of attention. One exception is the commentary provided by C. A. Bayly, who writes: "It seemed to me that the Wahhabi revolt against intrusive Ottoman rule and the decline of proper religious observance in the cities of Saudi Arabia should be regarded as a variety of world revolution."[2] This chapter returns to the Gulf in the late eighteenth and early nineteenth centuries not to exalt the Wahhabis as keepers of an isolated revolutionary tradition. Instead, it considers the Gulf at the interstices of a series of profound political changes. These include the reconfiguration of Eurasian empires, the rise of a new style of maritime European imperialism and trade, the reconstitution of sea-facing smaller polities or "successor states," and the paths traversed by sailors and slaves. Accordingly, it is possible to populate the Gulf's Age of Revolution with a richly varied set of perspectives.[3] Extrapolating outward from the Gulf, such a picture builds the argument that the Age of Revolution was a tangle of political possibilities.

Such a tangle was particularly knotty in sea-facing places set against Europe, fringed both by connected Eurasian empires in rivalry and the states they birthed. The contestation of the Gulf came from many directions: from France and Britain, from Oman and the Wahhabis as much as from India.

The shadow of the Ottoman and Persian realms exercised a sizeable pull. The Gulf's coordinates in the Age of Revolution were fought over at multiple levels: local, interimperial, and transregional. The British aimed to redefine this space of water from Bombay. British expeditions invaded the Gulf from India, and the British thrust their treaties and commercial arrangements—which in themselves were responses to the Age of Revolution—over this sea. These instruments reversed the dreaming of the Gulf's ferment of revolt, though their penetration into the city-states facing the Gulf should not be overemphasized.[4] Critically, such imperial control was not a complete success. For the revolutionary character of the age carried well into the nineteenth century, as subjects under the rubric of intrusive empire reworked their claims in a supposedly liberal imperial age. The protest of sailors on ships that plied the route between Bombay and the Gulf, or the fact that ships could be built for Oman right under the nose of the British ruling in India, suggests that an older history of the maritime Gulf lived on.[5]

Before proceeding with this complicated story, it is important to clarify the sense in which the Age of Revolution is marshaled here as a concept.[6] First, the argument decenters and recontextualizes the story of an Islamic age of revolt, away from Europe, the Mediterranean, and Turkey. Those who write on the Islamic Age of Revolution present the Western and Eastern Mediterranean as an intersecting terrain of modernization and imperial control lasting into the Napoleonic expedition to Egypt.[7] Yet the Gulf's Age of Revolution releases the scholar from debating Ottoman diplomacy, the spread of news of the French Revolution in Turkey, and responses to it in turn. Relatedly, this chapter places the Wahhabi story within a more textured landscape, one that includes divisions of theology and state-making within the lands facing the Gulf as well as the histories of communities from South Asia and elsewhere who interacted with the Gulf, and whose skills, resources, and protest intersected with the Wahhabi moment. Second, the argument of this chapter is that revolutionism is wrapped with imperialism and imperial definitions of revolution in turn.[8] While empires sought to define revolt as irrational fanaticism or piratical despotism, the British successfully adopted some revolutionary principles within their arsenal of ideas. In this way, revolution could be folded into imperialism without being totally encompassed by it. Third, and in reference to this volume's concern with indigeneity, this argument is consistent with my writing elsewhere, which does not reify the Indigenous in the Age of Revolution but tracks "indigeneity" as a changeable category of belonging and classification.[9] Such an approach is compatible with the twinned insistence of this volume's editors that the Indigenous should encompass colonial modes of categorization as well as self and group endorsement and identification. Indeed, it is the diversity of peoples who enter this story who are worth considering; the search for indigenes or indeed the obsessive interest with the tyranny of the Wahhabis was partly a colonial product that points to European ignorance about histories of migration, theology, and historical memory. The Gulf was anything but a closed or isolated ground of a single indigeneity. At the same time, and in counterpoint, the take-up of a historic tradition—for instance, by Parsis in Bombay—was a mode of marshaling a lineage to make a group cohere within the Age of Revolution.

Without exalting a singular Indigenous, this chapter approaches the Gulf from a variety of vantage points and histories of mobility across space. It seeks to ground the Gulf within a history of diplomacy as much as a history of trade and ideas, and in relation to the people who carried the story on into the British empire, and especially how Bombay came to be interlinked with the Gulf. The sum of its parts is critical to the chapter's historiographical intervention. By virtue of its status as a crossroads, and given that "[i]ts orientation is outwards, towards the Indian Ocean," the Persian Gulf had many lives in the Age of Revolution.[10] These were violently overtaken but not flattened or obliterated by the British empire. Empire did not fill the whole picture, though it had a marked effect.

To orient the reader: after starting with the British assault on those they recognized as Wahhabi, the discussion moves on to how Oman found its way in the Age of Revolution and within the conflict over Wahhabi Ras al-Khaimah. From there, the chapter broadens into the changing political stakes in the Persian and Ottoman realms that generated the conditions of possibility for the Gulf's Age of Revolution. The last third of what follows looks across the waters to the story between Bombay and the Gulf—by considering the status of shipbuilders and the culture of protest and agency on ships in this line of sea.

Gulf Invasions

From Bombay, in 1809–10 and 1819–20, the British launched two invasive operations against Ras al-Khaimah, which sat at the apex of the Qasimi confederacy, a set of maritime Arab city-states in the present-day United Arab Emirates.[11] These military invasions, among the originary moments in the history of British invasions of the Gulf, were driven by fear of Qasimi piracy. Such fears coincided with the rise of British India's trade with the Gulf after

1790. Concerns about French activity in the Gulf and Persia fed into the first moment. The second was post-Napoleonic. Critical to the whole story was the British desire to stand by their ally, Oman.

Visual images of the 1809–10 expedition pay attention to how the British burnt the settlement of Ras al-Khaimah, inclusive of merchandise, naval resources, and buildings.[12] "Sixteen Views of Places in the Persian Gulph" provides a visual narrative of the military expedition, beginning with the departure from Apollo Gate, Bombay, and including an image of Ras al-Khaimah lying in choppy waters. A closer image shows troops preparing to land, using smaller vessels to get to the beach, and then two prints follow of Ras al-Khaimah burning (figs. 5.1, 5.2, and 5.3). While a British officer lies wounded in a sacrificial pose in the middle of one of the images, another shows local settlers desperately attempting to save their possessions. The visual rhetoric contrasts the manly devotion of the British military with the self-serving interests of the barely clothed people of Ras al-Khaimah. The official record reported a complete destruction of Ras al-Khaimah: fifty vessels, allegedly

Figure 5.1. "No. 7: The Troops Landing at Rus ul Kyma [Ras al-Khaimah]." I. Clark, W. William Haines, and R. Temple, "Sixteen Views of Places in the Persian Gulph," PAF4799, © National Maritime Museum, Greenwich, London.

Figure 5.2. "No. 8: The Storming of a Large Storehouse Near Rus ul Kyma [Ras al-Khaimah]." I. Clark, W. William Haines, and R. Temple, "Sixteen Views of Places in the Persian Gulph," PW4800, © National Maritime Museum, Greenwich, London.

Figure 5.3. "No. 9: Rus ul Kyma [Ras al-Khaimah] from the S.W. and the Situation of the Troops." I. Clark, W. William Haines, and R. Temple, "Sixteen Views of Places in the Persian Gulph," PW4801, © National Maritime Museum, Greenwich, London.

used for piracy, including thirty large *dhows*, were said to have been destroyed, and some captured property was passed on to Muscat.[13] In the expedition's instructions, burning vessels with fire was specifically advised. It was the appropriate response to the plunder of goods.[14]

Like all such invasions of the Gulf and despite the visual priming, the political results of the 1809–10 expedition were incomplete. In one account, the hold of Wahhabism among these states was accentuated as the political structures of the city-states that had composed Qawasim crumbled.[15] For his own part, the ruler of Muscat noted that unless another expedition was sent out he might be overwhelmed by the Qawasim backed by the Wahhabis. In response, the British opted to arm him with "several articles of Guns, muskets and ammunition."[16] However, when a second expedition left about ten years later, his request was eventually answered.

In 1819, Hasan bin Rahma of Ras al-Khaimah sought to prevent a British expedition by proposing a truce; this time, he sought to embrace the British legal culture of the sea and spoke of the need of "signals and boundaries," and the proper use of flags.[17] But it was too late: the second expedition destroyed twice as many boats and fortifications. As the wife of one of the leading lights of this expedition noted of the demolition of Ras al-Khaimah: "The atmosphere seemed absolutely on fire—there was no air to breathe, and I was burning with fever. I recollect the appearance of the horizon all in flames."[18] The uncontrollable use of fire problematizes and contextualizes the instrument that the British utilized in the immediate aftermath and that Hasan bin Rahma already understood: legal paperwork.

It is easy and correct to interpret these expeditions through the lens of the Wahhabis as participants in the Age of Revolution. The intensification of maritime plunder in the Gulf came as Wahhabism took hold among the Qawasim, from 1800, and especially from 1808. Millenarian Wahhabism emerged out of an alliance between a scion of a family of *qadis*, or Muslim judges, Shaikh Muhammad bin Abd al-Wahhab, and the rulers of Dir'iyyah, close to Riyadh in 1744–45. As a set of teachings, it stressed the Unity of Allah and criticized the sin of polytheism. Combining rigid dictates about prayer and fasting, it also sought to eliminate any kind of infidelity to a Unitarian doctrine by tearing apart shrines of saints, outlawing minor pilgrimages, and standing against the invocation of the names of angels, prophets, or even the Prophet Muhammad; all of this was labeled as *shirk*, or polytheist. The movement pursued a course of *jihad* in Arabia in the late eighteenth and early nineteenth centuries, so allowing the alliance to be politically useful to the Al Sa'ud family in creating a stronger state. From 1795, the Wahhabi-Saudi state undertook raids against Ottoman Iraq, sacking Karbala, the holy Shi'ite shrine; it made raids into Syria, Yemen, and the Hijaz, taking over Mecca and Medina in 1803–04, the indisputable centers of the Islamic world.[19] In the end, the response to Wahhabism came from Egypt, when Muhammad Ali launched a sustained attack on the new Wahhabi-Saudi state, retaking Mecca and Medina in 1815–16. Abdullah bin Sa'ud, the Saudi ruler, was sent to Constantinople and executed.[20]

Yet the glorification of Wahhabi revolt, and the interpretation of it as revolutionary, emerged partly from the period's colonial writings. One of the earliest accounts of Wahhabism among English observers comes from Harford Jones, the Resident of the East India Company in Baghdad. Jones wrote of the Wahhabis as "[a] sect of Puritan Arabs" who if not stopped might "be the occasion of considerable revolutions in this part of the Globe."[21] He defined the tenets of Wahhabism to include a "literal" embrace of the Qu'ran: "2dly. That a Mohammedan, who deviates, in religious duties, in the smallest degree from the literal forms, injunctions and precepts of the Koran is as much a Cafer or Unbeliever or Christian as a Jew; and that, therefore, to make war against him is the positive duty of every Wahambee, or as they call themselves, all true Mussulmans."[22] Even in this description, it is clear that the Wahhabis were not without a legal code. However, contemporary colonial observers defined Wahhabism as revolutionary in its lack of a code of conduct, and this framed the justified utilization of techniques such as fire in response. Simultaneously, the British intervention counted also as the imposition of a practice of paperwork on these agents, which was born of the Age of Revolution. The place of the Wahhabis as players in the Age of Revolution cannot thus be divorced from the colonializing power of instruments born of the Age of Revolution.

After the 1819 expedition, the British signed a series of truces with the rulers of the city-states of the Gulf, enabling this coastline to become, in popular British parlance, the Trucial Coast. This was an attempt to diffuse into the Persian Gulf the liberal imperial definition of good conduct at sea. According to the terms of the General Treaty of 1820, there would be a cessation of piracy and plunder, and such conduct was defined as orchestrated by "an enemy of all mankind." The illegality of piracy arose here in opposition to the legality of warfare: "An acknowledged war is that which is proclaimed, avowed, and ordered by Government against Government; and the killing of men and taking of goods without proclamation, avowal, and the order of a Government is plunder and piracy."[23] In this view, vessels needed to have national identities and alliances. Arab vessels became tied by the treaty to carrying by land and sea "a red flag, with or without letters in it." This flag's peculiar characteristics were spelled out: the red coloring was to be set "in a border of white, the breadth of the white in the border being equal to the breadth of the red . . . (the whole forming the flag known in the British Navy by the title of white pierced red)." William Grant Keir, who led the second expedition, explained his logic elsewhere. Given that a red flag was taken to indicate pirates, by combining it with a border of white it could signal peace.[24] By the treaty, each Arab vessel had to carry a registration paper with "the signature of the Chief," specifying the name of the vessel, its length, and breadth and capacity. In these ways, diplomacy tied the vessels to their chiefs and in turn generated their chiefly identity and subjugation, apparent in how they sent an envoy to the British Residency in the Persian Gulf.

The Arab city-states facing the sea had to live with what they had signed in 1820. The General Treaty of 1820 fed into the Perpetual Mandate Truce of 1853 and was reprinted into the twentieth century. From fire to bureaucracy, the British overtook the maritime violence of the Gulf, with methods that resonated with this age. The revolutionism of the Wahhabis was set against the British neutralization and adoption of revolutionary practices.

Maritime Muscat in the Age of Revolution

If the placement of the Wahhabis in the Age of Revolution needs to be approached alongside a sense of how the British saw themselves as countering this revolutionism, the Wahhabi story might be pluralized much further. The maritime violence in the Persian Gulf, undertaken in all directions, was the result of the slow collapse of the Ottoman Empire and the fall of the Safavid Empire, which gave rise to Qajar and Zand Persia in the late eighteenth century. These empires could not keep up with the imperial and military toolkit of France or Britain. Oman's new state based in Muscat is a good place to trace this history, as it was a successor at the rim of these great empires that attempted to pursue a sea-facing policy in order to benefit from the new style of empire orchestrated by the Europeans.

An Omani state in Muscat was consolidated in the 1780s as a turn away from the interior of Oman with its theologically conservative brand of Islamic teaching, Ibadism, and in an attempt to wrest control of the maritime trade of the Gulf by making Muscat the Gulf's new gatekeeper and port of choice. Its origin is sometimes attributed to Hamad bin Said.[25] Hamad's Muscat marked the disintegration of a unified Omani polity ruled from Rustaq, by his grandfather Ahmad bin Sa'id, who inaugurated the Al Bu Sa'id dynasty in 1749. This dynasty continues to reign in Oman today. Like his grandfather, Hamad was particularly interested in maritime trade. Under his hold of Muscat, commercial links were further developed with the Sind and Afghanistan, utilizing the collaboration of Muslim merchants. Yet competition with Bahrain and the Qawasim was intense, and Muscat lost territory to Qawasim after the death of Hamad.

Sea-facing trade and politics was intensified under Sultan bin Ahmad, the son of Hamad, who formalized a cooperative relationship between the British East India Company and Muscat, which fed into the military expeditions to Ras al-Khaimah. A treaty, or *qawlnama,* was signed with the "High and Potent English Company" in 1798, and a Resident was stationed at Muscat.[26] At the heart of this relationship was the British bid to make a base for free trade in the Persian Gulf, and the eager eye it cast over Bahrain.[27]

With this alliance, Muscat's dream of making itself an entrepôt of maritime trade came to fruition for a brief period. In the words of one historian: "Oman's great need in the nineteenth century was for strong leadership and military strength. Instead the country received ineffectual government from a dynasty of merchant princes whose talents and resources were almost wholly connected with the sea."[28] Yet it is inadequate to tell this story as the result of internal governmental weakness. For the turn to the sea reflected changing global circumstances as well as the plight of large land-based empires, and it points to a rather vibrant attempt on the part of Muscat's leaders to place themselves within such developments. This attempt was not ineffectual.

Muscat's diplomacy is particularly revealing of this interplay between the global and the regional, which did not see the Persian Gulf's particularity disappear. Oman actively turned away from the French to develop its agreement with the British, having observed that France made and did not keep its promises: for instance, for the appointment of a Resident who was expected in 1796. Omanis had also seen how Britain was taking an increasingly critical role in India. In the interim, the Omani state also successfully kept up a trade with the Dutch in Batavia, and Tipu Sultan of Mysore had a factory in Muscat. Indeed, even after signing the agreement with the East India Company in 1798, Muscat did not totally annul its relations with the French—to the chagrin of the British.[29] Some sympathy for the French lasted until the fall of French Mauritius to the British in 1810. Such agency arose from the changing political landscape at the crossroads of the Ottoman and Persian worlds, which produced in Oman a new confidence that could then be wielded in global diplomacy.

The strengthening of the Saudi state with the rise of Wahhabism had a negative impact on the place of Oman as the door to the Gulf.[30] When the Sultan invaded Bahrain for the first time in 1799, he angered Persia, and in 1801, when he staged another attempt on Bahrain, the Saudis intervened and expelled Muscat. Oman itself was invaded by the Saudis in 1803, and this gave rise to the need for an annual tribute from Muscat to the Saudi state. On a mission to get the Ottomans to assist him against the Saudis, the Sultan met his death in 1804. In the years after this event, and with the dominance of Sai'd bin Sultan at Muscat, the region entered an even more volatile period, rife with raids and counterraids and a tangled network of alliances between Qawasim, Bahrain, Muscat, the Saudis, Persia, the British, and the French. The 1809–10 expedition to Ras al-Khaimah occurred in this context. Despite a persistent desire to proclaim its independence and sovereignty, Oman now found itself in collaboration with Britain in military terms, too.

If the British expedition was undertaken without full knowledge of the internal politics of the region, it is notable that in the long run these British interventions had some impact on the economic landscape of the Gulf, such that raiding was no longer profitable and the region's politics became reconfigured as a result. This British policy of peace by treaty led traders to forego the security of Oman. Before this happened, however, the Wahhabis and their collaborators, the Qawasim, benefited from the changing circumstances of maritime trade in the Persian Gulf.

The late eighteenth century saw a resurgence of sea-based trades, connected to pearls, dates, wool, and opium in the Persian Gulf, and the rise of these trades required labor, which also came via the ocean, primarily as slaves from East Africa. These slaves arrived as a result of Omani merchants' contacts and the developing political alliance between Oman and Zanzibar, which would in the end see the Omani sultanate relocate to East Africa.[31] The sea-facing position of the burgeoning centers of the Gulf denoted how earlier factors that determined settlement in Arabia—such as access to water and the potential for agriculture—were no longer constraints.[32] Slavery itself was reconstituted as a result: it shifted from being primarily domestic and agricultural to being connected, for example, with pearling, with loading and unloading at port, and with work aboard *dhows* or other oceangoing craft. A major slaving entrepôt was Ras al-Khaimah, and others included Basra, Bushire, Bandar Abbas, and Dubai. From this coastal region, a large number of slaves were taken further into Iranian and Ottoman lands. In the port of Muscat, there arose an eclectic group of peoples who supported this maritime trade: Hindus, Armenians, and Jews were involved in lending money or providing insurance and did not need to adhere to Islamic law.[33] The connections to the wider Indian Ocean were also apparent in the fact that Bombay slowly became the leading entrepôt for pearls from the Persian Gulf as the century progressed.

In 1786, it is estimated that Muscat's customs duties equaled its internal tax revenues.[34] However, in the new context of quietude across water, which came with British free trade, Oman had to look elsewhere in order to bolster its coffers. It increasingly based itself in East Africa after 1820. Muscat's story, then, points to the creative path treaded by a polity facing the sea in the Age of Revolution and beyond. It came to terms with the muscular power of British diplomacy and trade. European empire constrained but did not bar its evolution.

Ship-Builders: Facing the Gulf and Empire

There are still other ways of understanding the life of the Persian Gulf in the global Age of Revolution beyond this narrative of political structures in change as they faced European empire. It is time to move to the history of communities and people. Here, too, modes of protest sat together with collaboration with the British. The earlier history of the maritime violence of the Persian Gulf lived on, and revolutionary practice found a path within the contortions of the British empire. Tracing this story requires a change of vantage point—to look at Oman from where the invasive expeditions set off: Bombay.

On 10 February 1819, a new ship was floated on the middle dock of Bombay Harbour. Named the *Shah Alum,* it did not receive the customary ritual of naming where wine was poured over a new vessel.[35] The *Asiatic Journal* reported that there was simply a "conspicuous effusion of rose-water and ottar," the latter of which was a perfume, and also that the ship was saluted by all the Arab ships in the harbor on the following morning. Critically, the *Shah Alum* was bound for Muscat and for the navy of Sa'id bin Sultan. It had been built by Parsi ship-builders who had by this time become renowned for their skill in making sturdy teak ships that could stand their own against European vessels. The *Asiatic Journal* noted the expectation that the *Shah Alum* would receive a benediction from a Muslim holy man. In fact, it was named by a European, upon the advice of the agent of the Muscat Resident at Bombay. The year the *Shah Alum* took to water was also the year of the second expedition against Ras al-Khaimah.

The late eighteenth and early nineteenth centuries saw a great deal of debate about the merits of oak versus teak as the wood of choice for shipbuilding and the relative value of Indian-built ships.[36] The debate drew in the context of the French revolutionary and Napoleonic wars: including observation on the shortage of ships and the arrival of Indian-built ships in London, carrying rice and wheat in 1795, in the midst of war with France.[37] The tensions around ship-building were handled by partitioning the British–Indian Ocean trading world by type of ship. Beyond the Cape of Good Hope to the west, the trade was restricted to British-built ships. Meanwhile, "country ships," or Indian-built ships, could be used by British private merchants in a trade that ran from India to the East Indies and the Malay Peninsula, to China, and to the Persian Gulf, but not to Europe.[38]

In such a story, the Parsi ship-builders and their wider community of merchant families, shipowners, money-lenders, brokers, and printers are seen as one of the most successful "comprador classes" of British imperialism.[39] Their easy adaptation to British culture is evident, for instance, in the series of portraits drawn of the Parsi "Master Builders" of the Bombay Dockyard to celebrate their dedicated and accomplished service to the British.[40] The first Master Builder of Bombay was Lavji Nasarvanji, who moved from Surat in 1735 and gave rise to the Wadia family of Bombay.

A portrait of his grandson Jamshedji Bamanji (c. 1754–1824) might indicate how Parsis accommodated themselves to British norms. Jamshedji Bamanji was the third Master Builder, and held this title jointly with his cousin, Framji Manakji, who was also portrayed for British eyes.[41] Jamshedji Bamanji's portrait is a richly textured image that highlights the effervescent beauty of Jamshedji's white robe, which in turn is wrapped within a gold-, red-, and green-embroidered pashmina shawl (fig. 5.4). The image carries the markers of technical skill, by including a divider and two rules, one of which is tucked into Jamshedji's robe. The second rule sits on the table and may have been the one gifted to him in 1804, inscribed in praise of his "continued Fidelity and long tried Services."[42] The workmanship of his clothes thus matches his own expertise in building ships, which is on show in the image. Out of the window, one can see the *Minden* (1810), "the first and only British ship of the line built out of the limits of the Mother Country," keeping with

Figure 5.4. J. Dorman, "Jamsetjee Bomankee Wadia [Jamshedji Bamanji Wadia], (c. 1754–1821)." BHC2803, © National Maritime Museum, Greenwich, London.

the plan in Jamshedji Bamanji's hands.[43] Consistent with the tradition of European portraiture and exploration, this painting includes a chair, a curtain, and a window out of which one sees the new world. Jamshedji's son was portrayed before a wide landscape of a mountain, coconut palms, and a sailing ship in clear water (fig. 5.5). Nevertheless, Jamshedji's portrait does not emphasize effortless genius or manly heroism, such as that deemed to characterize British explorers. Rather, it was a token of hard work. Jamshedji himself appears rather weary, with one eye almost totally closed and frowning. His cousin Framji Manakji poses with his spectacles in hand.[44]

Figure 5.5. J. Dorman (?), "Nourojee Jamsetjee [Naoroji Jamshedji] (1756–1821)." Library, Royal Asiatic Society of Great Britain and Ireland, London.

Parsis first arrived in Gujarat from Persia after the Arab conquest of Iran, perhaps in the eighth century, to escape persecution for their Zoroastrian faith.[45] They turned to ship-building at the port of Surat from the seventeenth century while taking up an increasingly urban style of life. They moved in increasing numbers to Bombay, reacting perhaps to recurrent famines, so that there were ten thousand of them in the city in 1811, most of whom arrived as farmers and artisans, but then turned to trade and industry. Their increasing wealth came partly out of profits in cotton and opium, and money-lending and brokerage. In time, they took a pioneering place in Indian politics; in Britain, the first three Asians to become members of the British Parliament were all Parsis.[46] In sum, and for the argument that they were subimperialists, it may be said that they adapted to the British empire with greater occupation mobility, compared, say, with Hindus or Muslims, or that they were unimpeded by a sense of a loss of status in political or administrative terms, like older elites. Instead, they embraced English language learning and maritime culture.

Yet this does not give the full picture of Parsi agency. The *Shah Alum* and also the *Tajbaux* (1802), *Caroline* (1814), and *Nausery* (1822), which were also built for Oman rather than Britain, complicate this story. That the Parsis were also building vessels for Muscat picks up the biographical history of this community as well as the long-standing reliance on the part of Arab sea-facing states for timber and ships from India. According to one estimate, eight ships were built for Muscat in Bombay between 1802 and 1835.[47] It is likely that other vessels operated by Arabs and Persians were also built elsewhere along the coast of India. Indeed, earlier in the eighteenth century, Nadir Shah of Persia had ships built and repaired ships in India.[48] In the aftermath of the 1809–10 expedition to Ras al-Khaimah, the British-Indian government enforced a ban on the import of timber to the Gulf in order to put a stop to what they saw as the menace of Wahhabi piracy. Yet it was possible for the Qawasim to continue to get their hands on timber, for instance, from Travancore, on the southwest Indian coast.[49] There was a similar discussion yet again in 1820, after the second expedition.[50] The British could not control the making of ships on the coast of India, just as they could not monopolize access to the valued hardwoods used for ship-building.[51] In fact, they were particularly anxious to get a good estimate of the forests on the southwest coast in Malabar and Kanara, which could be used for ship-building.[52] The arrival of an Indian-built vessel made a great impact in Muscat. The *Caroline*, for instance, came to Saʿid bin Sultan's navy just when he was assailed by the Wahhabis. In order to bolster morale, it is said that Saʿid bin Sultan boarded the vessel "attended by a thousand men, armed with lances, and among whom were a crowd of his own slaves." The ship was immediately engaged in firing on the enemy.[53] However, according to Francis Warden of the Bombay government, it was almost taken over by the Qawasim of Ras al-Khaimah.[54]

Right under the nose of the British, until the late 1820s, from which date the Bombay shipyard declined, finally giving way to steamships built of British iron, an earlier history of connection between the Persian Gulf and

Bombay continued to operate.[55] Parsis may have benefited from the British empire, but they should not for this reason be excluded from the class of people who were agents of the Age of Revolution.[56] Their early politics in Bombay bears out such a characterization, for they began to conceive of themselves as a nation and also took an active interest in their own history in Persia in response to the Christian missionary critiques of Zorastrianism.[57] A Parsi *panchayat* (an assembly of community governance, theoretically of five chosen leaders) was founded in Bombay to regulate the community in the early eighteenth century. By 1818, this assembly was run by eighteen members who were elected in a public meeting.[58] Among the families that took a leading role in this *panchayat* were the Wadia family. It took into its purview matters connected to marriage and adoption, property, and charity.

By the late 1830s, this *panchayat* was already in decline, accused of corruption, bigamy, and idolatry by a new generation of Parsis. Yet it was consolidated in concord with the global moment: Parsis began traveling to London from the early eighteenth century to proclaim their rights and to observe and critique the English. Among Parsi travelers to London were two ship-builders of the Wadia family, who were grandsons of Jamshedji Bamanji. Jehangir Naoroji and Hirjibhoy Meherwanji were sent to acquire new skills in shipbuilding at a time when the Bombay dockyard was in decline, arriving in 1838. These two builders visited the dockyards, but also the British Museum, the zoological gardens, and other sites of London, and wrote of the progress made "by that giant Steam" and how it was "becoming more extensively applied to marine purposes."[59]

Their observations about how Britain decided between "Reform or Revolution," by adopting the Reform Bill, drew on a visit to the British Parliament, where they witnessed a debate in progress.[60] They sat in the "foremost" seats in the gallery, dressed in what they called "our costume," seen by every member of Parliament. There they sat for eight and a half hours through the night, until two thirty in the morning. Naoroji and Meherwanji's published journal issues the judgment that "the British constitution is acknowledged to the best in the known world, and a perfect model to be imitated by others for the legislation of their countries." Yet they twinned this sentiment with a critique of the "bribery" that characterized elections, and how the Reform Bill had increased such "bribery" by allowing poor votes to be bought. These comments can be read in light of the problems that beset the Bombay Parsi *panchayat*. Debates about reform in Britain in the late 1830s were happening side-by-side with the questioning of rights in Bombay.

Bombay's links to the west via ships did not simply rest with socially mobile ship-builders; it also included the world of laborers, traders, and slaves aboard the vessels that plied this line of sea. In this respect, the Age of Revolution from the Persian Gulf to West India had less elite constituents who reworked the culture of constitutions, sometimes forging more violent forms of revolt. Despite their differences, these agents also shared the same mental world as the Parsis, stretching from Bombay to the Gulf.

Revolt between Bombay and the Gulf

The Persian Gulf and Bombay and other western Indian ports in Surat, Sindh, Kutch, Kanara, and Malabar were becoming increasingly connected by Arab vessels in the Age of Revolution.[61] In the early nineteenth century, there were some years where the number and tonnage of Arab vessels arriving and departing from Surat exceeded that of British ships.[62] These figures are likely to be underestimations, because some Arab ships sailed under British flags, while others were probably unrecorded. This increase in Arab maritime activity arose directly from the Napoleonic wars. Because of their supposed neutrality, Arab vessels were not attacked by either the British or the French. Such was the advantage that some European vessels—especially French and Dutch—took up Arab colors. While *baghlas* and their smaller equivalents, *battils,* were used for Arab trade between the west coast of India and the Gulf, European-style ships flying Arab colors became increasingly prevalent. Some of these latter ships were bought by Arab merchants from the French, who in turn had taken them captive from the British. A range of commodities went back and forth in this trade, including the export of Chinaware and grain from India and the import of aloes, copper, beads, horses, and pearls from Arabia. Slaves could also travel in both directions. It was only with sustained opposition by British merchants, who accused Arab merchants of spying and disguising French trade, that measures were tightened in the mid-1830s, so that Arab vessels were classed as comparable to any other foreign craft, thus finally annulling tariff preferences.

From this vantage point, the relationship between Muscat's rulers and Bombay fits into a wider context of regional connections between Arabia and western India, which were becoming more intense in these decades. It also included the role of money-lenders and traders, who were critical for the Indian connection to the Gulf.[63] In piecing together the relatively small number of travel journals in English for the early-nineteenth-century Persian Gulf, Arabia, and Persia, it is possible to reconstruct something of the experience of the laborers and slaves aboard the Arab vessels and also the wider class of "country ships" under British flags. James Silk Buckingham, the liberal critic of the East India Company, noted the high level of linguistic hybridity on the vessels that traveled between Muscat and Bombay: "[o]n board their own large ships, even the names of the masts, sails, and ropes, as well as the orders of command in evolutions, are, as in India, a mixture of Arabic, Persian, Hindee [Hindi], Dutch, Portuguese, and English."[64] Yet the breadth of these languages flattened out to make "Hindoostanee" the language most widely understood by the diverse crew of these vessels. There were also some remnants of Portuguese evident among them: Portuguese words for flag, compass, and squadron were used.[65]

The range of languages was also matched by the backgrounds of the crew. Lieutenant William Heude of the Madras army, who traveled from India to the Persian Gulf and overland to England in 1817, was on an "Arab ship" with British colors named *The Fuzil Kareem* for the first leg of the journey: "with a crew of 50 Lascars, and 90 passengers on board; of these, 30 were Persians, stout, able, and turbulent; the rest were Arabs, Turks, Jews, and Gentiles, of every quality and degree, of every trade and occupation that can be named. Merchants, and pilgrims to the holy tomb at Kurbulla [Karbala]; horse-dealers, soldiers, gentlemen, and slaves; they had reached Bombay from every part."[66] As they approached Muscat, twenty-five craft were sailing out to Bombay, under convoy with the *Caroline*, built by the Parsis.

Much of Heude's description was presented rather nonchalantly. The *Edinburgh Review* lambasted the author for being full of "idle and ill-told stories about drunken Turks," rather than having as his aim "the gratification of that rational curiosity respecting the countries he passes through."[67] This critique is important in making sense of Heude's account of an insurrection that overtook *The Furzil Kareem* on its journey out of Muscat. The Persians tried to strangle a *lascar* [usually an Indian sailor], after a quarrel, and when the mate interfered they rose against him. The commotion overtook the vessel in the early morning; the "mutineers" were driven "towards the poop" and "happily without bloodshed."[68] This is a useful reminder that the linguistic and social hybridity of these vessels does not indicate smoothly functioning relations between rival communities. The episode occurred just prior to the vessel meeting a "pirate dow": "[b]ound by no law, by no respect controlled, their wanton barbarous cruelty has set them beyond the pale of civilised intercourse, of mutual trust and sacred confidence."[69] The insurrectionary events on this "Arab ship" thus occurred in the same space of time as other revolutionary events connected with Wahhabism in the Persian Gulf. Observers, travelers, and sailors of all kinds brought these two things together: insurrection on board was interpreted alongside maritime plunder undertaken by alleged pirates. Both were said to be threats to the law and to involve unnecessarily "barbarous mutilation," though, in fact, both sailors in revolt and Wahhabi-inflected raiding were operating under separate understandings of the law.[70]

Because of the detailed records kept by the East India Company, including testimonies from captains, servants, slaves, and sailors in revolt, it is possible to trace the occurrence of revolt among *lascars* on the country ships after the 1780s.[71] *Lascars* were sailors who were part of a gang under the command of a headman or *serang,* who was a recruiter, and who negotiated a contract with a European sea captain for the labor of his gang. Though they were predominantly from India, the same gang could include men with diverse origins from across the Indian Ocean world. The partitioning of the trade of the Indian Ocean by type of ship was related in turn to the impact of the Navigation Laws, according to which British ships arriving and departing from London needed to have predominantly British crews, despite the heavy reliance on Indian *lascar* sailors.[72] In practice, this meant that *lascars* often took up work on vessels on the way to London, but such *lascars* found themselves stranded without work on getting to London, at times having to become passengers on the return journey. There was also increasing rivalry, resentment, and conflict on the part of *lascars* directed toward British officers and crew members on ships and the Company, connected to differences in pay and the exploitative use of *lascars,* given the legislative constraints of the Navigation Laws. The *lascar* issue became a point of debate for liberal reformers of the British empire and was picked up by humanitarian activists.[73] However, attempts at reform generated further bureaucracy rather than an improvement of conditions for *lascars.* The so-called lascar act, after the end of the Napoleonic wars, further precluded the legal use of Indian seamen on British vessels.[74] These wider conditions framed the types of insurrections that occurred among *lascars* in the circuit of country trade between Bombay and the Gulf.

Lascar revolt aboard country vessels involved complex alliances and grievances: the *serang* or his deputy could serve as a rebel leader or as a point of protest. There were times when isolated Europeans joined the rebel cause. The character of revolt could range from work stoppage to violent upheaval. By the middle of the nineteenth century, accounts of *lascars* who allegedly burnt ships in Calcutta, Bombay, and Madras were picked up by sensationalist journalists across the British empire as examples of "wilful incendiarism": fourteen were burnt in 1851.[75] The progress of revolt could be marked by the work of mimicry. Rebel captains could seek to imitate their deposed captains or to occupy their cabins. This was the case when the *Alert* was taken over by its *serang* in 1804, in the middle of a journey from Calcutta to Bombay; he took it to Al-Mukalla, in present-day Yemen, under Arab colors. News circulated that the rebels had murdered all the Europeans, and the British government of Bombay sent a cruiser for recovery of the ship. In published reports, the crew were cast in racial terms as "woolly headed men, originally slaves procured from the east coast of Africa by the Arabs, and by these metamorphosed into mussulmans [Muslims]."[76] The ship itself was said to have been "disfigured" to look "Arab."[77] The Bombay government was keen that to take charge of this "most horrible and successful conspiracy" and to secure "many of the pirates" on the *Alert's* return journey back to India.[78]

In another instance, revolt occurred between Bombay and the Gulf on board *The Bombay Merchant* in 1821. Here a relatively simple request, that the *serang* and the crew be allowed to go on shore when the ship arrived at Al-Mukalla, turned into a full-scale revolt when Captain Hyland declined the request, announcing that "only one at a time could be allowed to leave the vessel."[79] Eventually, "[t]he Serang and some of the crew laid hands on the Captain, who extricated himself with some difficulty from them." The captain gave up the ship and returned to India on another vessel. The *serang* commanded *The Bombay Merchant* successfully back to Bombay, where he managed to deliver the cargo "to the satisfaction of the owners." Captain Henry William Hyland's description of the events that overtook his ship is telling. In a petition to the Bombay government, he wrote of the "mutinous conduct" of the crew and described it as "insurrection and piracy," which could be avoided by "lawful prosecution to that condign punishment they are so deservedly entitled to."[80]

This petition is telling for the ideological slippage between the categories of protest in the Indian Ocean: pirates could be compared with rebel lascars, or racial and religious attitudes to Wahhabis could come to set the terms for the "superstitions" embraced by the passengers onboard "country-ships" sometimes on pilgrimage, or how *lascars* were converting increasingly to Islam. One instructive instance of this was the explanation provided by Captain Thompson, who played an instrumental role in crafting the General Treaty of 1820, about how he was able to make the agreement consistent with abolitionism: "the most remarkable article in which [the truce] was the declaring the Slave Trade to be piracy."[81] This blurring of contexts, or the concentric circles of the Age of Revolution, was also evident in the histories of the ships on which these events unfolded. The *Bombay Merchant* was used, for instance, in the taking of French Mauritius by the British in 1810.[82] More widely, ships passed between and were rebooted by the British, the French, and the traders and rulers of the Persian Gulf.

Conclusion

The tangle of political possibilities, or the number of concentric circles, that formed the Age of Revolution in the Persian Gulf is impressive. In the words of Francis Warden, the secretary of the Bombay government, writing in 1819: "complicated interests" and many "Powers" had "contended for superiority" in the Persian Gulf, in the midst of "various revolutions." Together with these interests, "the unsettled state" of Persia and the Ottoman world had given rise to Wahhabi power.[83] Instead of being cast as closed, this stretch of water may be approached as falling in the intermediate zone between the historic Safavid and Ottoman Empires, and also with the Mughal Empire of South Asia beyond. The rise of maritime politics, plunder, and commerce in this period came about partly as a result of the decentralization of land polities and the emergence of successor states to these great empires that in turn faced the sea, such as Muscat. The plurality of political interests also encompasses rival Europeans, and particularly the British and the French, as they tussled for control over shipping, trade, and strategic access to Asia and the Middle East.

The true complexity of the Age of Revolution in the Gulf cannot be understood simply by listing the tiers of polities, from large empires to successor states, or new maritime-facing polities to European rivals—or in other words by following Warden. Rather, communities of migrants, merchants, moneylenders, sailors, and slaves made the Persian Gulf come alive, and found these circles of historical memory and divisive politics particularly useful in finding their own path. Such a perspective is important lest the Persian Gulf is approached through a simple commitment to Wahhabis as agents in the Age of Revolution. It is also important lest the "Persian Gulf" is taken too simply to be the geographical region marked by this name on a modern map rather than a space on the mental globe of the Age of Revolution. Approached as such, it is possible to contribute to current attempts to critique the unhelpful lexical and politicized debate on whether to name this gulf "Persian," "Arab," or even "Ottoman" or "Islamic," and the associated program of excluding African or Asian connections with it.[84]

The British, with their legal norms and paper, started to insert their own notions of rights and citizenship into the Gulf, aimed at determining practices of labor, politics, and trade. Indeed, their dominance over France was evident by the late 1830s by the fact that French ships were being refitted in British Bombay.[85] Before this occurred, it was possible for Muscat to assert its confidence in its own sovereignty, while playing the Age of Revolution. Symmetrically, prior to the age of steam, the need for sailing ships could bolster the prospects of Parsis. The political context of the Napoleonic wars also benefited Arab shipping vessels before new legal norms came in during the 1830s. In these ways, the Persian Gulf and those who engaged with it could be characterized by types of agency, which arose from the bottom up. It was in reassembling the Persian Gulf as a contested space that political elites, trading communities, or technicians were able to find their way. Those who were able to remold the culture of historical empires, by inserting reformist religion or by taking up the mantle of long-term transregional connections in ship-building, did the best in the Age of Revolution.

It is tragic to see how this plural landscape of revolution became tied up with an imperial attempt to make revolution part and parcel of its arsenal of ideas. As time passed, Bombay sought to define the Persian Gulf, though it was not fully successful in this. This shift in turn indicated the ascendance of the British in India. Yet British travelers and officials also found their categories in contest and blurred by the stretch of water linking the Persian Gulf to India. Right under their noses, trade, pilgrimage, slavery, and ship-building could carry on apace. Though legal norms sought to define piracy, theft, illicit labor, and friendship, in practice there was a categorical confusion. Forms of protest and agency in the Age of Revolution did not only straddle different geographies, political times, and communities; such straddling also characterized the British imagination despite its pretensions to exact discursive definition. In addition, to pick up a strand of research that is not covered here, there was also an important set of connections to East Africa.

Extrapolating outward, the intent of this chapter has been to show how the watery space of the Gulf, a fault line between large Eurasian empires, was assaulted and defined from different directions while its historical memory could not be suppressed by European imperialists, even though the British empire was clearly on the ascent. In mounting this argument, the aim has been to work from the Persian Gulf, rather than from Europe, and also to foreground how the Persian Gulf looked from adjoining continental regions. Approaching this space in this way avoids the language of diffusion. This is replaced with a conceptualization of concentricity and entanglement. To speak of the Gulf's Age of Revolution as a concentric arrangement of powers and agents and a tangle of politics complicates a definitive "Indigenous" and a geographically determined sense of the authentic. The people who engaged with the Gulf had to come to terms with imperial decrees—tied with concepts of nation, liberal rights, and association. Yet the diverse paths of protest and alliance that they used to find their way were not closed down by imperial categories. Empire itself came to be in the landscape of the Age of Revolution. Space and heritage could be transmuted in so many ways from the Age of Revolution to the age of the British empire.

Notes

1. There are not many histories of the Persian Gulf. For some exceptions, see Lawrence G. Potter, ed., *The Persian Gulf in History* (Basingstoke: Palgrave Macmillan, 2009), and Lawrence G. Potter, ed., *The Persian Gulf in Modern Times* (Basingstoke: Palgrave Macmillan, 2014). See also William Floor, *Persian Gulf: A Political and Economic History of Five Port Cities, 1500–1730* (Washington, DC: Mage Press, 2006). For an account of India's connections to the Gulf, see J. Onley, *The Arabian Frontier of the British Raj: Merchants, Rulers, and the British in the Nineteenth-Century Gulf* (Oxford: Oxford University Press, 2007).

2. The literature on the global Age of Revolution is, of course, growing fast. But it is noteworthy that the Gulf does not come into focus in collections such as David Armitage and Sanjay Subrahmanyam, eds., *The Age of Revolutions in Global Context, c. 1760–1840* (Basingstoke: Palgrave Macmillan, 2010) or, indeed, in recent accounts of the global history of the French Revolution, such as Suzanne Desan, Lynn Hunt, and William Max Nelson, eds., *The French Revolution in Global Perspective* (Ithaca, NY: Cornell University Press, 2013). It appears briefly in Alan Forrest and Matthias Middell, eds., *The Routledge Companion to the French Revolution in World History* (Abingdon: Routledge, 2016), 129, and in C. A. Bayly's chapter "The Revolutionary Age in the Wider World, c. 1790–1830," in *War, Empire and Slavery, 1770–1830*, ed. Richard Bessel, Nicholas Guyatt, and Jane Rendall (Basingstoke: Palgrave Macmillan, 2010); quotation on 31.

3. For the classic works on the Gulf in this period, which foreground British intervention and piracy in turn, see J. B. Kelly, *Britain and the Persian Gulf, 1795–1880* (Oxford: Clarendon Press, 1968), and Charles E. Davies, *The Blood-Red Flag: An Investigation into Qasimi Piracy, 1797–1820* (Exeter: University of Exeter Press, 1997).

4. On this, see Nelida Fuccaro, "Rethinking the History of Port Cities in the Gulf," in *The Persian Gulf in Modern Times*, 23–46.

5. In stressing the maritime dimensions of the Age of Revolution in the Indian Ocean, I follow the work of Clare Anderson. See, for instance, Clare Anderson, “The Age of Revolution in the Indian Ocean, Bay of Bengal and the South China Sea: A Maritime Perspective,” *International Review of Social History* 58 (2013): 229–251.

6. This argument will be further developed in a forthcoming book tentatively titled *Revolutionary Empire,* which considers the small seas of this age in the Indian and Pacific Oceans.

7. Bernard Lewis, “The Impact of the French Revolution on Turkey,” *Turkiyaṭ Mecmuası* 11 (1954): 231–233, or, more reçently, Ian Coller, “The French Revolution and the Islamic World of the Middle East and North Africa,” in *The Routledge Companion,* 117–133.

8. On this, see Robert Travers, “Imperial Revolutions and Global Repercussions: South Asia and the World, c. 1750–1850,” in *The Age of Revolutions,* 144–166.

9. For this argument, see Sujit Sivasundaram, *Islanded: Britain, Sri Lanka and the Bounds of an Indian Ocean Colony* (Chicago: Chicago University Press, 2013), chap. 1, and also Sujit Sivasundaram, “Ethnicity, Indigeneity, and Migration in the Advent of British Rule to Sri Lanka,” *The American Historical Review* 115 (2010): 428–452. I have also discussed this general issue in a comparative perspective in Sujit Sivasundaram, “Appropriation to Supremacy: Ideas of the ‘Native’ in the Rise of British Imperial Heritage,” in *From Plunder to Preservation: Britain and the Heritage of Empire, c. 1800–1940,* ed. Astrid Swenson and Peter Mandler (Oxford: Oxford University Press, 2013), 149–170.

10. Potter, ed., *The Persian Gulf in History,* 1.

11. For a detailed dissection of these expeditions and their motivations, see Davies, “Afterword,” in *The Blood-Red Arab Flag,* 277–295.

12. R. Temple, I. Clark, and W. William Haines, “Sixteen Views of Places in the Persian Gulph,” National Maritime Museum Collections, Greenwich, PAF4793ff.

13. Report of Captain J. Wainwright, commanding HMS *La Chiffonne,* off Ras al-Khaimah to Rear Admiral Drury, 14 November 1809, in *The Expansion of Wahhabi Power in Arabia, Vol. 1: 1798–1848: British Documentary Records,* ed. A. L. P. Burdett (Cambridge: Cambridge University Press, 2013), 255–259.

14. Political Dept. Diary No. 339 of 1809, instructions issued to the Commanders of the expedition, in J. A. Saldanha, ed., *The Persian Gulf Précis* (Simla: 1906; Archive Edition, 1986), 3:46.

15. For the idea of the Ras al-Khaimah and associated ports as “headless,” see Davies, *Blood-Red Arab Flag,* 190.

16. Letter from Jonathan Duncan, Governor of Bombay, Fort St. George to the Rt. Hon. Lord Minto, Governor General, 6 April 1810, in *The Expansion,* 267–268, this quotation from 268.

17. See Davies, *Blood-Red Arab Flag,* 208; for an earlier truce between Ras al-Khaimah and the East India Company, including the clause “they [Qawasim] will respect the flag and property of the Honourable East India Company,” see “Agreement between Shaikh Sultan b. Saqr and the East India Company, 6 February 1806,” in *Records of the Emirates: Primary Documents, Vol. 1: 1820–1835,* ed. Penelope Tuson (Cambridge: Cambridge University Press, 1990), 3ff.

18. The words of Mrs. Thompson, wife of Captain T. Perronet Thompson, cited in H. Moyse-Bartlett, *The Pirates of Trucial Oman* (London: Macdonald, 1966), 130.

19. According to Risso, the Qawasim took about a one-fifth share of the booty arising from maritime violence at Ras al-Khaimah. See Patricia Risso, "Cross-Cultural Perceptions of Piracy: Maritime Violence in the Western Indian Ocean and Persian Gulf Region during a Long Eighteenth Century," *Journal of World History* 12 (2001): 293–319; 312.

20. For the execution, see Tuson, *Records of the Emirates*, 35. See also Kelly, *Britain and the Persian Gulf*, 45–47.

21. Letter from Harford Jones, Baghdad, to Jacob Bosanquet, Chairman of the Court of Directors of the East India Company, 1 December 1798, enclosing an essay on the Wahhabis, reproduced in *The Expansion*, 125–135, citations here from 125 and 130.

22. Burdett, *The Expansion*, 130.

23. All quotations and discussion based on "General Treaty with the Arab Tribes of the Persian Gulf, 1820," in *Records of the Emirates*, 13–15.

24. "Sir William Grant Keir's Reports on the Conclusion of the Treaties and Operations in the Arabian Gulf, January–February 1820," in *Records of the Emirates*, 47–117, information from 49–50. Yet there is evidence that the directions to use flags and signals were not fully followed, even in the immediate aftermath of the Keir agreement. See "Letter Dated 26th November 1821 from Mr. Meriton," in *The Persian Gulf Précis*, 3:129.

25. See, for instance, Calvin H. Allen, "The State of Masqa in the Gulf and East Africa, 1785–1829," *International Journal of Middle East Studies* 14 (1982): 117–127.

26. Material on the history of Oman here and in the following paragraphs draws from Risso, *Oman and Muscat*; quotation from appendix II. For the original, see C. U. Aitchison, *A Collection of Treaties, Engagements and Sanads Relating to India and Neighbouring Countries* (Calcutta: Government Press, 1933), 9:287–288.

27. Simon Layton, "Commerce, Authority and Piracy in the Indian Ocean World, c. 1780–1850" (PhD diss., University of Cambridge, 2013), 87. Layton pays particular attention to the role of Bahrain in British policy in the Persian Gulf and also as a topic that inflects the relationship between Oman and the British.

28. Kelly, *Britain and the Persian Gulf*, 11.

29. Risso, *Oman and Muscat*, 142. For the wider context of French-British competition in Muscat, see chapter 8 of Risso's book.

30. See Kelly, *Britain and the Persian Gulf*, 101ff, and Risso, *Oman and Muscat*, 175ff.

31. For slavery in the Gulf, see Ricks, "Slaves and Slave Traders." See also Matthew S. Hopper, "The African Presence in Eastern Arabia," in *The Persian Gulf in Modern Times*, 327–350. Also Abdul Sherriff, "The Slave Trade and Its Fallout in the Persian Gulf," in *Abolition and Its Aftermath in Indian Ocean Africa and Asia*, ed. Gwyn Campbell (New York: Routledge, 2005).

32. See Robert Carter, "The History and Prehistory of Pearling in the Persian Gulf," *Journal of the Economic and Social History of the Orient* 48 (2006): 139–209, 151.

33. See Patricia Risso, "Muslim Identity in Maritime Trade: General Observations and Some Evidence from the 18th-Century Persian Gulf/Indian Ocean Region," *International Journal of Middle East Studies* 21 (1989): 381–392, 387.

34. Risso, *Oman and Muscat*, 99.

35. This account of the launch of the *Shah Alum* arises from *Asiatic Journal and Monthly Miscellany* 8 (1819): 394, and Ruttonjee Ardeshir Wadia, *The Bombay Dockyard and the Wadia Master Builders* (Bombay: Godrej, 1957), 237.

36. See Wadia, *Bombay Dockyard*, chap. 6, and W. T. Money, *Observations on the Expediency of Shipbuilding at Bombay* (London: Longman, 1811). Note that the Money family was involved in the country trade themselves, while William, who drafted this text, worked in the Bombay Marine.

37. Amalendu Guha, "Parsi Seths as Entrepreneurs, 1750–1850," *Economic and Political Weekly* 5 (1970): M107–M115, and Michael Mann, "Timber Trade on the Malabar Coast, c. 1780–1840," *Environment and History* 7 (2001): 403–425, 404.

38. See Anne Bulley, *The Bombay Country Ships, 1790–1833* (Richmond: Curzon, 2000), 2–3.

39. Amalendu Guha, "The Comprador Role of Parsi Seths, 1750–1850," *Economic and Political Weekly* 5 (1970): 1933–1936.

40. For details on the Wadia family, see Dosabhai Framji Karaka, "Distinguished Parsis of Bombay," in *Parsis in India*, ed. J. B. Sharma and S. P. Sharma (Jaipur: Sublime Publications, 1999), 86–146, 93ff.

41. Details from Bulley, *The Bombay Country Ships*, 12ff. See also Wadia, *The Bombay Dockyard*, 172.

42. See the rules facing 202 in Wadia, *The Bombay Dockyard.*

43. From Wadia, *The Bombay Dockyard*, 208, cited from *Bombay Courier*, 23 June 1810.

44. See image facing Bulley, *The Bombay Country Ships*, 14.

45. John R. Hinnells and Alan Williams, "Introduction," in *Parsis in India and the Diaspora*, ed. John R. Hinnells and Alan Williams (London: Routledge, 2007), 1.

46. Guha, "Parsi Seths as Entrepreneurs," and Hinnells and Williams, "Introduction," 2.

47. See Bulley, *The Bombay Country Ships*, 33, and appendix B in Wadia, *The Bombay Dockyard.* For more on the trade in timber from India to Oman during this period, see Risso, *Oman and Muscat*, 4, 81.

48. See Money, "Observations," 65.

49. Kelly, *Britain and the Persian Gulf*, 116, 124, 129. For the ban, see also Francis Warden, "Historical Sketch of the Joasmee Tribe of Arabs from the Year 1714 to the Year 1819," in *Records of the Emirates*, 247.

50. Kelly, *Britain and the Persian Gulf*, 157–158.

51. Mann, "Timber Trade." There was also the worry that control over ship-building in India by Arabs would restrict trade; see Bulley, *The Bombay Country Ships*, 32–33.

52. Letter from the Madras Government dated 23 January 1805, expressing their agreement "regarding the appointment of our Agent for the purpose of ascertaining the extent to which the forests of that province [Malabar] and Canara may be available towards the objects of ship-building," P/343/20. See also other letters in this volume connected to inquiries directed to forests and wood.

53. Vincenzo Maurizi, *History of Seyd Said, Sultan of Muscat, with a New Introduction by Robin Bidwell* (Cambridge: Oleander Press, 1984), 95.

54. Warden, "Historical Sketch of the Joasmee Tribe of Arabs from the Year 1714 to the Year 1819," in *Records of the Emirates*, 251.

55. For the decline of the Bombay shipyard, see David Arnold, *Science, Technology and Medicine in Colonial India* (Cambridge: Cambridge University Press, 2000), 102ff; and for the wider context of building ships in India, see also Frank Broeze, "Underdevelopment and Dependency: Maritime India during the Raj," *Modern Asian Studies* 18 (1984): 429–457.

56. See, for instance, T. M. Luhrmann, *The Good Parsi: The Fate of a Colonial Elite in a Postcolonial Society* (Cambridge, MA: Harvard University Press, 1996), 17: "Because they tried to assimilate, and did not turn to revolution, they reveal the postcolonial consequences of their assimilation more powerfully than do most other colonial elites."

57. Christine Dobbin, "The Parsi Panchayat in Bombay City in the Nineteenth Century," *Modern Asian Studies* 4 (1970): 149–164.

58. This section relies on C. A. Bayly, *Recovering Liberties: Indian Thought in the Age of Liberalism and Empire* (Cambridge: Cambridge University Press, 2012), 118ff.

59. For an account of the journal, see Marwa Elshakry and Sujit Sivasundaram, eds., "Science, Race and Imperialism," in *Victorian Science and Literature*, ed. Gowan Dawson and Bernard Lightman (London: Chatto and Pickering, 2012), 1–6, citation from 4.

60. From "Houses of Parliament," in *Journal of a Residence of Two Years and a Half in Great Britain*, ed. Jehangir Naoroji and Hirjibhoy Meherwanji (London: William Allen, 1841), 164ff.

61. This paragraph draws heavily from N. Benjamin, "Arab Merchants of Bombay and Surat (c. 1800–1840)," *Indian Economic and Social History Review* 13 (1976): 85–95. See also Bulley, *The Bombay Country Ships*, 32–33.

62. Benjamin, "Arab Merchants," 85.

63. Onley, *The Arabian Frontier*; James Onley, "Indian Communities in the Persian Gulf," in *The Persian Gulf in Modern Times*, 231–266.

64. James Silk Buckingham, *Travels in Assyria, Media, and Persia* (London: Henry Colburn, 1829), 2:430.

65. Buckingham, *Travels in Assyria*, 2:430.

66. William Heude, *A Voyage Up the Persian Gulf* (London: Strahan and Spottiswoode, 1819), 19.

67. *Edinburgh Review* 32 (1819): 113–114.

68. Heude, *A Voyage Up the Persian Gulf*, 34–35.

69. Heude, *A Voyage Up the Persian Gulf*, 36.

70. Heude, *A Voyage Up the Persian Gulf*, 36.

71. Aaron Jaffer, "'Lord of the Forecastle': Serangs, Tindals and Lascar Mutiny, c. 1780–1860," *International Review of Social History* 58 (2013): 153–175, 170.

72. For the wider framework of lascar labor, the navigation laws, and so forth, see Michael H. Fisher, "Working across the Seas: Indian Maritime Labourers in India, Britain, and in Between, 1600–1857," *International Review of Social History* 58 (2013): 21–45.

73. Bayly, *Recovering Liberties*, 28ff.

74. Broeze, "Underdevelopment and Dependency."

75. Michael H. Fisher, "Finding Lascar 'Wilful Incendiarism': British Ship-Burning Panic and Indian Maritime Labour in the Indian Ocean," *South Asia: Journal of South Asian Studies* 35 (2012): 596–623.

76. George Annesley, Earl of Mountnorris [George Viscount Valentia], *Voyages and Travels to India, Ceylon, the Red Sea, Abyssinia and Egypt* (London: W. Bulmer, 1809), 80, and *The Naval Chronicle* 15 (1806): 476.

77. For further details on the *Alert*, see Aaron Jaffer, *Lascars and Indian Ocean Seafaring, 1780–1860* (Woodbridge: Boydell and Brewer, 2015), appendix, 193.

78. Letter of the Superintendent of the Marine, Robert Anderson, dated Bombay, 2 February 1805, P/343/20, BL. The term "pirate" was also applied to the lascar rebels in the letter dated Bombay, 7 February 1805, from Forbes & Co., P/343/20.

79. Jaffer, "Lord of the Forecastle," 166; quotation from *Asiatic Journal and Monthly Miscellany* 14 (1822): 98. See also Jaffer, *Lascars*, appendix, 199.

80. "The Memorial of Henry William Hyland Late Master of the Grab Brig Bombay Merchant," dated 26 September 1821, Bombay Public Proceedings, P/345/65, IOR, British Library.

81. Cited in Moyse-Bartlett, *The Pirates of Trucial Oman*, 111. This was a retrospective statement that, according to Moyse-Bartlett, was penned in Thompson's "middle age."

82. Bulley, *The Bombay Country Ships*, 80.

83. Francis Warden, "Extracts from Brief Notes Relative to the Rise and Progress of the Arab Tribes of the Persian Gulf," in *Records of the Emirates*, 24–25.

84. On this, see Potter, ed., *The Persian Gulf in History*, 14–16.

85. See "Statement Shewing the Expence Incurred in the Dockyards for the Honble Company's, Her Majesty's, French Government and Merchant Vessels from 1838 to 1842," in Papers of Captain Sir Robert Oliver (1783–1848), National Maritime Museum, Greenwich, MS94/006.

PART TWO

ENTANGLEMENTS

CHAPTER SIX

Red Power and Homeland Security

Native Nations and the Limits of Empire in the Ohio Country

COLIN G. CALLOWAY

The story of imperial contest and American conquest in the Ohio country has been told often and well. After the Seven Years' War, known in North America as the French and Indian War, at the Peace of Paris in 1763 France transferred the Ohio country to Britain without reference to the Indian nations who lived there. After the American Revolution, at the Peace of Paris in 1783 Britain transferred the Ohio country to the United States without reference to the Indian nations who lived there. As their homelands changed hands, and changed color on other people's maps, the Indigenous peoples of the Ohio country were caught between competing empires like, as one Indian said, cloth between the blades of scissors, and Euro-American expansion engulfed their world.[1] Here, as elsewhere, Indigenous peoples surely were victims of empire.

But knowledge of what eventually happened distorts our understanding of a time when Indian nations stalled the "course of empire" in the Ohio country, when Indigenous foreign policies trumped imperial ambitions, and when Indigenous power shaped imperial outcomes and threatened the future of the United States. In 1755, Indians in the Ohio country destroyed the biggest army Britain had dispatched to North America; in 1791, they destroyed the only army the United States possessed. Indigenous power fluctuated, it sometimes involved more bluff than substance, and it was not applied consistently in a single direction, but it was something that empires had to reckon with, and it was applied with consistent purpose to protect homelands and to preserve independence that, somewhat paradoxically, involved a measured dependence on European contact.

To argue that Indians defended their homelands is not particularly new or imaginative, of course, but that defense entailed more than simply holding a line against a colonial land rush at the western edge of empire (although in the Ohio country it involved that, too). Indians in the Ohio country looked outward from the center of an Indigenous world, and each community, tribe, or nation conducted shifting political, diplomatic, economic, military, and ritual relations with other Indian communities, tribes, and nations, as well as with imperial powers and their colonies. They pursued their own Indigenous agendas, not someone else's imperial agendas. Actions that Europeans and Americans dismissed as illogical and fickle possessed their own logic and consistency. Tribes did not switch sides on a whim; they shifted course as things changed around them, and they used competing imperial powers as those powers used them. They negotiated and sometimes dictated the terms on which Europeans entered and competed for their country, and they stated their objectives repeatedly in the written documents where they are supposed to be silent.

The Origins of the Seven Years' War

The struggle for the Ohio country was a kaleidoscope of contests among many nations, not a duel between two nations. The French, the British, and the Iroquois all claimed to control the region, but none did. By the middle of the eighteenth century, it was a refuge for displaced peoples and a crossroads of cultures. Shawnees who had left to escape the reverberations of war and disease in the mid-seventeenth century had returned and settled in the Scioto and Miami valleys. Delawares, pushed west by English pressure, settled on the Muskingum River. Wendats had established communities near Detroit and Sandusky. Splinter groups from the Iroquois confederacy—primarily Senecas and Cayugas known as Mingoes—moved in from the east. Miamis, Mascoutens, and Kickapoos edged in from the west. The Ohio Valley, said one Cayuga, was "a Republic composed of all sorts of Nations."[2] The forks of the Ohio, where the Allegheny and Monongahela merge to form the Ohio River, were the gateway to the West and the focus of imperial ambitions. France needed the Ohio River as the route connecting its settlements in Canada and the Illinois country, and ultimately to Louisiana, and based its claim on ritualized acts of "discovery." British colonists on the Atlantic seaboard and ministers in London poring over maps feared the French were building a huge arc of empire that threatened to strangle the British colonies. The British cited colonial charters that granted land as far west as the Pacific and reaffirmed their claims to the land by trying to leverage control over western tribes via the Iroquois: the British claimed the Iroquois as "subjects," and the Iroquois claimed dominance over other nations on the basis of seventeenth-century "conquests." The French likewise tried to maintain good relations with the Iroquois. The Iroquois made the most of the situation.[3]

Tanaghrisson, the Seneca "Half King" or ambassador from the central council fire of the Iroquois League at Onondaga, said the Ohio region where he lived was "a Country between." But being caught between and courted by competing imperial powers offered opportunities as well as challenges. "[F]ar from being the ignorant People they are generally supposed to be in Europe," wrote one observer, the Indians exploited the situation to "hold the scales & direct the Ballance" between French and English power.[4] Indian villages sometimes flew French and British flags simultaneously.[5] Tanaghrisson insisted that the Ohio country was Indian land, off limits to the English and the French alike, and he bragged that he was not afraid to kick them both out. In reality, he wanted to expel French soldiers and admit English traders and their merchandise. To achieve his goals, he played the French and the British against each other. Above all, he played George Washington.

In 1754, Tanaghrisson asked Virginia to build a trading house at the Forks of the Ohio.[6] He declared that the Indians would make war against anyone who tried to prevent it. With such a promise, he embraced an English alliance and defied the French with a level of commitment many other Ohio Indians did not share: they suspected British intentions and worried that the action might precipitate a conflict that would be fought in their country.[7] Tanaghrisson's bluff was soon called when a French army arrived, took possession of the post, and built Fort Duquesne.[8] It was a blow to Tanaghrisson's standing as well as to Virginia's ambitions in the Ohio country.

Hearing that George Washington was coming with a force of Virginia militia, Tanaghrisson sent him word that the Indians were ready to attack the French and were only waiting for his assistance.[9] Washington responded that he was pushing ahead and that a larger force would follow with artillery, munitions, and supplies, and signed himself "Connotacarious"—town destroyer, a name his great-grandfather had earned killing Susquehannock Indians (and that Washington would earn in his own right by burning Iroquois towns in the Revolution).[10] Each man spoke with a level of confidence in the power behind them that the realities of their respective situations scarcely merited. Tanaghrisson then warned Washington that a French force was on the move against him.[11] The French had made clear their determination to defend the Ohio country against British intrusions, and there were other reports of French activity in the area, but the only information Washington had that the French soldiers were actually coming to attack him came from Tanaghrisson.[12]

In fact, Ensign Joseph Coulon de Villiers, Sieur de Jumonville, and thirty-three soldiers had been dispatched to see what the Virginians were up to and to demand that they withdraw from French territory. Washington and Tanaghrisson joined forces and surprised the French at dawn. An Ohio Iroquois who participated in the ambush said the Indians "directed Col Washington with his men to go up to the Hill," while they circled left and right to cut off escape, and that Washington fired the first shot.[13] Washington kept his own accounts of the fifteen-minute skirmish deliberately brief and glossed over the details: "We killed M. de Jumonville, commanding this party, with nine others; we wounded one and made 21 prisoners," he wrote. "The Indians scalped the dead, and took most of their arms."[14] Other reports indicated that Tanaghrisson and his warriors cut down the French as they ran from the Virginians' guns.[15] The only French soldier to escape said Jumonville was killed as he tried to read aloud the summons to withdraw.[16] Washington insisted the French were spies and cited Tanaghrisson's opinion "that they had evil designs, and that it was a mere pretext; that they had never intended to come to us as anything but enemies, and that if we had ever been so foolish as to let them go, he would never help us to capture other Frenchmen."[17]

Tanaghrisson killed Jumonville. A Virginian soldier who did not take part in the fight heard from those who did that "the Half King took his Tomahawk and split the head of the French Captain. . . . He then took out his Brains and washed his Hands with them and then Scalped him." Another account reported that Tanaghrisson came up to the wounded Jumonville and said, "Thou art not yet dead, my father," and then tomahawked him. If these reports are true, by addressing the young officer as "father," and then killing him, the veteran Seneca employed the language of ritual and diplomacy, and dramatically rejected French authority; washing his hands in Jumonville's brains, he washed his hands of the French alliance.[18]

Claiming to speak for the Ohio nations, Tanaghrisson had warned the French to stop their advance into the Ohio country. When the French ignored his warnings and the Ohio Indians' resolve began to waver, Tanaghrisson tried to regain the initiative by pushing both the Indians and the British into more decisive action. He maneuvered the inexperienced Washington into attacking a French force that was not looking for a fight—that was not, officially at least, even an enemy—and then severed the peace that had existed between the Ohio nations and their French father. Tanaghrisson immediately sent a French scalp, inviting the Ohio nations to take up the hatchet. Virginia Governor Robert Dinwiddie, who had to explain things to the Board of Trade, stressed that "my orders to the Commander of our Forces was to be on the defensive" and hastened to pin the blame on the Indians, but his characterization of the event was not far off the mark: "[T]his little skirmish was by the Half King and their Indians. We were as auxiliaries to them."[19] Tanaghrisson, not Washington, deserves the dubious credit for starting "the first of the World Wars."[20]

Shaping a New Imperial Vision

Tanaghrisson did not live to see the war he started, but the Indians who did followed policies he would have understood. Many fought with the French, some fought with the British, and some fought first with one then with the other, but always in a consistent effort to keep their country independent of both. When General Edward Braddock marched against the French Fort Duquesne at the forks of the Ohio in 1755, he found himself with only eight Indian allies. Historians have usually blamed that on Braddock, citing a former captive's later recollection that the Delaware war chief Shingas blamed Braddock: the Indians asked if their lands would be protected under a British regime; Braddock sneered that "[n]o Savage shou'd inherit the Land," and Shingas retorted that the Indians were not about to fight for land they were not free to live on.[21] Other firsthand testimonies, however, indicate that Braddock treated his Indian allies with respect, did business by gift-giving and wampum diplomacy, and assured them their lands would be safe. Deeper-seated concerns about English treatment and encroachment on their lands evidently explained the Indians' defection. The hundreds of Indians who rallied to the French at Fort Duquesne did so for a variety of reasons, which included economic and kinship ties with the French and one another; those who came from mission villages on the St. Lawrence, the upper Great Lakes, or the Mississippi would not have been as concerned about the threat to Ohio Valley lands as were the Shawnees and Ohio Iroquois who joined the French alliance. Customarily attributed to British arrogance and ineptitude, Braddock's defeat at the Battle of the Monongahela graphically demonstrated the limits of empire in the Ohio country: inadequately trained British troops met a multinational assemblage of Native military power with French Canadian officers who were more experienced in fighting and leading Indians, and British training and tactics proved disastrous when confronted with Indian mobility, firepower, and marksmanship. The battle was "an unprecedented rout of a modern and powerful British army by a predominantly Indian army."[22] Instead of falling, Fort Duquesne became the hub of the French-Indian war effort in the West; instead of supporting the British, Shingas earned the sobriquet "the Terrible" for his raids on the frontiers of Virginia and Pennsylvania.

The Delawares and Shawnees made common cause with the French, but they fought for Delaware and Shawnee, not French, reasons. Eastern Delawares cited years of trade abuse, land theft, and unpunished murders that cried for revenge.[23] Shawnees were outraged by English imprisonment in South Carolina of six of their warriors, one of whom died in captivity.[24] "[Y]ou wonder at our joining with the French in this present War," an old Ohio chief told the English: "Why can't you get sober and once think impartially? Does not the Law of Nations permit, or rather command us all, to stand upon our Guard to preserve our Lives, the Lives of our Wives and Children, our Property and Liberty?" The Indians had no love for the French either, but the English were relentless in settling on the Indians' land, and "where one of those People settled, like Pidgeons, a thousand more would settle."[25] Any peace would have to include a guarantee of Indian territorial autonomy in the Ohio country.[26]

General John Forbes succeeded where Braddock had failed by securing such a peace. When William Pitt took over Britain's war effort, his strategy for North America included dismantling France's Indian alliances. As Forbes prepared another campaign to take Fort Duquesne, he initiated the diplomacy necessary to secure the cooperation, or at least the noninterference, of the Indian nations in the Ohio Valley. He understood that Indian allies who lived beyond the walls of Fort Duquesne were more important to its defense than the firepower within. The Indians were deeply suspicious of British peace overtures but insisted: "were we but sure that you will not take our Lands on the Ohio, or the West side of Allegeny Hills from us[,] we [could] drive away the French when we please." In other words, the British could have peace, and victory, if they guaranteed the security of Indian homelands.[27] At the Treaty of Easton in 1758, the British restored some lands between the Susquehanna River and the Alleghenies, pledged that no intrusions would be made west of the mountains without Native consent to the Crown, and promised to regulate fair trade. Having achieved the goals for which they had fought, the Indian delegates made peace. Forbes had a green light to advance; Fort Duquesne became essentially indefensible, and the French blew it up as the British closed in. The Treaty of Easton, wrote Colonel Henry Bouquet, "struck the blow which has knocked the French in the head."[28]

But Ohio Indians watched the French collapse with concern. A clear imperial victory—no matter which empire won—limited their playoff options. Sir William Johnson, the British superintendent of Indian affairs, claimed that had it not been for his unrelenting efforts to keep the Indians divided, they would have "greatly protracted" the war with France "in order to preserve the balance of power."[29] Ohio nations did not want French troops and forts in their country, but they hoped the destruction of Fort Duquesne would mark the end of European military occupation, not just a shift from one occupying nation to another. Having taken the opportunity to oust Frenchmen from their lands, they were not inclined to accept Englishmen in their place.[30] A Delaware chief named Keekyuscung warned the British that "all the nations would be against them" if they settled west of the mountains. "It would be a great war, and never come to peace again."[31] Despite British assurances that Indian lands were safe, the roads that Braddock and Forbes had cut to Fort Duquesne brought hundreds more British hunters, traders, and settlers over the mountains. Fort Pitt, which the British built on the ruins of Fort Duquesne, was a formidable symbol of imperial presence; it was also a military community of soldiers, traders, farmers, artisans, laborers, and camp followers sustained by farms, supply routes, and taverns.[32]

Britain acquired a vast North American empire at the Peace of Paris in 1763, but the Ohio nations had not ceded their country to anyone. Peace reinforced rather than removed their concerns for homeland security. Financially strapped at the end of an expensive global war, Britain dispensed with gift-giving, the essential lubricant of Indian diplomacy, and the British commander in chief, General Jeffery Amherst, ignored the dying General Forbes's advice to pay attention to the Indians. The presence of British troops, the absence of British gifts, and the attitude of the British high command portended ill for Indian independence. War belts circulated and Ohio warriors joined Pontiac's multinational war of independence against the world's greatest empire.

The Indians nearly obliterated that empire west of the Appalachians. And they made sure the British understood the causes of the conflict. Before the Senecas killed the commander at Fort Venango, they made him write down their list of grievances: lack of trade, high prices, and the presence of British forts on their land, which "induced them to believe they intended to possess all their country."[33] At Fort Pitt, Shingas, Turtle's Heart, and other Delaware chiefs blamed the besieged garrison for starting the war "by coming with a large army into the country and building Forts." "You know this is our country, and that your having possession of it must be offensive to all nations of Indians," they said.[34] The Shawnees likewise cited British fort-building as "one Chief Reason for entering into a War against you, as we had sufficient reason to think you intended taking our country from Us." Iroquois delegates said much the same thing.[35]

Pontiac's war accelerated imperial plans to implement a boundary line protecting Indian lands as a means of keeping the peace. The Royal Proclamation in October 1763 established the Appalachians as the boundary and prohibited private purchases of Indian lands; only the Crown's representatives could negotiate such transfers, and only licensed traders were permitted to operate there. George Washington said the proclamation was a temporary expedient to quiet the minds of the Indians, and he was right, but the British understood that the expedient could only work if the people who called the shots in the interior of the continent were on board and ratified the agreement. William Johnson understood that Indian country was an international space where diverse Indigenous nations pursued their own foreign policies, and in the winter of 1763–64 he dispatched messengers, calling an international summit meeting at Niagara in the summer. Two thousand delegates representing two dozen nations from Nova Scotia to the Mississippi and from the Ohio to Hudson Bay assembled at Niagara; some of them traveled months to get there. In the figurative speech and metaphorical language of Indian diplomacy, Johnson conveyed that the King acknowledged the Indian nations as owners of the land and offered them protection from unscrupulous traders and speculators. The Royal Proclamation was a guiding document of imperial policy and a unilateral declaration of imperial intent. In Indian country, however, declarations of imperial will had to be presented for approval by sovereign powers in negotiations conducted on terms of peace and mutual respect. Johnson and the chiefs exchanged wampum belts.[36]

Not all of the negotiators were looking for a new imperial order. Seneca warriors had destroyed a British column at Devil's Hole during the war, and Johnson talked tough about punishing them. He made them cede the Niagara corridor and grant the British safe use of the Niagara portage. But in agreeing to these terms, the Senecas gave up a strip of land they had given up twice before (in 1701 and 1726) and escaped any military reprisals for Devil's

Hole. In return, they had Johnson's assurance that the ceded land would be for military use, not settlement, and they remained free to hunt, fish, travel, and trade through the Niagara corridor as they had for generations.[37] At Venango, the Senecas had cited unfair trade and the threat of settlement as their reasons for resorting to war. At Niagara, they secured their goals by resorting to peace. Many Anishinaabe chiefs from the Great Lakes saw the meeting as a British effort at appeasement and an opportunity to push for a renewal of British trade at Michilimackinac and other locations, and they got what they wanted. Johnson had years of experience and expertise in dealing with the Six Nations, but at Niagara he was touching the edges of an Anishinaabe world he knew relatively little about, where imperial policies petered out, sometimes into irrelevance, and where "an infinity of nations" held sway.[38]

The Shawnees and Delawares did not attend the treaty at Niagara. Henry Bouquet led an army into the Ohio country and finally made peace on the Muskingum River in November 1764, first with the Mingoes and Delawares and later with the Shawnees, who still displayed "a dilatoriness and sullen haughtiness in their conduct." Some officials had called for punitive terms and the execution of ringleaders. But Bouquet's army was not an army of occupation, and he readmitted the Indians to the Covenant Chain of Friendship on condition that they made nominal concessions and returned their captives.[39] Meanwhile, in the Illinois and Wabash country Pontiac still headed a multitribal coalition ready and able to resist the empire, and he rejected the wampum belts the British sent him. "We want none of them," he said. "Tell your general to withdraw all of his people promptly from our lands. We do not intend to allow any of them to set foot there."[40] It took more British diplomatic initiatives and another year before Pontiac and the Wabash nations showed up at Detroit to make peace. Even then, they announced that France had no right to transfer their country to Britain, that they were allowing the British to use land for trading posts, and that they expected "proper returns." When Captain Thomas Stirling and one hundred soldiers of the Black Watch Regiment traveled down the Ohio River and took over Fort Chartres from the French, they did so cautiously and without fanfare to avoid giving offense. The Peace of Paris may have ushered in a glorious new era of British imperial dominance, but that dominance petered out in the Ohio country and Great Lakes, where, William Johnson reported, the Indians considered themselves "a free people" who had "never been conquered, Either by the English or the French, not subject to the Laws."[41] The

British sent peace emissaries to the Indians, returned to gift-giving and diplomacy as the way to conduct relations, and "had to plead with the Indians for consent to occupy the French forts."[42] This was Indian country, no matter what the Peace of Paris said, and Britain modified its vision of empire to fit the realities of power in Indian country.[43]

Contesting the Ohio Country

Wealthy land speculators and their agents and associates in London lobbied hard against the proclamation, and Johnson was soon busy negotiating a new boundary line with the Iroquois. The home government authorized him to secure an extension of the boundary down the Ohio River as far as the Kanawha River, to meet up with a new boundary negotiated with the Cherokees. At the Treaty of Fort Stanwix in the fall of 1768, in exchange for £10,000, the Iroquois ceded territory that stretched four hundred miles beyond the Kanawha to the mouth of the Cherokee or Tennessee River. It was a land grab by Johnson and his associates, but the Iroquois were willing collaborators; by ceding those lands, they diverted the oncoming tide of settlement down the Ohio and away from their own country.[44]

The Indians who actually inhabited and hunted those lands resisted the invasion, and the Shawnees tried to build a multitribal coalition to resist the British-Iroquois land deal. In the power vacuum left after Britain evacuated Fort Pitt and withdrew its troops from the West in 1772, speculators and squatters escalated their encroachments on Indian lands, Virginia went to war against the Shawnees in 1774, and the Shawnees grudgingly accepted the Ohio River as the new boundary. But that same year, in a move to restrict colonial settlement, Parliament passed the Quebec Act, making all the land west of the Ohio part of Quebec.

The American Revolution in the Ohio country was a war to throw off such imperial restraints and to throw open Indian land. Most Indians preferred to stay out of a conflict they regarded as a civil war, but British and American agents operating out of Detroit and Fort Pitt competed for the allegiance of the tribes. Most eventually allied with the empire that had tried to restrict access to their homelands and against the "Virginians"—a term they applied to aggressive and land-hungry Americans in general—who seemed determined to take their homelands for sale and settlement. In a region where local struggles for power and authority—between Virginia and Pennsylvania, between the Continental Congress and western settlers, between Indians and settlers, between Delawares and the Six Nations—often took precedence over the struggle for independence between colonists and crown, Indian populations confronted embryonic republics that demanded their land and their destruction.[45] Washington sent American campaigns into Indian country as retaliation for raids on frontier settlements but also to establish a claim to the Ohio country by the time peace talks were held. Britain might acknowledge American independence but still insist on the boundaries established by the Treaty of Fort Stanwix or the Quebec Act: in other words, relinquish its North American empire east of the Appalachians but hold on to the Ohio country.

The American showing in the Ohio country was not especially impressive. In February 1778, General Edward Hand, commanding at Fort Pitt, led an expedition of five hundred men toward the Cuyahoga River that managed to kill four Indian women, one man, and a boy. "In performing these great exploits," wrote Hand, one soldier was wounded and another drowned.[46] The Delawares were in a precarious position, but they still held some power. In its first formal treaty with an Indian nation, the Treaty of Fort Pitt in 1778, the United States needed a Delaware alliance, not Delaware land (and even laid out the possibility that tribes friendly to the United States might join the alliance and "form a state whereof the Delaware nation shall be the head, and have representation in Congress").[47] When General Lachlan McIntosh, who launched an expedition against Detroit that got nowhere near Detroit, called a council with Delawares and issued a warning to the tribes to make peace or face the wrath of the United States, the Indians "Set up a General Laugh."[48] McIntosh's soldiers did manage to kill one Indian: the Delaware chief White Eyes, who had signed the Fort Pitt treaty and was possibly their best Native friend in the Ohio country.[49] In the fall of 1779, Colonel Daniel Brodhead launched a campaign from Fort Pitt up the Allegheny River in conjunction with General John Sullivan's scorched-earth assault on Iroquois country. The armies burned towns; destroyed orchards, cornfields, and food supplies; and drove cold and hungry people into refugee camps at Niagara. But the campaign only stiffened Iroquois resolve and strengthened their alliance with the British. Iroquois raids resumed with even greater intensity in the spring.

The Revolution in the Ohio country and the war for the Ohio country continued long after the American victory at Yorktown in 1781. With peace on the horizon, the United States pushed to establish its hold on the region, but warriors from different nations, united in their resistance to American expansion, burned Hannastown, Pennsylvania, ambushed the Kentucky militia at Blue Licks, and routed William Crawford's expedition against Sandusky. Nevertheless, across the ocean in Paris in 1783 Britain recognized American independence and handed over to the United States all territory east of the Mississippi, south of the Great Lakes, and north of Florida. The Ohio Indians understood that territorial boundaries they had agreed on in colonial treaties could not be changed "without their Express Concurrence and Consent," but they were neither included in the Peace of Paris nor consulted about its terms, an act of betrayal they said "that Christians only were Capable of."[50]

The United States presumed to have acquired the Indians' land by right of conquest, but the Indians were not defeated subjects of a distant king; they were independent nations fighting to defend their homelands. Once they recovered from the shock of British betrayal, they continued their struggle to halt American expansion at the Ohio River and resumed their war for independence. Inconsistently aided and abetted by the British, they kept the United States at bay for a dozen years after the contests for empire were supposedly decided and historical outcomes supposedly assured.

In the Northwest Ordinance of 1787, the Confederation Congress laid out a plan for building a nation on Indian lands and at the same time pledged not to take the Indians' lands without their consent or to invade them except "in just and lawful wars authorized by Congress."[51] The nation's commitment to seizing land that the tribes were committed to defending meant that "just wars" were inevitable. In retrospect, the outcome also was inevitable. At the time, it was not so evident.

The union of states clashed with a union of Indian nations in the Ohio country. Led by the Shawnee Blue Jacket, the Miami war chief Little Turtle, Buckongahelas of the Delawares, and the Ottawa Egushawa, the Indian confederacy centered on the Maumee River in northwestern Ohio boasted that they held the Americans "in the most Supreme Degree of Contempt" and would "send their Women to fight us & with Sticks instead of Guns."[52] Instead, when General Josiah Harmar's forces invaded in 1790, the Indians evacuated their women and children.[53] Then they sent Harmar's army straggling home in humiliating defeat.

In 1791, General Arthur St. Clair led a campaign that was intended to destroy the villages along the Maumee River and build a fort there. Instead, the Indians destroyed the US army, inflicting casualties of 630 killed and 284 wounded. Indian losses were between twenty or thirty killed and perhaps fifty wounded. Logistical problems, lack of training and the limitations of the soldiers, and military misjudgments set up St. Clair's army to fail, but "St. Clair's defeat," like "Braddock's defeat," is a misnomer. It was an Indian victory achieved by a multinational army executing a carefully coordinated battle plan worked out by their chiefs. The Indian victory over Braddock had demonstrated the limits of the British empire in the Ohio country; the victory over St. Clair's demonstrated the limits of American empire. At a time when separatist movements in the West gravitated toward alliance with Spain and the British in Canada waited for the fragile republic to fall apart, Indian power, for a moment, threatened the very survival of the infant United States. It generated a deluge of reports and correspondence, and fueled rancorous debates in Congress and the press. It added to the growing divisions that led to the creation of the first political parties. It produced the first congressional investigation in American history, and it saw the birth of the principle of executive privilege, as the Washington administration considered whether to withhold documents that implicated the secretary of war and secretary of the treasury in the contractor fraud that had left St. Clair's troops ill-fed and ill-equipped. It produced reforms that increased the federal government's role in shaping western development and increased the army's role as an instrument of national expansion.[54]

As the United States scrambled to build a new army, it resumed boundary negotiations with the Indian confederacy. US commissioners held out prospects of a compromise line—mainly as a ploy to buy time and divide the confederacy—but the Shawnees and others who had led the fight for the Ohio River boundary refused to budge or to acknowledge American claims to their homelands. "We never made any agreement with the king, nor with any other nation, that we would give to either the exclusive right to purchase our lands," they told the commissioners. "If the white people, as you say, made a treaty that none of them but the king should purchase of us, and he has given that right to the United States, it is an affair which concerns you and him, and not us. We have never parted with such a power."[55]

But General Anthony Wayne, with a new and improved American army, defeated a weakened confederacy at the Battle of Fallen Timbers in 1794, and the British failed to deliver the support they had led the Indians to expect. At the Treaty of Greenville the next year, chiefs who had defended the Ohio boundary since before the revolution acknowledged that the fight was over and ceded most of Ohio to the United States. It was not the end of Indian resistance, either military or cultural, but it ended a struggle for the Ohio country they had sustained for forty years.

Conclusion

Euro-American expansion across the Ohio country fits neatly into the East-to-West narrative that dominates American history. Escaping the tyranny of that narrative requires not only facing east from Indian country, as Daniel Richter has recommended,[56] but also looking outward from Indian country, where still powerful Indigenous nations faced north, south, and west, as well as east, and built alliances with other Indian nations as they conducted foreign policies, waged war, and made peace with imperial powers and colonial governments. The power that Indian nations in the Ohio country were capable of bringing to bear was not easily swept aside. It could not be ignored, then, and it should not be ignored now. Indigenous struggles for the security of their homelands shaped the contest of empires, slowed the march of empire, and left enduring impacts on the imperial nation that built itself on Indian land.

Notes

1. John Heckewelder, *History, Manners, and Customs of the Indian Nations Who Once Inhabited Pennsylvania and the Neighboring States* (Philadelphia: Historical Society of Pennsylvania, 1876), 104.

2. Michael N. McConnell, *A Country Between: The Upper Ohio Valley and Its Peoples, 1724–1774* (Lincoln: University of Nebraska Press, 1992), chaps. 1–5; Richard White, *The Middle Ground: Indians, Empires, and Republics in the Great Lakes Region, 1650–1815* (Cambridge: Cambridge University Press, 1991), chap. 5. Cayuga quote in Edmund B. O'Callaghan, ed., *Documents Relating to the Colonial History of the State of New York*, 15 vols. (Albany: Weed, Parsons, 1853–57), 10:206.

3. Fred Anderson, *Crucible of War: The Seven Years' War and the Fate of Empire in British North America, 1754–1766* (New York: Knopf, 2000), 16–21; Francis Jennings, *The Ambiguous Iroquois Empire: The Covenant Chain Confederation of Indian Tribes with English Colonies from Its Beginnings to the Lancaster Treaty of 1744* (New York: W. W. Norton, 1984).

4. *The Journal of Major George Washington* (Williamsburg, VA: Colonial Williamsburg Foundation, 1959), 6–7 (Tanaghrisson speech); Lois Mulkearn, ed., *George Mercer Papers Relating to the Ohio Company of Virginia* (Pittsburgh: University of Pittsburgh Press, 1954), 96.

5. Andrew Gallup, ed., *The Céloron Expedition to the Ohio Country, 1749: The Reports of Pierre-Joseph Céloron and Father Bonnecamps* (Bowie, MD: Heritage Books, 1997), 40.

6. *Colonial Records of Pennsylvania*, 16 vols. (Harrisburg, PA: Published by the state, 1851–53), 5:734–35.

7. David Dixon, "A High Wind Rising: George Washington, Fort Necessity, and the Ohio Country Indians," *Pennsylvania History* 74 (Summer 2007): 341.

8. *Colonial Records of Pennsylvania*, 6:29–30; W. W. Abbot, Dorothy Twohig, et al., eds., *The Papers of George Washington: Colonial Series*, 10 vols. (Charlottesville: University Press of Virginia, 1983–95), 1:85–87; Anderson, *Crucible of War*, 46–49.

9. Donald H. Kent, ed., "Contrecoeur's Copy of George Washington's Journal for 1754," *Pennsylvania History* 19 (January 1952): 11–12; Mulkearn, *George Mercer Papers*, 88; *Colonial Records of Pennsylvania*, 6:31.

10. Kent, "Contrecoeur's Copy of George Washington's Journal for 1754," 13–14; Fred Anderson, ed., *George Washington Remembers: Reflections on the French and Indian War* (Lanham, MD: Rowman & Littlefield, 2004), 16, 31–32, 118, 137–38.

11. Kent, "Contrecoeur's Copy of George Washington's Journal," 19.

12. Kent, "Contrecoeur's Copy of George Washington's Journal," 20–21; Donald Jackson and Dorothy Twohig, eds., *The Diaries of George Washington*, 6 vols. (Charlottesville: University Press of Virginia, 1976–79), 1:194–95; Dixon, "A High Wind Rising," 343.

13. "An Ohio Iroquois Warrior's Account of the Jumonville Affair, 1754," in David L. Preston, *Braddock's Defeat: The Battle of the Monongahela and the Road to Revolution* (New York: Oxford University Press, 2015), 27, 351–53.

14. Kent, "Contrecoeur's Copy of George Washington's Journal," 21; Abbot, Twohig, et al., eds., *The Papers of George Washington*, 1:110–12.

15. Anderson, *Crucible of War*, 53–59; Dixon, "A High Wind Rising," 344; *Colonial Records of Pennsylvania*, 6:195.

16. Kent, "Contrecoeur's Copy of George Washington's Journal," 21–22; Joseph L. Peyser, trans. and ed., *Letters from New France: The Upper Country 1686–1783* (Urbana: University of Illinois Press, 1992), 196–97.

17. Kent, "Contrecoeur's Copy of George Washington's Journal," 21–22; Jackson and Twohig, eds., *The Diaries of George Washington*, 1:197–98; *Papers of George Washington: Colonial Series*, 1:110–12.

18. "Affidavit of John Shaw," in *The Colonial Records of South Carolina: Documents Relating to Indian Affairs, 1754–1765*, ed. William L. McDowell Jr. (Columbia: South Carolina Department of Archives and History, 1970), 4; Hayes Baker-Crothers and Ruth Allison Hudnut, "A Private Soldier's Account of Washington's First Battles in the West: A Study in Historical Criticism," *Journal of Southern History* 10 (1952): 24; Anderson, *Crucible of War*, 57–58.

19. *Papers of George Washington, Colonial Series*, 1:114.

20. Dixon, "High Wind Rising," 345.

21. Beverly W. Bond Jr., ed., "The Captivity of Charles Stuart, 1755–57," *Mississippi Valley Historical Review* 13 (June 1926): 63–65.

22. Preston, *Braddock's Defeat*, esp. 81–82, 109–18; quote at 327.

23. Alison Duncan Hirsch, ed., *Pennsylvania Treaties, 1756–1775*, in *Early American Indian Documents: Treaties and Laws, 1607–1789*, ed. Alden T. Vaughan, 20 vols. (Bethesda, MD: University Publications of America, 1979–2004), 3:2, 7, 15, 19, 148.

24. Ian K. Steele, "Shawnee Origins of Their Seven Years' War," *Ethnohistory* 53 (2006): 657–87; Callaghan, ed., *Documents Relating to the Colonial History of the State of New York*, 10:423; Hirsch, ed., *Pennsylvania Treaties*, 445.

25. Hirsch, ed., *Pennsylvania Treaties*, 423–25.

26. Michael A. McDonnell, *Masters of Empire: Great Lakes Indians and the Making of America* (New York: Hill and Wang, 2015), 170–71, 177; Daniel P. Barr, "'This Land Is Ours and Not Yours': The Western Delawares and the Seven Years' War in the Upper Ohio Valley, 1755–1758," in *The Boundaries between Us: Natives and Newcomers along the Frontiers of the Old Northwest Territory, 1750–1850*, ed. Daniel P. Barr (Kent, OH: Kent State University Press, 2006), 30–37.

27. *Pennsylvania Archives*, First Series, 12 vols. (Harrisburg, PA: Published by the state, 1852–54), 3:534–35; "Journal of Christian Frederick Post," in *Early Western Travels, 1748–1846*, ed. Reuben G. Thwaites (Cleveland: Arthur H. Clark, 1904), 1:212–16.

28. S. K. Stevens, Donald Kent, and Autumn L. Leonard, eds., *The Papers of Henry Bouquet*, 6 vols. (Harrisburg: Pennsylvania Historical and Museum Commission, 1972), 2:611.

29. Johnson quoted in Keith R. Widder, *Beyond Pontiac's Shadow: Michilimackinac and the Anglo-Indian War of 1763* (East Lansing: Michigan State University Press, 2013), 184.

30. White, *Middle Ground*, 255–56.

31. Thwaites, ed., *Early Western Travels*, 1:274, 278.

32. Anderson, *Crucible of War*, 284–85, 328–29; McConnell, *A Country Between*, 166–67; David L. Preston, *The Texture of Contact: European and Indian Settler Communities on the Frontiers of Iroquoia, 1667–1783* (Lincoln: University of Nebraska Press, 2009), 221, 245–46, 251–52.

33. Callaghan, ed., *Documents Relating to the Colonial History of the State of New York*, 7:532.

34. Armand Francis Lucier, comp., *Pontiac's Conspiracy and Other Indian Affairs: Notices Abstracted from Colonial Newspapers, 1763–1765* (Bowie, MD: Heritage Books, 2000), 143; Stevens, Kent, and Leonard, *Papers of Henry Bouquet*, 6:261–62.

35. "Gladwin Manuscripts," *Collections of the Michigan Pioneer Historical Society* 27 (1897): 671–72.

36. John Borrows, "Wampum at Niagara: The Royal Proclamation, Canadian Legal History, and Self-Government," in *Aboriginal and Treaty Rights in Canada*, ed. Michael Asch (Vancouver: University of British Columbia Press, 1997), 155–72; Alan Ojiig Corbiere, "Parchment, Wampum, Letters, and Symbols: Expanding the Parameters of the Royal Proclamation Commemoration," *Canada Watch* (Fall 2013): 17–18.

37. Daniel Ingram, *Indians and British Outposts in Eighteenth-Century America* (Gainesville: University Press of Florida, 2012), chap. 4.

38. Widder, *Beyond Pontiac's Shadow*, 197–98; McDonnell, *Masters of Empire*, 232–38; Michael Witgen, *An Infinity of Nations: How the Native New World Shaped Early North America* (Philadelphia: University of Pennsylvania Press, 2012).

39. William Smith, *An Historical Account of the Expedition against the Ohio Indians, in the Year 1764* (Philadelphia, 1765), 23 ("haughtiness"); Richard Middleton, *Pontiac's War* (New York: Routledge, 2007), 181.

40. *Journal of Captain Thomas Morris* (London: James Ridgway, 1791; reprinted, Readex Microprint, 1966), 7–8.

41. Patrick Griffin, *American Leviathan: Empire, Nation, and Revolutionary Frontier* (New York: Hill and Wang, 2007), 34.

42. Middleton, *Pontiac's War*, 197–99 ("had to plead"); Robert G. Carroon, ed., *Broadswords and Bayonets: The Journals of the Expedition under the Command of Captain Thomas Stirling of the 42nd Regiment of Foot, Royal Highland Regiment (The Black Watch) to Occupy Fort Chartres in the Illinois Country, August 1765 to January 1766* (Chicago: The Society of Colonial Wars in the State of Illinois, 1984).

43. White, *Middle Ground*, 269–71; Ian K. Steele, *Warpaths: Invasions of North America* (New York: Oxford University Press, 1994), 246–47.

44. Colin G. Calloway, *Pen and Ink Witchcraft: Treaties and Treaty Making in American Indian History* (New York: Oxford University Press, 2013), chap. 2; William J. Campbell, *Speculators in Empire: Iroquoia and the 1768 Treaty of Fort Stanwix* (Norman: University of Oklahoma Press, 2012).

45. Griffin, *American Leviathan;* Daniel P. Barr, *A Colony Sprung from Hell: Pittsburgh and the Struggle for Authority on the Western Pennsylvania Frontier, 1744–1794* (Kent, OH: Kent State University Press, 2014), 175–93.

46. Consul W. Butterfield, ed., *Washington-Irvine Correspondence: The Official Letters which Passed between Washington and Brig.-Gen. William Irvine and between Irvine and Others concerning Military Affairs in the West from 1781 to 1783* (Madison, WI: David Atwood, 1882), 15–16; Reuben G. Thwaites and Louise P. Kellogg, eds., *Frontier Defense on the Upper Ohio* (Madison: Wisconsin Historical Society, 1912), 215–23; W. W. Abbot et al., eds., *The Papers of George Washington: Revolutionary War Series*, 22 vols. (Charlottesville: University of Virginia Press, 1985–), 14:182.

47. Charles J. Kappler, comp., *Indian Affairs: Laws and Treaties,* 2 vols. (Washington, DC: Government Printing Office, 1904), 2:3–5.

48. Louise Phelps Kellogg, ed., *Frontier Advance on the Upper Ohio, 1778–1779* (Madison: Wisconsin State Historical Society, 1916), 178–80; Randolph C. Downes, *Council Fires on the Upper Ohio* (Pittsburgh: University of Pittsburgh Press, 1940), 220.

49. Kellogg, ed., *Frontier Advance*, 20–21; Downes, *Council Fires on the Upper Ohio*, 217.

50. Colin G. Calloway, *Crown and Calumet: British-Indian Relations, 1783–1815* (Norman: University of Oklahoma Press, 1987), 5–13.

51. "Ordinance of 1787," in *The Territorial Papers of the United States*, ed. Clarence Edwin Carter, 28 vols. (Washington, DC: Government Printing Office, 1934–75), 2:39–50.

52. Sargent to St. Clair, August 17, 1790, Arthur St. Clair Papers, 1788–1815, Ohio State Library; Carter, ed., *Territorial Papers*, 2:301.

53. Gayle Thornborough, ed., *Outpost on the Wabash, 1787–1791: Letters of Brigadier General Josiah Harmar and Major John Francis Hamtramck and Other Letters and Documents Selected from the Harmar Papers in the William L. Clements Library* (Indianapolis: Indiana Historical Society, 1957), 266.

54. Colin G. Calloway, *The Victory with No Name: The Native American Defeat of the First American Army* (New York: Oxford University Press, 2015); William H. Bergman, *The American National State and the Early West* (Cambridge: Cambridge University Press, 2012); Andrew R. Cayton, "Radicals in the 'Western World': The Federalist Conquest of Trans-Appalachian North America," in *Federalists Reconsidered*, ed. Doron Ben-Atar and Barbara B. Oberg (Charlottesville: University of Virginia Press, 1998), 77–96.

55. "Message to the Commissioners of the United States," in *First Peoples: A Documentary Survey of American Indian History*, 5th ed., ed. Colin G. Calloway (Boston: Bedford/St. Martin's, 2016), 244.

56. Daniel K. Richter, *Facing East from Indian Country: A Native History of Early America* (Cambridge, MA: Harvard University Press, 2001).

CHAPTER SEVEN

Between Reform and Revolution

Class Formation and British Colonial Rule at the Cape of Good Hope

NICOLE ULRICH

The Age of Revolution was a period characterized by significant social and political upheaval that facilitated an epochal shift, marking the global acceleration of modern capitalism. Scholars increasingly agree that the Age of Revolution did "not necessarily spread outward from Europe and North America into colonies and empires," and cannot be conceived of as a uniquely Western event.[1] Rather, as historians such as Clare Anderson have argued, it is better understood as "complex sets of interconnected phenomenon" that "circulated in all directions" across the globe and that raised issues related to legitimate political authority, economic change, social hierarchies, rights, and political agency.[2]

The Cape of Good Hope was colonized by the Dutch East India Company (*Vereenigde Oost-Indische Compagnie*, or VOC) in 1652 and plugged into global circuits of trade and labor migration.[3] The colony was not isolated from the political and social upheavals of the late eighteenth and early nineteenth centuries. British forces occupied the Cape in 1795 during the Revolutionary Wars, ending 143 years of VOC rule. The occupation gave rise to what historians have termed the "transition period," in which the Cape was handed between the British empire (which occupied the Cape between 1795 and 1803, and again from 1806 to 1813) and the revolutionary Dutch Batavian administration (which briefly reclaimed the Cape from 1803 to 1806).[4]

The "transition period" marked a significant turning point in the political history of the colony. Chris Bayly notes that one of the most important outcomes of the Age of Revolution was the emergence of stronger, more intrusive imperial states with colonial officials who appropriated and reformulated the radical ideas of the Age in order to establish state legitimacy.[5] In the case of the Cape, the British occupation marked the start of a new phase of imperialism that was state led: the colonial bureaucracy was modernized and intruded into new areas of life. It was within this context that colonial officials sought to reform the labor regime inherited from the VOC. The new labor regime was still predicated on unfree labor, but the labor system was regulated to temper some of the more violent excesses and grant laborers some rights.

Just as much as the Age of Revolution was not a purely Western affair, it cannot simply be attributed to the agency of bourgeoisie elites. To be sure, elites and states were ultimately the main beneficiaries. However, as Peter Linebaugh and Marcus Rediker have highlighted in *The Many-Headed Hydra: Sailors, Slaves, Commoners and the Hidden History of the Revolutionary Atlantic*, the popular classes played a central role in instigating revolt and developing more radical understandings of egalitarianism, political representation, and freedom.

The aim of this chapter is to broaden our understanding of political and social change at the Cape at this important historical juncture and investigate what these changes meant for labor. While this requires an examination of the British colonial state and creation of a new labor regime, it is also necessary to consider the way in which the colony's popular classes were constituted and reconstituted, and how laborers and the poor both prompted, and responded to, labor reform under British occupation. In order to do this, the chapter will consider popular political resistance and forms of belonging. Special attention is given to laboring women and men with Indigenous Khoesan ancestry and the role they played in the making of what would become the modern proletariat of southern Africa.

Labor and Indigeneity

The Cape of Good Hope served as a convenient resting point for the VOC's fleets traveling between the Netherlands and the VOC's operational base in Batavia. Even though VOC colonial rule was fragmented, it was predicated on political and territorial conquest and the entrenchment of private property.[6] The Company introduced a unique, and somewhat limited, form of citizenship at the Cape: respectable servants, mainly European, were released from their contracts and awarded the status of "free-burgher" to take up farming in order to stimulate agricultural production to aid the reproduction of VOC crews that stopped over at Cape Town's port. However, by far the largest section of inhabitants (recognized by the VOC colony as under its government) were slaves and servants governed through harsh labor codes and subject to a criminal justice system based on upholding social and political inequalities through violence and fear.

As the colony grew and diversified, three regionally based, yet interdependent, economic sectors emerged.[7] These consisted of, firstly, the urban-centered port economy dominated by the Company, which relied on the labor of low-ranking VOC servants (sailors, soldiers, and a small number of artisans) as well as slaves. This sector also included retail and small-scale manufacturing run by free-burghers and free blacks, which drew on the labor of slaves and the "free" poor.[8] The second sector involved the production of wheat and wine in the more fertile hinterland, on farms owned by free-burghers.[9] This sector relied mainly on slaves. In addition, farmers also made use of other laborers, particularly those of Khoesan (or partial Khoesan) ancestry and low-ranking Company servants permitted to become *pasgangers*.[10] Thirdly, from the 1700s, a stock-farming sector emerged on the colonial borderlands.[11] Stock farmers owned slaves, but most relied on family labor supplemented by laborers of Khoesan ancestry and poorer free-burghers.

This economy was embedded in a very specific social structure. Although the upper class was predominantly European, or white, the popular classes were motley, drawn from Africa, Asia, and Europe. Slaves were initially mainly sourced from Indonesia, India, and Madagascar, but toward the end of the 1700s, from East Africa as well.[12] The large number of slaves, mostly men, who worked the wheat and wine farms of the hinterland has led many to view the Cape as a rural and slave society. While VOC-owned slaves never increased beyond 1,000, the number of privately owned slaves was about 14,747 in 1793, the overwhelming majority being rural.[13]

However, while slavery was important, slavery existed alongside other forms of labor, including forced labor. Low-ranking VOC servants were another significant part of the popular classes. By the late eighteenth century, the number of Company servants—mainly sailors and soldiers recruited from across Europe—stationed at the Cape had grown to between three thousand and four thousand.[14] These numbers were augmented by the great many VOC and other sailors and soldiers who temporarily stopped off at the Cape on the voyage between the East Indies and Europe.

There was also a small group of free working poor outside of VOC employ. The free working poor would have included poorer free blacks (e.g., manumitted slaves and convicts), destitute or dependent free-burghers, and others. There are no figures for this category, partly because scholars conflate the free, in general, with well-to-do free-burghers who employed others and are thus unable to perceive poorer free-burghers as socially marginal.

Nor are there overall figures for laborers of Khoesan ancestry. This was almost certainly a substantial group. Historians have estimated that roughly 23,000 Khoesan were living inside the colony by the 1780s, and we must presume most were working for colonists, even if only on temporary contracts.[15] The lack of figures for Khoesan laborers reflects, in part, their peculiar legal position and their subordinate status in Cape society under VOC rule.

Here a note on terminology is required. The current use of "Khoesan," "San," and "Khoe" (sometimes "Khoi") in place of "Bushmen" and "Hottentots" is meant to contest the derogatory terminology used to refer to Indigenous hunter-gatherer and herding communities (as opposed to African farming societies) in the Cape. However, the categories used—both past and present—are complex and politically charged. For instance, postapartheid South Africa is witness to the rapid emergence of an overt, vocal, self-described Khoesan nationalism.[16] Central to this movement's discourse is its claim to represent "first peoples" with a continuous history preceding both African farming communities and European settlers in the area now called South Africa.

Further, a close reading of the historical record also suggests the fluidity of categories and cautions against the notion that "Khoe" and "San" were fixed categories, consistently referring to the same essential groups. Shula Marks notes that in the VOC records, officials were, at first, very careful to detail specific clan names.[17] However, once the colony became less reliant on local people as trading partners, in the first few decades of the eighteenth century, officials became less particular and used "Hottentot" and "Bushmen" in new ways. Most notably, the term "Bushmen" was increasingly used to refer to rebellious groups as "thieves" or bandits, of whom colonial officials and European settler-farmers constantly complained.

George MaCall Theal, the core figure in the "colonial/settler" school of South African history, read the archival record to mean that Cape Peninsular "Hottentots" were subdued and acculturated out of existence by 1713, while "Bushmen" continued to harass colonial authorities and farmers through constant stock raids, especially on the borderlands.[18] This argument was echoed in the 1930s by the "liberal" school. For instance, William Miller Macmillan wrote: "Hottentot resistance . . . to the advance of Dutch settlers was hardly as vigorous even as that of the more primitive Bushmen."[19]

In these two schools, the terms had come to signify different levels of agency by very distinct groups, different levels of "civilization," and racial distinctions as well. From the 1970s onward, the "revisionist-Marxist" school and a new layer of liberal scholars contested such arguments, claiming that VOC officials did not actually see the Khoe and San as racially separate at all but rather distinguished the two groups on the basis of their way of life.[20] The Khoe were, in this reading, herders who owned stock, while the San were hunter-gatherers who did not. Thus, leading revisionist Shula Marks argued that the division between Khoe and San was a class division as much as a cultural, ethnic, or linguistic one.

While Marks's analysis differed in many respects with that of liberals such as Richard Elphick and Candy Malherbe, these historians agreed that due to social and economic stress, the distinction between Khoe and San increasingly broke down toward the end of the 1700s. Some San were able to acquire cattle ("becoming" Khoe), and increasing numbers of Khoe lost their stock ("becoming" San). This reasoning led to a new preference for the term "Khoesan," as a way of amalgamating the two.

However, while distinguishing Khoe from San on the basis of the form of their independent economies is revealing, it is less useful when it is noted that independent Khoesan economies were systematically destroyed by colonial expansion. Members of these groups were steadily integrated into the colony's labor systems, and the broader political economy of the VOC, comprising a majority of the Cape population. This brought Khoesan into proximity with other parts of the popular classes, a process associated with a substantial degree of social connection and cultural change. What, then, defined being "Khoe" or "San" or "Khoesan" (or, in the terms of colonial officials, "Hottentots" or "Bushmen")? Thus, despite their advances, the work of Marks as well as Elphick and Malherbe have not adequately located these Indigenous peoples' dispossession within the larger processes of class formation and class struggle at play. Related to this, scholars also need to consider how political choices and responses influenced the meaning of these categories, as it would appear that colonial officials and free-burghers would more readily identify those groups who challenged their authority as bandits and thieves (or "Bushmen") than those considered allies.

Identity and Protest

European colonialism and capitalist enclosure disrupted African societies across southern Africa. Many aspects of traditional life proved resilient despite dispossession. Nevertheless, the disruptions caused by capitalism and colonialism also opened possibilities for the development of novel social formations, identities, and solidarities.

As I have argued elsewhere, laborers and the poor at the Cape should not just be viewed as an economic category, or social rank.[21] The popular classes formed a distinct social entity and constituted themselves as collective agents. The mainstream historiography presents the Cape as a plural society of racially and ethnically distinct "population" groups corresponding to class and occupation, which consist of the segmented and unequal worlds of white free-burghers, European VOC employees, Asian slaves, Khoesan servants, and so forth. But while class divides were central, different parts of the popular classes—different occupations and labor types—never existed in social silos. Slaves and servants were drawn together through familial connections, mutual aid, fellowship, and recreation across the divides of ethnicity, race, and labor type. Such relationships played an integral part in the formation of multiracial and multinational class-based forms of belonging and formed the basis for remarkable struggles and solidarities.

At the same time, the state played an important countervailing role by enforcing differences between different laboring groups. For instance, being "Khoesan" was partly constituted by issues related to governance. Most notable was their ambivalent legal status under the VOC: people of Khoesan descent were legally free yet were excluded from colonial institutions and increasingly forced into labor.[22]

After peninsular Khoesan groups were defeated through war in the 1670s, only VOC-sanctioned patriarchs were officially able to retain access to land and resources in the colony.[23] These "captains" or "chiefs" were expected to discipline their own subjects. The VOC failed to develop any official labor codes for those Khoesan drawn into the colony as workers, especially on the colonial borderlands. Those who entered employment voluntarily through initially reasonably flexible clientage arrangements were increasingly reduced to unfree servants, while others (mainly women and children) were captured during border raids by *commandos* and forced into a system of indentured servitude akin to the slavery seen on the wine and grain farms elsewhere.

Despite their distinctiveness, laborers with Khoesan ancestry shared a common class experience of physical violence and control, and they were part of and integrated into the Cape's popular classes. Khoesan worked and lived alongside other slaves and servants and formed intimate relations with them. As observed by Otto Friedrich Mentzel, "Hottentot women, in the service of the colonists, do not dislike the slaves, and easily let themselves be persuaded to live with them."[24] There are numerous references in the court records to slave men who had developed lasting partnerships with Khoesan women, confirming Mentzel's claims. For instance, Mieta, a Khoesan woman from Roodezand who appeared before the court in 1798, had thirteen children with the slave Felix van Boegis.[25]

Khoesan women in Cape Town were also known to cohabit and have children with sailors, soldiers, and other servants. The most prominent example is the iconic Saartjie Baartman, who fell in love with a poor Dutch soldier, Hendrik van Jong, while she was working in Cape Town for a free black family.[26] Figures such as Baartman remain important. Given the significantly skewed gender ratios in the colony, especially regarding slaves, historians need to pay more attention to the role Khoesan women servants played in the reproduction of class-based, and often racially mixed, families and communities.

Another key site in which Khoesan played a key role in the making of the popular classes was via "fugitive" bands on the borderlands. These bands often started as the remnants of traditional clans: resisting full integration into the colony, they often offered refuge to other fugitives, including runaway Khoesan laborers, slaves, and VOC servants, as well as deserters from other African polities.[27] Such bands played an important role in the development of alternative, dissident communities.

The familial and communal relations that laborers with Khoesan ancestry developed with other sections of the laboring classes suggest that the complexity of the "Khoesan" category went well beyond the fact that the "Khoe" and "San" distinction was blurred by the impact of dispossession and proletarianization. By the late 1700s, a significant proportion of those classified as "Bushmen" or "Hottentots" by the Company, and as "Khoesan" by later historians, were of mixed Asian, African, and European ancestry. Colonial categories developed to reflect some of the complexities and changes: for example, "Bastaard" became used to refer to people of mixed Khoesan and European parentage, while "Bastaard-Hottentot" referred to mixed Khoesan and slave parentage. These categories were closely tied to legal status: for example, children with Khoesan fathers and slave mothers were regarded as slaves.

The Cape's popular classes were thus not just more integrated than often recognized but also far more rebellious than the mainstream literature concedes. Under VOC rule, the popular classes developed a rich, and varied, tradition of "resistance" that included desertion, the creation of fugitive communities, arson, threats against and attacks on masters, and collective insurgency.[28] In many instances, these modes of resistance were overt and confrontational, collective in nature, embedded within social networks, socially inclusive of different sections of the popular classes, and informed by very clear moral codes and a popular sense of justice.

By the mid-to-late 1700s, the VOC entered into a period of decline that was, in part, linked to the fall of the Mughal Empire and the Safavid dynasty in the 1720s. (It is interesting to note that Bayly identifies the fall of the Mughal Empire as one of the key precipitators of the Age of Revolution). The weaknesses of the VOC were exposed and intensified by the Fourth Anglo-Dutch War (1780–1784).[29] Numerous VOC possessions were lost, and it was only with the assistance of the French troops that an attack on the Cape in 1780 was thwarted, allowing local VOC rule to be extended for a further decade and a half.

From the 1770s and 1780s, social and political revolutions and upheaval were taking place across the north Atlantic. Historians of the Cape have certainly considered the impact that the spread of revolutionary political ideas had on local elites such as the richer free-burghers. For instance, elite burghers, who were inspired by the American Revolution and by the Patriots in the Netherlands, objected to the Company's monopolistic trade policies and demanded more representation in government. In 1784, the "Cape Patriots" petitioned the States-General, winning some concessions such as trade with foreign ships, albeit only after VOC needs were satisfied.[30] By the 1790s, political turmoil had spread to the free-burghers on the colonial borderland. British spies reported that these burghers were informed by the "ridiculous notion, that like America, they could exist as an independent state."[31] However, the republicanism of these burghers was exclusive and narrow. They did not generalize their beliefs in freedom, equality, and fraternity to other sections of the population, least of all their slaves or Khoesan servants.

However, little attention has been paid to the larger patterns of struggle among the Cape's popular classes during the Age of Revolution. The evidence suggests that this was both a time of popular unrest and of popular radicalism. In line with a long-established tradition of "direct action" in the colony, the VOC had to deal with ongoing revolts and mutinies. For instance, in 1784 Chinese sailors mutinied on the *Java* en route to the Cape.[32] In 1789, soldiers attached to the Wurtemberg regiment mutinied and demanded better food and the same pay as the regular VOC garrison.[33]

Due to the fractured historiography of the popular classes at the Cape, there is not really a base from which to measure accurately whether we can see an increase of popular resistance. However, two very significant developments can be identified. First, there are indications that slaves started to question entrenched patterns of deference in new ways. Slave historian Nigel Worden notes that the case of the slave Caesar, from Madagascar, indicates that slaves had started to invoke the claim to have certain rights.[34] One evening in June 1793, Malan, the master, asked Caesar and two fellow workers why they had not yet gone to bed, as they were expected to get up early and plow the fields. Caesar replied, "I am going to make my bed just now, there is enough time, I will span the cattle early tomorrow."[35] Malan ordered Caesar to be silent, but Caesar insisted that "I must have my right to speak."[36] Malan retaliated by beating Caesar with a broom. Yet Caesar insisted: "I do not want to be silent, and I must retain my right to speak," while adding, "*Baas* [boss] must stop beating me like this."[37] Caesar asserted his ability to manage his own time and, strikingly, also claimed that even though he was a slave, he had certain inalienable rights.[38] This claim indicates that slaves like Caesar were influenced by the prevailing political climate, in which the language of rights was widespread.

In the second instance, there was an intensification of a number of related disorderly acts on the borderland involving large numbers of laborers of Khoesan ancestry. From 1770 onward, many, especially those working in the stock-farming sector on the borderland, deserted their masters and joined fugitive bands, and participated in armed raids on frontier colonial farms. According to Marks, by the 1780s, some fugitive bands had grown to several hundred strong, and by the 1790s, there were reports of a band of almost a thousand people.[39] Here it is important, again, to be cautious in the use of categories. It should not be assumed that the fugitive bands were simply Khoesan bands, or an expression of a Khoesan identity. The bands were not homogenously "Khoesan" and—as noted by scholars such as Marks—they included a wide range of deserters and rebels from both the Cape colony and surrounding African societies.[40]

Modern Colonialism and Class Formation

The British fleet arrived in Table Bay in June 1795. The British occupation was not simply a military or political affair and led to notable changes in Cape colonial society. Social and economic divides remained firmly in place, but both the elite and popular classes changed in composition. Laborers and the poor also created novel identities and openly participated in new kinds of communities.

On arrival, the British fleet caused alarm among the elite. Wild rumors spread that they would all be impressed as sailors, or even be banished to Botany Bay, Australia.[41] Some also believed that the British would encourage slaves to rise up and revolt.[42] Recognizing that the Revolutionary Wars were deeply ideological, Vice Admiral Keith Elphinstone and Major-General Craig sought to alleviate such concerns. They stressed the British commitment to the protection of private property and promised, for the first time, free trade.[43] According to historian Timothy Keegan, the initial distrust of the British was soon replaced with mutual relations of reliance.[44] Local elites were freed from the monopolistic practices of the VOC, and, in return for their loyalty to the British colonial state, they enjoyed new opportunities for economic enterprise and for patronage.[45]

The Cape elite also included new British merchants, who—through their linkages with London markets—stimulated commerce and production with access to credit and financial institutions.[46] They were a key stimulus for commercial agriculture in the colony, especially with regard to the wool industry. These gentlemen were firm empire patriots. In 1799, a number of the "gentlemen in the Civil Department" and the "principal English inhabitants," including the likes of the travel writer and imperial ideologue John Barrow, the slave trader Alexander Tennant, and the merchant W. Venables, issued a public letter offering their services to "defend this valuable Colony against the Enemies of our most gracious Sovereign."[47]

Linebaugh and Rediker argue that the transatlantic "proletariat" of the time played a key role in the revolutionary overthrow of *ancien regimes*. At the very same time, they note that the revolutions changed the transatlantic "proletariat," which became increasingly segmented.[48] Seduced by significant gains—including higher wages, property, and national citizenship—industrial waged workers separated themselves from the more marginalized and unemployed. It would appear that the motley and revolutionary transatlantic proletariat split in two: leading to mutually exclusive narratives of "the working class" and "black power" that, they maintain, continue to dominate proletarian politics today.

What, then, was involved in the social and political reconstitution of the colony's popular classes that would lay the foundations for the modern proletariat? Did the popular classes at the Cape become increasingly segmented, as Linebaugh and Rediker argue was the case of the transatlantic "proletariat"? Like the Cape's elite, the popular classes also changed in terms of composition under British occupation. VOC sailors and soldiers were replaced by roughly five thousand soldiers and three thousand sailors (Scots, Irishmen, northern Englanders, "lascars" from India, and a sprinkling of sailors recruited from the West Indies and North America) employed by the British army and navy.[49] These new sailors and soldiers were accompanied by a new category of labor—domestic servants who traveled to the Cape with their wealthy masters.

Another important shift included the creolization of the slave population. By 1806, slaves born in the Cape constituted a substantial proportion (about 40 percent) of slaves in the colony.[50] The trend, it is argued, served to homogenize slaves in terms of ethnicity and language.[51]

New laborers who arrived with the British occupation and Cape slaves continued to participate in a broad multiracial and multiethnic fellowship. This inclusive fellowship was partially stabilized into what historian Andrew Banks calls the underclass culture of leisure that centered on dancing, gambling, and drinking in taverns and on the streets and that continued into the nineteenth century.[52]

There is much to suggest that, as in the case of life under the VOC, popular social inclusivity was not limited to leisure and was more deeply rooted in social and family relationships. This is best illustrated by the family arrangements of Louis from Mauritius, one of the leaders of the 1808 revolt against slavery (on that revolt, see section on Labor Radicalism in this chapter). A slave, Louis was hired by a free black woman named Anna. This arrangement reflected the common practice whereby slaveholders in Cape Town hired out their slaves to make money, rather than rely on the labor of their slaves directly. Like many slaves before, Louis created his own networks of belonging and referred to Anna as his "wife," even though such a union had no legal sanction.[53] According to historian Jackie Loos, Anna belonged to a large extended family that spanned four generations.[54] It consisted of her mother, her married sisters and their husbands, and their various children. One of Anna's daughters, Silvia, lived in Stellenbosch and was also already married with her own children. Anna's sister, Coba, was married to Abraham Anthonissen, whose parents were freed slaves. Despite his parents' slave past, Anthonissen had fared relatively well. He supported ten children and could also afford to hire a poor white free-burgher, Hendrik van Dyk, who later married Anthonissen's eldest daughter. Loos paints a picture of a lively family living in close quarters in rented premises and cooperating to generate an income.[55] Louis's family structure suggests that, as under the VOC, families of laborers and the poor were often based on extended familial networks and transcended racial and legal divides.

At the same time, at the start of the nineteenth century, we also see the development of new, distinct religious and national identities emerge within the Cape's popular classes. The small Muslim community that became visible in Cape Town during the 1790s gained in coherence. At the start of the nineteenth century, a *madrasah* and a mosque were opened. It is thought that the Muslim community grew from about 1,000 in 1800 to about 7,500 in 1842.[56]

It was not only Islam that appealed to the popular classes: increasing numbers of laborers of Khoesan ancestry and freed slaves were attracted to Christianity. By 1808, the Moravians had established mission stations at Genadendal and Groenekloof, and by 1814 the London Mission Society had set up Bethelsdorp, Zuurbraak, Hoogekraal, and Theopolis as permanent mission stations.[57] These new religious communities were internally stratified and offered forms of belonging that were not class specific. However, some of these religious communities retained a strong proletarian orientation and played a significant political role, providing participants with leadership and new strategies that were appropriated by the popular classes. For instance, it has been argued that, in addition to its perceived spiritual benefits, Islam offered slaves and poorer free blacks access to an alternative culture and social networks that were distinct from those of their Dutch or British masters and rulers.[58]

Perhaps one of the most notable political developments of this period—and which points to the same kind of segmentation experienced by the transatlantic proletariat as identified by Linebaugh and Rediker taking place at the Cape—was the creation of new national communities. At the start of the 1800s, the motley bands on the colony's northern borderlands gave rise to the *Griqua* nation, north of the colony.[59] The Griqua nation was based on *Baastards* (Khoesan of mixed race) but also included Khoi, ex-slaves, renegade Europeans, Tswana, and Korana San who all claimed a common ancestor on political grounds and negotiated with the colonial state (with the assistance of missionaries) as an independent people. The Griqua people are racially mixed but, like other modern nations, are internally stratified and, once solidified, have become exclusive of other groups.

Governance and Labor Reform

In line with what Bayly identifies as the rise of the stronger, and more intrusive, states, both the British and Batavian administrations devised new ways to legitimize colonial and class power. It was within this context that key institutional reforms were enacted: the administration of the Cape was centralized under the British War Office, the state bureaucracy was streamlined and the civil service professionalized, surveillance and record keeping was improved, and the state extended itself into new areas of life such as education and public health initiatives and the regulation of medicine.[60] In addition, the colonial state now sought to insert itself into the relationship between masters and their slaves/servants.[61]

Such labor reforms were part of what Wayne Dooling identifies as a "thoroughgoing revolution in productive relations": a crisis that prompted the reorganization of the relations between masters, the state, and labor.[62] This crisis was intimately linked to slave emancipation and did not take place in isolation but was part of global contests over acceptable forms of labor, and of the treatment of working people across the empire.

The most formidable opposition to slavery came from slaves themselves, leading to a wave of armed revolts across the British empire (e.g., risings in Jamaica in 1760, the Virgin Islands in 1790, and British-occupied St. Lucia in 1796) and elsewhere (including Berbice in Guyana in 1763; Cuba in 1795, 1798, 1802, and 1805; St. Domingue in 1791 followed by the Haitian Revolution; Curaçao and nearby Venezuela in 1795; and the United States of America in 1800 and 1805). As noted by Iain McCalman, the abolitionist campaign against slavery also had massive proletarian and popular support in Europe, not least in Britain, and can be located within the wider world of contemporary radicalism and popular politics.[63] The ideas associated with religious nonconformists, and the Enlightenment, including around equality, natural law, and inherent rights, were critical, and slave revolts were a central part of the Age of Revolution. Without popular radicalism, it is unlikely that abolition of the slave trade and slavery would have taken place.

In addition, increasing numbers of "respectable" men and women also became convinced of the immorality of slavery.[64] While the efforts of these groups were very important, they also had the effect of containing abolition within more limited parameters. In Britain, the Abolition Committee was founded in 1787 and led by gentlemen campaigners such as Granville Sharp, Thomas Clarkson, and William Wilberforce. The committee stressed the horrific conditions on slave ships and the high mortality rates of both slaves and the sailors involved in the transatlantic slave trade.[65] Even though its campaign for the abolition of the slave trade developed a mass base, the campaign did not center on popular insurgency, but on lobbying Parliament to change the law.

Slaveholders organized through bodies like the West Indian Committee vehemently opposed abolition. Even so, slavery as a system continued to lose legitimacy in the face of a global battle for abolition, encompassing many strands, revolutionary as well as reformist.

By the 1790s, the political climate in Britain had been decisively transformed by the American, French, and Haitian Revolutions. Michael Craton, James Walvin, and David Wright note that while support for abolitionism grew among the radical "correspondence societies" and other clubs, fear of "Jacobinism" among the British Lords stifled efforts at parliamentary reform.[66] This lull may explain why the importation of slavery did not diminish under early British rule at the Cape but instead became one of the most profitable areas of trade before 1807/08.[67]

However, the imperatives of state legitimacy in the context of global upheaval provided a powerful spur for change. In the Cape, the colonial state also sought to reduce the autonomy of private employers and position itself as the locus of rights and punishments. While this did not translate into the widespread adoption of free, waged labor, existing forms of unfree labor at the Cape were reformed and ameliorated through reforming the law and criminal justice system, which had historically played a key role in determining the treatment and discipline of labor.

The legitimacy of the British legal system rested on the notions—or the illusion—of equality before the law and impartial governance.[68] This differed significantly with the VOC, which established a justice system overtly based on entrenching inequality, on gaining confessions through torture, and on gruesome public punishment. In 1797, the War Office noted of the Cape that "the practice of proceeding by Torture against persons suspected of Crimes and of punishment after Conviction in many Capital cases, by breaking upon the Wheel and other barbarous modes of execution prevails."[69] George Macartney, First Earl of Macartney and governor of the Cape from 1796 to 1798, was instructed to "abolish these forms of Trial and Punishment, and provide other more lenient and equitable proceedings."[70]

Another marked change was that British officials identified Khoesan as a key category of labor for the future.[71] For instance, the British observer

Barrow believed that if such laborers were treated more kindly by masters, they could be encouraged to take on vital work once carried out by slaves. He wrote in 1806: "There is not, perhaps, any part of the world, out of Europe, where the introduction of slavery was less necessary than the Cape of Good Hope. . . . To encourage the native Hottentot in useful labour, by giving them an interest in the produce of that labour, to make them experience the comforts of civilized life, and to feel they have a place and value in society, which their miserable policy has hitherto denied to them, would be the sure means of diminishing, and in time, of entirely removing the necessity of slavery."[72] The VOC only partially integrated laborers of Khoesan ancestry into colonial institutions, and then mainly into the criminal justice system. Now the British administration viewed these same laborers as British subjects. In this context, British authorities focused their attention on the relations between Khoesan laborers and their "Boer" masters,[73] who, these authorities believed, needed to be disciplined into their respective class roles. In contrast to wealthy slave owners who were viewed relatively sympathetically by the British administration, "Boers," especially stock farmers on the borderlands, were cast as indolent, unsophisticated, and cruel masters in need of state regulation, and their Khoesan employees were viewed as "an innocent and oppressed race of men" that required "countenance and protection" from government.[74]

It is important to stress that the aim of the government was to maintain some degree of control: free labor in the Cape, including European laborers in the colony, was widely regarded as disorderly and hardly viewed as the preferred form of labor. For instance, in July 1808, Governor Du Pre Alexander (the second Lord Caledon) echoed the universal complaint of wealthy British inhabitants who "suffered from the conduct" of European domestic workers. After the costs and trouble of bringing these domestic servants to the Cape, they soon found themselves "without a single attendant."[75] He argued: "The cause is obvious. European servants, in a country where they cannot be immediately replaced, assume a consequence ill becoming a state of service, so accustomed to domineer over slaves, they become impatient of control, claim a free agency which the law of the land does not allow them and which, were it otherwise, would set at large upon the colony a description of people of all others the most troublesome and useless."[76] An example was made of Sarah Bradbury, who abandoned the service of her mistress to get married. She was arrested for breaking her contract and sent back to England to stand trial.[77]

The Cape's new imperial rulers favored forms of labor control that were less brutal, with excessive violence discouraged, but firm, harsh labor controls remained, as did heavy reliance on various forms of bonded and forced labor.

Labor Radicalism

It was not only elites who reimagined labor and rights under British rule. Among the popular classes, there were growing demands for rights and freedom. The new forms of moderate and reformist political strategies engendered by changing state policy, and fostered by missionaries, existed alongside long-established traditions of direct action and growing popular radicalism.

Under the VOC, laborers and the poor found it difficult to report masters to the court for abuses, and slaves were punished if they could not prove their claims sufficiently.[78] However, under British rule it became feasible for slaves and servants to systematically adopt indirect action—reformist, legally based political strategies—to improve their conditions. The role played by missionaries was complex. On the one hand, missionaries played a key role in instilling European, middle-class values and notions of "respectability," and are seen as agents of capitalism and colonialism.[79] On the other hand, there were those missionaries who were inspired by evangelical humanism, and who often deeply opposed the harsh injustices experienced by the unfree, enslaved, and colonized. They intruded into the realm of popular politics and assisted slaves and servants, especially of Khoesan ancestry, to articulate their grievances in an organized manner. In so doing, they modeled moderate political action centered on the ability of a few well-respected leaders to lobby British and local statesmen to adopt new and progressive labor legislation.

At the same time, the entrenched traditions of direct action and radicalism persisted. It was, in fact, during the Age of Revolution, and, more specifically, the "transition period" of British rule at the Cape, that three mighty popular rebellions took place: naval mutinies in 1797, the "Servants' Rebellion" of 1799–1803, and an armed revolt against slavery in 1808. Part of the global cycles of struggle at the time, these rebellions saw locally based sailors, servants, and slaves reject limited reforms and raise deeper questions about how best to realize their rights and the role of the colonial state in their struggle for freedom.

With as much as 40 percent of sailors in the British Navy impressed at this time,[80] and sailors suffering from various deprivations and unfreedoms, many were deeply disaffected. In 1797, sailors at Simon's Bay mutinied, hoisting the red flag, as part of the empire-wide naval mutiny started at Spithead in Britain in April that year.[81] Instead of killing their commanding officers or deserting, the sailors at Simon's Bay forced Admiral Pringle to negotiate and implement improvements.

VOC crews had sometimes used mutiny to strike, but not in Cape waters, where the execution of officers and piratical ship seizures were characteristic of major shipboard revolts. Thus the 1797 Simon's Bay mutiny marked a distinct departure from previous modes of maritime protest in the region. The deeply democratic and egalitarian nature of sailors' political action, including the mutinies of 1797, have been detailed elsewhere.[82] In the Cape, sailors were able to use their military advantage to force the admiral to improve their working conditions. It seems that many sailors accepted notions that rights resided in British custom and law, and articulated their demands within this framework.

The sailors returned to duty on 12 October, and initially, it appeared that their protest was successful. However, their struggles were far from over, and by November, developments undermined their faith in British fair play. Central to sailors' demands were complaints about officers' brutality: a controversial Captain Stephens drew especial ire. Admiral Pringle insisted that Stephens be tried properly by the court. However, Stephens's court-martial, held on 6 November on board the *HMS Sceptre* in Table Bay, did little to address sailors' concerns. Rather, it was used to reclaim the authority of the officers and the admiral. The sailors shifted from a rhetoric centered on the claims of "free-born Englishmen" used during the initial mutiny to, at the trial, insisting that their rights were not subordinate to naval customs but to law and rights. For instance, in the charges brought against Stephens, sailors noted that "the Ships Company does not appeal to Customs as it has been custom perhaps before the Existence of the British Navy for people in low situations to be opprest [*sic*] by those in power therefore the purpose of all laws has generally been to protect the weaker members of society."[83] The sailors argued for the rule of law over custom yet also did not really trust the courts as a basis for popular redress. Their behavior at the trial was such that on 7 November, the second day of the trial, the court held two sailors in contempt. This led to the second mutiny in Table Bay. This time, the sailors did not have the military advantage, and the mutiny was brutally crushed.

The sailors' action needs to be understood in the context of revolutionary ideas about rights, which were being reframed by the writings of radicals such as Thomas Paine, and the stirring calls and declarations of the Atlantic Revolutions. Sailors questioned the limited view that rights resided in British tradition and law, as they, too, were part of a popular and political milieu where rights were claimed as intrinsic—derived from reason, God, or nature rather than custom or the state. In other words, despite popular interest in exploiting the space opened by British rule and British reforms, serious questions were being raised about the benefits and possibilities of reformist strategies. The Cape's new British rulers were certainly able to win the allegiance of the elite, but the popular classes proved much more difficult to contain.

The "Servants' Rebellion" took place only two years after the 1797 mutinies. Historians usually consider the "Servants' Rebellion" to be part of the Third Frontier War / Xhosa War. This formulation forces the Servants Rebellion into a nationalist narrative that privileges the struggles between Xhosa and the British imperial power. Radical popular response to both class and national oppression are obscured, and so are the laborers of Khoesan ancestry who, together with other deserters, attempted to resist colonial dispossession and proletarianization through a longer tradition of action based on armed raids and establishing independent maroon-type communities.

The rebellion started when servants living on the eastern colonial borderlands deserted en masse to join fugitive bands on the eastern colonial borderlands, which raided colonial homesteads.[84] As noted, such raids were not new, and large raids that had taken place before that were openly political and aimed to challenge colonial authority. In one instance, in 1772, a rumor circulated that the (free-burgher controlled) *commando* in the Roggeveld planned to kill all the Khoesan in independent *kraals*. Numerous servants deserted their free-burgher masters when they heard the news, forming a band of about seventy men, women, and children. The band was captured and transported to Cape Town for trial.

The travel writer and scientist Karl Peter Thunberg, who witnessed the very same prisoners in Cape Town, believed that the incident was part of a broader rejection of colonialism expansion. He wrote: "They [the prisoners] did not deny their crimes, but asserted that they acted so in their own defence, the Europeans making every year fresh encroachments upon their lands and possessions, and forcing them continually farther up the country, whence they were driven back again by other Hottentots or else killed."[85] Nevertheless, there is no doubt that the recent defeat of the VOC by the British empire helped precipitate the massive upsurge of 1799–1803. These runaways not only contested colonial dispossession and class exploitation, as done in the past, but also presented these as intimately linked. Barrow, for example, met Klaas Stuurman, one of the "captains" of the rebels, who, "without interruption, began a long oration, which contained a history of their [Khoesan] calamities and sufferings under the yoke of the Boers; their injustice, in first depriving them of their country, and then forcing their offspring into a state of slavery, their cruel treatment on every slight occasion, which it became impossible for them to bear any longer."[86] Like the sailors in the 1797 mutinies, these servants rejected the violent and inegalitarian social order to which they were subjected. They, too, questioned reformist approaches, but much more stridently, rejecting their servile class status by seeking to reclaim lands and access to resources and become their own masters.

Relationships between groups that were predominately Khoesan, and Xhosa chieftaincies that occupied territory to the east of the Cape colony, varied across space and time. However, Jeff Peires argues, as the colony expanded to the east and Xhosa chieftaincies consolidated westward of the Kei River, Khoe and San disintegrated between the two.[87] There were instances in which Xhosa chieftaincies fought against Khoi groups, especially those who "defied them or refused them tribute" and, at times, Xhosa could be "exceptionally brutal" toward the San.[88] Those Khoi or San polities that were defeated by Xhosa chieftaincies were forcefully incorporated, such as the mighty Inqua Khoi in the 1700s and the group led by the Khoi "chieftainess" Hoho after 1750.[89]

However, there were also cases of cooperation, alliances, and overlap between Khoesan and Xhosa polities. Peires notes that there were instances in which Xhosa would join San bands, while the Gqunukhwebe, a Xhosa chieftaincy that occupied the area between the Sundays River and the Fish River from the 1780s, was largely Khoi in composition and attracted slaves and laborers of Khoesan ancestry from the colony.[90] Indeed, in the case of the Servant's Rebellion, rebels allied with the Xhosa chief Chungwa in 1799 when the British military attempted to force the Gqunukhwebe clan east across the Fish River.[91]

Unlike in the past, the rebel bands now united as a confederacy. By September 1799, a conservative estimate of the confederacy's size gave it as 700 men with 300 horses and 150 guns.[92] Rebel forces grew, as they raided outlying farms for arms, ammunition, and horses, and took control of the southeastern portion of the Graaff-Reinet district. In so doing, they succeeded not only in halting the latest land enclosures but also managed to push the colonial border back.

Fearing that a military campaign against the rebels would not succeed, the colony's British rulers sought, rather, to undermine the rebellion by destabilizing the alliance between rebel servants and Xhosa in the area and by co-opting rebel captains with promise of land. Further, believing that the main impetus for the revolt was the cruel treatment of servants by "Boer" masters, state authorities stepped up attempts to reform and mediate class antagonisms.[93] This involved efforts at state regulation of labor relations and the promise of basic legal protections against arbitrary violence and mistreatment. For instance, in 1801 the fiscal urged that contracts with Khoesan servants be formally registered with the court, something quite unprecedented. While this would bind these servants to masters, preventing them from deserting by enabling legal sanctions, it was also meant to stop farmers from beating their servants "*ad libitum*."[94]

Despite these efforts, the British rulers were unable to quell the rebellion. It was only after the Cape was ceded back to the Batavians in 1803 that the rebellion dissipated. Colonial farmers were encouraged to return to the lost areas, and the new district of Uitenhage was established in the Zuurveld.

Those involved in the "Servants' Rebellion" sought to end their exploitation and ill-treatment at the hands of their masters by fighting against colonial encroachment. Their struggle can be contrasted to the clear and systematic process of state and nation formation of the "Griqua" on the northern reaches of the colony. Rather, the servant rebels rejected reformism, showing that broad class-based action was necessary to address the devastating, and proletarianizing, effects of colonialism.

The "Servants' Rebellion" did not give rise to a permanent community, even a class-based one, and it is not yet clear as to what happened to these rebels once the rebellion dissipated. However, the British colonial government did pass the "Hottentot Code" in 1809 to further regulate relations between masters and servants on the colonial borderland. As noted by Dooling, the colonial government enacted measures to prevent violence and the abuse of laborers of Khoesan ancestry.[95] These laborers had the right to complain to local authorities if their wages were withheld, and masters were not allowed to extend labor contracts to recover debts and were compelled to provide laborers with adequate food, clothing, and shelter. Masters could also be fined or prosecuted by local authorities if found guilty of mistreating their servants. However, such protection came at a cost. The 1809 Code bound laborers to their masters: those without a "fixed place of abode" or who could not produce a pass were classified as "vagrants."[96]

Within five years of the "Servants' Rebellion," the colony was rocked by the largest rebellion against slavery in its history. The 1808 revolt was unprecedented in scale and scope, and it was not confined to slaves, as it drew in other sections of the popular classes.[97] It took place against the backdrop of the British empire's moves toward gradual abolition, starting with the end of the slave trade. However, rebels demanded more than the mere amelioration of bondage and developed their own vision of immediate and complete abolition from below. In the words of one of the rebel leaders, Abraham of the Cape, they were prepared to "hoist the bloody flag and fight themselves free."[98]

The Abolition Act came into full effect at the Cape on 1 January 1808, prohibiting the British trade of slaves to foreigners and to newly conquered territories and signaled a major victory for abolitionism. The system of slavery was under visible attack: it's weakening inspired radical opponents of slavery with the view that freedom was possible and potentially imminent. Slaves, sailors, soldiers, *sans-culottes*, servants, and colonial subjects in various parts of the world, including the Cape, had shaken the world with recent risings. There were those in the Cape who felt that, with the abolition of the slave trade, the time had come to do so again.

It was in this context that the previously mentioned Louis from Mauritius, who worked in a Cape Town tavern, conspired there with deserted Irish sailors and other slaves in the countryside to incite a slave revolt. The plan was to travel to farms in the interior, mobilize slaves to revolt and "make fast all the farmers, to take away all their arms and ammunition, and to bring them as prisoners to Cape Town with their wagons and horses."[99] Once the armed rebels reached Cape Town, they were to seize the first battery and dispatch a "letter" to the governor demanding he grant slaves their freedom.[100] If he refused, the rebel forces would "fight themselves free," break open the prison and release the prisoners, and take possession of the military's magazines.[101]

The revolt started on the morning of 27 October on Vogelgezang Farm, owned by a Petrus Gerhardus Louw. The details of the revolt fall outside this chapter, but it was well organized and remarkably nonviolent—not a single human life was lost. By the time the governor dispatched the infantry and cavalry to crush the revolt late that evening, thirty-four farms had risen and a large party of rebels were on the move toward Salt River at Cape Town. The military halted the procession and captured approximately three hundred rebels. Only fifty rebels—mostly slaves but also sailors and a couple of laborers of Khoesan ancestry—were arrested and tried.[102]

Given that slavery was under attack internationally, it is not surprising that slave owners testifying at the trial were quick to stress that "they themselves gave no cause whatsoever for the revolt" and insisted that not one of the slaves on trial had complained about ill treatment.[103] Such claims were questionable but, in any case, missed the point that the 1808 rebels wanted abolition, not amelioration. Nevertheless, the very fact that the issue of the treatment of slaves was so central to the proceedings highlights some of the major shifts that were taking place related to the reorganization of labor relations. British authorities claimed to protect masters as well as slaves. This meant that slave owners' authority was no longer absolute but confined by moral norms: the fair treatment of slaves and their right to voice protest.

Governor Lord Caledon sought to find a balance between the standing VOC legislation and the court, which proposed harsh sentences, and the political concerns of the War and Colonial Offices.[104] As a result, only five of the ringleaders were sentenced to be hanged, although their corpses were still condemned to rot in the open. Other rebels received lesser sentences, including banishment, sentences of hard labor for fifteen years or more, confinement to chains for up to five years, and whippings. Compared to the past VOC rule, and given the scale of the revolt, these sentences were—for the time—remarkably lenient.

With the defeat of the servant rebels in 1803, and then the antislavery rebels in 1808, more radical challenges to the existing order, including its labor systems, were briefly silenced. Negotiations between employees, masters, and the state now centered on the appropriate means to discipline and treat unfree workers, as opposed to their emancipation. Legislation in the 1820s regulated, for example, slaves' hours worked, food, and clothing, and in 1826, the court appointed a Guardian of Slaves to ensure that these regulations were implemented.[105]

Hopes for freedom in the Cape were renewed with Lord Somerset's proclamation that aimed to uplift and promote the conversion of slaves to Christianity, and 1825 saw a slave known as Galant lead a small rebellion.[106] Galant's prosecutor noted that his uprising reflected "the fire of discontent at the frustrated hope of general freedom."[107]

Conclusion: Facing Empire

In 1814, the Cape was officially ceded to the British empire. The British empire was not the first imperial power that colonized the Cape of Good Hope. Nevertheless, British rule proved significant, ushering in a substantially new form of colonialism centered on a modern and efficient state. With the formation of new nationalities, such as the Griqua in the north, the Boers in the interior, and, beyond the colony, groups like the Zulu, the temptation is to focus on the British empire's external relations with these new polities and expansion.

However, this chapter draws attention to the impact that British rule had on class formation and labor reform *within* the Cape from 1795 to 1814. Focusing on laborers with Indigenous Khoesan ancestry, this chapter has examined the ways in which the Cape's motley popular classes, long drawn into the global political economy of empire, responded to their new rulers and modified their identities and modes of protest that would inform the region's modern proletariat. Despite some segmentation along national lines, an inclusive multiracial popular culture persisted. Even though some laborers and poor strove for respectability and political moderation, now made possible by changing legislation and ruling class attitudes, others continued to raise a serious revolutionary challenge to both colonial occupation and class exploitation.

These two contending approaches—reformist and revolutionary—would become deeply entrenched in the modern proletariat that developed in the nineteenth century, as would divides based on national and ethnic identities. Changes in the state led to important changes in popular politics, but popular struggles, in turn, played a key role in changing the state.

The Age of Revolution left a notable imprint, and both the uneven popular victories of the Age, alongside the ultimate victory of elite visions of labor and power in the Age, were also evident at the Cape. In 1828, Ordinance 50 laid the basis for servants of Khoesan ancestry to become free laborers, and in 1838 slaves were finally emancipated. Such developments were not simply granted from above but forced from below by the hard-fought, protracted battles of the Cape's laborers and poor.

Yet, as illustrated by the elaboration of an internal passport system (or pass laws) in the 1800s, the persistence of masters and servants laws in some areas, the importation of Indian indentured labor to the new British colony of Natal[108] from the 1860s, and the subsequent systems of unfree labor used in diamond and gold mining from the 1870s, unfree labor was far from dead and remained central to modern British imperialism in southern Africa.

Notes

1. Clare Anderson, "The Age of Revolutions in the Indian Ocean, Bay of Bengal, and South China Sea: A Maritime Perspective," *International Review of Social History* 58, no. S21 (Mutiny and Maritime Radicalism in the Age of Revolution: A Global Survey) (2013): 230.

2. Anderson, "The Age of Revolutions in the Indian Ocean, Bay of Bengal, and South China Sea," 230.

3. See, for instance, Kerry Ward, *Networks of Empire: Forced Migration in the Dutch East India Company* (Cambridge: Cambridge University Press, 2009).

4. For work on the transition period, see William Freund, "Society and Government in Dutch South Africa: The Cape and the Batavians, 1803–6" (PhD diss., Yale University, 1971), and "The Cape under the Transitional Governments, 1795–1814," in *The Shaping of South African Society, 1652–1840*, 2nd ed., ed. Richard Elphick and Herman Giliomee (Cape Town: Maskew, Miller, and Longman, 1989), 324–357.

5. Christopher A. Bayly, *The Birth of the Modern World* (Malden, MA: Blackwell Publishing, 2004).

6. Wayne Dooling, "Social Identities and the Making of Private Property: The Cape and Lagos Colony Compared," in *Contingent Lives: Social Identity and Material Culture in the VOC World*, ed. Nigel Worden (Cape Town: Historical Studies Department, University of Cape Town, 2007), 266–278.

7. Richard Elphick and Herman Giliomee, "The Origins and Entrenchment of European Dominance at the Cape, 1652–c. 1840," in *The Shaping of South African*, 521–566, esp. 534.

8. For more detail on the urban economy, see Nigel Worden, Elizabeth van Heyningen, and Vivian Bickford-Smith, *Cape Town: The Making of a City: An Illustrated History* (Cape Town: David Philips, 2004).

9. The most comprehensive studies of slavery in this sector include Nigel Worden, *Slavery in Dutch South Africa* (Cambridge: Cambridge University Press, 1985), and Robert Shell, *Children of Bondage: Social History of the Slave Society at the Cape of Good Hope, 1652–1838* (Johannesburg: University of the Witwatersrand Press, 2001).

10. Low-ranking Company servants were sometimes permitted to become *pasgangers*, which meant that they were allowed to pay others to take over their usual duties, while they earned extra money by engaging in a wide range of activities ranging from wig-making to carpentry. Many were employed to teach free-burghers' children or serve as *knechten* (supervisors/overseers).

11. See Leonard Guelke, "Freehold Farmers and Frontier Settlers, 1657–1780," in *The Shaping of South African Society*, 66–108.

12. James Armstrong and Nigel Worden, "The Slaves, 1652–1834," in *The Shaping of South African*, 109–183, see esp. 112–120, and Worden, *Slavery in Dutch South Africa*, 31.

13. Armstrong and Worden, "The Slaves," 123, and Worden, *Slavery in Dutch South Africa*, 11.

14. Worden, van Heyningen, and Bickford-Smith, *Cape Town*, 49.

15. Worden, *Slavery in Dutch South Africa*, 11.

16. June Bam, "Contemporary Khoisan Heritage Issues in South Africa: A Brief Historical Perspective," in *The Pre-Colonial Catalytic Project*, ed. Lungisile Ntsebeza and Chris Saunders, vol. 1 (Cape Town: Centre for African Studies, 2014), 123–136.

17. Shula Marks, "Khoisan Resistance to the Dutch in the Seventeenth and Eighteenth Centuries," *Journal of African History* 3, no. 1 (1972): 69.

18. Marks, "Khoisan Resistance," 56–57.

19. William Miller Macmillan, *Cape Coloured Question* (London: Faber and Gwyer, 1927), 26–27, quoted in Marks, "Khoisan Resistance," 56.

20. See Marks, "Khoisan Resistance," 55–80, and Richard Elphick and Vertrees C. Malherbe, "The Khoisan to 1828," in *The Shaping of South African Society*, 3–65.

21. Nicole Ulrich, "Popular Community in 18th-Century Southern Africa: Family, Fellowship, Alternative Networks, and Mutual Aid at the Cape of Good Hope, 1652–1795," *Journal of Southern African History* 40, no. 6 (2014): 1139–57.

22. For more on the status of Khoesan, see Elphick and Malherbe, "The Khoisan to 1828," and Nicole Ulrich, "Rethinking Citizenship and Subjecthood in Southern Africa: Khoesan, Labor Relations and the Colonial State in the Cape of Good Hope, c. 1652–1815," in *Citizenship, Belonging and Political Community in Africa: Dialogues between Past and Present*, ed. Emma Hunter (Athens: Ohio University Press, 2016), 43–73.

23. See Elphick and Malherbe, "The Khoisan to 1828," 3–65.

24. Otto Friedrich Mentzel, *Geographical and Topographical Description of the Cape of Good Hope*, trans. and ed. G. V. Marias and J. Hoge (Cape Town: Van Riebeeck Society, 1944), 2:300.

25. Hans Heese, *Reg en Onreg: Kaapse Regspraak in die Agtiende Eeu*, C-Reeks: Narvorsingspublikasies, No. 6 (Bellville: Insituut vir Historiese Narvorsing, Universiteit van Wes-Kaapland, 1994), Western Cape Provincial Archive, Cape Town (WCPA), Criminal Justice (CJ) 797, 45, p. 236.

26. See, for instance, Clifton C. Crais and Pamela Scully, *Sara Baartman and the Hottentot Venus: A Ghost Story and a Biography* (Princeton, NJ: Princeton University Press, 2010), and Rachel Holmes, *The Hottentot Venus: The Life and Death of Saartjie Baartman: Born 1789–Buried 2002* (London: Bloomsbury, 2007).

27. Marks, "Khoisan Resistance," 73.

28. Nicole Ulrich, "Cape of Storms: Surveying and Rethinking Popular Resistance in the Eighteenth-Century Cape Colony," *New Contree* 73 (2015): 16–39.

29. Jonathan Israel, *The Dutch Republic: Its Rise, Greatness and Fall, 1477–1806* (Oxford: Clarendon Press, 1995), 1096.

30. Worden, van Heyningen, and Bickford-Smith, *Cape Town*, 82.

31. "Memorandum on the Condition of the Colony by Kersteins, n/d," in *Records of the Cape Colony*, ed. George McCall Theal (London: Public Records Office, 1793–1796), 1:168.

32. K. van der Tempel, "'Wij Hebben Amok in Ons Schip': Aziaten in Opstand Tijdens drie Terugreizen of het Einde van de Achttiende Eeuw," in *Muiterij: Oproeren Berechting op Schepen van de VOC*, ed. J. R. Bruijn and E. S. van Eyck van Heslinga (Haarlem: De Boer Maritiem, 1980), 123–147.

33. Worden, van Heyningen, and Bickford-Smith, *Cape Town*, 81.

34. WCPA, CJ, 796 *Sententiën*, 1790–1794, ff. 279–284, in *Trials of Slavery: Selected Documents concerning Slaves from the Criminal Records of the Council of Justice at the Cape of Good Hope, 1705–1794*, trans. and ed. Nigel Worden and Gerald Groenewald (Cape Town: Van Riebeeck Society, 2005), 614.

35. WCPA, CJ, 796 *Sententiën*, 1790–1794, ff. 279–284, in *Trials of Slavery*, 614.

36. WCPA, CJ, 796 *Sententiën*, 1790–1794, ff. 279–284, in *Trials of Slavery*, 614.

37. WCPA, CJ, 796 *Sententiën*, 1790–1794, ff. 279–284, in *Trials of Slavery*, 615.

38. Worden and Groenewald, *Trials of Slavery*, 612.

39. Marks, "Khoisan Resistance," 74.

40. Marks, "Khoisan Resistance," 73, 75.

41. "Address of Sir George Keith Elphinstone, K.B. and Major General Craig to the Governor, Council Magistrates, and Inhabitants of the Settlement and Town of the Cape of Good Hope," 24 June 1795, *Records of the Cape Colony*, 1:74–75.

42. "Address of Sir George Keith Elphinstone, K.B. and Major General Craig to the Governor, Council Magistrates, and Inhabitants of the Settlement and Town of the Cape of Good Hope," 24 June 1795, *Records of the Cape Colony*, 1:74–75.

43. Address to the Inhabitants of the Colony of the Cape of Good Hope, 9 September 1795, *Records of the Cape Colony*, 1:117–118.

44. Timothy Keegan, *Colonial South Africa and the Origins of the Racial Order* (Cape Town: David Philip, 1996), 50.

45. Keegan, *Colonial South Africa*, 50; Dooling, *Slavery, Emancipation and Colonial Rule*, 11.

46. Dooling, *Slavery, Emancipation and Colonial Rule*, 11.

47. Letter from Messrs. John Holland, John Hooke Green, and Others to Major General Dundas, 5 January 1799, *Records of the Cape Colony*, 2:333.

48. Peter Linebaugh and Marcus Rediker, *The Many-Headed Hydra: Sailors, Slaves, Commoners and the Hidden History of the Revolutionary Atlantic* (Boston: Beacon Press, 2000), 333–334.

49. Worden, van Heyningen, and Bickford-Smith, *Cape Town*, 93.

50. Shell, *Children of Bondage*, 47.

51. Robert Ross, *Cape of Torments: Slavery and Resistance in South Africa* (London: Routledge and Kegan Paul, 1983), 21–22; Nigel Worden, "Revolt in Cape Colony Slave Society," in *Resisting Bondage in Indian Ocean Africa and Asia*, ed. Edward Alpers, Gwyn Campbell, and Michael Salman (London: Routledge, 2007), 10–23; Robert Shell, *Children of Bondage*, 328–329; Worden and Groenewald, *Trails of Slavery*, 21–22.

52. Andrew Banks, *The Decline of Urban Slavery at the Cape* (Cape Town: Centre for African Studies, 1991).

53. WCPA, CJ 516, First Examination of Louis, Article 5, 21.

54. Jackie Loos, *Echoes of Slavery: Voices from South Africa's Past* (Cape Town: David Philip, 2004), 70.

55. Loos, *Echoes of Slavery*, 71.

56. J. Mason, "'Some Religion He Must Have': Slaves, Sufism and Conversion to Islam at the Cape," working paper, Southeastern Regional Seminar in African Studies, Armstrong Atlantic State University, Savannah Georgia, 1999, 6.

57. Freund, "The Cape under the Transitional Governments," 340.

58. Banks, *The Decline of Urban Slavery*, 110–119.

59. Martin Legassick, "The Northern Frontier to c. 1840: The Rise and Decline of the Griqua People," in *The Shaping of South African Society*, 382. For more on the history of the Griqua, see Martin Legassick, *The Politics of a South African Frontier: The Griqua, the South Sotho-Tswana, and the Missionaries, 1780–1840* (Klosterberg: Basler Afrika Bibliographien, 2010), and Robert Ross, *Adam Kok's Griquas: A Study in the Development of Stratification in South Africa* (Cambridge: Cambridge University Press, 1976).

60. For detailed discussions of institutional change, see William Freund, "The Cape under the Transitional Governments, 1795–1814," in *The Shaping of South African Society*, 324–357, and Martijn van den Burg, "The Age of Revolutions at the Cape of Good Hope, 1780–1830: Contradictions and Connections," *Journal of Colonialism and Colonial History* 16, no. 2 (2015): doi:10.1353/cch.2015.0022.

61. Wayne Dooling, *Slavery, Emancipation and Colonial Rule in South Africa* (Scottsville: University of KwaZulu-Natal Press, 2007), 12.

62. Dooling, *Slavery, Emancipation and Colonial Rule*, 7.

63. Iain McCalman, "Anti-Slavery and Ultra-Radicalism in Early Nineteenth-Century England: The Case of Robert Wedderburn," *Slavery and Abolition* 7 (1986): 91–92.

64. Michael Craton, James Walvin, and David Wright, *Slavery, Abolition and Emancipation* (London: Longman, 1976), 195–199.

65. See Marcus Rediker, *The Slave Ship: A Human History* (New York: Viking, 2007).

66. Craton, Walvin, and Wright, *Slavery, Abolition and Emancipation*, 232–233.

67. Worden, van Heyningen, and Bickford-Smith, *Cape Town*, 82–83.

68. Douglas Hay, "Property, Authority and the Criminal Law," in *Albion's Fatal Tree*, ed. Douglas Hay, Peter Linebaugh, E. P. Thompson, and Cal Winslow (New York: Pantheon Book, 1975), 17–63.

69. "Instructions to Our Right Trusty and Right Well Beloved Cousin and Councillor George Earl of Macartney, K.B. . . . ," 13 December 1796, *Records of the Cape Colony*, 2:3–20.

70. "Instructions to Our Right Trusty and Right Well Beloved Cousin and Councillor George Earl of Macartney, K.B. . . . ," 13 December 1796, *Records of the Cape Colony*, 2:3–20.

71. Keegan, *Colonial South Africa*, 54.

72. John Barrow, *Travels into the Interior of Southern Africa*, 2nd ed. (London: Cadell and Davies, 1806), 1:192.

73. "Boers" were previously European (especially Dutch or German) farmers and free-burghers under the VOC colonial order.

74. Barrow, *Travels into the Interior of Southern Africa*, 1:375.

75. "Letter from Earl of Caledon to Viscount Castlereagh," Castle of Good Hope, 1 July 1808, *Records of the Cape Colony*, 6:367–370, 369.

76. "Letter from Earl of Caledon to Viscount Castlereagh," Castle of Good Hope, 1 July 1808, *Records of the Cape Colony*, 6:367–370, 369.

77. "Letter from Viscount Castlereagh to Earl of Caledon," Downing Street, 5 February 1808, *Records of the Cape Colony*, 6:281; Letter from Earl of Caledon to

Viscount Castlereagh, Castle of Good Hope, 1 July 1808, *Records of the Cape Colony*, 6:367–370; "Letter from Lord Castlereagh to the Earl of Caledon," Downing Street, 12 May 1809, *Records of the Cape Colony*, 6:496–501.

78. Wayne Dooling, "The Good Opinion of Others: Law, Slavery and Community," in *Breaking the Chains: Slavery and Its Legacy in the Nineteenth-Century Cape Colony*, ed. Nigel Worden and Clifton Crais (Johannesburg: Witwatersrand University Press, 1994), 29.

79. See, for instance, Legassick, *The Politics of a South African Frontier*, 75–78.

80. Chris Magra, "Anti-Impressment Riots and the Age of Revolution," in "Mutiny and Maritime Radicalism in the Age of Revolution," ed. Anderson et al., special issue, *International Review of Social History* 58, no. 21 (2013): 134.

81. This summary is based on Nicole Ulrich, "International Radicalism, Local Solidarities: The 1797 British Naval Mutinies in Southern African Waters," in "Mutiny and Maritime Radicalism in the Age of Revolution," ed. Anderson et al., special issue, *International Review of Social History* 58, no. 21 (2013): 61–85.

82. For the egalitarian traditions of sailors, see Marcus Rediker, *Between the Devil and the Deep Blue Sea: Merchant Seamen, Pirates and the Anglo-American Maritime World, 1700–1750* (Cambridge: Cambridge University Press, 1987), and for self-organization at Spithead and Nore, see J. P. Moore, "'The Greatest Enormity That Prevails': Direct Democracy and Workers' Self-Management in the British Naval Mutinies of 1797," in *Jack Tar in History: Essays in the History of Maritime Life and Labour*, ed. Colin Howell and Richard Twomey (Fredericton: Acadiensis, 1991), 76–104.

83. National Archive (NA), United Kingdom (UK): Admiralty Records (ADM) 1/5488, Court-martial of Captain George Hopewele Stephens, Charges, 7–8.

84. For a fuller account of the Servants' Rebellion, see Susan Newton King and Vertrees C. Malherbe, ed., *The Khoikhoi Rebellion in the Eastern Cape, 1797–1803* (Cape Town: Centre for African Studies, University of Cape Town, 1981).

85. Carl Peter Thunberg, *Travels at the Cape of Good Hope, 1772–1775*, ed. V. S. Forbes and trans. J and I. Runder (Cape Town: Van Riebeeck Society, 1986), 47.

86. Newtown-King, "Part I: The Rebellion of the Khoi," in *The Khoikhoi Rebellion in the Eastern Cape, 1797–1803*, 15.

87. Jeff B. Peires, *The House of Phalo: A History of the Xhosa People in the Days of Their Independence* (Berkley: University of California Press, 1982), 22.

88. Peires, *The House of Phalo*, 22, 24.

89. Peires, *The House of Phalo*, 22–23.

90. Peires, *The House of Phalo*, 24, 56.

91. Peires, *The House of Phalo*, 57.

92. Newtown-King, "Part I: The Rebellion of the Khoi," 25.

93. Newtown-King, "Part I: The Rebellion of the Khoi," 28–29.

94. Dooling, *Slavery, Emancipation and Colonial Rule*, 66.

95. Dooling, *Slavery, Emancipation and Colonial Rule*, 62–65.

96. Dooling, *Slavery, Emancipation and Colonial Rule*, 63.

97. For a full account of the rebellion, see Nicole Ulrich, "Abolition from Below: The 1808 Revolt in the Cape Colony," in *Humanitarian Intervention and Changing*

Labour Relations: The Long-Term Consequences of the Abolition of the Slave Trade, ed. Marcel van der Linden (Leiden: Brill, 2011), 193–222.

98. WCPA, CJ 802, *Sententiën*, 759.

99. WCPA, CJ 516, First Examination of Hooper, Article 10, p. 67.

100. WCPA, CJ 516, First Examination of Louis, Article 69, p. 37; First Examination of Abraham, Article 71, p. 168.

101. WCPA, CJ 516, First Examination of Louis, Article 69, p. 37.

102. WCPA, CJ 802, 725–30. The court also investigated a *free-burgher*, Pieter Theron, suspected for participating in the revolt. He was able to provide a number of alibis, and the case against him was dropped.

103. WCPA, CO 11, Letter from G. A. Miller et al. to Caledon, 3 December 1808.

104. WCPA, CJ 90 and (Government House) GH, 34/3, Letter from Caledon to Court of Justice, 29 December 1808.

105. Armstrong and Worden, "The Slaves," 109–183, see esp. 165.

106. John E. Mason, *Social Death and Resurrection: Slavery and Emancipation in South Africa* (Charlottesville: University of Virginia Press, 2003), 66, 46.

107. Quoted in Mason, *Social Death and Resurrection*, 66.

108. Adjacent to the Eastern Cape, formed in 1843 after the annexation of a short-lived Boer republic established in 1839.

CHAPTER EIGHT

Christianity, Commerce, and the Remaking of the Māori World

TONY BALLANTYNE

Although the Age of Revolution is often seen as the crucible of a modern secular order, it actually energized a series of debates that helped secure "religion" as a global category that stood at the center of both cultural practice and political contestation.[1] It was within the later stages of the revolutionary age that the evangelical revival, which had kindled on both sides of the Atlantic in the 1730s and 1740s, became a powerful engine for the globalization of Christianity. New voluntary associations gave shape to a powerful surge in religious enthusiasm and political energy, propelling a wave of missionary work that carried the gospel and the culture of Protestantism to distant imperial frontiers, especially in Asia and the Pacific.

This chapter uses the establishment of the Church Missionary Society (CMS) mission to New Zealand in 1814 to explore the opening up of the Pacific as a key global frontier for evangelization and to map some of the connections between religion, economics, and politics within an acquisitive imperial age. My central aim here is to return to a key concern of the old imperial history tradition: "How and why did the empire expand?" Although Britain did not formally assert its sovereignty over New Zealand until 1840, imperial networks and processes of various kinds effectively incorporated significant parts of those islands into the empire in the early nineteenth century. One key engine of incorporation was missionary work, and I am particularly interested in why and how the CMS mission was established.

This chapter suggests that the genesis of the mission lay in the convergence between the interests of Samuel Marsden, the colonial chaplain of New South Wales, and the interests of an influential cohort of rangatira (chiefs) from the Bay of Islands in the northeast of Te Ika a Māui (New Zealand's North Island). Marsden and the rangatira shared a commitment to the benefits that might flow from the "improvement" that the mission promised, especially the extension of agriculture and the growth of trade. But as the chapter demonstrates, although Marsden and key Māori leaders might have had some important common interests, they were drawn to the idea of "improvement" as a result of very different cultural aspirations and with very different ends in mind.

The relationships and common interests that underpinned the establishment of the mission profoundly and irrevocably entangled te ao Māori (the Māori world) with the British empire. As an analytical metaphor, "entanglement" builds upon my earlier work, which has shown how the modern British empire was a dynamic web-like formation, a shifting and complex assemblage of connections that linked the metropole and its colonies, ran directly between colonies, and incorporated informal frontiers of imperial activity into an integrated, if lumpy and uneven, system.[2] Recently, I have argued that "entanglement" offers a more powerful analytical lens than does "meetings" or "encounters" in understanding the operation of empire in the Pacific.[3] This approach has drawn inspiration from African scholarship on colonialism and its abiding consequences. Carolyn Hamilton's study of Shaka Zulu stressed the heuristic power of "entanglement" in explicating the colonial order. Hamilton argued that rather than understanding colonial institutions and practices as straightforward transplantations and impositions of European norms, colonial forms were actually produced out of the "complex historical entanglement of indigenous and colonial concepts."[4] Lynn M. Thomas has extended Hamilton's arguments about the entangled nature of African colonial societies to stress the ongoing uneven interplay between "local and imperial" aspirations and processes in colonial spaces.[5]

Sarah Nuttall has more recently suggested that the analysis of "entanglement" should stand at the center of work on colonialism and postcolonial societies. "Entanglement is a condition of being twisted together or entwined, involved with; it speaks of an intimacy gained, even if it was resisted, or ignored or uninvited. It is a term which may gesture towards a relationship or set of social relationships that is complicated, ensnaring, in a tangle."[6] My interest here is in both how divergent societies become entangled and how entanglements develop between different domains of human activity (e.g., the concepts and practices that we typically donate as discreet: "religion," "economics," and "politics"). In the first part of this chapter, my focus is on Samuel Marsden and the development of his plan for a CMS mission to New Zealand, a scheme that I read against the backdrop of the Pacific's incorporation into

British commercial and imperial networks as well as Marsden's understanding of the power of "improvement." The middle part approaches the genesis of the mission through the lens of Māori kinship politics and the importance of trade, agriculture, and warfare in te ao Māori. It concludes by returning to the metaphor of "entanglement" and the ways in which it can enrich our understandings of the genesis, pattern, and legacies of modern imperial orders.

It is possible to narrate the genesis of the CMS mission to New Zealand in 1814 as essentially a story about the interconnectedness between trade, empire, and evangelization, driven by the global impact of the evangelical revival and expanding British commercial and territorial interests in the Pacific. The mission was formally established in December 1814, with the creation of the first missionary settlement at Hohi, in the Bay of Islands, in the northeast of Te Ika a Māui. Further stations were established at Kerikeri (1819), Paihia (1823), and Waimate (1830) as the incoming missionaries built relationships with influential rangatira (chiefs) and attempted to negotiate a path through a complex and dynamic local political terrain.

The development of the mission has often been framed as a story of encounters, and while some scholars have recently emphasized the importance of connections across the Tasman Sea to colonial New South Wales in the development of the mission, the tendency generally has been to read these engagements within a national frame, interpreting them as foundational to New Zealand's "race relations" or as central to the development of "two worlds," Māori and Pākehā.[7] What generally has been occluded in such framings is the question of empire and ways in which Indigenous social change was woven into imperial networks and global forces, albeit unevenly in time and space. And, equally fundamentally, what is erased within both national narratives and scholarship within the church history tradition is the extent to which the whole enterprise of evangelization was deeply embedded in the history and language of empire.[8]

As a result of Cook's three voyages from 1768, the Pacific was framed as a space that not only could be profitably woven into British commerce but where also the civilizing and religious uplift of English influence could remake native societies. The Pacific's potential as a sphere for evangelization was recognized by William Carey, the Northampton Baptist who was influential in fashioning the theological underpinnings of the new wave of British Protestant activity in Asia and the Pacific from the 1790s. Carey was convinced of the "obligation" of British Christians to actively bring the gospel to the world by his own imaginative encounter with the Pacific: "reading Cook's voyages was the first thing that engaged my mind to think of missions."[9]

Carey was a key catalyst in the establishment of the Missionary Society, which brought together Anglicans and nonconformists committed to the evangelization of non-Christians. It sponsored the first British mission to the Pacific, dispatching the missionary vessel the *Duff* in 1796.[10] This experiment with missionary work in Tahiti, Tonga, and the Marquesas was fraught with misunderstanding, scandal, and conflict, effectively disintegrating within a decade.[11] If Carey was a key spur to the evangelization of Pacific societies, it was Samuel Marsden, the assistant chaplain to the colony of New South Wales, who drove forward the rekindling and extension of the London Missionary Society's evangelization of the Pacific and who was the influential sponsor of the CMS's mission in New Zealand.

Raised in Yorkshire in a family with strong Methodist connections, Marsden was a key agent of the "Anglican providentialism" that C. A. Bayly argued was at the heart of the British empire emerging out of the revolutionary age.[12] Within New South Wales, where he rose to the position of principal chaplain in 1800, Marsden was a powerful champion of economic improvement and the reforming moral force of evangelicalism. His influence was not confined to the spiritual realm as he became a significant functionary in the colonial state, serving as both a magistrate and superintendent of government affairs. Marsden saw New South Wales as a key center from which British economic and religious influence might be exercised. While he became deeply skeptical of the capacity of Australian Indigenous communities—"I am convinced we cannot do more for them than to give them a Loaf of Bread when hungry and a Blanket when cold"—he was optimistic about the ability of Polynesians, especially Māori, to embrace both improvement and Christianity.[13]

In 1808, Marsden wrote to the CMS proposing the foundation of a mission to New Zealand. He suggested the creation of a small mission, initially made up of three "Mechanics": "a Carpenter. Another a Smith and a third a Twine Spinner." These lay missionaries would bring practical crafts and knowledge to Māori—producing edged iron tools, introducing new boat-making skills, and assisting with the manufacture of European twine and fishing-nets—while teaching them the rudiments of Christian belief and practice.[14] Marsden believed that the missionary settlement would be effective, as these "trades would apply to their immediate wants, and tend to conciliate their minds and gain their Confidence."[15]

Thus Marsden's plan was based on the "improvement" of Māori through the introduction of the "Civilized Arts." In his April 1808 proposal to the CMS, Marsden suggested:

> The attention of the Heathens, can only be gained and their vagrant Habits corrected, by the Arts. Till their attention be gained and the moral and industrious habits are induced, little or no progress can be made in teaching them the Gospel. I do not mean that a native should learn to build a Hut or make an Axe before he should be told any thing of Man's Fall and Redemption, but that these grand Subjects should be introduced at every favorable opportunity while the Natives are learning any of the simple Arts.—To preach the Gospel without the aid of the Arts will never succeed amongst the Heathens for any time.[16]

Three years later, he reiterated this vision:

> My friend one of the chiefs who has lived with me and acquired a knowledge of agriculture will introduce cultivation among his countrymen. This will add greatly to their civilization and comfort and prepare the way for greater blessings. I may be too fond perhaps of the garden, the field and the fleece. These would be the first object of my attention was I placed among a savage nation. The man who introduced the potato into Ireland and England merited more from those nations than any General who may have slain thousands of their enemies.[17]

Marsden appreciated that his stress on the primacy of "civilized arts" was contentious and that his critics felt that he prioritized "the garden, field and fleece" ahead of the gospel itself.

Marsden's theory of evangelization was molded by two immediate contexts. First, it was shaped by the failure of early experiments to convert Australian Aboriginal communities to Christianity and to interest them in the routines and material culture of "Civilization."[18] Marsden later explained this to Lachlan Macquarie, governor of New South Wales, suggesting that Aboriginal disinterest in new technologies and trade meant that evangelizing them was destined to fail as "[c]ommerce promotes industry—industry civilization and civilization opens up the way for the Gospel."[19] Second, Marsden's blueprint for the New Zealand mission was a response to the spectacular unraveling of the CMS's first attempts at evangelizing in Oceania. While the missionaries sent to Tahiti, Tongatapu, and the Marquesas on the *Duff* were "mechanics"—lay missionaries who were skilled in the trades—

like those Marsden intended to send to New Zealand, the CMS's strategy emphasized evangelization over civilization.[20] The collapse of this initial experiment in evangelizing the Pacific convinced some influential evangelicals that the cultivation of "Civilization"—through agriculture, commerce, and practical education—should precede coordinated efforts to convert "native peoples" to Christianity, a position strongly supported by J. F. Cover, who served on Tahiti, and William Henry, who evangelized on Tahiti, Huahine, and Moorea.[21]

The emphasis on "Civilization" in Marsden's plan for New Zealand reflected his own conviction in the universal "improving" power of agriculture, commerce, and hard work, whether these were deployed in his native Yorkshire, in colonial New South Wales, in the islands of Oceania, or on the fledgling mission stations of New Zealand.[22] But for the translation of this plan into reality on the ground in New Zealand, Marsden was dependent on the economic networks and political institutions that Britain had established in Australia and the Pacific. From its foundation in December 1814, the CMS mission in northern New Zealand was embedded in the webs of empire, even though New Zealand was not formally incorporated into the empire in 1840.

The mission was dependent on British imperial capital and commercial networks. Key here was Robert Campbell, from Calcutta's Campbell, Clarke and Co., who quickly became New South Wales's most influential merchant after his arrival in the colony in 1798. A close associate of Marsden's, Campbell became the key moneyman for the reinvigorated efforts of the London Missionary Society's activities in the Pacific, functioning as its Pacific agent from 1807.[23] Campbell subsequently fulfilled a similar function for the CMS's New Zealand settlements, supplying goods for the operation of the mission and for the private consumption of missionaries, mission workers, and their families.[24]

The commercial connections created by men like Campbell were not only essential to the function of missionary settlements but also simultaneously developed other initiatives that accelerated New Zealand's entanglement in the commercial networks of empire. Campbell was an important catalyst behind the expansion of the extractive industries that lacked the resources of New Zealand's coastlines—especially timber and seals—to British imperial commodity flows and markets.[25] Marsden's relationship with Campbell reinforced his belief that the Pacific was an important domain for the exercise of British moral and commercial influence.[26] And Marsden was convinced that even though it was not yet a formal colony, New Zealand occupied a key position within the region, as he explained to Josiah Pratt of the CMS: "New Zealand must be always considered as the great emporium of the South Seas, from its local situation, its safe harbors, its navigable rivers, its fine timber for ship-building, its rosin, its native flax."[27]

Marsden's imagined future of the Pacific was underpinned by an understanding that the interests of true religion and the British empire were aligned. This reflected his conviction that state power and religious authority should be mutually reinforcing: the "Throne and the Altar generally fall together."[28] Marsden deployed Britain's imperial interests as a foundation of his case for evangelizing Māori. When Marsden first proposed founding a New Zealand mission to the CMS in 1808, he stressed New Zealand's commercial and strategic value because of its proximity to both New South Wales and Norfolk Island.[29] Marsden routinely suggested that exploiting New Zealand's strategic position and commercial potential was in Britain's interest when he sought support for missionary work in those islands. In 1820, for example, Marsden stressed to the CMS that the spars that could be manufactured from New Zealand timber meant that "New Zealand will be of great national importance." He suggested that missionary settlements at Hohi and Kerikeri allowed Britain to "derive all the advantages they may wish for from New Zealand without the expenses of forming a colony."[30] Later in the same year, Marsden anticipated the arrival of the HMS *Coromandel* and HMS *Dromedary* to collect timber. He suggested that "[t]here would have been difficulties in the way of the ships getting their cargo if the Mission had not paved the way for them. I think these ships will lay the foundation of a permanent intercourse between the British Government and these islands."[31]

In keeping with the deep moral sensibility of evangelicalism, Marsden was a critic of irreligious aspects of British society, frequently challenging the violence and "immorality" of British sailors in the Pacific as well as imposing a harsh culture of discipline on the convicts of New South Wales. But as the preceding discussion has suggested, he was a strong supporter of the British state and the possibilities of a moral imperial order underpinned by agriculture, markets, and Christianity. Unlike a later generation of CMS missionaries in New Zealand and key figures in the society in Britain, who were deeply critical of what they saw as the excesses of empire and the particular dangers of large-scale colonization, Marsden rarely offered any general critique of colonialism or its pernicious impact on Indigenous communities.[32] In the first two decades of the New Zealand mission, Marsden consistently framed its development within an idiom of empire: he described the missionaries and their associated workers as "settlers," discussed the New Zealand "missionary settlement," and on occasion used the term "colony" to describe the missionary enterprise. Both London-based CMS administrators and the New Zealand–based mission workers echoed this language.[33]

Marsden's embrace of empire was even more explicit in 1817, when he endorsed a plan to create a "small colony at New Zealand." This plan was developed by the Reverend Andrew Cheap and supported by the reverends Robert Cartwright and John Youl. In their view, the creation of a colony grounded in British industriousness and moral seriousness would complement the evangelizing work of the fledgling CMS establishments. "To introduce the arts of civilization at New Zealand by the establishment of a small colony is a very desirable object, and we think that there would be little difficulty in doing this as far as the New Zealanders would be concerned, since they are so anxious for Europeans to reside amongst them." This new colony, they argued, presented the CMS with a valuable commercial opportunity. Cheap suggested that a vessel would be based at the new colony and identified the ideal as the *Active*, the ship Marsden purchased to supply the Pacific and New Zealand missions. The *Active* would source the valued commodities—timber and flax as well as whale oil—that were harvested from the New Zealand frontier for imperial markets, allowing the CMS to offset the costs of running its New Zealand stations. Most importantly, they suggested that such a colony would be sponsored and overseen by "real friends of religion," and as such, neither the future of the existing mission or the Māori themselves would be jeopardized.[34]

This plan never came to fruition, but its framing anticipated some of the recurrent concerns in the heated debates over New Zealand's suitability for colonization in the 1830s. Moreover, it provides further clear evidence that Marsden's vision of New Zealand was articulated in a context that regularly stressed the potential value of those islands to the British, and that Marsden understood that the growth and success of the mission was dependent on the empire. This position was openly rejected by the majority of CMS missionaries working on the New Zealand frontier in the early and mid-1830s, many of whom were fiercely opposed to New Zealand's formal incorporation into the empire and plans for the "systematic colonization" of the islands espoused by the New Zealand Company.[35]

More broadly, this discussion underlines the centrality of both Christianity and commerce in shaping understandings of the place of the island Pacific and New Zealand, in particular, within the new imperial formations that emerged out of this new global imperial age. It is important to underline that the military-fiscal state, which two generations of scholarship have identified as propelling the transformation of the United Kingdom as well as in Britain's colonial holdings in North America and Asia, did not develop on this important new imperial frontier.[36] The foregoing discussion also suggests that the Pacific and Australasia—key regions of the new "second" British empire—diverged significantly from the military-fiscal model.[37] In the early Australian colonies, substantial powers were invested in the governors and a coercive state apparatus underwrote the functioning of a penal system that did not promote either the kind of agrarian or commercial development that could support a military-fiscal state.[38]

In New Zealand and the Pacific, where Britain did not exercise formal sovereignty over territory, the growing reach of the postrevolutionary empire was shaped by the interplay of Christianity and commerce rather than the kind of military-fiscalism that dominated India's development from the 1750s to the 1820s, and which remained a powerful influence on what other historians have called the colonial "garrison state" through the nineteenth century.[39] The interlacing of "Christianity and Commerce" has been seen as a core and enduring feature of Victorian imperialism, but in the Pacific they were firmly linked and stood at the heart of British imperial activity from the beginning of the nineteenth century.[40] The emergence of that imperial nexus in the Pacific around 1800 is an important reminder that the fundamental lineaments of the modern British empire took shape in the crucible of the age of revolution and its aftermath.[41]

Chiefly Power and Indigenous Geopolitics

But the shape of that empire was never solely determined by the needs and aspirations of Britons. Marsden's plan for New Zealand might have been articulated in 1808, and he quickly recruited the first cohort of missionaries, but events in New Zealand meant that the first mission was not established until 1814, when local conditions were finally conducive. C. A. Bayly's *Imperial Meridian* emphasized the foundational importance of the hollowing out of great Muslim empires in shaping the form and character of British imperial order in the revolutionary age.[42] But *Imperial Meridian*'s argument underlined a broader point: that British empire-building in the Age of Revolution was never simply the outcome of an imperial will-to-power that was then neatly translated into colonial structures. Rather, empire took diverse and shifting shapes in particular locations, locations with deep histories and whose different political, economic, and social configurations were central in determining the timing and nature of the entry points exploited by incoming Europeans. The weight of these local contexts and conditions strongly shaped the processes of imperial encroachment and incorporation as well as the subsequent pattern of colonial development.[43]

In the New Zealand context, the genesis of the mission needs to be understood against the nature of rangatiratanga (chiefly culture) and the changing pattern of relationships between kin groups. The rangatira Te Pahi recognized the immediate benefits that might flow from facing, and engaging, the agents of empire and Christianity. Te Pahi clearly understood the rewards that Tuki and Huru gained from their sojourn in Norfolk Island (after being kidnapped by the *Daedalus* in 1793), and their subsequent connection to NSW's Lieutenant Governor King. Te Pahi in particular grasped the value of the seed potatoes gifted to Tuki and Huru by King. These new introductions produced larger and more hardy crops than the more sensitive Polynesian kūmara, and they were a crop that visiting ships were keen to trade for. Te Pahi traveled to Norfolk Island "against the wishes of his dependents" because he believed that the anxiety of his kin would be overshadowed by the very real advantages that would flow to his people from establishing relationships with the colonial authorities. Lieutenant Governor King maintained his custom of gift-giving, presenting Te Pahi with a box of seedling fruit trees, iron utensils and tools, a prefabricated house, and a silver medallion struck to mark their friendship.[44] After receiving these gifts, Te Pahi invited visiting vessels to anchor off his island at Te Puna, enabling him to engage in lucrative cross-cultural trade and access the ships carrying potatoes and prepared flax back to Port Jackson.[45] John Savage's 1807 description of the Bay of Islands identified Te Puna as the "capital" of the north, suggesting that it became the central site for cross-cultural trade as Te Pahi's people grew excellent potatoes and enthusiastically traded them for iron.[46]

However, Te Pahi's wealth and power and the gravitational pull of Te Puna on shipping sparked conflict. The path of cross-cultural trade was uncertain, especially as some Europeans did not enter reciprocal relationships, instead plundering Te Puna's potato fields and resorting to violence and kidnapping, including Te Pahi's daughter Atahoe.[47] Te Pahi's complaints about these raids and outrages roused little response from Lieutenant Governor King's successors: the chief's relationship with King was personal, rather than an enduring structural relationship. Later, authority figures in colonial New South Wales were not only skeptical of Te Pahi but mocked him. Within the Bay, Te Puna's position as the primary entrepôt altered the existing balance of political and commercial power, feeding animosity toward Te Pahi and triggering a sequence of conflicts that ultimately led to his death. In 1809, Te Pahi was in Whangaroa when the Port Jackson–based *Boyd*, seeking timber, was attacked and destroyed. The attack was investigated by other vessels and crews in the region, under the leadership of Alexander Berry (supercargo on the whaling ship *City of Edinburgh*) and with guidance from Bay of Islands chief Matengaro. This initial investigation suggested that Te Pahi instigated the attack, an understanding that was fostered by Tara, Te Pahi's rival who controlled the anchorage and trade at Kororareka on the south side of the Bay of Islands.[48] In retaliation for Te Pahi's supposed role in the *Boyd* incident, a party of whalers stormed Te Pahi's island, killing approximately sixty of his kin. Te Pahi himself evaded capture but was killed within weeks as a result of a skirmish with the people of Whangaroa.

Even though Te Pahi's death made the stakes of facing empire clear, Ruatara, a young chief also closely connected to both Te Puna and Te Pahi, was convinced of the benefits of cross-cultural contact.[49] Marsden was delighted that Ruatara had agreed to serve as the protector of the CMS mission at Hohi and noted that Ruatara had "made arrangements with his people for a very extensive cultivation of the land, and formed a plan for building a new town, with regular streets, after the European mode, to be erected on a beautiful situation, which commanded a view of the harbor's mouth, and the adjacent country round. We, together, inspected the ground fixed on for the township, and the situation of the intended church."[50] Marsden believed there was a strong alignment in his interests and those of Te Pahi and Ruatara, leaders who he held in high regard and considered as friends. A different view emerged from the missionaries on the ground at Hohi, who repeatedly warned Marsden that the motivation of the rangatira who "protected" the mission actually diverged in significant ways from Marsden's hope that the "civilized arts" would function as an instrument ultimately to convert Māori. Thomas Kendall, the missionary schoolteacher, explained to Marsden: "The natives approve of Europeans settling amongst them, through motives of self-interest. . . . We must not try them beyond their strength, and it becomes us, as it will do any others who may settle with us or near us, for the sake of the natives as well as our own, to be watchful, and not to injure them by placing too much confidence in them. The natives are eager after trade. . . . Felling axes, large or small chopping axes, hoes, spades, shovels, large and small fish-hooks, etc., please them well."[51]

Rangatira in the Bay of Islands actively sought to engage agents of empire and were interested in Marsden's gospel of improvement, but not because they wanted to initiate a revolution and radically refashion the cultural underpinnings of their own society. Te Pahi, Ruatara, and Hongi Hika did exhibit interest in Christian practice and cosmology, but the initial motivation for them each developing connections with Marsden was centered on European technology and possibilities of agriculture.[52]

Despite their fundamentally different cultural underpinnings, the aims of improvement and the culture of chieftainship converged in important ways. The ideology of improvement aimed to extend commerce and enhance the efficiency and productivity of agriculture through the technology of cultivation. The consequences of these transformations—increased agricultural surpluses and trade—were valued aspects of rangatiratanga (chieftainship). A central responsibility of leadership in the Māori world was overseeing the production, storage, and distribution of food.[53] The ability to accumulate large surpluses of foodstuffs, especially highly prized items, was an efficacious display of the mana (power, charisma) of a leader.[54] Such surpluses were dispersed through trading relationships or at hākari, ritual feasts that accompanied hui (meetings; forums). There is evidence to suggest that such feasts grew in size and significance within the context of cross-cultural contact, and high-yielding potatoes were well suited to ostentatious displays of productive capacity.[55] These potatoes were much hardier than the frost-sensitive kūmara, and this allowed rangatira to both bring new areas into cultivation and increase the output of production. The extensive cultivation of potatoes for trade meant that chiefs were required to increase the labor inputs into production, becoming an important driver of the extension of slavery in Māori society.[56] The precise link between the embrace of potato production and the marked intensification of intertribal warfare between the 1810s and 1830s is contentious, but there is some evidence that potatoes were a significant material base for the extended raids of taua (war parties), and war captives were routinely put to work in potato fields. In a strong reading of this evidence, James Belich suggested that these conflicts, which are typically known as the "Musket Wars," should be renamed the "Potato Wars."[57] Potatoes were thus at the heart of the transformation of the Māori world: reinforcing and amplifying some traditional cultural norms, reshaping the pattern of economic life, and facilitating, at least in part, an age of expanded conflict and migration.

The food plants, animals (especially pigs), and technologies that rangatira such as Te Pahi and Ruatara sourced through their connections to influential figures in colonial New South Wales, such as King and Marsden, were vitally important in enhancing the mana and influence of these leaders. Those concerns were especially important in the Bay of Islands of the early nineteenth century, as it was an arena in which a complex and dynamic set of sociopolitical processes—enacted through gift-giving, marriage alliances, warfare, plunder, and migration—reshaped the contours of Indigenous power and affiliation. The genealogical ties, political alliances, and chiefly rivalries that molded life in the region were extremely dynamic and complex, and as we have already seen with Te Pahi, they also had high stakes attached. The work of Jeffrey Sissons, Wiremu Wi Hongi, and Pat Hohepa has used genealogical narratives to establish that the region's political terrain was shaped by two primary "alliances" of hapū (subtribes, clans)—hapū that were part of the consolidation of the larger Ngā Puhi iwi (tribe). The group they identify as the "northern alliance" was based at Kaikohe, Te Waimate, Kerikeri, Waitangi, Te Puna, and Rangihoua. A tight web of genealogical connections linked these collectives, and Te Pahi, Ruatara, and Hongi Hika (who emerged as the patron and protector of mission in the mid-1810s) were among the influential rangatira of this group.[58] This coalition was in competition with the so-called southern alliance, which was based in an arc of settlements in the south and southeast of the Bay, including Ōkura, Kawakawa, Paihia, Waikare, Matauwhi, and Kororāreka.

Relationships with Europeans were woven into the rivalries between these two contending groups. Open conflicts were initiated and legitimated by various *take* (causes, origins, sources), and the complex skein of genealogical connections that underpinned the region's social formation meant that conflicts could have a cascading effect, particularly as *utu* (retribution, balance) could be sought many years after an affront or slight. The pattern of these sociopolitical dynamics was reshaped by the uneven impact of Euro-American traders and relationships with missionaries, which meant that some individuals and groups had ready access to new technologies and trade goods while others did not. By 1814, the "northern alliance" was in a dominant position, at least in part as a result of Te Pahi's successful cultivation of potatoes and his resulting ability to attract American and European vessels to his anchorage on the north side of the Bay. For Te Pahi, potatoes were an effective trade medium that allowed him to secure regular supplies of iron, a commodity that enhanced the effectiveness and efficiency of both tools and weapons.[59] When the lay missionaries William Hall and Thomas Kendall visited the Bay of Islands in June 1814 to lay the foundations of the mission, the "northern alliance" had sourced trading relationships to procure European muskets.[60] Those muskets were not only useful in conflicts against local rivalries but were also deployed in a long sequence of devastating raids to the south, raids in which the "northern" and "southern" hapū came together in unified Ngā Puhi taua (war parties).

Within the context of the Bay of Islands itself, the "southern alliance" rangatira resented the military and economic benefits that their rivals were accruing. Quite quickly, Samuel Marsden was aware of the extent to which the mission had become entangled in Indigenous politics and conflicts. When Marsden made his second visit to New Zealand in 1819, Te Morenga and Waitara, rangatira from the inland Taiamai district, protested that trade with Europeans had been monopolized by Ruatara and Hongi Hika as a result of their connections with the CMS. They complained that "by this means the power and wealth of Shunghee [Hongi] had greatly increased." Hongi did strictly police trade, preventing his rivals from engaging with Europeans and Americans who anchored near or visited his settlements. These chiefs, connected to the "southern alliance," told Marsden that what they "wanted was an equal advantage of trade, which they could not enjoy without the residence of a missionary amongst them."[61] Two weeks after Marsden departed, Te Morenga's people and Hongi's were at war, a conflict triggered by the theft of some shellfish. In the ensuing conflict, a *taua* (war party) from Taiamai plundered the mission station at Kerikeri, which had been established under Hongi's patronage and in the shadow of his Kororipo pā (fortified settlement).[62]

Māori leaders and communities continued to be able to exercise considerable control over incoming Europeans in northern New Zealand until at least the mid-1830s. Missionaries only slowly grew in confidence and authority. That process began after the establishment of the CMS mission at Paihia, in the southwest of the Bay of Islands. Well located and with rich soils, Paihia offered the mission a sounder economic base, even if the station was initially dependent on the patronage of Te Koki, a "southern alliance" chief with close connections to Marsden.[63] In 1824, the new leader of the New Zealand mission, Reverend Henry Williams, initiated the construction of a fifty-ton schooner. This vessel, the *Herald*, allowed the mission to regularize communications with New South Wales and greatly enlarged the reach of the missionaries within New Zealand. Williams and other missionaries traveled down the North Island's east coast south to Tauranga and around the North Cape to the west coast. These voyages reconfigured the economic foundation of the mission, as new trading relationships were established with communities that accepted simple iron tools and fishhooks as mediums of exchange for pork rather than demanding muskets. As a result, the missionaries were, for the first time, able to control the movement of food, tools, livestock, and trading goods that sustained the mission. This diluted the power of the rangatira who served as their patrons and protectors, giving the missionaries a new degree of independence. That independence was significantly extended after the death of great chief Hongi Hika in 1828, and the subsequent establishment of a mission inland at Waimate, in Hongi's old domain, was a marker of the mission's greater confidence, a confidence that was central to the beginnings of significant Māori interest in Christian teachings in the early 1830s. As I have demonstrated elsewhere, missionaries gained greater influence in the Māori world when they enjoyed a more secure economic base and were less dependent on the patronage of chiefs. They became increasingly significant as peacemakers and advocates for the gospel when their own mana was clearly displayed, including through their ability to produce more food, engage in long-distance trade, and successfully introduce a wider range of crops and technologies.[64]

Entanglements and Unexpected Impacts

As this material suggests, an appreciation of the changing contours of the Indigenous sociopolitical formation and the cultural logics of Indigenous action are crucial to understanding the foundation of the CMS mission and subsequent reshaping of Māori society. But those frameworks are by themselves insufficient if we are to understand why Britons and Māori were increasingly drawn together: our understanding of those entanglements is partial if it is framed only in terms of Indigenous perspectives and local histories.[65] Locally grounded narratives, of course, can have great social weight and cultural meaning, but in order to understand empire and colonization, a knowledge of the interface between these Indigenous dynamics and operation of imperial institutions and networks is crucial.

A final example in connection with Samuel Marsden is helpful here. Because of the long commitment Marsden demonstrated to New Zealand and his deep engagement with at least two generations of influential Māori leaders from the Bay of Islands, Marsden himself was incorporated into te ao Māori. Marsden welcomed the rangatira who traveled to Poihākena (Port Jackson or Sydney), and he offered substantial hospitality, an attribute highly valued in Māori life. Marsden generously provided for the immediate material needs of the rangatira and their families, he showed them new technologies and practices, he explained British and Christian ideas, and he drew Māori visitors into the life of his family. The son of the "southern alliance" rangatira Tara named Kawiti Tiitua formed a very high opinion of Marsden after his 1811 visit to New South Wales, especially as Marsden was the only person in the colony who recognized Kawiti's status as a "king." Marsden respected Kawiti's mana, even offering Kawiti "as much land as he liked" from his holdings at Parramatta. Kawiti was delighted by this, suggesting that he would return to the Bay of Islands and gather together one hundred of his men who he would take back to New South Wales to work on Marsden's property.[66]

Marsden's recognition of the centrality of manaakitanga—hospitality that recognizes and enhances mana—in the Māori world was integral to the mana he himself came to wield, and it was a key framework of the mission's establishment. We can see this in a letter that Marsden wrote in March 1814 for Thomas Kendall and William Hall to carry to Ruatara during their exploratory voyage in the winter of that year. This letter was framed in idioms of friendship and reciprocity. It opened with an explicit recognition of Ruatara's mana, being addressed to "Duaterra King." The body of the letter stressed the common interests that united the two men, their families, and the potential of "improvement." Marsden explained that he was sending Ruatara wheat seed and a teacher for Ruatara's "Tamoneekes [tamariki: boys] and Kocteedos [kotiro: girls]." Marsden's son Charles was sending Ruatara a cockerel as a present, while Elizabeth, Marsden's wife, was gifting the rangatira a shirt and jacket. Marsden also promised to provide Ruatara with anything else that he desired. In return, Marsden requested that Ruatara use his chiefly power to protect the missionaries and to ensure that the *Active* was loaded for its return to New South Wales: Marsden explained he wanted muka (dressed flax), potatoes, fishing lines and nets, and mats. The letter ended by informing Ruatara of the well-being of Marsden's family and intimate circle, naming each individual who the rangatira had met during his sojourns in Parramatta.[67] The affective bonds of family and friendship were also enacted through Elizabeth Marsden's gift of a red gown to Rahu, Ruatara's wife. Here again, the Marsdens were recognizing the mana of Ruatara and his kin: red was the color most prized by Māori, and it was associated with chiefly status.[68]

This letter, couched in intimate knowledge and personal connections, demonstrates Marsden's adept navigation of cross-cultural relationships with Māori. But the friendship it articulated and the reciprocity it enacted were grounded in empire and drew Māori more firmly into connections with New South Wales, with Britain, and with the empire as a whole. Intimacy could be both genuine and a means to enable the extension of evangelization and empire. The conversational tone and affective freight of such cross-cultural dialogues must not blind us to consequences of such "strategic intimacies."[69]

Although the primary concern of this chapter has been to explore the cultural priorities that encouraged both Māori and Britons to support the establishment of the CMS mission, it is important to end by noting the profound consequences that also resulted from "facing empire." Almost forty years ago, in an underappreciated essay, J. M. R. Owens stressed the "unexpected impacts" of evangelization and the inability of missionaries to dictate the terms of cross-cultural engagement or control Māori understandings of Christian doctrine.[70] The embeddedness and entanglement of missionaries in te ao Māori was a vital condition of their work, but it meant that they operated in a world underpinned by translation, negotiation, and accommodation. Recent scholarship is paying more attention to such transactions. Alison Jones and Kuni Jenkins have recently offered a compelling reassessment of the authorship and meaning of some key early texts that are commonly seen as the product of the labors of the pioneering CMS missionaries. They suggest, for example, that *A Korao no New Zealand; or, the New Zealander's First Book* (1815) should not be simply attributed to the missionary Thomas Kendall, as this volume was "a remarkable product of Maori teaching." It was indeed a coproduction between missionary and Māori.[71]

There is no doubt that we need to recover the conversations and debates that played out between missionary and Māori. But we must not entirely dislocate these engagements from the deeper contexts and frameworks that enabled and shaped them: these were exchanges, but these exchanges entangled Māori in empire. "Entanglement" reminds us that by their very natures, empires were incorporationist regimes, which drew in resources, land, skill, labor, and knowledge into expansive systems of extraction and mobility. After communities were woven into these webs of interdependence, their ability to control and direct the pattern and impact of the flows of technologies, commodities, animals, plants, germs, and ideas was attenuated. And after Māori communities were incorporated into the world of empire, however partially and fitfully, that history and consequences of connection could not be erased. Māori, like other colonized communities, discovered that the convergent interests and cultural conjunctures that drew them into the empire in the first place ultimately enriched and empowered the agents of empire in the long term and undercut some of the key foundations of the Indigenous order, with deep and abiding consequences. Empires broke open old systems, remaking worlds and transforming future possibilities. Facing empire was a very high-stakes game.

Notes

1. C. A. Bayly, *The Birth of the Modern World 1780–1914* (Oxford: Blackwell, 2004); Tony Ballantyne, "The Persistence of the Gods: Religion in the Modern World," in *World Histories from Below: Disruption and Dissent, 1750 to the Present*, ed. Antoinette Burton and Tony Ballantyne (London: Bloomsbury, 2016).

2. See Tony Ballantyne, *Orientalism and Race: Aryanism in the British Empire* (Basingstoke: Palgrave, 2002); *Between Colonialism and Diaspora: Sikh Cultural Formations in an Imperial World* (Durham, NC: Duke University Press, 2006); and *Webs of Empire: Locating New Zealand's Colonial Past* (Wellington: Bridget Williams Books, 2012).

3. Tony Ballantyne, *Entanglements of Empire: Missionaries, Maori and the Question of the Body* (Durham, NC: Duke University Press, 2014), especially 16–18, 251–52, 257. An important earlier use of "entanglement" in the Pacific was Nicholas Thomas's *Entangled Objects: Exchange, Material Culture and Colonialism in the Pacific* (Cambridge, MA: Harvard University Press, 1991).

4. Carolyn Hamilton, *Terrific Majesty: The Powers of Shaka Zulu and the Limits of Historical Invention* (Cambridge, MA: Harvard University Press, 1998), 3–4.

5. Lynn M. Thomas, *Politics of the Womb: Women, Reproduction, and the State in Kenya* (Berkeley: University of California Press, 2003), 19.

6. Sarah Nuttall, *Entanglement: Literary and Cultural Reflections on Post-Apartheid* (Johannesburg: Wits University Press, 2009), 1.

7. Most notably, Vincent O'Malley, *The Meeting Place: Maori and Pakeha Encounters, 1642–1840* (Auckland: Auckland University Press, 2012); Anne Salmond, *Between Worlds: Early Exchanges between Maori and Europeans, 1773–1815* (Auckland: Viking, 1991); James Belich, *Making Peoples: A History of the New Zealanders: From Polynesian Settlement to the End of the Nineteenth Century* (Auckland: Penguin, 1996).

8. Allan Davidson, Stuart Lange, Peter Lineham, and Adrienne Puckey, eds., *Te Rongopai 1814 "Takoto Te Pai!": Bicentenary Reflections on Christian Beginnings and Developments in Aotearoa New Zealand* (Auckland: Anglican Church, 2014).

9. Eustace Carey, *Memoir of William Carey, D.D.* (London: Jackson and Walford, 1836), 18.

10. George Smith, *The Life of William Carey, D.D.: Shoemaker and Missionary* (London: John Murray, 1885), 114.

11. William Smith, *Journal of a Voyage in the Missionary Ship Duff, to the Pacific Ocean in the Years 1796, 7, 8, 9, 1800, 1 & c.* (New York: Collins and Co., 1813); John Garrett, *To Live among the Stars: Christian Origins in Oceania* (Suva: University of South Pacific Press, 1982), 13–18.

12. C. A. Bayly, *Imperial Meridian: The British Empire and the World 1780–1830* (London: Longman, 1989), 137.

13. Quoted in J. D. Bollen, "English Missionary Societies and the Australian Aborigine," *Journal of Religious History* 9, no. 3 (1977): 284.

14. Māori, in fact, possessed strong craft traditions and were skilled boat-builders, highly proficient makers of cord and nets, and produced a range of highly functional tools.

15. Samuel Marsden to Reverend Josiah Pratt, 7 April 1808, MS-0498/001/003, Hocken Collections (hereafter HC), University of Otago, Dunedin.

16. Samuel Marsden to Reverend Josiah Pratt, 7 April 1808, MS-0498/001/003, HC.

17. Marsden to John Stokes, 26 November 1811, in *Some Private Correspondence of the Rev. Samuel Marsden*, 44–45.

18. Marsden had a personal stake in this experiment: he had been hopeful that he could improve and convert an Aboriginal boy named "Tristan," who was attached to the Marsden household from around 1794. Tristan accompanied the Marsdens on their voyage to England in 1807 but fled the family during their brief sojourn in Rio de Janeiro. Tristan liked alcohol and left the family after "his master" (as Mrs. Elizabeth Marsden described her husband, Samuel) disciplined him for his drunkenness. A. T. Yarwood, *Samuel Marsden: The Great Survivor* (Carlton: Melbourne University Press, 1977), 112–13.

19. John Gascoigne, *The Enlightenment and the Origins of European Australia* (Cambridge: Cambridge University Press, 2006), 157. Here Marsden was explaining that because Australian Indigenous communities had no interest in trade, so the Gospel would remain beyond their reach.

20. Neil Gunson, *Messengers of Grace: Evangelical Missionaries in the South Seas 1797–1860* (Melbourne: Oxford University Press, 1978), 270.

21. Ballantyne, *Entanglements of Empire*, 52.

22. On Marsden's experience and understandings of empire, see Ballantyne, *Entanglements of Empire*, 45–46, 101–103, 113.

23. Yarwood, *Samuel Marsden*, 111.

24. Margaret Steven, *Merchant Campbell, 1769–1846: A Study of Colonial Trade* (Melbourne: Oxford University Press, 1965), 273, 279.

25. Steven, *Merchant Campbell, 1769–1846*, 31, 112–17, 145–46, 213–14, 231, 254, 283.

26. In return, Marsden worked to forward Campbell's interests: he wrote to William Wilberforce to ask him to protect colonial merchants, including Campbell, from the East India Company's attempts to control British commercial activity in the Pacific Ocean. Yarwood, *Samuel Marsden*, 133. It is notable that Campbell named one of his sons Frederick Marsden Campbell.

27. Marsden to Pratt, 22 September 1814, printed in *A Sermon Preached at the Parish Church of St. Andrew by the Wardrobe and St. Anne Blackfriars on Tuesday, 2 May 1815. . . . Also the Report of the Committee to the Annual Meeting, Held on the Same Day . . .* (London, 1815), 625.

28. Quoted in Yarwood, *Samuel Marsden*, 158.

29. Samuel Marsden to Reverend Josiah Pratt, 24 March 1808, "Records Relating to the New Zealand Mission," MS-0498/001/001, HC.

30. Marsden to Reverend Josiah Pratt, 7 February 1820, in J. R. Elder, ed., *The Letters and Journals of Samuel Marsden, 1765–1838* (Dunedin: Coulls Somerville Wilkie, 1932), 329–30.

31. Marsden to Reverend Josiah Pratt, 22 September 1820, in Elder, ed., *The Letters and Journals of Samuel Marsden, 1765–1838*, 329–30.

32. For discussion of those critiques, see Tony Ballantyne, "Moving Texts: Materiality, Mobility, and the Emotions of Imperial Humanitarianism," *Journal of Colonialism and Colonial History* 17, no. 1 (2016), and Elizabeth Elbourne, "The Sin of the Settler: The 1835–36 Select Committee on Aborigines and Debates over Virtue and Conquest in the Early Nineteenth-Century British White Settler Empire," *Journal of Colonialism and Colonial History* 4, no. 3 (2003).

33. Marsden to CMS, 3 May 1810, in *Marsden and the New Zealand Mission*, 28–29; Marsden to Miss Mary Stokes, 15 June 1815, in *Some Private Correspondence of the Rev. Samuel Marsden*, 54–55; *A Sermon Preached at the Parish Church of St. Andrew by the Wardrobe and St. Anne Blackfriars on Tuesday, 3 May 1814. . . . Also the Report of the Committee to the Annual Meeting, Held on the Same Day . . .* (London, 1814), 302–303; *Missionary Papers*, No. III, Michaelmas 1816, unpaginated; Kendall to Joshua Mann, 14 July 1817, and Kendall to Marsden, 1 August 1822, "Thomas Kendall. Letters &c. 1816–1827," PC-0151, HC.

34. Marsden, Cartwright, and Youl to Pratt, 27 March 1817, in *Letters and Journals of Samuel Marsden*, 226–28.

35. Ballantyne, *Entanglements of Empire*, chapter 6.

36. See John Brewer, *The Sinews of Power: War and the English State, 1688–1783* (London: Unwin Hyman, 1989); Patrick K. O'Brien and Philip A. Hunt, "The Rise of a Fiscal State in England, 1485–1815," *Historical Research* 66 (1993): 129–76; Lawrence Stone, ed., *An Imperial State at War: Britain from 1689 to 1815* (London: Routledge, 1994).

37. Bayly also suggested that the West Indies was an important exception to this pattern, for even if entangled in the rapid expansion of the British imperial state's military capacity, the structure of its economy did not hinge upon revenue-gathering.

38. There were persistent fears that these fledgling settlements were tainted by a kind of colonial absolutism. See Jeremy Bentham, *A Plea for the Constitution: Shewing the Enormities Committed . . . in and by the Design . . . of the Penal Colony of New South Wales* (London: Wilks and Taylor, 1803); Gascoigne, *The Enlightenment and the Origins of European Australia*, 39–42. Paul McHugh has suggested that a distinctive settler-colonial form of absolutism, which was a counterpoint to a more dominant pluralistic tradition, also was articulated in the second quarter of the nineteenth century and evolved, having considerable influence in New Zealand as the century progressed. Paul McHugh, "'A Pretty Gov[ernment]!': The 'Confederation of United Tribes' and Britain's Quest for Imperial Order in the New Zealand Islands during the 1830s," in *Legal Pluralism and Empires, 1500–1850*, ed. Lauren Benton and Richard J. Ross (New York: New York University Press, 2013), 235–36.

39. See Bayly, "The British Military-Fiscal State and Indigenous Resistance, 1750–1820," in *An Imperial State at War: Britain from 1689–1815*, 322–54; Douglas M. Peers,

Between Mars and Mammon: Colonial Armies and the Garrison State in Early Nineteenth-Century India (London: Tauris Academic Studies, 1995); Tan Tai Yong, *The Garrison State: Military, Government and Society in Colonial Punjab 1849–1947* (New Delhi: Sage, 2005).

40. See, for example, Brian Stanley, "'Commerce and Christianity': Providence Theory, the Missionary Movement, and the Imperialism of Free Trade, 1842–1860," *The Historical Journal* 26, no. 1 (1983): 71–94; Andrew Porter, "'Commerce and Christianity': The Rise and Fall of a Nineteenth-Century Missionary Slogan," *Historical Journal* 28, no. 3 (1985): 597–621.

41. Bayly, *Imperial Meridian*; C. A. Bayly, "The British and Indigenous Peoples, 1760–1860: Power, Perception, and Identity," in *Empire and Others: British Encounters with Indigenous Peoples, 1600–1850*, ed. Martin Daunton and Rick Halpern (Philadelphia: University of Pennsylvania Press, 1999), 21–22.

42. Bayly, *Imperial Meridian*. This was a strong argument within Eurasia, but less convincing, perhaps, for understanding imperial activity in the Pacific or, for that matter, the Caribbean.

43. C. A. Bayly, *Indian Society and the Making of the British Empire* (Cambridge: Cambridge University Press, 1990). For a similar argument with a focus on religion, see Tony Ballantyne, "Religion, Difference, and the Limits of British Imperial History," *Victorian Studies* 47, no. 3 (2005): 427–55.

44. King's "Notes, 1806," in Robert McNab, ed., *Historical Records of New Zealand*, 8 vols. (Wellington, 1908), 1:263–64.

45. *Sydney Gazette*, 15 June 1806 and 12 April 1807.

46. John Savage, *Some Account of New Zealand: Particularly the Bay of Islands, and Surrounding Country* (London: J. Murray, 1807), 9, 54–56.

47. On the kidnapping of Atahoe and George Bruce, who functioned as Te Pahi's key intermediary, see Anne Salmond, *Between Worlds: Early Exchanges between Maori and Europeans 1773–1815* (Auckland: Viking, 1997), chapter 15.

48. Angela Ballara, "Te Pahi - Te Pahi," from the *Dictionary of New Zealand Biography: Te Ara—the Encyclopedia of New Zealand*, updated 30 October 2012.

49. Samuel Marsden understood that Kaparu, the younger brother of Te Pahi, was Ruatara's father and that his mother was Hongi Hika's sister. While recent research questions these identifications, Marsden's belief in these important kin connections was significant in shaping the relationship he forged with Ruatara. On these genealogical issues, see Angela Ballara, "Ruatara," from the *Dictionary of New Zealand Biography: Te Ara—the Encyclopedia of New Zealand*, updated 30 October 2012.

50. Samuel Marsden, "Observations on the Introduction of the Gospel: Journal: Reverend Samuel Marsden's First Visit to New Zealand in December 1814," MS-0176/001, HC.

51. Kendall to Marsden, 25 July 1817, *Marsden's Lieutenants*, 141.

52. On their interest in Christianity, especially the Sabbath, see Marsden, "Observations on the Introduction of the Gospel"; Marsden to CMS, 19 November 1811, MS-0498/008/240, HL.

53. Maharaia Winiata, "Leadership in Pre-European Maori Society," *Journal of the Polynesian Society* 65, no. 3 (1965): 212–31.

54. For two classic readings of the importance of mana and competitiveness in Māori society, see Ann R. Parsonson, "The Expansion of a Competitive Society: A Study in Nineteenth-Century Maori Social History," *New Zealand Journal of History* 14, no. 1 (1980): 45–60, and Ann Parsonson, "The Pursuit of Mana," in *The Oxford History of New Zealand*, ed. W. H. Oliver (Wellington: Oxford University Press, 1981).

55. W. Colenso, "On the Vegetable Food of the Ancient New Zealanders before Cook's Visit," *Transactions and Proceedings of the New Zealand Institute* 13 (1880): 18.

56. Salmond, *Between Worlds*, 422.

57. Ballara, *Taua*, 397–98. Compare Ballara's cautious reading of the role of potatoes in providing the material base for the extension of Māori warfare—she suggests that they may have only become very significant in the 1830s—with Belich's more assertive reading: Belich, *Making Peoples*, 159.

58. Jeffrey Sissons, Wiremu Wi Hongi, and Pat Hohepa, *Nga Puriri o Taiamai: A Political History of Nga Puhi in the Inland Bay of Islands* (Auckland: Reed, 2001), 36–42.

59. See John Savage's comments about Te Pahi's use of potatoes: Savage, *Some Account of New Zealand*, 54–57. Angela Ballara emphasizes the centrality of potatoes as a medium of "external" trade geared toward iron, muskets, and other new forms of technology (*Taua*, 22).

60. Thomas Kendall Journal, 16 June 1814, and Thomas Kendall Journal, 9 March 1814–13 February 1815, both in MS-Papers-0921, ATL.

61. John Rawson Elder, ed., *Marsden's Lieutenants* (Dunedin: Coulls Somerville Wilkie, 1934), 204–205.

62. See Sissons et al., *Nga Puriri o Taiamai*, 48–49; Ballara, *Taua*, 193.

63. Te Koki's son Te Ahara had lived with Marsden at Parramatta in New South Wales. After Te Ahara died, Marsden promised Te Koki that he would send a missionary to his people. Ballantyne, *Entanglements of Empire*, 75–76.

64. Ballantyne, *Entanglements of Empire*, 76–77.

65. For a similar argument, see Bayly, "The British and Indigenous Peoples," 21. Cf. Samuel Carpenter's review of *Entanglements of Empire* in the *New Zealand Journal of History* (October 2015).

66. Marsden to Pratt, 20 November 1811; *Marsden and the New Zealand Mission*, 40–41.

67. Marsden to Ruatara, 9 March 1814, "Correspondence 1814–1815," PC-0119, HC.

68. Alison Jones and Kuni Jenkins, *He Korero: Words between Us: First Maori-Pakeha Conversations on Paper* (Wellington: Huia, 2011), 79; Nicholas suggested that the dress was a gift from Marsden himself: Nicholas, *Narrative of a Voyage to New Zealand*, 2:199.

69. Tony Ballantyne, "Strategic Intimacies: Knowledge and Colonization in Southern New Zealand," *Journal of New Zealand Studies* 14 (2013): 4–18.

70. J. M. R. Owens, "The Unexpected Impact: Wesleyan Missionaries and Maoris in the Early 19th Century," *Wesley Historical Society of New Zealand: Proceedings* 27, no. 6 (1972): 1–37.

71. Jones and Jenkins, *He Korero*, 119–27.

CHAPTER NINE

Broken Treaty

Taungurung Responses to the Settler Revolution in Colonial Victoria

ROBERT KENNY

In early July 1837, John Coppock, acting on behalf of William Henry Yaldwyn, an English squire hoping to make enough profit from a colonial pastoral adventure to save his ailing family estate in Sussex, established the Barfold sheep run on the banks of the Campaspe River, about 100 kilometers north of Melbourne. Its 57,000 acres of rolling wooded grasslands took in both banks of the Campaspe and stretched west to the Coliban River. Barfold was the second run to be established north of the Dividing Range in what was then known as the Port Phillip District of New South Wales and which would become the Colony of Victoria. Six weeks earlier, in late May, Charles Ebden had established Carlsruhe Station immediately to the south of Barfold, also on the banks of the Campaspe and stretching west toward the Coliban. Ebden had put nine thousand sheep on his forty thousand acres, along with one thousand cattle and thirty or so horses. His entourage included twenty-two assigned convicts and ten free workers.[1]

On December 2, William Yaldwyn, who had been delayed by the confinement of his wife, finally arrived at Barfold. He brought three thousand sheep to add to the one thousand that John Coppock had brought down in July, plus three hundred cattle and twenty horses. Among his workmen were eighteen assigned convicts. A few days later, Alexander Mollison took possession of seventy thousand acres of land south of Barfold and west of Carlsruhe. Mollison had with him five thousand sheep, six hundred cattle, twenty-eight bullocks, and twenty-two horses, along with twenty-five men. Mollison called his run Colliban. Two days after this, on December 7, Captain Sylvester Brown laid claim to sixty thousand acres along the eastern boundary of Barfold, giving his run the name Darlinghurst. He had with him approximately five thousand sheep and four hundred cattle and twenty or so workmen. The next occupations had to wait till after the dry of summer. In March 1838, William Bowman with five thousand sheep claimed all the area west of Barfold's boundary on the Coliban River up to the foot of Mt. Alexander, about seventy thousand acres. He named it Stratford Lodge. A few weeks later, Henry Monro claimed fifty thousand acres along the northern boundary of Barfold, bringing with him several thousand sheep. It is unclear if Monro gave his run a name, but it was known as the Campaspe plains run. Shortly after this, Captain Charles Hutton laid claim to at least eighty thousand acres north of Monro's run. Included in Hutton's claim was the junction of the Coliban and Campaspe Rivers.[2]

Within twelve months, almost two thousand square kilometers of the Coliban and Campaspe valleys had been claimed and occupied by approximately 35,000 sheep, 4,000 cattle, sundry bullocks and horses, and around 200 European men. That these enterprises came when and where they did was not fortuity. Through 1836, these pastoralists, backed by British finance, had been forming partnerships and companies, buying stock, and recruiting workers. Typically, they had brought their enterprises together on temporary runs around the town of Yass, near the upper reaches of the Murrumbidgee River and at the official southern limits of settlement in NSW. There they prepared to head south to take up runs in northern Port Phillip. In October 1836, Thomas Mitchell's survey party passed through the area. Mitchell's discoveries were not the prompt for the pastoralists' desire to move south, but the track Mitchell's large cumbersome party carved through the country proved a heaven-sent road from the Murrumbidgee down into the Coliban and Campaspe valleys. Heaven-sent for the pastoralists, that is; for the Indigenous peoples of the area—the Taungurung—it would prove to be a road from hell. Along the Major's Line, as the track became known, the pastoralists traveled, departing from it in various directions as it reached the Campaspe near the present hamlet of Redesdale. The line itself was used to mark the northern boundary of the Barfold run.

Those traveling along the Major's Line in 1837 found any Indigenous peoples they encountered either friendly—even helpful—or, at worst, indifferent. Both William Yaldwyn and Alexander Mollison kept diaries of their journeys (which encountered each other), and both are interesting for the almost complete lack of mention of Aboriginal presence. And yet we get the impression from them that the "Blacks" are never too far away and are occasionally sought for assistance. Mollison's entry for July 3, 1837, casually notes: "We went onwards along the track with a native black, to a creek called

Bunwurrima, distance 3½."[3] Yaldwyn's journal notes similar occasional engagements.[4] While some of their men expressed nervousness of "Blacks," no incidents of confrontation are reported in these journals of 1837.

Then, on April 11, 1838, at least seven shepherds belonging to a party led by George and William Faithfull were surrounded and speared to death as they encamped on the Major's Line as it crossed the Broken River near present-day Benalla.[5] At about the same time, on Bowman's run on the west bank of the Coliban, a shepherd was attacked but escaped uninjured. The next month, on the same property, a shepherd was found speared, his stomach cut open and the internal organs removed (see below). A couple weeks later—June 9—several hundred of Yaldwyn's and Bowmen's sheep were stolen from the Barfold run. A party of Yaldwyn's and Bowmen's men tracked these sheep to rise on the Coliban River about ten kilometers north, where they found the sheep corralled in European-styled holds. In the resultant clash, a number of Aboriginal warriors were killed. In August the same year, a horse was found mutilated on Brown's Darlington station. The following May, two shepherds were killed on Hutton's Campaspe plains run and seven hundred sheep driven off. A few days later, in what was to be deemed an illegal police action, the majority of the sheep were recovered and "5 or 6 natives" were killed. These sheep had also been corralled. In July, another flock was stolen, this time from the Darlington run. Brown's overseer, William Cox, pursued and killed natives near present-day Mia Mia. In the same month, there was an attempt to steal a flock of sheep from Monro's run. In the attempt, Monro was seriously speared. This incident seems to have taken place near where Yaldwyn's and Bowman's sheep had been found the previous year. On November 18, 1839, a young mare disappeared from Ebden's Carlsruhe station. It was never found. On December 23, a bay yearling, missing since the previous day, was found strangled in the same vicinity. On December 26, Mollison's grey gelding was found killed near one of Ebden's outstations. That same evening, one of Mollison's mares was found injured from an attack. On January 16, 1840, a large flock of Monro's sheep was taken from Myrtle Creek on the left bank of the Coliban and driven off to Mt. Alexander. These are just the major incidents we know about.

While new pastoralists arrived in adjacent areas, sometime in 1840 Charles Hutton and Henry Monro decided they had had enough of the perils of the Coliban and Campaspe valleys and left the area. Ironically, twelve months later the "clashes" seemed to end. Indeed, by then, the previous owner-occupiers of the valleys had all but "disappeared."

The conquest of the Coliban-Campaspe valleys was ruthless. We are justified to suspect the number of Aboriginal deaths was grossly underreported (most of the accounts were recorded after the execution of those responsible for the Myall Creek massacre in 1838). Before 1837, no Europeans lived in the area: indeed, only two parties of Europeans are known to have passed through the area, and both in the latter part of 1836. But by the end of 1839, the western Taungurung people had been effectively removed from their country. We can understand fairly easily what brought the settlers down Mitchell's Line in 1837–38. But understanding why the Taungurung seemed at first to accommodate the settlers and to then turn on them and in the way they did is vastly more difficult.

The Clash of Imperatives

The "overlanding" parties herding stock down from the Murrumbidgee to establish pastoral leases in northern Port Phillip mirrored the influx south of the Dividing Range over the previous eighteen months, as pastoralists from Van Diemen's Land (Tasmania) ferried stock across Bass Strait to Port Phillip Bay. Throughout 1838, similar conquests took place in the Goulburn and Ovens valleys to the east of the Coliban and Campaspe valleys, and in the Loddon and Avoca valleys to the west. The deep cause for these moves was in one of the last triumphs of the Industrial Revolution, the mechanization of British woolen textile production. Saxon Merino wools, fine-textured and long, were particularly suited to this mechanization.[6] The wooded grasslands of Taungurong country, indeed of all Aboriginal country throughout southeastern New Holland, rough as they were compared to the ordered downs of the German principality, seemed perfect for Saxon Merinos.[7] The dispossession of the country was part of what James Belich has called the "Anglo explosion," when the English-speaking population of the world rapidly spread in settler colonies through Australasia, and the North American west and South Africa, creating an economic—and ecological—"Settler Revolution."[8]

In response, the British parliamentary antislavery leader, Thomas Fowell Buxton, established a Select Committee on Aborigines in the British colonies. The committee took evidence in 1835–36. The Report of Buxton's Select Committee would find many of the atrocities of colonization to have "passed unnoticed and unreproved."[9] One of the greatest was the attempt to exterminate the Aborigines of Van Diemen's Land (later, Tasmania). The lieutenant-governor of Van Diemen's Land, George Arthur, urged treating with the Aborigines to avoid such bloodshed again. Treating would allow settler and Aborigine to share in the development of settlement[10] in a view that was almost utopian.[11] Although often portrayed as the instigator of the Tasmanian Black Wars, Arthur understood he had inherited a tragic situation that could have been mitigated if the original governors in Van Diemen's Land had treated with the natives.[12] The British Colonial Secretary Lord Glenelg, with his Evangelical sympathies and connections to Clapham,[13] was as cognizant of the fate of Aboriginal Australians as he was of the commercial imperative in the Australian colonies. Writing to the NSW Governor Richard Bourke in 1836, Glenelg described "the whole surface of the country [of southeastern NSW]" as "of almost unrivalled value for the production of the finest description of wool."[14] Little wonder he had a reputation for administrative ennui. In London, it might have seemed possible to defer indefinitely, but not in the settler colonies themselves.[15] By the end of 1835, the government could dither no more.

Glenelg's letter to Bourke responded to a legal dilemma.[16] In June 1835, John Batman, a pastoralist from northern VDL, returned from an expedition across Bass Strait to the unsettled Port Phillip Bay area, claiming to have treated with the Aboriginal peoples of that area—the Kulin peoples—and, thereby, acquiring 600,000 acres of land for the use of himself and the other members of the Port Phillip Association. "Batman's Treaty" is one of the most contested acts in Australian historiography.[17] Indeed, no other act reveals as much of the complexity of perceptions of Australian settler colonization, and of Aboriginal Australia.

Batman's claim was met with a good deal of skepticism by his VDL pastoral peers in 1835—no doubt in part because it was seen as an act of theft that usurped their own right to steal. At the core of this skepticism was the belief that Aboriginal Australians had no leaders who could legitimately undertake such negotiations and no sense of land tenure. Although the Treaty gained a legitimacy through the late nineteenth century in Victoria as the founding act of the colony,[18] through the twentieth century in historiography skepticism reasserted itself and the treaty was conventionally seen as little more than a hoax inflicted on the Kulin. If the Kulin who met with Batman that June day in 1835 signed anything, later historians suggested, it was "their own death warrants."[19]

From late last century, scholarship—and public perception[20]—has been more nuanced, reading the meeting as one of miscomprehension but also one of significant negotiation. The late anthropologist Diane Barwick claimed that while Batman thought he was purchasing the land, the Kulin had been conducting a *tanderrum* ceremony to allow Batman and company temporary access to the land.[21] The deed Batman had with him, drawn up by his lawyer-associate Joseph Tice Gellibrand, was based on enfeoffment, a form of feudal land tenure that still had viability, if antiquated, under English common law in the nineteenth century.[22] It had a ritual aspect very similar to that of the *tanderrum*: the handing over of a token of the land in Kulin lore, in this case a handful of soil. Indeed, many of the actions of the Kulin who met with Batman were consistent with ritual behavior, and so were many of Batman's.[23] Was the "treaty" a coincidence of ritual and thus a classic case of mutual cultural incomprehension?

Given that in Barwick's own account the group of Sydney Aborigines Batman had with him, and who had been in his employ for many years, would have been "familiar with such ceremonies" as a *tanderrum*,[24] complete mutual miscomprehension is doubtful. In addition, the tone of Batman's journal, correspondence, and comments to and by associates shows he strongly believed he had come to some agreement with the Kulin. It is hard to believe his reaction grew from a knowingly fraudulent act.[25]

Barwick's revisionist view, however, failed to address two important facets. First, it presumed the Kulin, despite established trade and message routes to such places, knew nothing of the dispossession that had been in progress for more than forty years to their north and thus discounted any probability that the Kulin negotiated with Batman in an attempt to mitigate the impact of settlement. Second, it underplays the fact that Batman's attempt to treaty sprang from a wish to appease the powerful voices in London concerned with the fate of Indigenous peoples in the wake of expanding colonization.[26] It is also important here to understand the nature of the deed itself. An enfeoffment was essentially a system of reciprocity, that is, a sense of land use rights close to that of the Kulin.[27] Tenure was only retained as long as the conditions of the enfeoffment were fulfilled, whether by lord or by serf. Batman's deed was a lease, and any rights granted ceased if the "annual rental of tribute" was not forthcoming (the term is used in the treaty).[28] The Kulin under this were granting Batman and his associates temporary access to the land, even if temporary could mean a long time in Aboriginal eyes.[29]

The Kulin federation consisted of five closely related language groups of central Victoria: the Wathaurong, whose country was west of the Werribee River, encompassing present-day Geelong; the Dja Dja Wurrung, whose country centered on the Loddon valley to the northwest of the Dividing Range; the Taungurung, north of the Divide from the Coliban valley east to the Goulbourn valley; the Woiwurrung (Wurundjeri), centered on the Maribyrnong and Yarra valleys; and the Boon Wurrung, whose country stretched along the north and east coasts of Port Phillip Bay and down to Wilson's Promontory. Present-day Melbourne is mainly on Woiwurrung and Boon Wurrung countries. It is almost certain that Batman's meeting with the Kulin took place on Woiwurrung country but included clan heads, or *ngurungeata,* from other Kulin clans, and that the area dealt with in the negotiation was on Woiwurrung and Wathaurong countries. (It is also worth noting that the 600,000 acres—often commented on as excessive—was to be divided between seventeen members of the association. This would have resulted in runs smaller than those taken up in the Coliban and Campaspe valleys.)

Batman's negotiations presented a legal and moral quagmire—not without intention, and perhaps not as unwelcomed at the heights of government as it might seem. Governor Arthur's evidence to Buxton's committee and the sentiment of that committee and its supporters was that of recognizing Indigenous prior ownership. Such a recognition was what Batman and his associates rested their claims on. But such a recognition also threatened the legality of the Australian colonization from 1788 on. That colonization had been founded on a British claim to the country that presumed no prior ownership, but that presumption had never been legally articulated. Batman's actions forced it to be. Two months after Batman's treaty signing, the NSW governor, Richard Bourke, issued a proclamation:

> Whereas, it has been represented to me, that divers of His Majesty's Subjects have taken possession of vacant Lands of the Crown, within the limits of this Colony, under the pretence of a treaty, bargain, or contract, for the purchase thereof, with the Aboriginal Natives; Now therefore, I, the Governor, in virtue and in exercise of the power and authority in me vested, do hereby proclaim . . . that every such treaty, bargain, and contract with the Aboriginal Natives . . . is void and of no effect against the rights of the Crown; and that all Persons who shall be found in possession of any such Lands as aforesaid . . . will be considered as trespassers, and liable to be dealt with in like manner as other intruders upon the vacant Lands of the Crown within the said Colony.[30]

Here was the first clear articulation of what would become known as the principle of *Terra Nullius.* Aboriginal country was now vacant Crown land, stripped of habitation. It denied Aboriginal ownership of country and drove them from the category "human" into the category "nature," inhabitants of a wilderness, themselves as wild as the streams and trees. This text is as close as possible to the foundational declaration of Settler Australia, which would remain its presumptive rationale until at least the Mabo Decision of 1992. Batman might have hoped for something less clear, and Buxton's Committee for something clearly opposite.

For Bourke, it was a matter of control. There was, outside the settled areas, a vast "wilderness" essentially unknown beyond the coast. And as unknown, it was uncontrollable. The proclamation ensured that endeavors such as Batman's were as empty of legality as was Aboriginal ownership. But the proclamation in itself could not stop settlers adventuring into unknown areas where their behavior could go unmonitored. Bourke's military and policing resources were limited—his seat of government was a thousand kilometers away. Declaring the nascent port of Melbourne illegal would do nothing to stop its growth. Short of sending an army down to clear out the settlers, nothing could. Bourke convinced Glenelg to allow the settlement of Port Phillip and land sales. In July 1836, at Bourke's instigation, the NSW Legislative Council passed the Squatters Act, which attempted to regulate squatting beyond the official zone of settlement by requiring squatters to purchase an annual license.[31] Now, going in and claiming unknown lands was legal. In September, Bourke sent a police magistrate, William Lonsdale, down to Melbourne and began conducting organized land sales.

But what exactly was coming under license? The only official expedition south of the Murrumbidgee River had been undertaken by Hamilton Hume and William Hovell in 1824–25. They had taken a fairly direct line southwest to Port Phillip, skirting the western edge of the Australian Alps. In 1830, Charles Sturt had navigated the Murrumbidgee down to the Murray, which he named, and then the Murray down to Lake Alexandria and the sea. But between the coast and the Murrumbidgee, west of Hume and Hovell's route, the area remained incognita, at least officially. How many pastoralists had ventured illegally farther south is unknown. At the end of 1835, Bourke ordered the NSW surveyor Major Thomas Mitchell to complete his survey of the Darling River in western NSW down to its junction with the Murray River.[32] Bourke's desire for Mitchell to complete his expedition may have had nothing to do with the dilemma created a few months earlier by Batman, but Bourke included in his instructions this, in context, curious proviso: "If in your course upwards [of the Murray] you should meet with different streams, flowing into that along which you are travelling, you will follow that which you deem to afford the most promising appearance. . . ." Bourke added: "[It is] desirable that you should return to the settled parts of the colony by a route on the western side of the range of mountains named the Australian Alps, entering the settled parts of the colony by Yass or any more convenient point."[33]

Mitchell interpreted this proviso generously,[34] but it is also possible that Bourke intended him to (we have no record of conversation between the two men). Mitchell eventually broke away from the Murray route altogether to head southwest, then west across the district, and then south down the Glenelg River (which he named) at the far west of the Port Phillip District to the sea. Returning up the Glenelg some way, Mitchell then traveled east across country, deciding to make an excursion south again to visit Portland Bay. In the Mitchell legend, promoted in Mitchell's published journals and nearly all subsequent histories, the surveyor was astonished to find at Portland the Henty family well established in pastoral pursuits. Given that the Henty's establishment was common knowledge in Van Diemen's Land from 1834, it is hard to believe that it was completely unknown in Sydney by the time Mitchell left and that his expedition just happened to end up at Portland. From Portland, Mitchell returned across the unknown areas of Port Phillip, making detours every now and then, including to Mt. Macedon, where he spied in the distance the new port town of Melbourne. His description is disparaging, and in his official recommendation he suggested that the new port for the district should be at Cape Northumberland near the mouth of the Glenelg River on the coast he had surveyed. His recommendation came to nothing. Indeed, it was the presence of this new port that was a major factor in the attraction of the Port Phillip district, from here the wool could be sent to Yorkshire.[35]

Given that Mitchell suffered no serious rebuke for his generous interpretation of his excursion on the left bank of the Murray, it is hard to believe that Bourke's sending him on his third expedition when he did was not in some way expected to reveal much more of the hinterland of Port Phillip than was as yet officially known. It was not a minute too soon. As we have seen with the Coliban and Campaspe valleys, the pastoralists were poised for a land grab.

Listening to the Silent Archive

Compared with some places and times in the Australian past, the colonization of Port Phillip abounds with historiographical resources. Official documents, correspondence, diaries, memoirs, and visual representations crowd the archives and throw extraordinary light on the actions, motivations, and even the mind-set of the settlers. Yet this light also casts deep shadows. We catch only glimpses of Indigenous activity and motivations, as augmented as it may be by present-day Indigenous remembering. This is particularly true for the history of the settlement of the Coliban and Campaspe valleys. In the foyer of the First Peoples Exhibition at the Bunjilaka Aboriginal Cultural Centre at the Melbourne Museum is a relief map of the state spread across a table. Buttons at various points on this map when pressed give you an example of the Indigenous language of that area. In the center of the map, there is an area where there are no buttons to push; that area represents the Coliban/Campaspe valleys. There are examples of the Taungurung language to be found to the east and north of this area, and indeed there is now a handsome volume of Taungurung vocabulary. But of the original nine clans of the Taungurung, as the present-day Taungurung community website puts it, "[s]adly there are descendants of only five of those clan groups that survive today."[36]

The glimpses we have from the non-Indigenous records are tempered, of course, by the worldviews of the settlers, and their motivations were clear. They had come as the party of industry. They manufactured wool. The raw materials they sought were grass and water. The factories they ran were alive. But alive as they were, the sheep were a utility and a utility only, as was the land. Whatever beliefs the pastoralists held beyond the mercantile—and nearly all would have been at least nominally Christian—they saw the land that they entered as a resource, and their immediate moral authority the market. Few of them had come to stay; William Yaldwyn only held Barfold for eighteen months and probably spent little more than a few months on the property. Holding their runs was contingent on profit. If they did not produce, the runs were abandoned or sold. In this, they resembled the pastoral nomads of various regions of the world (say, Mongolia), driving their stock from one pasture to another. But these—let us call them traditional pastoralists—owned allegiance to the wide expanse of country they roamed from season to season. They understood its variations and gifts, and they understood its preservation. Such understanding was deep and tied within their emotional and cultural being. The first pastoralists who came to the Port Phillip district, however, were typically from another place, and it was to that other place that they gave political, emotional, even aesthetic allegiance. Those who did harbor an idea of staying—who saw a long view in their settlement—envisaged that that settlement would transform the land and redeem it from nature.

The Taungurung that the pastoralists in the Coliban and Campaspe valleys confronted were, like the other peoples of the Kulin nation, intrinsically and intimately attached to their country—and attached to it as it was. As I have argued elsewhere,[37] the Aboriginal country into which the settlers intruded was an enchanted landscape, to be engaged with inseparably as spiritual and material. It was a totemic landscape in which there was, as Catherine and Ronald Berndt put it, an "essential unity between people and their natural environment,"[38] a world full of signs of the Dreaming. It was a world into which any access granted was a matter of more than material concern. It was a matter of preserving the spiritual balance, and it would be expected that any strangers granted such access would adhere to the law of country, the law of spiritual and material balances. In this enchanted world, what might be thought of as a commodity also had a spiritual reality. This is why we must appreciate that there was more than a human intrusion.

When the Kulin heads negotiated with Batman in 1835, they negotiated only with fellow humans; Batman and his associates came without animals. They did not ride horses—they traveled on foot. What either side understood about the other's understanding of grazing stock is open to speculation. Indeed, it is probable that the Kulin who negotiated with Batman had never seen sheep, horses, or cattle, although they may have heard of strange beasts. On seeing the tracks of Mitchell's wagons and bullocks, the people of the southern Wimmera—who had not seen a European but heard of them—thought they were the tracks of white men and women. Similarly, a stray bullock from Mitchell's party was thought to be a white man, and a terrifying beast, by people in the Western District. These were unaccounted-for creatures, terrifying enough as tracks or as an individual animal.[39] What happened when they intruded en masse?

Taungurung country stretches across a large part of north-central Victoria.[40] A map would show Mitchell's journey, after crossing the Murray at what is now Albury, track entirely through Waveroo and Taungurung country. The present town of Benalla is near the beginning of the intrusion into Taungurung country and not far from the meeting of Taungurung and Waveroo; it was there that the first notable action against settlers—the "Faithful Massacre"—occurred.

Like maps, history tends to provide a panorama, allowing us to see events in a temporal as well as a spatial long view, driving us to deduce causes and impacts as obviously related, apparent at the time, and inevitable. This drive to make narrative sense, what Paul Ricoeur would call "narrativity," important as it is to us as humans, can deny the experience of events at ground level.

What did the Taungurung see in 1837? Each party that entered their country was startlingly similar: twenty or so men, some on horseback, others walking, some riding carts, along with around five thousand sheep, a few hundred cattle, bullock drays, and various horses without riders. The most familiar of these intruders were the men (and they were almost invariably men). Their skin color might have been different, as certainly was their clothing, not to mention their smell, but they walked as other humans did, spoke to each other as humans did, worked in teams as other humans did, and ate and drank as other humans did. But what to make of the majority of the intruders? All the cattle? The horses? Most of all, the thousands of sheep—so many that they may have become, suddenly, the largest population of any mammal species in Taungurung country? For a start, the newcomer humans seemed to be in the thrall of these animals, helping them to pasture, helping them cross rivers, waiting as the smaller ones gave birth, guarding them at night, and riding them. And yet they also treated them harshly, especially the bullocks, which they whipped to get them to drag drays. In many ways, these new animals were like dogs, but in many ways not.[41] The horses and bullocks and cattle were so much *bigger* than any kangaroo. So much bigger than humans. We know from the diaries kept by Yaldwyn and Mollison that the parties in mid-to-late 1837 criss-crossed each other's paths and that stock—particularly bullocks—were constantly straying on the journey, and that river crossings and various other circumstances caused delays. When Mitchell's survey party crossed this area the other way twelve months earlier, it was a disciplined caravan that took a little more than two weeks to travel from the Coliban to the Murray. Mollison's party took almost six months. The 1837 parties were undisciplined and messy, and the disturbance they made to the Taungurung country they passed through must have been enormous.

Knowing it as intimately as they did, knowing it as a living, spiritual place, the Taungurung would have seen a hoard blundering through streams, meadows, and woodlands, little caring for, or indeed noticing, the damage they caused. And this hoard looked to be a spiritual as well as a material intruder. Some reports of the very first contact hint that the Taungurung, and others, were helpful in suggesting good pasture for the sheep, but it may have been that the Europeans were being led to areas where they could cause the least harm. That is, the concern was more for country than for the Europeans. What we can be sure of is that the Taungurung were never far away from the traveling settlers, with many of them reporting that bands of Taungurung were traveling "parallel" with the settler parties.[42] The Taungurung were watching and observing. The lack of hostility to these hoards in the first twelve months or so may have been produced from a belief that they were just traveling through, down to the area around Melbourne, where some accommodation was granted. Then the sheer volume of those who came to stay made accommodation impossible by mid-1838. So, too, did the behavior of the settlers. Although they understood their country with both temporal and spatial long views, what the Taungurung saw when the pastoralists entered it was a grounded moment, a long moment that grew from disturbance to cataclysm. That is, in the twelve months from Ebden's intrusion to the Faithful incident, they may have moved from a willingness to accommodate to a recognition of an unrectifiable breach with their past—both spiritual and physical. A breach that had to be responded to.

Interpreting Indigenous Violence

In his groundbreaking book *Aborigines in Colonial Victoria 1835–86*, Michael Christie described various Aboriginal groups as "dispersing" flocks as part of the wide resistance to the settlement throughout the Port Phillip District. For Christie, such action was seen as part of a guerrilla war meant to disrupt the activity of the settlers.[43] Christie's interpretative model of behavior, not unreasonably, was that of post-WWII anticolonial nationalist campaigns in various parts of the world. It demanded materialist explanations and tended to concentrate on the human alone. Others have argued that such dispersals were meant as attacks on the settler economy. But we miss their importance if we concentrate too much on the human-to-human engagement. When settler posses found the stolen sheep, they usually found them corralled with makeshift fences. Most were alive. Often, some sheep had been mutilated—"butchered"—and their fat removed.[44] It is the mutilation we should take note of.

The first serious attack on settlers by the Taungurung was the "Faithful Massacre," as it quickly became known, in April 1838. Judith Bassett, in the most detailed examination of this event,[45] argued that it had to be understood as a ritual retaliation by a small group of Taungurung and Waveroo,[46] in retaliation for an attack shortly before, and that, contrary to accounts such as those by Christie that it was a large group of up to three hundred and part of a broad-based resistance to the settler invasion, it was a discreet act. While I am convinced by Basset's account of the attack as focused and ritual, and carried out by a small group assigned to the task, I think it can nevertheless be seen as part of a broad resistance but that that resistance, rather than looking like a twentieth-century anticolonial guerrilla campaign, rested on predominantly ritual action, determined more to evoke spiritual power than to inflict material harm.

It is clear, as Bassett argues, that the attack on the banks of the Broken River was very carefully planned and organized. As the settler David Reid, who had been with the Faithful party but not involved in the incident, explained in his memoir.[47]

> Early in the morning the shepherds started with their sheep, that is to say, having been camped all together during the night, in the morning after breakfast the sheep were divided into several flocks, enabling sheep to graze the better, two or three men had the driving of each flock. No blacks were at this time visible. After . . . a half to three quarters of an hour the men at the camp heard these men with the sheep cooeeing and crying out for assistance and on impulse . . . all rushed away from the drays. Immediately . . . a party of blacks emerged from a bed of reeds . . . and surrounded the drays.

As Reid makes clear, the shepherds had left their firearms in the drays. The attacking party had effectively cut the men off from their weapons. "It seems that the blacks must have had all this planned," Reid added. The shepherds were surrounded and systematically speared to death. Then, "the blacks not only pillaged the drays but drove off the sheep as well, but becoming, no doubt, tired and unaccustomed to drive sheep and having satisfied their hunger by killing some, they left the remainder to the mercies of the warrigals or native dogs. Out of the large number of sheep which Mr. William Faithful had in this unfortunate expedition not more than some two or three thousand were recovered."[48]

Reid would no doubt have agreed with later historian A. G. L. Shaw, who described the motivation for the attack as "plunder."[49] But the main items taken from the drays appear to have been clothing. Within a few weeks, the Taungurung warriors would be showing themselves very adept at driving sheep. Like many, Reid believed hunger was the motivation for killing the sheep. And it is clear here that the dogs were set on them as they would be in other incidents. Bassett claims the motivation was retaliation for a fatal altercation a little earlier nearby. No doubt that altercation contributed motivation, but let us look at the upshot of the incident: the loss of several thousand of Faithful's sheep. This was probably the prime intention. Killing the shepherds was simply to remove the guardians of the sheep. It is clear the attack was extremely well organized, and organized with a good knowledge of the shepherds' behavior.

Four weeks after the Faithful incident, on the other side of Taungurung country in the Coliban valley, Thomas Jones, one of William Bowman's shepherds, was killed. Around the time of the Faithful incident, Bowman had complained to the police magistrate in Melbourne, William Lonsdale—then the highest official in Port Phillip—that he "found the natives at my place who ran off as soon as they saw me. They had taken all my men's bedding."[50] Then on May 19, Jones's body was found. Another shepherd, Samuel Faloon, described the scene: "[W]e found Jones lying dead we found two large spears sticking in his body and his stomach open and the inside taken away his clothes were torn and his hat taken away, he had also several severe cuts on his head with a blunt instrument." Faloon added: "[T]he day before the murder they had taken a flock away . . . on the same day several blacks came to one of the huts and took away the bedding."[51] It is clear that these were coordinated, and not random, attacks.

Of course, it is possible that a dog or eagle may have torn open Jones's body after death, but the description matches too closely that given of another killing near the Ovens River in Waveroo country a year or so later: "[The blacks had] broken his skull with a tommyhawk, maimed him in the hand, bruised him with sticks and had cut a circular piece of flesh about nine inches [in] diameter out of his abdomen which they had taken away with them."[52] Compare to this the description of the ritual use of fat and human organs from A. W. Howitt's classic ethnographic study *The Native Tribes of South-East Australia*: "[T]he medicine-men of hostile tribes sneak into the camp in the night, and . . . garrotte one of the tribe, drag him a hundred yards or so from the camp, cut up his abdomen obliquely, take out the kidney and caul-fat . . ." Howitt explains the purpose: "The fat is greatly prized. . . . they believe the prowess and virtues of the victim will pass to those who use the fat." Lynne Hume, in a more recent study, also discusses the use of fat in sorcery.[53] Howitt also quotes descriptions of "medicine-men" seeking objects belonging to an enemy, to likewise steal the prowess of the enemy.[54] So many of the objects stolen—particularly the bedding—appear to have had no practical use. Their theft is more convincingly explained as the taking of objects to use in sorcery than as "plunder."

On June 9, three weeks after Jones's death, Samuel Futter, one of William Yaldwyn's shepherds, was tending a flock of Yaldwyn's sheep on the banks of the Coliban. Nearby, one of Bowman's shepherds was also tending a flock. Bowman's shepherd came to Futter, alarmed, and said: "There are blacks here I can see their dogs." Futter went back with him and found the dogs "among" the sheep; they had, according to Futter, already killed fourteen. Then Taungurung warriors appeared, about twenty of them, armed with spears and dispersed in twos, running at the shepherds. The shepherds fled. The warriors chased them for "three-quarters of a mile" before leaving them and returning to the sheep. The shepherds went to report to Yaldwyn's overseer, John Coppock, who organized a group of his men to retrieve the sheep. When they got to the site of the attack, they found more of the sheep had been killed. Futter described that he "saw some hanging on the trees."[55] Coppock said that he found "carcasses of sheep . . . some cut up, and a great many totally destroyed."[56] The other sheep had gone. Coppock and his men tracked them for three miles north to a hill on the Coliban and found them corralled in a bow yard "made as a white man would make it."[57] It was now near dusk. The Taungurung warriors had fortified their position "behind fallen trees and sheets of bark." When the Europeans approached, according to Coppock, "they threw up their hands and dared us to come on some said Come on you white b—-s, I distinctly heard these words." In the ensuing battle, no European was injured, but a number of the warriors were killed—Coppock's men were well armed. Futter stated, "I do not know how many blacks were killed only what I was told I saw only two myself." Coppock estimated that the warriors numbered about fifty or so. As it was now dark, the Europeans retreated. When Futter got back to his hut, he found "the tarpaulin of which it was made and nearly everything in it" had been taken. The next morning, Coppock's party returned to collect the sheep and the items taken from the huts over the previous few days. "The blacks had disappeared and we found the sheep a short distance off. . . . [W]e found a great many of the sheep had been killed, some were cut up." Futter claimed that "some of them were cut up as a butcher would do in quarters."

How many Taungurung were killed that day is open to question. Seven or eight seems the colonial consensus.[58] But it was reported that "90 rounds of ball cartridge [were] expended."[59] It is probable that almost all the warriors were killed. There were many reasons to underreport such killings. As the hanging of the seven Europeans for the deaths of thirty Wirrayaraay people at Myall Creek, virtually at the same time as this incident, demonstrated, the colonial administration was serious about treating Aboriginal Australians as equal before the law. We can compare this reticence about

Aboriginal deaths in the late 1830s to the recollections made, usually in private later in the century, which admit—from the safety of decades—a more cavalier attitude to the killing of Indigenous people.[60]

When the Melbourne police magistrate William Lonsdale heard of the June 1838 killings, he sent troops to bring Coppock in for an explanation. They found Coppock already on the road to Melbourne to report them. Coppock claimed, "The attack was so sudden that we could not enter upon any explanation." Yet Lonsdale, in his letter forwarding Coppock's deposition to the colonial secretary in Sydney, wrote: "[The blacks] have some time past been very troublesome in the country about Mr. Yaldwyn's station they disappear & return within unexpected periods." Lonsdale believed the attackers were "some of the same who were concerned in the attack on Mr. Faithfuls party."[61] This sense of a connection is one reason they suggested that the group knew some English. One thing is for sure: the shepherds knew no Taungurung. A shout in that language could have been misheard—for instance, the Taungurung root for "steal" is *baadha*; for "die" *wiig*; for "fight," *wiy-arr.*[62]

It is hard to tell how many of the settlers actually believed that it was only a small renegade group instead of a widespread reaction to the European intrusion, but it worked within a rhetoric of overall Indigenous acquiescence to the usurpation of their land. Such thinking was no doubt bolstered by the frequent, seemingly friendly visits from Taungurung at other times to ask for food. Interestingly, though, David Reid believed such visits were designed to reassure the settlers and put them off guard. Perhaps they were, but they were almost certainly reconnoiters. As the actions at Broken River and in the Coliban valley show, the Taungurung had been observing the Europeans' behavior closely and learning to replicate it. The idea of the attack being the work merely of renegades does not stack up when we consider that the colonial records of almost every incident of sheep theft in these years suggest the deaths of around "6–8" Taungurung.

The sheep were not dispersed. On the contrary, as Lonsdale observed, "in this instance the blacks adopted more method than they usually do and the yards in which they put the sheep were made after the manner of the white shepherds"—that is, the sheep that had not already been killed. Food had not been the motivation for killing, even though the sheep may have been "butchered." When Coppock's party arrived, they found sheep cut up and many hanging from trees. This hanging could have replicated the hanging of carcasses to drain the blood as part of the European butchering process, a practice observed by the Taungurung. But the warriors had left the carcasses behind, no doubt deliberately to be found in this state by the Europeans, who, as the fortifications testify, they expected to be in pursuit.

Jones had been killed and his organs taken three weeks earlier from the same vicinity. Bedding and other goods had been stolen at the same time. Why wait three weeks to attack again? Assume for a moment that these were thefts to be used to gain ritual control over the Europeans. Such an assumption explains the delay—and the spasmodic nature of the attacks in general—as a period of waiting to see if the sorcery worked. If this had been the case, the Taungurung soon realized the sorcery had not worked: the Europeans, human and animal, remained. The Taungurung then changed emphasis and ritually mutilated sheep in the manner of the Europeans, perhaps believing this was a ritual to negate the sheep's powers (before they ate them). As I have argued before, the relationship between Europeans and their sheep was probably seen as totemic.[63] The other animal to be most often attacked was also the animal the Europeans would have been seen as most close to: horses. One interesting aspect about the horses is that the settlers did not themselves suspect the Taungurung of attacking them. They could not find any rationale for an Indigenous attack—they had not been eaten and were not considered food. And yet the attacks bear the hallmarks of ritual. One of the horses is described as strangled, garroted. At least two had been attacked in the mouth, their tongues cut out. Individually, the horses were far more highly valued than the other animals. And the settler relationship to them was visibly far more intimate—they were ridden, after all.

While these mutilations and killings of animals were certainly part of an attack on the settlers, they were also an attack on the perceived powers of the animals. As Alfred Crosby pointed out some time ago, "the efficiency and speed with which [European domestic animals] can alter environments, even continental environments, are superior to those for any machine we have thus far devised."[64] To a people finely attuned to the environment, this potential must have been evident within months. To a people who believed that environment to be an enchanted place, these animals must have seemed like devils. The Taungurung attacks were acts of resistance, but acts that called on powers beyond the material. In the end, of course, they failed, but they were concisely planned and based on astute observation of European behavior.

Conclusion

If the Kulin nation, including the Taungurung, had negotiated with Batman to limit the intrusion of settlers, that, too, failed. But the Kulin who negotiated may have had no way of knowing that they were not just allowing a few strange, but essentially fellow, humans temporary access to their countries; they were opening the flood gates to an invasion of hundreds of thousands of even more alien beasts that would turn their countries not just upside down but inside out. When this became evident, they could not have felt other than a tragic sense of betrayal, and they took action.

In Victorian Indigenous memory, the treaty is seen now as very much an act of cultural misconception. In the First Peoples Exhibition at the Bunjilaka Aboriginal Cultural Centre at the Melbourne Museum, the treaty marks the entrance of the European into this Aboriginal world. A *tanderrum* misconstrued is the sense conveyed, and thus a *generosity* abused. And as we see in the foregoing, Taungurung attacked European animal stock in response to how much this betrayal was seen in the invasion of these animals into the environment, into country.

Notes

1. This chapter reprises the arguments I made in my 2008 paper "Tricks or Treats: The Case for Kulin Knowing in Batman's Treaty," *History Australia* 5, no. 2 (2008): 38.1–38.14, and in *The Lamb Enters the Dreaming: Nathanael Pepper and the Ruptured World* (Melbourne: Scribe, 2007), through the focus on the settlement of the Western Tauranguag country in the Coliban and Campaspe valleys of central Victoria and taking into account recent scholarship.

2. This survey is drawn from J. O. Randell, *Pastoral Settlement in Northern Victoria, Vol. 1: The Coliban District* (Melbourne: Queensberry Hill Press, 1979), and *Vol. 2: The Campaspe District* (Melbourne: Chandos, 1982); R. V. Billis and A. S. Kenyon, *Pastoral Pioneers of Port Phillip*, 2nd ed. (Melbourne: Stockland, 1974).

3. A. F. Mollison, *An Overlanding Diary*, ed. J. O. Randell (Melbourne: Mast Gully Press, 1980), 17. "The track" is Mitchell's Line.

4. Yaldwyn's journal can be found in J. O. Randell, *Yaldwyn of the Golden Spurs: The Life of William Henry Yaldwyn 1801–1866: Sussex Squire and Australian Squatter—Member of the Legislative Council of Queensland* (Melbourne: Mast Gully Press, 1980).

5. The most detailed discussion of this incident is Judith Bassett, "The Faithfull Massacre at the Broken River, 1838," *Journal of Australian Studies* 13, no. 24 (1989): 18–34.

6. D. T. Jenkins and K. G. Ponting, *British Wool Textile Industry 1770–1914* (Aldershot: Scolar Press, 1987).

7. James Belich has argued that the importance of sheep has been exaggerated in accounts of the economic development of Port Phillip. This may be the case, but it was

wool, and the hoped-for profits from it, that brought the pastoralists into Port Phillip in the first few years. (Belich, *Replenishing the Earth: The Settler Revolution and the Rise of the Anglo-World, 1783–1939* [Oxford: Oxford University Press, 2009], 257–277.)

8. James Belich, "The Rise of the Anglo World: Settlement in North America and Australasia, 1784–1918," in *Rediscovering the British World*, ed. P. A. Buckner (Calgary: University of Calgary Press, 2006), 39–57. See also Russell Smandych, "Colonialism, Settler Colonialism, and Law: Settler Revolutions and the Dispossession of Indigenous Peoples through Law in the Long Nineteenth Century," *Settler Colonial Studies* 3, no. 1 (2013): 82–101.

9. *Report of the Parliamentary Select Committee on the Aboriginal Tribes (British Settlements)*. Reprinted, with Comments, by the Aborigines' Protection Society (London, 1837), v.

10. Marnie Bassett, *The Hentys* (London: Oxford University Press, 1954), 251.

11. See Standish Motte, *Outline of a System of Legislation, for Securing Protection to the Aboriginal Inhabitants of All Countries Colonized by Great Britain; Extending to Them Political and Social Rights, Ameliorating Their Condition, and Promoting Their Civilization. Drawn Up at the Request of the Committee of The Aborigines' Protection Society, for the Purpose of Being Laid before the Government* (London, 1840).

12. M. C. Levy, *Governor George Arthur: A Colonial Benevolent Despot* (Melbourne: Georgia House, 1953), 105; A. G. L. Shaw, *Sir George Arthur, Bart: Superintendent of British Honduras, Lieutenant-Governor of Van Diemen's Land and of Upper Canada, Governor of the Bombay Presidency* (Melbourne: Melbourne University Press, 1980), 133.

13. Glenelg entry, *Australian Dictionary of Biography* (Melbourne: Melbourne University Press, 1966–2002).

14. Glenelg to Bourke, April 13, 1836, *Historical Records of Victoria* (Melbourne: Victorian Government Printing Office, 1981), 1:25.

15. See Bourke's letter to Glenelg, October 10, 1835, *Historical Records of Victoria* 1:26. See also Shaw, *Sir George Arthur, Bart*, 15–19.

16. For a detailed account of the machinations in Glenelg's changes of heart, see James Boyce, *1835: The Founding of Melbourne and the Conquest of Australia* (Melbourne: Black Ink, 2011), 127–135.

17. Since I have dealt in detail with this theme in my 2008 article "Tricks or Treats?," here I shall reprise my discussion as briefly as possible. Since 2008, when that article appeared, the most important further studies of the treaty are Boyce's *1835*, which shows the importance of the opening up of Port Phillip in the subsequent history of Australia, and Bain Attwood's *Possession: Batman's Treaty and the Matter of History* (Melbourne: Melbourne University Press, 2009), which focuses on the reception of the treaty in Victoria through the nineteenth century into the twentieth century.

18. See Attwood, *Possession*.

19. Paul Carter, *Living in a New Country: History, Travelling and Language* (London: Faber and Faber, 1992), 138. Carter's later work modifies this view.

20. See comment below on the First Peoples exhibition, Museum Victoria.

21. Diane Barwick, "Mapping the Past: An Atlas of the Victorian Clans 1835–1904, Part 1," *Aboriginal History* 8, no. 2 (1984): 100–131, 122.

22. See discussion of this in M. W. Bean, *The Decline of English Feudalism 1215–1540* (Manchester: Manchester University Press, 1968), 1–6.

23. See William Thomas's description in T. F. Bride and C. E. Sayers, eds., *Letters from Victorian Pioneers* (Melbourne: Heinemann, 1969), 439, and Sylvia J. Hallam, "A View from the Other Side of the Western Frontier: Or 'I Met a Man Who Wasn't There . . . ,'" *Aboriginal History* 7, no. 2 (1983): 134–157.

24. Barwick, "Mapping the Past," 107.

25. Intriguingly, Barwick also suggested that the area in both the main treaty and the subsequent treaty dealing with the Geelong area (which has always been understood as an opportunist fiction by even Batman's supporters) "so neatly fit the territories of the Wurundjeri-balluk and the Yaluki-willam and those of the two clans near Geelong whom they married . . . that the interpreters and owners must have achieved some mutual comprehension—whatever they thought of Batman's intentions." (Diane Barwick, *Rebellion at Coranderrk* [Canberra: Aboriginal History, 1998], 24.)

26. See Kenny, "Tricks and Treats."

27. Bean, *The Decline of English Feudalism*, 1–6.

28. These terms are used in the deed.

29. See Henry Reynolds, *The Other Side of the Frontier: Aboriginal Resistance to the European Invasion of Australia* (Melbourne: Penguin Books, 1990), 65.

30. *Historical Records of Victoria*, 1:12–14.

31. Alastair Davidson, *The Invisible State: The Formation of the Australian State 1788–1901* (Cambridge: Cambridge University Press, 1991), 69; A. G. L. Shaw, *A History of Port Phillip District* (Melbourne: Melbourne University Press, 1996), 68.

32. Gregory C. Eccleston, *Major Mitchell's 1836 "Australia Felix" Expedition: A Re-evaluation* (Melbourne: Monash Publications in Geography, 1992), 27.

33. Eccleston, *Major Mitchell's 1836 "Australia Felix" Expedition*, 27.

34. Eccleston, *Major Mitchell's 1836 "Australia Felix" Expedition*, 27.

35. Bride, *Letters*, 87; in many of the settlers' journals, Melbourne is simply referred to as "the Port."

36. Loraine Padgham, "Taungurung: A Brief History," Taungurung News, http://taungurung.net/2011/04/taungurung_a_brief_history.html, accessed October 4, 2017.

37. Kenny, *The Lamb Enters the Dreaming*, passim, but particularly 153–156.

38. R. M. Berndt, *The First Australians* (Sydney: Ure Smith, 1967), 294–295.

39. See discussion of these incidents in Kenny, *The Lamb Enters the Dreaming*, 164ff.

40. See Barwick, "Mapping the Past." Barwick's mapping of the Taungurung clans substantially concurs with the descriptions given on the current Taungurung community website: Padgham, "Taungurung."

41. See Kenny, *The Lamb Enters the Dreaming*, 146–179; Bruno David, *Landscapes, Rock-Art and the Dreaming: An Archeology of Preunderstanding* (London: Leicester University Press, 2002), 17–18.

42. See descriptions in David Reid Papers, "Typed from Manuscript Notes of the Early Times in Australia, as Recited by an Old Pioneer, David Reid, Esq. J. P. of

Moorawatha, near Howlong; Taken Down by J. C. H. Ogier, 1905," MS 7961, State Library of Victoria.

43. M. F. Christie, *Aborigines in Colonial Victoria 1835–86* (Sydney: Sydney University Press, 1979).

44. See discussion of this in Kenny, *The Lamb Enters the Dreaming*, 173–176.

45. Judith Bassett, "Faithful Massacre"; see also Randell, *Pastoral Settlement*, 1:26–30; Bride, *Letters*, 219.

46. Interestingly, George Robinson notes the Taungurung and Waveroo in company in his 1840s journals.

47. David Reid Papers.

48. David Reid Papers.

49. Shaw, *A History*, 114.

50. Quoted in Randell, *Pastoral Settlement*, 1:124.

51. Samuel Faloon Deposition, Police Magistrates Depositions, VPRS 2136, Public Record Office Victoria, 380.

52. Ian D. Clark, ed., *The Journals of George Augustus Robinson, Chief Protector, Port Phillip Aboriginal Protectorate*, Vol. 1: *1 January 1839–30 September 1840*, 2nd ed. (Ballarat: Heritage Matters, 2000), 263.

53. Lynne Hume, *Ancestral Power: The Dreaming, Consciousness and Aboriginal Australians* (Melbourne: Melbourne University Press, 2002), 124.

54. A. W. Howitt, *The Native Tribes of South-East Australia*, Facsimile of 1904 edition (Canberra: Aboriginal Studies Press, 1996), 367.

55. Futter deposition, July 7, 1838, Police Magistrates Depositions, VPRS 2136, Public Record Office Victoria, 411–413.

56. Coppock deposition, June 29, 1838, Police Magistrates Depositions, VPRS 2136, Public Record Office Victoria, 394–396.

57. Futter deposition.

58. Randell, *Pastoral Settlement*, 1:90.

59. Edward Parker, quoted in Randell, *Pastoral Settlement*, 1:91.

60. Reid Papers; James McLaurin, "Memories of Early Australia," MS 8527, State Library of Victoria.

61. Lonsdale to Col. Secretary, 38/84, July 2, 1838, Lonsdale Letterbook 1836–1840, VPRS 1, Public Records Office Victoria, 250.

62. *Taungurung: liwik-nganjin-al ngula-dhan yaawinbu yananinon*, comp. Lee Healy (Melbourne: Victorian Aboriginal Corporation for Languages, 2011).

63. Kenny, *The Lamb Enters the Dreaming*, 176–179.

64. Alfred Crosby, *Ecological Imperialism: The Biological Expansion of Europe 900–1900* (Cambridge: Cambridge University Press, 1986), 173.

PART THREE

CONNECTIONS

CHAPTER TEN

Envoys of Interest

A Cherokee, a Ra'iatean, and the Eighteenth-Century British Empire

KATE FULLAGAR

One late summer evening in 1774, on the grounds of a country estate in Cambridgeshire, England, a small party sat down to enjoy a particularly well-prepared shoulder of mutton. The chef was Mai, a visitor from Ra'iatea in the South Pacific who had cooked the meat in Polynesian fashion. "Having dug a deep hole in the ground," explained one guest, "he placed the fuel at the bottom of it, and then covered it with clean pebbles; when properly heated, he laid the mutton neatly enveloped in leaves, at the top, and having closed the hole, walked constantly around it, very deliberately, observing the sun." The guest went on: "the meat was afterwards brought to the table, and much commended."[1]

Twelve years earlier, farther south in the port town of Plymouth, a larger party of English folk had gathered to enjoy the performance of another visitor from the New World. In June 1762, the Appalachian Cherokee warrior Ostenaco had sailed to shore on a tender singing "a solemn dirge with a very loud voice." His song was an offering of thanks to his Maker for his safe arrival from the colonial port of Williamsburg, Virginia. "The loudness and uncouthness of his singing," reported one observer, "drew a vast crowd of boats, filled with spectators, from all the ships in the harbor."[2]

Throughout the eighteenth century, there were similar scenes of Indigenous custom played out on British shores. Mostly, the pattern of response by Britons was the same. One or two eyewitnesses commented on the unfolding of the scene, and then they offered a discussion of what the foreign mores on display told other Britons about their own customs. These discussions usually went on to join larger debates about what the presence of Indigenous people in Britain illuminated about British society in general. The narrator of Mai's feast, for instance, held up the visitor's cooking as a critique of "fastidious gourmands" in London who would "deride . . . simple method[s]." For are not their own "pheasants, or partridges," he asked, "now frequently brought to table wrapped in vine leaves?" The narrator went on to suggest that Mai represented the "natural" politeness of the noble savage, which was meant as a refutation of the overrefinement of eighteenth-century British culture. Conversely, the reporter on Ostenaco's dirge described the Cherokees' practice as "frightful." He proceeded to tell other anecdotes about Ostenaco's visit that were intended to congratulate British society for being so much more advanced than anything a Cherokee might know.

Rarely did British commentators engage with what the Indigenous custom might mean for the visitors themselves. They did not stop to consider what certain cooking practices or ritual songs revealed about the visitors' lives, as they were transplanted half a world away. Indigenous visitors to Britain were overwhelmingly narrated as windows into Britain's own imperial society. This perspective has colored almost all subsequent scholarship on eighteenth-century Indigenous visitors to Britain.[3] Historians have, on the whole, regarded such travelers as conduits through which to understand the Georgian British empire. Although a valuable way to gain insight into this significant phenomenon, such a practice has also had the effect of diminishing the visitors' own historical presence. At best, these historians have underscored through their subject how Indigenous people featured in the imperial past more than has been acknowledged. But they have not seen in them ways to assess precisely how empire, in turn, featured in different Indigenous pasts.

To their credit, a few scholars, inspired by the decolonizing trends of the 1970s, have tried to read against the grain of eighteenth-century assumptions about the significance of Indigenous visitors. This minority has sought to overturn the notion of Indigenous travelers as ciphers for imperial history, and to show them instead as actors in their own present. John Oliphant, for instance, has argued that Ostenaco's trip to Britain is better seen as the result of a personal grab for "enhanced influence."[4] Eric McCormick, similarly, has explained the success of Mai's journey as a consequence of qualities "peculiar to himself" rather than of British predeterminations.[5] These more Indigenous-centered perspectives are refreshing, but they have consistently replaced the "cipher" narrative with a model of self-seeking opportunism. Agency only ever seems to emerge in this literature in the form of pragmatic individualism. Moreover, even though these scholars have sought to question notions of Indigenous visitors as passive figures in imperial history, they have not gone so far as to test the central place that empire is so often supposed to have had in Indigenous lives.

This chapter aims to situate Indigenous travelers in their own contexts. Unlike most other studies of Indigenous travelers, which focus on single visitors and place the visit itself squarely at their center, this chapter takes a combined comparative and biographical approach. That is, it looks at the parallel life histories of Ostenaco and Mai in order to see beyond interpretations of personal power plays as well as to rethink the momentousness of the imperial encounter for each.

Comparison helps reveal commonalities between separate Indigenous actors that may not otherwise stand out—most notably, here, the similar ways in which Ostenaco and Mai acted for interests larger than the self. Only when compared to the dogged policy of Mai to pursue familial vengeance, for example, do Ostenaco's actions seem also to suggest a lifelong larger cause. In Ostenaco's case, the object of that cause grew over time from town to region to nation. Such overall collectivist behavior rejigs earlier understandings of Indigenous travelers as canny or "wily" self-servers.[6]

Biography helps us put the role of empire—at least during the Age of Revolution—into a more modest perspective. When scanning the whole of a life, the advent of British strangers is scaled down; it takes its place among a variety of other factors shaping individual Indigenous behavior. In the cases of Ostenaco and Mai, the imperial encounter turned out to be significant but not particularly more so than their encounters with fellow and enemy Indigenous groups. At the end of their lives, negotiating with white Britons probably did not register for either man as his most important memory. Such a probability puts the historian of empire in a little-experienced position of marginality; it makes the historian of empire start to question the parameters of her field.

The chapter divides in simple fashion between an account of Ostenaco's life and then of Mai's life; it discusses the literature on each and reveals the ways in which their biographies, when viewed together, suggest both more complex motivations and less imperial circumscription for eighteenth-century Indigenous travelers than hitherto supposed. Ostenaco and Mai were envoys of interest to their local communities, their British interlocutors, and, these days, to the reconception of British imperial historiography.

Ostenaco: Cherokee Leader

Ostenaco was an influential Cherokee warrior of the eighteenth century who lived from about 1715 to about 1779. His life spanned the period from the first European arrivals in his southern Appalachian homelands to the wars for American Independence. Ostenaco still awaits a full biography, though he has figured in a few articles and wider surveys. The generalist view has been that Ostenaco represents in his person the powerlessness that colonization eventually brought to all Cherokees.[7] The more particularist view sees that, despite colonization, Ostenaco still controlled his own actions, which were apparently to advance his personal "prestige and power."[8]

Neither perspective is groundless. The Cherokees did find themselves significantly reduced and embattled by century's end compared to their position one hundred years earlier. And, indeed, Ostenaco's many switches in policy throughout his life could well suggest that he was mostly out to gain kudos for himself during the overall process of decline. Both observations, however, are better accommodated by flipping the dominant views on their heads: Ostenaco's apparently inconsistent about turns signify instead the *realpolitik* moves of a leader protecting changing collective interests. Such maneuverings, taken together, represent an exemplar of resistance to annihilation, rather than any symbol or confirmation of it.

Ostenaco's initial political loyalty was to his town of Tellico. The town of Tellico was located in the Overhills region, one of four main clusters of Cherokee towns in the eighteenth century. By 1740, Ostenaco had achieved the high-ranking warrior title of Outacite, or Mankiller, of Tellico.[9] Through the 1740s, Ostenaco's main objective was to extend Tellico's special relationship with the fledgling British colony of South Carolina. Tellico led the Cherokee trade with Britain at this time, exchanging lucrative deerskins for arms, metals, and glassware. In turn, Charlestown (as it was called then) monopolized the Cherokee connection among the British. Ostenaco championed this exclusive trade because he believed such protected, movable wealth ensured the greatest security for his small community.[10]

In 1751, his town-based allegiances were tested when a rival Overhills town, Chota, suggested that the trade of the region as a whole might be improved by introducing potential competition from British Virginia, or even from surrounding French colonies. Ostenaco's instinct until then had been to assuage South Carolina's leadership in order to maintain Tellico's position as most preferred Cherokee town. After a series of mishaps with Tellico's own leadership at the same time, however, Ostenaco shifted to Chota's view, helped open up negotiations with Virginia, and moved himself to a satellite town of Chota.[11]

Earlier historians have seen this abrupt switch in policy as a prime instance of Ostenaco's self-interested behavior,[12] but later events suggest that it was instead his first redefinition of collective interests: he had come to see that regions rather than towns stood fairer chances for success against the region-like colonies of a rapidly organizing British empire. From this point on, in the colonial records at least, he started to use the word "we" to refer to all Overhills people rather than just those from Tellico.[13] In addition, it is worth noting that Ostenaco never challenged the Chota leadership and never seemed to suffer ridicule from his own contemporaries for this switch: few fellow Overhills suspected him of solely individualist maneuvers.

Between 1753 and 1755, Overhills Cherokees enjoyed the fruits of their gamble: South Carolina was forced to concede a freer trade, and the Overhills benefited from more advantageous terms. The new line of communication to Virginia, however, eventually produced its own set of problems. From 1755, Overhills Cherokees became entangled in Virginia's separate battle for the Ohio valley. Ostenaco fought for Virginia several times, motivated always by a need to keep multiple colonial trading sites in play.[14]

In one sense, the connection worked. At the conclusion of one battle, Ostenaco brought home with him a contingent of Virginian soldiers to build a fort near Chota. The Overhills Cherokees had long wished for a colonial fort to keep their homes and kin safe from rival Indian groups while they were away for increasingly longer times hunting or fighting for colonists. By 1757, the region had a fort built for them by Virginia *and* one built for them by South Carolina.[15] In another sense, though, the Virginians proved tougher partners than the Carolinians. Flailing in their own battles of the Seven Years' War, these colonists reneged more and more frequently on their promises of trade or prizes to the Cherokees. By 1759, the ongoing continental war had worn down South Carolina's sense of obligation, too. Displeased already at the Cherokees' determination to play them off with Virginia, South Carolina also began to cut corners in their deals and promises.

Tensions escalated, eventually coming to a head in late 1759 when the South Carolina governor, William Lyttelton, arrested a contingent of Cherokee leaders that had come to Charlestown to stem the unraveling of relations. Cherokee political leaders argued with Lyttelton for weeks for their release. They managed to save a few key figures, but in March 1760 an armed showdown between the groups led tragically to the colonists' butchering of all remaining twenty-two hostages.[16]

Ostenaco had not been among the Charlestown contingent; he had been asked by his leaders to stay behind in the Overhills to keep the peace. When he heard about the massacre, his belief in the profits of partnership dropped like a stone. "If peace were made even 7 times," he is reported to have said at this moment, he "would always disregard and break it."[17] The event produced his second key policy switch. Ostenaco resolved at this point to reject all British overtures and take an aggressive stance against every colony. Significantly, the switch entailed also another redefinition of his collective interests. When he had moved near Chota, Ostenaco had simultaneously enlarged his loyalties from town to region. In declaring war on the British, he widened them further still from region to nation.[18]

Ostenaco ordered a sustained attack on the South Carolina fort at Chota in retaliation for the hostage massacre. His superiors persuaded him to halt it while Cherokees in Charlestown gave peace one last stab. But by June 1760, South Carolina had called in Jeffrey Amherst's British North American army, and war was inevitable. Ostenaco engineered one of the bloodiest acts of the ensuing Anglo-Cherokee conflict by renewing the bombardment of the fort at Chota until he forced its surrender in August 1760. He oversaw the release of the two hundred soldiers still inside and almost certainly helped mastermind the brutal attack on the captives' return march home. Of the two hundred rank-and-file soldiers limping back to Charlestown, it looked like around twenty-two died in the attack. The numbers accorded with eighteenth-century Cherokee notions of restorative justice. No document places Ostenaco squarely as the architect of the event, but several observers noted how quickly he appeared soon afterward, calling for a cessation of hostilities now that blood on both sides had been "quieted."[19]

Ostenaco could not have been surprised, though, to find that South Carolina declined to see it that way. Violence between both continued for another year. At the end of 1761, after Amherst dispatched another huge force of British soldiers to South Carolina, which razed dozens of towns and destroyed thousands of acres, the Cherokees sued for peace. Having been one of the fiercest proponents of the war, Ostenaco was among the most reluctant to sign a treaty. By midwinter, however, even he conceded that surrender was better than further hardships. It was a third switch in policy, but it was as ever consistent with his avowal to act always in the best interests of the Cherokee collective before him in the moment.

Ostenaco's behavior through the peace process spoke volumes about his canny rather than defeatist approach to this latest policy change. While Chota's political leaders were down in Charlestown ratifying the peace with South Carolina, Ostenaco brokered a separate peace with Virginia. The colony of Virginia had not contributed much to the Anglo-Cherokee war, but in Cherokee minds it was just as culpable in starting the conflict as South Carolina. Ostenaco wanted to secure peace with all nearby parts of the British empire; after all, South Carolina was, at precisely that moment, ensuring ratification from all four Cherokee regions. Far from an individualist intent on gaining a personal advantage, Ostenaco was in this play merely keeping pace with Britain's own methods of statecraft. Ostenaco probably also knew that a separate peace with a "sister" colony that had given so little to the recent local war would deeply annoy Charlestown, and thus would keep South Carolinians on their toes when it came to assuming Cherokee subservience in the future.[20]

In December 1761, Ostenaco received the Virginian representative, Henry Timberlake, at Chota. "The bloody tomahawke, so long lifted against our brethren the English must now be buried deep, deep in the ground," intoned Ostenaco when they met.[21] He treated Timberlake with every mark of hospitality, so it took the soldier a few weeks to realize that he was in fact being kept as a guarantee for the peace process going on in Charlestown. If the peace talks down there failed, Timberlake would be the first to feel Cherokee ire. As the Virginian eventually cottoned on: "their revenge falls on any of the same country that unfortunately comes within their reach."[22]

Finally, in March 1762, Ostenaco heard that the South Carolina peace was complete. He offered to escort Timberlake back to his capital, Williamsburg. Once there, Ostenaco put his next plan into action. He requested a berth to see King George III himself, to make sure once and for all that every British colony would take the overall Cherokee peace seriously. Timberlake was amazed to hear such a request, and even more surprised to see the Virginian governor, Francis Fauquier, consent to it. Timberlake had not dealt with the Cherokees long enough to understand how influential they still were with southern governors, despite their recent defeat in battle.[23]

Against this background, Ostenaco's "solemn dirge" upon arrival in Britain begins to look more like a sign of his seriousness regarding national business and less like a quirky outburst of exotic ritual. Ostenaco met the king on 8 July, took in a whirlwind tour of the best and brightest of London, and was home again by October. His speech to George III had been clear about the hardships of the recent war for the Cherokees, but also about his people's sincere wish to build a new and lasting truce. "Some time ago my nation was in darkness, but that darkness is now cleared up. . . . There will be no more bad talks in my nation."[24]

Neither the king nor his secretary of state, Lord Egremont, made any binding promises to Ostenaco in reply, but the old warrior may have felt justified in believing that his journey to London was not unrelated to the crown's actions toward Native Americans the following year. In October 1763, the British crown proclaimed a boundary line in North America in order to protect Indian lands from settler encroachment. Numerous factors, of course, were behind the royal proclamation, but, as Ostenaco would have known, it was Lord Egremont who drafted the original act. To what extent the secretary of state had been influenced by his Cherokee visitor, bringing tales of bloody and unproductive war, deserves more speculation than it has thus far received.[25]

As is well known, the royal proclamation of 1763 did not deliver on its potential. The crown did not have the manpower, cash, or will to enforce the line.[26] Ostenaco saw crucial amendments to the boundary made as early as 1765. At a talk near Charlestown, he was among the assorted Cherokees who agreed to adjust it to the settlers' advantage, though he noted at the time that while "the price the white people give for land . . . is very small . . . land lasts forever."[27]

Ostenaco decided to support treaties rather than armed resistance for the rest of the 1760s—it was a much leaner decade for the Cherokees than the 1750s had been, and, as a national leader now, he continued down the path most feasible at the time. Nonetheless, his calculated cooperation had a limit. In 1775, when the speculator Richard Henderson pressed for a massive amendment to the boundary around the Cherokees' northernmost hunting grounds, Ostenaco felt that enough was enough. Henderson wanted to carve out nearly thirty thousand square miles, which was more than all the other conceded "amendments" till then combined.[28] The Henderson event is well known in wider Cherokee history as the moment when Attakullakulla's son, Dragging Canoe, stomped out of the talks, declaring dissent from his father's diplomacy-led generation and war on all white settlers—whether colonial or revolutionary. Few historians have noted that one member of his father's generation, old Ostenaco, decided quietly to join him.[29]

Ostenaco could not agree with Dragging Canoe on the issue of renewed war—perhaps he had seen too much of the colonists' resources fifteen years earlier. But he did agree that negotiation was now at an end. It took a couple more years for Ostenaco to complete this fourth and final switch in policy, but by 1777 he had migrated with Dragging Canoe and the mostly young "Chickamauga" dissidents, as they became known, west into what is now Tennessee. Interestingly, the move involved yet another redefinition of allegiance—this time from nation to subnational faction, which, certainly, was a narrowing of focus, but it was hardly a reduction down to the self.

Around 1778, Ostenaco drops out of all records, and it is presumed that he died soon afterward.[30] It remains significant, however, that this one-time advocate for colonial trade, later war leader against British aggression, then stalwart peace negotiator ended his days removed entirely from white activities. His total rejection of any relationship with whites proved to be his most frustrating play of all. Loyalists such as the colonial Indian agent John Stuart needed him to model peaceful acquiescence to his Cherokee brethren. Revolutionaries such as Thomas Jefferson wanted him to take the bait for war, in order to have reason to defend a land grab later. Ostenaco did neither, thwarting his imperial contemporaries to the end by redefining the collective for whom he believed he could act viably at the time. The encounter with empire profoundly shaped the events of Ostenaco's life, but it did not determine the ways in which he faced them. Ostenaco's mind was always more focused on his own people, variously construed, than on outsiders. His interests were collective, nimbly protected, and consistently Indigenous.

Mai: Ra'iatean Son

The scholarship on Mai is richer than that on Ostenaco, though there has been only one serious biography—Eric McCormick's *Omai: Pacific Envoy* (1977). Mai has interested historians chiefly as a feted "noble savage" in Britain between 1774 and 1776. In this role, Mai appears usually as "socialite phenomena among an elite class" or as the "darling of London society"—a judgment on Georgian vacuity, perhaps, but nonetheless an unfortunate attenuation of an otherwise complicated life.[31] Even McCormick declared in his preface that Mai's greatest historical significance was as a "catalyst" for British discussions about themselves in the eighteenth century. His book, in fact, made a solid case for Mai being a great deal more than that, even if McCormick himself never went further than asserting that the Islander's "success" owed much to his "individual . . . qualities."[32] In sum, historians have generally considered Mai only in terms of his journey to Britain—sometimes as a plaything of others, sometimes as a canny individualist, but rarely as a Pacific subject with a Pacific agenda.

Appraising Mai's whole life, the two-year trip to Britain recedes somewhat into the background. What stands out more prominently is the burning ambition he harbored ever since he was a child to reclaim his ancestral lands from nearby marauding Bora Borans. The journey to Britain was but one effect of this consistent desire. In some ways, then, Mai was like Ostenaco in how he approached the imperial encounter as a means of furthering collective interests. In Mai's case, those interests were familial rather than social. Unlike Ostenaco, though, Mai remained remarkably steady in his methods, doggedly pursuing one singular goal throughout his relations with British voyagers and hosts.

Mai was born about 1753 on the island of Ra'iatea, just more than one hundred miles northwest of Tahiti. Later sources suggest he was the second son of a *raatira* family, members of the middling rank in Ra'iatean society—neither noble nor serf but landowning and probably administrative.[33] In the early 1760s, just as Mai was coming of age, his island home was invaded by Bora Borans. His father was killed in the ensuing war, along with hundreds of others. Bora Borans took control of Mai's family estate while he and his surviving relatives fled to Tahiti.[34]

Settled in the north of Tahiti, Mai's family would have found some kudos as Ra'iateans, for their island was considered the motherland of Tahitian spirituality.[35] But their refugee status did not necessarily make them safe. A few years later, in 1767, the first European ship to discover Tahiti sailed into a northern harbor. Captain Samuel Wallis had been charged by the British government to explore islands "in the southern hemisphere . . . convenient for . . . the product of Commodities usefull in Commerce."[36] When he entered Matavai Bay, however, Wallis acted more like a conquistador wreaking havoc on hundreds of the inhabitants. Mai was wounded in the resultant violence.[37]

Far from curdling his view of Europeans, though, Wallis's extraordinary attack inspired Mai to think about ways in which they might help further a by-now-entrenched ambition. For even as a teen, Mai appeared to be driven by a desire to avenge his father's memory and regain the ancestral estate from the Bora Borans. A few years after Wallis's departure from Tahiti, Mai volunteered as a combatant in another island's war with the Bora Borans. Fighting for Huahine (an island midway between Ra'iatea and Tahiti), Mai was taken, with six others, as a prisoner of war. The seven captives were transported to Bora Bora itself. According to a later recounting, however, they all managed to escape by stealing a canoe and fleeing back to Huahine. It was on

Huahine that Mai met with another European vessel, Captain James Cook's *Resolution*, in 1773.[38]

While some Islanders understandably stood wary of the tall ship, Mai tried to ingratiate himself with the crew as soon as they docked. He found favor with the captain of the accompanying vessel, Tobias Furneaux of the *Adventure*. Cook did not particularly approve of Mai, but he knew that other Islanders before him had proved to be useful aides in navigating Pacific waters. As well, he knew that his one-time fellow explorer, Joseph Banks, wished to host, and scrutinize, a Pacific man back home in England. Mai would not have been his first choice, Cook claimed, but he gave in to the enthusiasm of his inferiors. "He is a fellow of quick parts," opined the officer James Burney, "very intelligent, has a good memory & takes great notice of every thing he sees."[39] The naturalist George Forster agreed: "he was warm in his affections, grateful and humane . . . polite, intelligent, lively."[40]

For his part, Mai was determined to gain a berth on the vessel because he wanted to find out how to secure the kinds of weapons that Wallis had wielded six years earlier. His singular mission was to acquire firepower in order to realize his dream of vengeance. Although little recognized by modern scholars, few of Mai's later English acquaintances missed it: he "would never listen to any plan, except that of destroying the bora bora chiefs & freeing his Native Island," noted officer James King.[41] "His desire to shoot his enemy the King of Bolabola [*sic*] is always uppermost," observed a minister in Cambridge.[42] The elderly lady who attended him in Joseph Banks's house had the whole thing down pat: Mai "says he wants to return with men & guns in a Ship," she recited, in order "to drive the Bola Bola Usurpers from his property."[43]

What scholars have been keen to note are the various activities in which Mai engaged during his two years in Britain—his inoculation by Thomas Dimsdale; his country excursions to Yorkshire and Cambridgeshire; and his many appearances at the fashionable parties, spas, museums, and palaces of London. Historians have often lamented the difficulty of getting at what Mai himself made of these quintessentially Georgian pursuits. Certainly, the evidence on this question is thin, and, indeed, such thinness does in itself represent much of what is frustrating about "cross-cultural" history. However, one reason why Mai seems passive in the records concerning his British activities may well be that, indeed, he was. That is, Mai may have simply been uninterested in most of the events put on for his benefit, or for the benefit of those associated with him. The fact that no treaty resulted from his meeting with the king, or that no new botanical or anthropological knowledge emerged from his various meetings with eager natural philosophers, might speak to his "active" lack of engagement with such things. Mai appeared not to protest his outings, but he was perhaps unmotivated to make them his own, as it were, or to catalyze something out of them, because he did not read them as advantageous to his specific goal.

On this reading, one of the few exceptions would be the *umu*, or pit feast, that Mai made in Cambridgeshire. The meal's methods accord with older Pacific practices for offering thanks and honoring dignitaries.[44] Unlike everyday meals, such a feast was customarily performed by men. Lord Admiral Sandwich, present on the occasion, understood Mai's work that day as an example of how Mai "always wished to make himself useful."[45] In the context of Mai's repeated requests for weapons and armed assistance against his enemies, however, it seems more likely to have been Mai's calculated move to appeal to the head of Britain's Royal Navy.

Frustratingly for Mai, neither this nor other appeals turned out as he had hoped. By the time he set off on his homeward passage on Cook's third and final expedition to the Pacific, Mai was carrying far fewer arms or promises from the British than he had planned. Cook disapproved of arming Pacific Islanders and stipulated that Mai should instead be given what he considered more practical implements—tools, seed, and livestock. Banks, however, still managed to exert some influence on the voyage leaders and ensured that Mai carried back at least a portion of his desired weaponry. Mai also took back odder gifts, including a jack-in-the-box, perfume, peacocks, and a full suit of armor.[46]

To what extent Mai got to use his reduced British weaponry is hard to say, since Cook did not deposit him back on Ra'iatea. Mai asked Cook repeatedly to return him to the island of his birth, but Cook signaled his unease about this idea as soon as they entered the Tahitian archipelago. At the island of Tahiti, Cook made clear his worry that Bora Boran–dominated Ra'iatea was still too dangerous for an angry young native-born man and started negotiating with the Tahitian paramount chief instead to repatriate him there. Mai instantly thwarted those plans by offending the chief, Tu, in several ways—bragging of the British king's power, offering honors to Tu's rival, and slighting Tu's marriageable sister.[47] Some historians have followed Cook's cue at this point and agreed with the British captain that such behavior signified Mai's unreliable or callow character.[48] Yet, as Nicholas Thomas has argued, "there may have been more to Mai's activity than met Cook's eye; there may have been strategy that he did not see."[49] Mai was more likely trying to achieve his aim of returning to Ra'iatea than indulging in "impudent" or "careless" impulses.[50]

Mai managed to fend off a Tahitian return, but he had to accept Cook's decision to return him finally at Huahine (halfway between Tahiti and Ra'iatea). Negotiations with the Huahine chiefs for a parcel of land for Mai proceeded more smoothly, though at one point Mai broke into the talks to declare that if it was not possible, he'd be happy to go on to Ra'iatea, where Cook would help him drive out the Bora Borans. Annoyed, Cook clarified that this was not going to happen.[51] Cook's men helped Mai establish a small allotment and hut on Huahine before bidding him a final farewell. Mai was said to "burst into tears" at the moment of leave-taking, for what we might guess now to be a complex range of reasons.[52]

When still in Tahiti, Mai had secured for himself a large sailing canoe (complete with six complementary sailor-servants). With it, he might have been able to sail over to Ra'iatea at some point to engage the Bora Borans. Probably, though, he did not have occasion to, since his enemies arrived in Huahine soon after Cook's departure. Later British voyagers learned that Mai died after the resultant showdown, probably around 1779.[53]

Mai never did, then, reclaim his ancestral lands. But he died having given it his best shot. The revelation of his determined focus on his familial mission for most of his life makes it seem unlikely that his dying thoughts would have lit upon the Britons he had met in the mid-1770s—despite the way that historians have generally imagined him. When seen as a whole life, his story suggests that he employed the imperial encounter more thoroughly for his aims than the empire in the end ever managed to employ him.

When set alongside Ostenaco's story, too, those aims become clearer: the comparative mode underscores the larger interests at play for both men in ways that may not otherwise stand out. Together, Mai's vengeful ancestral goals and Ostenaco's expanding collective leadership foils the notion that Indigenous agency only becomes apparent in imperial history when in the service of self-promotion.

Envoys of Interest

Eighteenth-century Britons, and their later historians, were deeply interested in the phenomenon of an actual representative from the New World visiting the heartland of empire. They noticed their quirks, their habits, their reactions. And they noticed these visitors noticing them. Though assuredly still dealing in stereotypes, such Britons (unlike their later Victorian successors) utilized a relatively capacious conception of the term they most favored for such people—that of "savages." That is, while Britons mostly ascribed the idea of "savagery" to people from the New World, many yet wondered if such a state was not a telling rebuke to their own supposed civility. Just as the participant at Mai's Cambridgeshire feast thought that an *umu* represented some critique of British customs, others also often pointed to the behavior of visiting indigenes as a way of satirizing themselves.

But fascination for New World visitors was generally for one end only: the reflection back onto Britain's own culture. Very few commentators let the arrival of an Indigenous person on their shores draw them into discussions of Indigenous worlds, and least of all into meditations on how these visitors made sense or use of the imperial mechanisms by which they came. At one level, it should not be surprising that most scholars have followed suit in their investigations of these visits. The intensity of the Eurocentric perspective in the sources left to us is overwhelming. It is also, of course, mirrored in the intensity that many Indigenous visitors brought to the same encounter. Most of them, Mai and Ostenaco included, undertook their journey purely because they were so wrapped up in their own cultural ends.

Switching to the Indigenous view on these visits, however, opens up some fresh ways of understanding the moment of contact. The switch invites us to see the longer histories behind the Indigenous actors involved, which may in turn make the momentousness of imperial intrusion suddenly contract. When we compare similar but different Indigenous visitors, we also start to see how their motives were often more intricate and embedded in those longer histories than first acknowledged. When Ostenaco and Mai faced empire, on vastly different spots on the earth, what they saw was less an end and more a means—a means, most particularly, to a continued, Indigenous future.

Notes

1. Joseph Cradock, *Literary and Miscellaneous Memoirs* (London: J. B. Nichols, 1828), 1:127–28.

2. Henry Timberlake, *Memoirs of Lieut. Henry Timberlake* (London: Ridley et al., 1765), 115.

3. Including my own: see my *The Savage Visit: New World People and Popular Imperial Culture in Britain 1710–1795* (Berkeley: University of California Press, 2012). See also, for just a few examples, Eric Hinderaker, "The 'Four Indian Kings' and the Imaginative Construction of the First British Empire," *William and Mary Quarterly*, 3rd ser. 53 (1996); Alden T. Vaughan, *Transatlantic Encounters: American Indians in*

Britain 1500–1776 (Cambridge: Cambridge University Press, 2006); Tim Fulford, Debbie Lee, and Peter J. Kitson, *Literature, Science and Exploration in the Romantic Era: Bodies of Knowledge* (Cambridge: Cambridge University Press, 2004), chap. 2; and Laura Brown, *Fables of Modernity: Literature and Culture in the English Eighteenth Century* (Ithaca, NY: Cornell University Press, 2001), chap. 5. This tendency has been partway rectified in Coll Thrush, *Indigenous London: Native Travellers to the Heart of Empire* (New Haven, CT: Yale University Press, 2016).

4. John Oliphant, *Peace and War on the Anglo-Cherokee Frontier 1756–63* (London: Palgrave Macmillan, 2001), 195.

5. Eric McCormick, *Omai: Pacific Envoy* (Auckland: Oxford University Press, 1977), 132.

6. This is how Keith Vincent Smith describes another famous Indigenous traveler of this era in his article, “Bennelong among His People,” *Aboriginal History* 33 (2009): 11.

7. See, for example, W. Anderson, “The Cherokee World Before and After Timberlake,” in *Culture and Conflict: Cherokee British Relations 1756–1765*, ed. A. F. Rogers and B. R. Duncan (Cherokee, NC: Museum of the Cherokee Indian, 2009), 9, and more recently Daniel Tortora, who claims that eighteenth-century empire was an “unmitigated disaster” for the Cherokee: *Carolina in Crisis: Cherokees, Colonists, and Slaves in the American Southeast, 1756–1763* (Chapel Hill: University of North Carolina Press, 2015).

8. See D. H. Corkran, *The Cherokee Frontier: Conflict and Survival, 1740–62* (Norman: University of Oklahoma Press, 1962), 263; and see Oliphant, *Peace and War*, 22.

9. See especially E. R. Evans, “Notable Persons in Cherokee History: Ostenaco,” *Journal of Cherokee Studies* 1, no. 1 (1976): 41–54, and D. H. Corkran, “Ostenaco,” in the *NCpedia* http://ncpedia.org/biography/osteneco-judds-friend (accessed January 2016). For the history of Cherokee towns, see T. Boulware, *Deconstructing the Cherokee Nation: Town, Region, and Nation among Eighteenth-Century Cherokees* (Gainesville: University Press of Florida, 2011).

10. See James Glen in a letter to Robert Bunning, undated, in *Documents Relating to Indian Affairs 1750–54 [DRIA]*, ed. W. L. McDowell (Columbia: South Carolina Archives Department, 1958), 1:109, and *DRIA*, 1:244.

11. See Corkran, *The Cherokee Frontier*, 39–40.

12. See Evans, “Ostenaco,” 44; Oliphant, “The Cherokee Embassy,” 1; Oliphant, *Peace and War*, 191, 195; Corkran, *The Cherokee Frontier*, 263.

13. See, for example, Governor Glen to Little Carpenter, 4 July 1753, in *DRIA*, 1:452.

14. See Doug Wood, “ ‘I Have Now Made a Path to Virginia’: Outacite Ostenaco and the Cherokee-Virginia Alliance in the French and Indian War,” *West Virginia History* 2, no. 2 (2008): 31–60.

15. On this incident and on Cherokee forts generally, see D. Ingram, *Indians and British Outposts in Eighteenth-Century America* (Gainesville: University Press of Florida, 2012), 27–58.

16. See Oliphant, *Peace and War*, 111; Boulware, *Deconstructing the Cherokee Nation*, 118.

17. *South Carolina Gazette*, 21 June 1760.

18. And in this move, Ostenaco became one of the first Cherokee to embody Boulware's identification of an incipient national identity emerging around the mid-eighteenth century, *Deconstructing the Cherokee Nation*, 27.

19. See Oliphant, *Peace and War*, 137–39; Corkran, *The Cherokee Frontier*, 219–21.

20. See Corkran, *The Cherokee Frontier*, 263–66; Oliphant, *Peace and War*, 191.

21. Timberlake, *Memoirs*, 17.

22. Timberlake, *Memoirs*, 42.

23. See Timberlake, *Memoirs*, 47–56.

24. Cited in Timberlake, *Memoirs*, 147. For the visit, see also Fullagar, *The Savage Visit*, 88–101.

25. See Oliphant, "The Cherokee Embassy," 9–10. See also Colin Calloway, *The Scratch of a Pen: 1763 and the Transformation of North America* (New York: Oxford University Press, 2007), 93–94, citing Egremont, saying of the legislation: "Such an Instance of our goodwill to the Indians, would fix them more firmly in our Interest."

26. See Colin Calloway, *The American Revolution in Indian Country* (Cambridge: Cambridge University Press, 1995), 188–89; Gary Nash, *Red, White and Black: The Peoples of Early America* (Englewood, NJ: Prentice Hall, 1974), 298–305.

27. See "Jud's Friend's Talk to Governor Tyron in Answer to his Excellency's Talk Delivered Yesterday at Tyger River Camp," *Colonial Records of North Carolina [CRNC]*, ed. W. Saunders (Raleigh: P. M. Hale, 1886–90), 7:464–66. See also "Copy of a Talk from the Headman and Warriors of the Cherokee Nation Dated Fort Prince George 20th October 1765," *CRNC*, 7:115–17.

28. See Boulware, *Deconstructing the Cherokee Nation*, 157.

29. See Corkran, "Ostenaco."

30. See Evans, "Ostenaco," and Corkran, "Ostenaco."

31. G. Dening, *Beach Crossings: Voyaging across Times, Cultures, and Self* (Melbourne: Melbourne University Press, 2004), 40; K. Wilson, *The Island Race: Englishness, Empire, and Gender in the Eighteenth Century* (London: Routledge, 2003), 63.

32. McCormick, *Omai*, vii, 132.

33. See James Burney, Private Journal (1772–73), reprinted in B. Hooper, ed., *With Captain James Cook in the Antarctic and Pacific* (Canberra: National Library of Australia, 1975), 70. See also McCormick, *Omai*, 1, and Anne Salmond, *Aphrodite's Island: The European Discovery of Tahiti* (Berkeley: University of California Press, 2009), 284.

34. McCormick, *Omai*, 3. Salmond, *Aphrodite's Island*, 36.

35. On Ra'iatea's role in the *longue durée* of Pacific history, see Patrick Vinton Kirch, *On the Roads of the Winds: An Archaeological History of the Pacific Islands before European Contact* (Berkeley: University of California Press, 2000), 245–301.

36. Admiralty instructions cited in H. Wallis, ed., *Carteret's Voyage Round the World 1766–1769* (Cambridge: Cambridge University Press, 1965), 2:302.

37. See Daniel Solander, excerpted in J. C. Beaglehole, ed., *The Journals of Captain James Cook on His Voyages of Discovery* (Cambridge: The Hakluyt Society, 1967), 2:949, and Burney, Private Journal, 70. See also Salmond, *Aphrodite's Island*, 284; McCormick, *Omai*, 12, 58.

38. As narrated in Burney, *With Captain James Cook*, 70–72.

39. Burney, *With Captain James Cook*, 70.

40. Forster cited in Salmond, *Aphrodite's Island*, 284.

41. James King in Beaglehole, *The Journals*, 3:187.

42. Cited in McCormick, *Omai*, 130.

43. Mrs. Hawley cited in Sarah S. Banks, [unpublished] Memorandums, August–November 1774, Papers of Sir Joseph Banks, NLA MS9. See also Sarah Banks (Joseph's sister) mentioning Mai's desire for guns three other times in this manuscript.

44. See Helen Leach, "Did East Polynesians Have a Concept of Luxury Foods?" *World Archaeology* 34, no. 3 (2010): 442–57.

45. Cited McCormick, *Omai*, 112.

46. On his gifts, see "Account of Presents Sent Out with Omai," 1776, the Papers of Sir Joseph Banks, NLA MS9. On Cook's preference, see Cook in Beaglehole, *The Journals*, 3:239. See also the astronomer William Bayly, who observed on the voyage back that "I cannot help remarking that those who had the care of fitting out Omi, used him exceeding ill, by giving him a collection of the worst things that could be procured . . . when he came to examine the contents of his Boxes and Casks, he was very near going out of his Senses, finding himself little richer, either in knowledge or Treasure, than when he left his native country": Bayly in Beaglehole, *The Journals*, 3:193.

47. See Cook's account in Beaglehole, *The Journals*, 3:193. See also the narrative account in Salmond, *Aphrodite's Island*, 428–36.

48. See, for example, Dan O'Sullivan, who thinks him unreliable (and much else) in his *In Search of Captain Cook* (London: I. B. Tauris, 2008), 154–57, or Glyn Williams, who thinks him callow in "Tupaia: Polynesian Warrior," in *The Global Eighteenth Century*, ed. F. Nussbaum (Baltimore: Johns Hopkins University Press, 2003), 41.

49. Nicholas Thomas, *Cook: The Extraordinary Voyages of Captain James Cook* (New York: Penguin, 2003), 336.

50. See Cook in Beaglehole, *The Journals*, 3:183, and Burney in Beaglehole, *The Journals*, 3:183. See also quotes in similar vein from Officer John Rickman, cited in McCormick, *Omai*, 203.

51. See Cook in Beaglehole, *The Journals*, 3:234.

52. See both Bayly's and Cook's accounts in Beaglehole, *The Journals*, 3:240.

53. See William Bligh's 1789 account cited in Beaglehole, *The Journals*, 3:239; William Ellis's 1829 account cited in Beaglehole, *The Journals*, 3:240; and John Watts's 1788 account cited in McCormick, *Omai*, 265.

CHAPTER ELEVEN

Makahs, Māori, and the Settler Revolution in Pacific Marine Space

JOSHUA L. REID

On May 5, 2004, a hīkoi (gathering) of more than 25,000 people arrived in Wellington, the capital of New Zealand, to confront the Labour Government over their foreshore and seabed policy. Fearing that the 2003 Court of Appeals decision in *Ngati Apa v. Attorney-General*—more commonly known as *Ngati Apa*—had given Māori iwi (people) and hapū (clans) the right to limit white New Zealanders' access to coastal spaces, the government enacted the Foreshore and Seabed Act in 2004.[1] This vested full legal ownership of New Zealand's foreshore and seabed in the Crown, thereby extinguishing customary Māori property rights protected by the 1840 Treaty of Waitangi. Worse, the act also prevented Māori from going to court to test whether they had customary rights to specific places. The social-democratic Labour Government disagreed that Māori had lost any rights, instead arguing that the act had established a way for Māori groups to claim large-scale exclusive rights—territorial customary rights—and smaller-scale nonterritorial customary rights orders. Others contended that the thresholds to acquire either type of rights were impossibly high and the benefits accrued so minimal that claimants only applied for a handful of the latter and did not seek any of the former. Many Māori argued that the act discriminated against them because it "amount[ed] to expropriation of taonga [treasured possessions]" and only applied to their customary rights while protecting pākehā (white) private and public rights, a position supported by the assessment of the Waitangi Tribunal, a body that investigates treaty breaches.[2] The foreshore and seabed controversy spawned a political party, the Māori Party; a United Nations human rights investigation; and a domestic Ministerial Review Panel that recommended in 2009 that the act be repealed. Following this recommendation, the government replaced the Foreshore and Seabed Act with the Marine and Coastal Area (Takutai Moana) Act in 2011.[3]

In 2007 and more than 6,200 nautical miles away, Makah hunters illegally harpooned a gray whale in the Strait of Juan de Fuca, near Cape Flattery, the most northwestern point of the contiguous United States. Before the hunters could dispatch the whale, three Coast Guard vessels interceded. Officers arrested the whalers, despite the fact that the Makah are the only tribal nation in the United States with a treaty right to whale. In 1855 (fifteen years after New Zealand's Treaty of Waitangi), Makah negotiators had reserved whaling, sealing, and fishing rights for their people in the Treaty of Neah Bay. With federal government support, the Makah Nation had successfully harpooned and landed a gray whale in 1999. Yet subsequent court cases filed by animal rights activists blocked them from exercising their treaty whaling rights, hence casting the later hunt as illegal. By 2007, these hunters had become frustrated with the lengthy delay blocking them from engaging in a cultural practice that defines who they are as the Qʷidiččaʔa·tx̌ ("kwi-dihch-chuh-aht," the People of the Cape).[4]

The actions of the Māori demonstrators and Makah whalers, and the resultant mainstream responses, shared several commonalities. First, these were both protests against government actions barring them from customary rights to the sea that Indigenous negotiators guaranteed for themselves and their descendants through treaties. Second, mainstream New Zealand and US societies underestimated—and continue to underestimate—Indigenous convictions about protecting their rights to marine spaces and resources. Non-Natives appear puzzled over the "special" rights Indigenous peoples claim and question the legitimacy of treaty rights—especially those in marine spaces, which the dominant societies see as a watery commons.[5] Part of the non-Native confusion over Indigenous rights to the sea emerged from a third commonality: a blindness to the interplay of marine space and human practices, especially as it relates to Māori and Makahs both currently and historically.

But Native protests over rights to the ocean and its resources should have come as no surprise—Makahs and Māori have been protecting these rights since the beginning of the Settler Revolution in what was then the British West of the late eighteenth and early nineteenth centuries. When considering the Settler Revolution, a concept proposed by historian James Belich, and the related settler-colonial processes, scholars usually explore the loss of ancestral lands, the impact on Indigenous communities, and the ways in which tribal nations inevitably resisted when settlers encroached upon homelands. In his comparative history of the Anglo Wests from 1783 to 1939, Belich typifies the terrestrial focus of these historiographies, explaining that a "Settler Revolution," which focused on the acquisition of Native lands and sale of commodities, fueled explosive growth of the Anglo-World.[6] These Wests emerged from the American Revolution, with the US West first materializing in Transappalachia and the British West taking shape among Loyalist Anglophone settlers in Canada and in far-flung settlements from Botany Bay, Australia, to Cape Colony, South Africa. More broadly, settler colonialism is predicated on the "logic of elimination" of Indigenous homelands, cultures, peoples, and bodies.[7]

From the 1780s to the mid-nineteenth century, however, encounters in the early Pacific British West—specifically Murihiku, the extreme southern portion of Aotearoa's (New Zealand's) South Island, and the Strait of Juan de Fuca, which separates Washington State from British Columbia—reveal that the Settler Revolution and settler colonialism were not only about land. They were also about marine spaces and resources such as the skins of fur seals and sea otters. From the perspectives of southern Māori and Makahs, competition over these resources predated land dispossession. As with cross-cultural encounters in the earlier Atlantic world, where relationships linked disparate regions and where different peoples established strategies and formed opinions that persisted throughout the colonial era in eastern North America, similar interactions in the early Pacific British West established long-running patterns that shaped subsequent relations between Indigenous peoples and settler-colonial governments.[8] Moreover, a marine-oriented analysis of this early period also uncovers how southern Māori and Makahs sought to engage with the expanding settler-colonial economy while retaining control over their marine spaces and resources. This finding complicates the narrow ways the Settler Revolution and even settler-colonial theory have sometimes recreated a binary between settlers and Native communities and perpetuated the assumption that Indigenous peoples lack agency, only appearing in narratives as victims.[9] By restoring the deeper history of these first maritime interactions, we can better see why Indigenous marine spaces remain important in the Pacific today.

Murihiku and Cape Flattery

The marine spaces around Murihiku and Cape Flattery act as crucial cultural components of the southern Māori and Makahs, and these worldviews evolved over the centuries prior to European arrival. In the late eleventh century, Polynesians used star navigation techniques and "seamarks"—currents, driftwood, bird sign, and cloud formations—to first find and settle Aotearoa from their ancestral homeland, Hawaiki.[10] As with North Island Māori, waka (canoe) traditions rooted in whakapapa (genealogy) explain the maritime origins of the South Island's Indigenous communities. Perhaps as early as 1100 CE, the waka *Uruao* brought people down the South Island's east coast; after exploring to the Foveaux Strait, these people settled Waihao in the Canterbury region. Later, a second waka, the *Tākitimu*, traveled down the island's west coast, and Māori settlers occupied Tamatea (Dusky Sound) and the Foveaux Strait. A third waka, the *Ārai-te-uru*, attempted to bring kūmara (sweet potato) from Hawaiki to the South Island, but powerful waves caused it to lose its cargo and wreck off Matakaea. Survivors settled the Otago region, over which looms hills thought to be the petrified remains of the shipwrecking waves. Together, the descendants of these waka became the Waitaha Māori.[11]

The earliest settlers invested their marine spaces with social and cultural meanings. Stories from long ago connect Aotearoa to the surrounding ocean. In one creation story, the Polynesian hero Māui caught an enormous fish, and when he pulled it up from the ocean depths, he "found it was land, on which were houses and stages on which to put food, and dogs barking and fires burning, and people working."[12] This became Te Ika a Māui (the fish of Māui, or the North Island), while the South Island came from Māui's canoe (Te Waka a Māui), and Rakiura (Stewart Island) to the south was once the canoe's anchor. In another creation story, more specific to the South Island, the sons of Sky Father Raki set out to see Earth Mother Papatūānuku, which was then a large piece of land in a vast ocean. After exploring Papatūānuku in their waka, they paddled out to find other lands. Failing to spot any, one of the sons began chanting to return the waka to the sky. Tired, though, he gave the wrong chant and submerged the canoe, which tipped to one side and turned to stone. This became Te Waka o Aoraki (The Canoe of Raki's World), the South Island. One of the other sons worked to make the coast habitable, but Te Waka o Aoraki was so remote that it took some time until people came from Hawaiki to live there.[13] Like these creation stories, thousands of marine place names appear to be derived from culturally important stories that remain relevant today. Māori also populated marine spaces with taniwha, powerful mythical beasts that could wreak havoc if mariners failed to appease them properly. Details in these waka traditions and stories gave meaning to the environment, emphasizing the distinct characteristics of the region and its waters, including dangerous sea conditions, locations of resources, and the impossibility of growing kūmara (sweet potato) in Murihiku.[14]

Māori settlers exploited the lands and waters as if they were a collection of "resource islands," spots where food and wood could be gathered. Some resource islands—such as places where pounamu (greenstone) could be found, crops could be grown, and game like moa, tītī (mutton birds), and fur seals could be hunted—were much rarer but even more important. As hunters drove the large, flightless moa bird to extinction around 1500 CE, seals became perhaps the most important source of meat protein for southern Māori. They hunted fur seals, hair seals, sea leopards, sea lions, and sea elephants, and those to the extreme south of Murihiku used the skins for cloaks, hats, and mats. Seal oil was thought to have curative powers, and mothers gave babies pieces of cooked seal fat to suck on as medicine.[15]

Prior to the non-Native arrival in Murihiku, southern Māori settled the coast, especially along the Foveaux Strait, which afforded them access to numerous fishing grounds that provided the protein foundation for their diet.[16] Years later, pākehā (whites) tramping around New Zealand stumbled upon enormous coastal middens, some over 160 feet long and 4 feet deep.[17] The homelands of a single Māori community consisted of a collection of resource sites scattered over hundreds of kilometers and linked by sea routes easily accessible because of oceangoing skills and technology. For example, Māori from Kaikōura on the South Island traveled to the Foveaux Strait islands, where they had usufruct rights to harvest up to 250,000 fat, juvenile tītī each fall. Each winter, sealers from Foveaux Strait paddled into the many labyrinthine fjords of Murihiku, while those around Otago hiked across the island to hunt seals on the island's western side.[18] Critical resource sites included fishing grounds located miles offshore, such as one that James Cook's *Endeavour* came across while sailing along the South Island's eastern coast. Cook's sailors encountered fifty-seven Māori fishers in four double canoes, twelve miles off Kaikōura on February 15, 1770.[19] Fishers used landmarks seen at sea, eventually recorded in carefully guarded mid-nineteenth-century "mark books," to locate offshore fishing grounds. Using triangulation, these highly accurate books enabled fishers to locate sites only thirty feet across at twenty miles offshore. Local ariki (chiefs) owned these important resources that they inherited, maintained, and protected, and people of all ranks depended on them. Logically, Māori domain extended well into the ocean and did not stop at the high-water mark, a position that they still maintain.[20]

The wealth of the sea drew others to the South Island. Beginning in the late sixteenth century, migrations brought Ngāti Mamoe people, originally from the North Island's Hawkes Bay, to the South Island, where they clashed with the resident Waitaha, but with whom they eventually intermarried. Beginning around 1710 CE, Ngāi Tahu peoples initiated a "chain of migration[s]" from the North Island to the South Island, arriving in Murihiku around the 1760s. Like earlier migrants, Ngāi Tahu first fought and then intermarried with those already there, while trade in surplus preserved fish and coastal birds contributed to the social integration of southern Māori, an assemblage of multiple peoples who interacted with the first pākehā to this region in the late eighteenth century.[21]

Similarly, the Makah relationship with marine space evolved over the centuries prior to the arrival of Europeans and Anglo-Americans. Makahs have been living in the Cape Flattery region and exploiting its marine resources for thousands of years.[22] Like their Nuu-chah-nulth kin on Vancouver Island's west coast, they have always been mariners. Due to their prime location along the Pacific Coast, Makah traders acted as middlemen in maritime, Indigenous commercial networks extending north of Vancouver Island, south to the Columbia River, and east into Puget Sound. The People of the Cape harvested unique marine resources from whales, halibut, and seals, which enabled them to trade for other fish, cedar, slaves, dentalium, and art. They understood the physical characteristics, such as the currents and weather, of marine space and species. Some of the Makahs' most important stories of long ago times anchor them to the marine waters around Cape Flattery. For instance, several family histories tell of a massive flood that scattered people across the Northwest Coast. Those who landed at Cape Flattery became the Qʷidiččaʔa·tx̌ and learned how to hunt whales from Thunderbird, a supernatural being who caused thunder and lightning.[23]

Like the Māori of Murihiku, generations of technological adaptations and local knowledge allowed Makahs to best exploit the sea. For example, from mid-April through July, they fished for halibut from banks located up to sixty miles offshore. They used specific gear and methods that reflected their knowledge of halibut and its habitat. Fishers departed before dawn, arriving by noon at the banks where they cast out lines carrying a sinker and two specially designed hooks, čibu·d ("chih-bood"), made from a hemlock or yew knot. These hooks were curved so that dogfish that infested the fishing banks slipped off when they struck, but halibut rarely escaped. The sinker dropped the line down sixty fathoms to the fishing bank. Once the halibut took the hook, the fisher hauled up the catch and clubbed it dead. In an afternoon, several people in a canoe thirty to thirty-five feet long could fill their vessel with ten to forty halibut, depending on the size. Once ashore, women processed the catch, preserving it to last during the winter. Working this way, the People of the Cape harvested more than 1.5 million pounds of fresh halibut annually, according to one estimate in the nineteenth century.[24]

Of all their customary practices, whaling best demonstrates how Makahs relied on Indigenous knowledge to exploit marine resources. These whalers have hunted leviathans for two thousand years. Through the mid-nineteenth century, most whalers caught one or two whales annually and as many as five in good years. A crew of eight, assembled by the harpooner, sometimes remained on the ocean for days, fifty to one hundred miles offshore pursuing whales. A whaler harpooned his prey several times, and to tire out the whale, he attached sealskin floats with each successful strike. While the paddlers kept the canoe close to the struck whale, the harpooner bled it to death with a lance. Once the whale was dead, a diver sewed shut its mouth to prevent it from sinking. Then the crew towed the whale back to the coast, sometimes taking three days to get it ashore, where they butchered it and apportioned it among the village. Staying out for this length of time and paddling across such great distances required Makah whalers to rely on their knowledge of the ocean environment and their navigational and weather-prediction skills within a large marine area. Additionally, they conducted extensive ritual preparations in order to gain the spiritual power to hunt such strong creatures.[25]

This relationship with marine space influenced Makah society and culture. For example, whaling families composed the ranks of nobility among the People of the Cape and often lived as large extended families in a single longhouse. Whaling traditions—the right to be a harpooner, equipment, names of prominent whalers, rituals, dances and songs, and sacred bathing pools—were all kept within particular families and passed from one generation to the next. Makahs observed strict usufruct rights over propertied marine waters and guarded them from neighboring communities. Marine space was the site of their most important stories, and the People of the Cape, like the southern Māori, had named nearly all features within this space.[26]

The first outsiders to sail into Makah waters at the end of the eighteenth century found a region well understood, heavily used, and crossed with complex notions of property.

Maritime Encounters and Interactions

Makahs and southern Māori interacting with Anglos in the Pacific British West expressed their rights to customary marine space. The People of the Cape first encountered Europeans in Makah waters with the 1788 voyage of British captain John Meares. After sailing east across the Pacific from Canton, China, Meares initially landed at Vancouver Island. He established a small trading post among the Mowachahts at Nootka Sound and then sailed down the coast of the island and agreed to an exclusive trading pact with Wickaninnish, a powerful Clayoquot chief. Under this agreement, the other leaders of communities on both sides of the Strait of Juan de Fuca were to trade their furs to Wickaninnish, who, in turn, would trade them with Meares. This agreement primed Wickaninnish to consolidate power in the strait.[27]

When Meares arrived at Tatoosh Island a day after agreeing to the Clayoquot's proposal, Makahs dictated terms for operating within their space. Chief Tatoosh came out with several large canoes, each holding twenty to thirty armed warriors. News of the Meares-Wickaninnish pact had already reached Tatoosh, and he demonstrated his displeasure, informing them "that the power of Wicananish ended here, and that we were now within the limits of his government, which extended a considerable way to the Southward." The chief likely felt that Meares should present him with gifts and offer him an arrangement comparable to the one Wickaninnish had secured. Because Meares failed to initiate trade with the proper gift protocols, Tatoosh did not allow his people to exchange any sea otter pelts or other goods with the British. The following day, Tatoosh and a contingent of four hundred warriors circled the *Felice*, as if "the greatest part of them had never seen such a vessel before."[28] While Meares's official version focused on the Makahs' apparent curiosity in his ship, in reality this naval veteran could not have missed the signals Tatoosh was sending with a prominent display of sea power.[29]

The Meares-Wickaninnish agreement disgruntled other Indigenous communities. Two weeks later, while Meares's longboat, under the command of First Officer Robert Duffin, was exploring deeper into the strait—they hoped that this was the fabled Northwest Passage—Makahs and related Pacheedahts of Vancouver Island's southern side attacked in several canoes carrying forty to fifty warriors. Lining both sides of the shore, they rained arrows and stones onto the vessel, piercing it in “a thousand places.” The survivors felt that the conflict had been “close” as they “fought for their lives.” After escaping, the boat limped back to the *Felice*, and a small canoe of Wickaninnish's people came alongside, offering to “sell” two freshly severed heads of Tatoosh's people—they likely offered these heads as an indication of siding with the British. The Clayoquot chief had attacked two of Tatoosh's men because the latter had declared war on him.[30]

The actions of Tatoosh and the Makahs and Pacheedahts demonstrated their willingness to respond violently to encroachments on the sociopolitical fabric of this marine space. Timed to coincide with the attack on the longboat, Tatoosh's war declaration indicated an alliance between Pacheedahts and Makahs against Meares and Wickaninnish, who had tried to limit British trade with other local villages by funneling valuable sea otter pelts through Clayoquot. The carefully executed Makah-Pacheedaht violence prevented Meares from going any farther into the strait. Much to his frustration, the Makah-Pacheedaht attack prevented him from determining whether this was the Northwest Passage.

From Tatoosh's perspective, this action only brought benefits. He had prevented the Meares-Wickaninnish alliance from spreading its maritime trade dominance farther into the strait, and the attack had happened in Pacheedaht waters, which left Makah waters safe for future trading. His alliance with the Pacheedahts allowed Tatoosh to position himself as an important broker in the maritime fur trade. Only a few weeks later, Makahs began incorporating visiting European and American vessels into their marine trade network. After Meares's brief visit to Tatoosh Island, Charles Duncan, captain of the British sloop *Princess Royal*, traded for all the sea otter skins Makahs had.[31] In the weeks between Meares's and Duncan's visits, Tatoosh and the People of the Cape had procured enough furs from farther down the coast to trade with passing vessels. During two voyages to the Pacific Northwest, Robert Gray's *Columbia* frequented the Cape Flattery villages. On April 5, 1789, Robert Haswell, third mate, noted in his log that “the [Cape Flattery] Coast abounds with Natives and good Sea otter skins.”[32] Two years later, the *Columbia* returned in the midst of the halibut season. Having caught an “incredible number” of halibut, Makahs traded some with the crew upon their return. The next day, canoes from several Makah villages came out to the *Columbia*. Tatoosh and others boarded the vessel and exchanged many skins for copper, nails, and beads; but the crew complained that the

People of the Cape carried away more furs than they traded.[33] Evidently, they had learned the furs' value and were willing to hold out for a higher price from another ship. Additionally, Makahs adapted to changing Anglo desires and offered different articles for trade. For example, the American Captain Boit purchased several war garments from Tatoosh in 1795, while the *New Hazard* purchased gallons of whale oil and four slaves from Makahs in 1811.[34] These interactions demonstrate a crucial and active role exerted by Makahs at controlling their relationship with Anglo vessels, traders, and captains who ventured into their marine space.

As the maritime fur trade declined due to collapsing sea otter populations in this part of the Northwest Coast, Makah chiefs found new opportunities in the Pacific British West's expanding markets. The maritime fur trade's successes drew American and British fur trading companies such as the Pacific Fur Company (1811–1814) and the North West Company (1813–1821) to the region, and they quickly moved to control the land-based fur trade. Although the Columbia River outposts of these companies lay two hundred miles south of Cape Flattery, Makahs made periodic trips there to sell beaver and sea otter skins.[35] But the newest and most important Northwest Coast arrival was the Hudson's Bay Company (HBC), which bought out the North West Company operation and built fourteen trading posts from the Columbia River to northern British Columbia. By the late 1820s, small New England vessels also frequented Makah waters as they sailed in and out of Puget Sound, attempting to intercept furs bound for British traders and collecting timber bound for Oahu, the Pacific whaling fleet's hub.[36]

Neah Bay, a Makah village east of Cape Flattery, emerged as "the critical spot" for HBC traders and other entrepreneurs.[37] Makah authorities sold sea otter pelts—the dwindling few they could acquire—fresh fish, slaves, and dentalium shells for tea, rice, tobacco, molasses, sugar, salt, coral, and Chinese-made sandalwood and camphor boxes, which became popular potlatch gifts.[38] The most important Makah commodity in the second quarter of the nineteenth century, however, was whale oil, which HBC ships purchased at more than one hundred gallons at a time. "Cape Flattery oil," as the Anglo traders called it, ended up in London, where it was distilled into benzene to light homes and businesses. By the 1830s, the HBC schooner *Cadborough* was trading regularly for Makah whale oil; one report to Congress estimated that Makahs had sold more than thirty thousand gallons of oil to passing vessels in 1852 alone.[39] These exchanges illustrate the ways that the People of the

Cape engaged with the new opportunities of the expanding settler-colonial world.

Similar to the convergence of peoples in the North Pacific, some of the earliest Māori-Anglo opportunities and conflicts in Murihiku centered around issues over marine space and resources. The first pākehā intrusion demonstrated the potential pressures outsiders would put on Māori marine resources. While sailing aboard the 368-ton *Endeavour* in Tamatea (Dusky Sound) on the South Island's southwest corner from March through May of 1773, Captain Cook and his crew took prodigious quantities of fish, waterfowl, and seals. Having been at sea for 117 days before arriving at Tamatea, the crew was desperate for fresh food. While the interactions they had with several Māori families remained peaceful, these hunters and fishers certainly noticed the toll the outsiders took on Tamatea's resources, the very same ones that had drawn them to this valuable place.[40]

The published accounts of this expedition fueled interest in hunting fur seals in the ocean's far corner. One of the first industries of Australia's New South Wales, the British penal colony established in 1788, sealing followed a series of rushes as gangs of hunters exterminated seals in one area and moved on to another. Sealers initially focused on hunting the rookeries in Bass Strait, which separates Tasmania from the Australian mainland, and shipped the salted skins to Canton. As hunting threatened the Bass Strait seal population, sealers turned to the Murihiku waters detailed by Cook. Staying for nearly eleven months, the first gang of twelve sealers landed at Tamatea in November 1792, harvesting 4,500 skins yet only seeing three Māori, who fled when the pākehā first arrived.[41] By the beginning of the nineteenth century, sealers had pushed into Foveaux Strait and begun hunting on Rakiura (Stewart Island). A decade later, they pursued seals around the Otago Peninsula, located halfway between the southeastern tip of the South Island and Waitaki River. Early successes drew vessels from Russia, France, and the United States, in addition to British operations from England and colonial India. By 1830, almost no fur seals could be found in Aotearoa's hunting grounds.[42]

Initially, some southern Māori communities developed amicable relations with sealers. Upon his 1803 return to Port Jackson, New South Wales, Captain Oliphant of the thirty-one-ton schooner *Endeavour*, one of the first vessels to hunt in Murihiku, noted that "the natives of New Zealand [were] very friendly, and ready to render every assistance he could possibly require."[43] Sealing gangs from the brig *Fox* lived with Māori on Rakiura, and some Anglos became relatively conversant in the Māori language, while Native traders along the Foveaux Strait exchanged potatoes—introduced by Anglo sealers in the early nineteenth century—and woven mats for metal tools.[44] Despite these early friendly exchanges, a general fear of Māori cannibalism continued to shape English perceptions of New Zealand: Arthur Phillip, the first governor of New South Wales, asked English authorities for the power to "confine the criminal [convicted of murder and sodomy] till an opportunity offered of delivering him as a prisoner to the natives of New Zealand, and let them eat him."[45] And Māori were not the only ones with a violent reputation.

Like other mammal hunting industries, sealing encouraged violence.[46] A Māori elder who had witnessed nineteenth-century sealers at work described the violence:

> Each man had a club in one hand and a sort of hook in the other which acted like a shepherd's crook or a fisherman's gaff. The sealers stood behind one another at intervals in a row. If you did not "patu te ihu" (tap the nose) exactly they were not killed and could bite savagely and inflict severe injury. As the sealer hit one on the nose another would be dodging behind him and he could turn quickly and gaff it and hit its nose, and swing back to hit another on his first side and so on. It was quick and expert work and there was no time for hesitation and no room for fumbling.[47]

Gangs worked together, sometimes making a lane to drive seals between them, knocking them down and lancing them dead under the flipper.[48] Sealers received a proportionate share, a "lay," of the skins and oil they collected, which encouraged men to kill as many as possible. Vessels dropped sealing gangs ashore and sailed away, returning months—sometimes years—later to pick up the hunters and skins. Often poorly supplied, gangs endured extreme privations and other hardships that made them desperate and heightened the tendency for violence. Owners of sealing operations expected gangs to procure their own food, water, and shelter while hunting on remote islands and shores where rookeries were located. This meant that sealers often clothed themselves in and slept on sealskins and ate the flesh of what they hunted. Those left to their own devices for lengthy hunts suffered from scurvy, starvation, thirst, and exhaustion. When vessels sailed away and became lost at sea, these hardships only worsened.[49]

The competitive scramble for fur seals, a diminishing natural resource, primed the industry for conflict, especially between non-Native hunters and Māori communities who relied on the same limited prey. By 1803, the

Tamatea rookeries had been emptied, a process that repeated from one rush to the next. An 1824 letter to the *Sydney Gazette and New South Wales Advertiser* noted that "the southern and western coasts of New Zealand have been infested with Europeans and New Zealanders, who, without consideration, have killed the pups before they are prime, and the clap matches [females] before pupping, for the sake of eating their carcasses. . . . [S]eals will be totally extinct within about three years on the coast."[50] The "innumerable wild dogs" left behind by sealers exacerbated the steep environmental toll of the industry by "ravag[ing]" the young seals and consuming shorebirds.[51] What the dogs did not get, the hordes of black and brown rats from Europe—brought unwittingly to Murihiku as stowaways aboard ships—devoured.[52]

As sealers emptied out rookeries and seabird nests, tensions escalated across Murihiku. Māori actions seemed to indicate that they saw the actions of non-Native sealers as theft.[53] In 1810, Honekai, a Ngāi Tahu ariki, "took offence at the activities of a sealing gang" and led an attack on a gang of six sealers left at Rakiura's South Cape.[54] Honekai and his warriors killed the gang, except James Caddell, a young laborer who married Tokitoki (one of Honekai's nieces), which raised him in status. Caddell became known as the infamous "Jimmy the Mowry."[55] As sealers shifted to the fully stocked rookeries of the Macquarie and Solander Islands farther offshore during the 1810s, tensions relaxed. But once sealers returned to Murihiku waters in the 1820s, Māori took violent actions to protect their resources. The conflict-riddled voyage of the *General Gates*, a sealing vessel from Boston under the command of Captain Abimeleck Riggs, exemplified the escalating efforts to expel sealers.[56] The *General Gates* placed its first gang of six ashore, with provisions and a whaleboat, somewhere north of Tamatea. Six weeks of hunting resulted in more than 3,500 skins and drew the attention of southern Māori who captured them on October 11, 1821, after burning their huts, skins, and remaining provisions. Their captors marched them about two hundred miles north and brought them to the area's "King and Queen," who ordered the execution, roasting, and consumption of one sealer. Over the course of several days, Māori killed and ate three more sealers. Under cover of an evening thunderstorm, the last two survivors fled in their whaleboat, which the Māori captors had brought to their leaders. After floating off the coast for three days, they were picked up by the brig *Maquary* and taken to Sydney.[57]

A larger sealing gang from the *General Gates* also encountered troubles. After Captain Riggs had left them at Chalky Bay in Tamatea with eight months' worth of supplies, the sealers encountered resistance led by the

Foveaux Strait ariki Te Pahi, Te Wera, and Te Pai, accompanied by James Caddell. Māori stole the sealers' supplies after killing the apprentice tasked with guarding them. Then they hunted the sealers themselves, capturing and killing two. When Captain W. L. Edwardson of New South Wales's brig *Snapper* encountered them in December 1822, he noted that "[t]he unfortunate men were in a most deplorable state and looking like skeletons: they had lived miserably in horrible suffering, fearing famine as well as the natives."[58] For months, the hunted sealers had been on the run.

Before sailing to Canton, the *General Gates* dropped a third gang on Rakiura. This group included an Australian "black Native woman," from Kangaroo Island, and her toddler. Shortly after the gang commenced hunting, Māori from across Foveaux Strait and Ruapuke, a nearby island, "killed them all, the last American making a desperate fight," according to Māori who shared this story several years later.[59] The woman and her child escaped, surviving on raw birds and seals for eight months until being rescued and taken to Sydney by Captain Dawson of the schooner *Samuel*. According to Māori oral histories from later in the nineteenth century, their people had "not approve[d]" of the sealers' presence, so they killed and ate them. When Captain Riggs returned in June or July 1823 and found his sealers dead, he "sailed . . . down" some canoes he encountered, leaving no survivors.[60]

Rather than viewing this Māori resistance as random violence committed by savages—the way such actions are often understood—we should see these as attempts to enforce control over particular marine resources and the spaces in which they could be found. Captain Riggs and the *General Gates*'s sealers clearly did not recognize the authority of Māori ariki over sealing grounds. Similar to other Europeans, these sealers perceived the ocean as a vast, uncontrollable space only suitable for transportation or harvesting resources such as fish and seals.[61] This view led the sealers to assume that no one owned the marine space itself or the resources in it until someone took the positive action to harvest them.

The multigenerational kinship connections among the Māori ariki who led these attacks, though, illuminate some of the structures of ownership and authority over marine spaces and resources that justified the violent responses against the sealers. Honekai, a Ngāi Tahu ariki, led the initial 1810 Rakiura strike and brought the captive Caddell into his family by marrying the youth to a niece. After Honekai's death around 1815, his son, Te Whakataupuka, inherited his mana (authority). A web of relations connected Te Whakataupuka to the Foveaux Strait ariki, who were loyal to him and attacked the second sealing gang in Chalky Bay. Te Whakataupuka was also related to whichever ariki—possibly Tupai (his uncle) from Ruapuke and Te Wera—had attacked the third gang on Rakiura. It is unclear who the unnamed "King and Queen" were who executed members of the first gang. They likely were Otago Māori—related to Te Whakataupuka through marriage—who frequented that part of the South Island's west coast.[62] So these attacks on the *General Gates*'s sealers were a coordinated strategy, orchestrated by Te Whakataupuka, in response to encroachments on his resources and mana. By the summer of 1827, Te Whakataupuka appeared to have chosen a more accommodating approach to the sealers and trade goods they brought, even allowing John Boultbee, an English sealer, to reside under his authority in one of his villages for several weeks.[63] With Te Whakataupuka's pacific overtures to Anglos, Māori violence against sealers dwindled.

Additionally, economic concerns likely motivated the violent acts of resistance and subsequent cooling of tensions from Te Whakataupuka and related ariki. Although the archival records of Murihiku sealing remain blind to Māori engagement in the sealing industry, oral histories hint at the economic importance of this activity for early nineteenth-century Native communities. Māori elders a century later reported that the older generation had visited the islands far to the south, first as sealers aboard white-owned vessels during the first decade of the nineteenth century. Later, Māori "ran small vessels of their own on sealing enterprises."[64] We can roughly date the involvement of Native sealing operations through another oral history: "A gang of [Anglo] sealers killed out the seals relentlessly [at the Antipodes Islands], and foolishly left the carcases [*sic*] rotting on the seashore. The consequence was that the seals coming the next year would not land but went elsewhere and they deserted the place for 10 or 12 years. A Maori gang came after the reckless gang ruined the rookery and found no seals. My father was in this party and he said, 'Only the birds were left,' so they named that group the Deserted [Antipodes] Islands."[65]

From 1804 to 1808, Anglo sealers heavily hunted the Antipodes Islands, about 530 miles southeast of Rakiura. Perhaps the Māori gang's discovery of the empty rookeries fueled Honekai's anger, which caused him to attack the Anglo sealers in 1810. Just as competition among various pākehā sealers fueled violence, competition between Māori and Anglo gangs may have prompted the resistance. Not only were outsiders taking an important food source, but they were also stealing a valuable commodity. With the profit from a single seal averaging eleven shillings and ten pennies at times, this represented a substantial opportunity for Māori sealers to acquire trade goods in kind.[66]

But as seals became overhunted and the regional economy turned toward whaling at the end of the 1820s, Māori ariki such as Te Whakataupuka found new opportunities through peaceful accommodations with Anglos. Since at least 1827 and probably earlier, Te Whakataupuka had already been cultivating and selling potatoes, introduced in the early nineteenth century, to passing vessels.[67] A year later, he gave permission to Captain Peter Williams and Benjamin Turner to build the first Murihiku shore whaling station at Preservation Inlet.[68] In what was possibly the first South Island land sale, the Māori ariki sold this land to Williams for sixty muskets in 1829 and protected the small pākehā settlement.[69] This exchange provided Te Whakataupuka with the necessary firearms to resist temporarily Te Rauparaha's Ngāti Toa incursions from the North Island. As part of the Musket Wars (1818–1832), Māori from Waikato on the North Island had expelled Te Rauparaha's people who fled to the South Island, pushing into Ngāi Tahu lands.[70] From Te Whakataupuka's perspective, engaging the settler economy allowed him to confront a more dangerous foe. Indeed, Māori participation in South Island shore whaling grew as the industry expanded.[71] Native entrepreneurs also branched out into other parts of the settler economy. By the late 1850s, "[m]ore than a hundred vessels built in [New Zealand] [were] the property of the natives who not only carry on a great portion of the coasting trade, but are also in active intercourse with the neighboring islands, and the colony of New South Wales in Australia."[72] Even prominent members of Anglo society, such as the Bishop of New Zealand, relied on Māori-owned and -captained schooners for their transportation needs.[73] Owning ships from the 1840s to 1860s was a profitable enterprise that made significant contributions to the colonial economy.[74]

Te Whakataupuka was not the only Māori leader engaged with the expanding settler-colonial world in Murihiku. Māori traded fish to visiting European vessels, and some found its way to markets in Sydney. For example, during the 1830s, Māori around Otago sold fish by the boatload to Octavius Hardwood, a storekeeper at the small pākehā settlement there, and the crew of the *Lucy Ann*, which landed twenty-two barrels of salted fish and two tons of potatoes at Sydney. With the establishment of Dunedin and Christchurch in 1848, along with several whaling stations, Ngāi Tahu expanded their fishery to sell their catches in local markets.[75] These Māori fishers and traders highlighted the ways in which Native peoples sought to make the most of new economic opportunities.

Conclusion

As settler-colonial governments—specifically the British colony of New Zealand and the US federal government in the Oregon Country south of the forty-ninth parallel—took hold in those parts of the Pacific in the mid-nineteenth century, southern Māori and Makahs continued to protect their rights and access to marine spaces, resources, and emerging economies. In this era, these protections took shape in treaties negotiated with their respective governments. In June 1840, several southern Māori ariki, including Tūhawaiki of Ruapuke Island—Te Whakataupuka's nephew and the one who had inherited his uncle's mana—added their signatures to the Treaty of Waitangi that numerous North Island Māori leaders had negotiated earlier that year with New Zealand's first Crown governor, William Hobson. Makahs negotiated and signed the Treaty of Neah Bay in 1855 with Washington Territory's first governor, Isaac Stevens. As important tools in the age of the Settler Revolution, these types of treaties secured specific rights for Indigenous peoples and extended limited rights to non-Native citizens.[76]

Although the scope, specific context, and actual negotiations differed greatly between these two treaties, they share a commonality in that southern Māori and Makahs believed—and continue to believe—that these documents protected critical marine properties and Indigenous participation in the settler maritime economy. The English- and Māori-language versions of the Treaty of Waitangi both reference fisheries in the second article. The English-language version "confirms and guarantees to the Chiefs and Tribes of New Zealand, and to the respective families and individuals thereof, the full, excusive, and undisturbed possession of their Lands and Estates, Forests, Fisheries, and other properties which they may collectively or individually possess, so long as it is their wish and desire to retain the same in their possession." Missionary translators condensed "Lands and Estates, Forests, Fisheries, and other properties" into "ratou kainga me o ratou taonga katoa," which basically means "their home and all their treasured possessions."[77] The key Māori word in this phrase is *taonga* (treasured possessions), which includes anything of value, such as propertied items and socially and culturally important objects, resources, and ideas. Taonga includes fisheries, even specifically the "business and activity of fishing," an interpretation that has been upheld by the Waitangi Tribunal in multiple investigations.[78] Similarly, the Treaty of Neah Bay explicitly protects Makah fisheries in article 4: "The right of taking fish and of whaling or sealing at usual and accustomed grounds and stations is further secured to said Indians [Makahs] in common with all citizens of the United States."[79] Makah leaders considered this treaty right to include commercial dimensions. As one Makah chief, Q̓alču·t ("kuhl-choot"), argued during the negotiations: "I ought to have the right to fish, and take whales and get food when I like. I am afraid that if I cannot take halibut where I want, I will become poor." Responding to Makah statements about the economic importance of their whale fishery, during the treaty negotiations Governor Stevens verbally promised that the federal government would "send you barrels in which to put your oil, kettles to try it out, lines and implements to fish with."[80]

The two treaties formed the foundation on which the Māori and Makah protests of the first decade of the twenty-first century rest. Our usual understandings of these treaties focus on the transfer of lands and the gross imbalance of power that privileged non-Natives over Indigenous communities. Yet as the history of the earliest, marine-oriented encounters in the Pacific British West demonstrates, southern Māori and Makahs also valued continued access to the sea and its resources around Murihiku and Cape Flattery. Examining the Settler Revolution and settler-colonial processes from the perspective of these Indigenous peoples reveals that the earliest contestations in the Pacific British West were over marine spaces and resources. Additionally, an Indigenous marine perspective highlights the ways in which southern Māori and Makahs engaged in the expanding settler-colonial economy as they sought to maintain autonomy over their lives and communities amid the revolutionary changes of the early nineteenth century. These patterns of fighting for Indigenous control over spaces and resources and of participating in new economic opportunities continued into the post-treaty years, when generations of Māori and Makahs suffered some of the heaviest-handed policies of control and elimination. The protests of 2004 and 2007 are simply the most recent iterations of their struggles over marine space.

Notes

1. *Ngati Apa v. Attorney-General* [2003] 3 NZLR 643. I am using Angela Ballara's definition of *iwi* (people: persons composing a community, tribe, race, or nation) and *hapu* (clan: group with a common ancestor). See *Iwi: The Dynamics of Māori Tribal Organisation from c. 1769 to c. 1945* (Wellington, NZ: Victoria University Press, 1998), 17.

2. Waitangi Tribunal, *Report on the Crown's Foreshore and Seabed Policy (Wai 1071)* (Wellington: Waitangi Tribunal, 2004), 81–125, quotation on 8.

3. Jacinta Ruru, "A Politically Fuelled Tsunami: The Foreshore/Seabed Controversy in Aotearoa Me Te Wai Pounamu/New Zealand," *Journal of the Polynesian Society* 113, no. 1 (2004): 57–72; Aroha Harris, *Hīkoi: Forty Years of Māori Protest* (Wellington: Huia Publishers, 2004), 142–155; Angeline Greensill, "Foreshore and Seabed Policy: A Māori Perspective," *New Zealand Geographer* 61, no. 2 (2005): 158–160; Richard P. Boast, "The Foreshore and Seabed, Again," *New Zealand Journal of Public and International Law* 9, no. 2 (2011): 271–283; United Nations, Sixty-Second Session, Commission on Human Rights, Economic and Social Council, *Report of the Special Rapporteur on the Situation of Human Rights and Fundamental Freedoms of Indigenous People, Rodolfo Stavenhagen, on His Mission to New Zealand*, E/CN.4/2006/78/Add.3, March 13, 2006, http://www.converge.org.nz/pma/srnzmarch06.pdf.

4. Keith Ervin and Lynda V. Mapes, "Gray Whale Shot, Killed in Rogue Tribal Hunt," *Seattle Times*, September 9, 2007; Charles Joseph Kappler, ed., *Indian Affairs: Laws and Treaties, Vol. 2 (Treaties, 1778–1883)* (Washington, DC: Government Printing Office, 1904), 682–685; Joshua L. Reid, *The Sea Is My Country: The Maritime World of the Makahs* (New Haven, CT: Yale University Press, 2015), 269–270.

5. Joshua L. Reid, "From 'Fishing Together' to 'To Fish in Common With': Makah Marine Waters and the Making of the Settler Commons in Washington Territory," *Journal of the West* 56, no. 4 (2017): 48–56; Bruce E. Johansen, *Enduring Legacies: Native American Treaties and Contemporary Controversies* (Westport: Praeger, 2004), 305–332.

6. James Belich, *Replenishing the Earth: The Settler Revolution and the Rise of the Anglo-World, 1783–1939* (Oxford: Oxford University Press, 2009), 9.

7. Patrick Wolfe, *Settler Colonialism and the Transformation of Anthropology: The Politics and Poetics of an Ethnographic Event* (London: Cassell, 1999).

8. Andrew Lipman, *The Saltwater Frontier: Indians and the Contest for the American Coast* (New Haven, CT: Yale University Press, 2015), 86.

9. For an introduction and response to critiques of settler colonialism, see Alissa Macoun and Elizabeth Strakosch, "The Ethical Demands of Settler Colonial Theory," *Settler Colonial Studies* 3, nos. 3–4 (2013): 426–443; Patrick Wolfe, "Recuperating Binarism: A Heretical Introduction," in the same volume, 257–279.

10. James Belich, *Making Peoples: A History of the New Zealanders, from Polynesian Settlement to the End of the Nineteenth Century* (Honolulu: University of Hawai'i Press, 1996), 31.

11. Atholl Anderson, *The Welcome of Strangers: An Ethnohistory of Southern Maori, A.D. 1650–1850* (Dunedin, NZ: University of Otago Press in association with Dunedin City Council, 1998), 13–16; Anne Salmond, *Between Worlds: Early Exchanges between Maori and Europeans, 1773–1815* (Auckland, NZ: Viking, 1997), 45.

12. "General Maori Information, Book 9," June 19, 1957, MS 582/E/1, Papers of James Herries Beattie, Hocken Library, Dunedin, New Zealand.

13. Salmond, *Between Worlds*, 45; Anderson, *The Welcome of Strangers*, 13.

14. "Notes on Maori Place Names and Folk-Lore Copied from James Cowan's Notebook, Jan. 1915," MS 582/E/5, and "General Maori Information, Book 4,"

Dec. 1942, MS 582/E/14, Beattie Papers; William Colenso, *Ancient Tide-Lore and Tales of the Sea from the Two Ends of the World*, reprint ed. (Christchurch, NZ: Kiwi Publishers, 1996).

15. Maarire Goodall, "Sealing and Whaling," [n.d.], MB 140 N(1) 16, T. Howse Personal Papers, 1986–1994, MacMillan Brown Library, Canterbury University, Christchurch, New Zealand; Ian Smith, "Pre-European Maori Exploitation of Marine Resources in Two New Zealand Case Study Areas: Species Range and Temporal Change," *Journal of the Royal Society of New Zealand* 43, no. 1 (2013): 26–27, and 33; Harry Evison, *Te Wai Pounamu (the Greenstone Island): A History of the Southern Maori during the European Colonization of New Zealand* (Christchurch: Aoraki Press, 1993), 15; Herries Beattie, *Traditional Lifeways of the Southern Maori: The Otago University Museum Ethnological Project, 1920* (Dunedin: University of Otago Press, 1994), 49, 156–157, and 333; Waitangi Tribunal, *The Ngai Tahu Sea Fisheries Report (Wai 27)* (Wellington: Waitangi Tribunal, 1992), 59. For "resource islands," see Belich, *Making Peoples*, 38–44.

16. Te Rangi Hīroa (Peter H. Buck), "The Maori Craft of Netting," *Transactions and Proceedings of the New Zealand Institute* 56 (1926): 597; Waitangi Tribunal, *The Ngai Tahu Sea Fisheries Report*, 39.

17. See "Hamilton Notebook [Vol. 2]: Diary, 26 December 1892-1 January 1893 [of a trip to Tautuku]," Augustus Hamilton Papers, 1875–1910, MS 131, Box 7, F2, Auckland War Memorial Museum Library, New Zealand.

18. John Rodolphus Kent, July 2, 1823, *Journal of the Proceedings of His Majesty's Colonial Cutter Mermaid from the 8th Day of May to the 15th Day of August 1823 Inclusive, Kept by John Rodolphus Kent, Commander*, MS A4037 (Micro CY1167), Mitchell Library, Sydney, Australia; Evison, *Te Wai Pounamu*, 5.

19. John Hawkesworth, ed., *An Account of the Voyages Undertaken by the Order of His Present Majesty*, vol. 2 (Dublin: J. Williams, 1775), 223–224.

20. Evison, *Te Wai Pounamu*, 30; Waitangi Tribunal, *The Ngai Tahu Sea Fisheries Report*, 42 and 118–120.

21. Te Maire Tau, Atholl Anderson, and A. H. Carrington, *Ngāi Tahu: A Migration History: The Carrington Text* (Wellington: Bridget Williams Books, 2008), 26; Te Maire Tau, *The Oral Traditions of Ngāi Tahu (Ngā Pikitūroa O Ngāi Tahu)* (Dunedin: University of Otago Press, 2003), 185–263; Waitangi Tribunal, *The Ngai Tahu Sea Fisheries Report*, 68. For an older interpretation of Ngāti Mamoe migration to the South Island, see Salmond, *Between Worlds*, 46–48. All of these migrations are difficult to date accurately because Māori whakapapa count these historical events generationally.

22. Gary Wessen, "Prehistory of the Ocean Coast of Washington," in *Northwest Coast*, ed. Wayne Suttles, Handbook of North American Indians (Washington, DC: Smithsonian Institution, 1990), 412–421; David R. Huelsbeck, "Whaling in the Precontact Economy of the Central Northwest Coast," *Arctic Anthropology* 25, no. 1 (1988): 1–15.

23. Maria Pascua, interview by author, October 13, 2008, Makah Cultural and Research Center, Neah Bay, WA; Frances Densmore, *Nootka and Quileute Music*, Smithsonian Institution, Bureau of American Ethnology, Bulletin 124 (Washington, DC: Government Printing Office, 1939), 109–110; Edward Sapir et al., *The Whaling*

Indians: West Coast Legends and Stories: Tales of Extraordinary Experience (Hull: Canadian Museum of Civilization, 2000), 57–58; James Gilchrist Swan, "The Indians of Cape Flattery, at the Entrance to the Strait of Juan De Fuca, Washington Territory," in *Smithsonian Contributions to Knowledge* 108 (Washington, DC: Smithsonian Institution, 1870), 7–8.

24. Henry Markishtum, *Seattle Mail and Herald*, December 9, 1905; James Swan to Miles C. Moore [governor, W.T.], August 30, 1889, "Fishing," box 1P-1-2, Moore Papers, Governor's Papers, Washington State Archives, Olympia. Swan drew this statistic from a fisheries report sent to the Smithsonian's Spencer Baird in October 1880. For a more complete description of this fishery, see Reid, *The Sea Is My Country*, 213–218.

25. James Swan, "Indian Method of Killing Whales," *Port Townsend Register*, May 20, 1860; T. T. Waterman, "The Whaling Equipment of the Makah Indians," *University of Washington Publications in Anthropology* 1, no. 1 (1920): 1–67; Huelsbeck, "Whaling in the Precontact Economy of the Central Northwest Coast." For a more complete description of Makah whaling, see Reid, *The Sea Is My Country*, 144–151.

26. Frances Densmore, *Nootka and Quileute Music* (Washington, DC: Government Printing Office, 1939), 3; Gilbert Malcolm Sproat, *Scenes and Studies of Savage Life* (London: Smith, Elder and Co., 1868), 225; T. T. Waterman, "Geography of the Makah," [n.d.], box 10/9, Erna Gunther Papers, University of Washington Special Collections, Seattle. See also Joshua L. Reid, "Marine Tenure of the Makah," in *Indigenous Knowledge and the Environment in Africa and North America*, ed. David Gordon and Shepard Krech III (Athens: Ohio University Press, 2012), 243–258.

27. John Meares, *Voyages Made in the Years 1788 and 1789 from China to the North-West Coast of America* (Amsterdam: Da Capo Press, 1967), 134–150; Vincent Aloysius Koppert, "Contributions to Clayoquot Ethnology" (PhD diss., Catholic University of America, 1930), 1; Philip Drucker, *The Northern and Central Nootkan Tribes* (Washington, DC: Government Printing Office, 1951), 240–243.

28. Meares, *Voyages*, 154, 156.

29. For more on the concept of Native peoples and sea power, see Matthew Bahar, "People of the Dawn, People of the Door: Indian Pirates and the Violent Theft of an Atlantic World," *Journal of American History* 101, no. 2 (2014): 401–426.

30. Duffin's account of the longboat's expedition is included as appendix 4 in Meares, *Voyages*, 176, 177.

31. Frederic William Howay, ed., *The Dixon-Meares Controversy, Containing, Remarks on the Voyages of John Meares, by George Dixon, an Answer to Mr. George Dixon, by John Meares, and Further Remarks on the Voyages of John Meares, by George Dixon* (Toronto: The Ryerson Press, 1929), 112.

32. Frederic William Howay, ed., *Voyages of the Columbia to the Northwest Coast, 1787–1790 and 1790–1793*, 2nd ed. (Portland: Oregon Historical Society Press, 1990), 75.

33. This account is from the narrative of John Hoskins, the ship's clerk, and John Boit, the fifth mate. See Howay, *Voyages of the Columbia to the Northwest Coast*, 197, 371–372.

34. John Boit, *Log of the Union: John Boit's Remarkable Voyage to the Northwest Coast and around the World, 1794–1796* (Portland: Oregon Historical Society, 1981), 53;

Stephen Reynolds, *The Voyage of the New Hazard to the Northwest Coast, Hawaii and China, 1810–1813* (Salem: Peabody Museum, 1938), 37.

35. Peter Corney and William DeWitt Alexander, *Voyages in the Northern Pacific: Narrative of Several Trading Voyages from 1813 to 1818, between the Northwest Coast of America, the Hawaiian Islands and China, with a Description of the Russian Establishments on the Northwest Coast* (Honolulu: T. G. Thrum, 1896), 58.

36. Reid, *The Sea Is My Country*, 93–97.

37. Richard Mackie, *Trading Beyond the Mountains: The British Fur Trade on the Pacific, 1793–1843* (Vancouver: University of British Columbia Press, 1997), 231.

38. Paul Kane, *Wanderings of an Artist among the Indians of North America: From Canada to Vancouver's Island and Oregon through the Hudson's Bay Company's Territory and Back Again* (London: Longman, Brown, Green, Longmans, and Roberts, 1859), 221, 238; Mackie, *Trading beyond the Mountains*, 55.

39. Charles Wilkes, *Narrative of the United States Exploring Expedition during the Years 1838, 1839, 1840, 1841, 1842*, vol. 4 (Philadelphia: Lea and Blanchard, 1845), 487; George Gibbs, *Indian Tribes of Washington Territory* (Fairfield: Ye Galleon Press, 1972), 35. For a more complete examination of these exchanges, see Reid, *The Sea Is My Country*, 97–105.

40. Hawkesworth, *An Account of the Voyages Undertaken*, 2:450–458.

41. Captain [William] Raven to Lieutenant-Governor King, November 2, 1793, enclosure in *Historical Records of New South Wales (HRNSW), Vol. 2, 1793–1795*, edited by F. M. Bladen (Sydney: Charles Potter, 1893), 94–96.

42. For an overview of the sealing industry, see Robert McNab, *Murihiku and the Southern Islands: A History of the West Coast Sounds, Foveaux Strait, Stewart Island, the Snares, Bounty, Antipodes, Auckland, Campbell and Macquarie Islands, from 1770 to 1829* (Invercargill, NZ: W. Smith, printer, 1907), 38–210, 250–265; Salmond, *Between Worlds*, 282–313; Rhys Richards, *Murihiku Re-viewed: A Revised History of Southern New Zealand from 1804 to 1844* (Wellington: Lithographic Services, 1995), 17–45; Tony Ballantyne, *Webs of Empire: Locating New Zealand's Colonial Past* (Wellington: Bridget Williams Books, 2012), 126–130.

43. *Sydney Gazette and New South Wales Advertiser (SG)*, October 16, 1803, 2.

44. *SG*, August 25, 1810, 2.

45. "Phillip's Views on the Conduct of the Expedition and the Treatment of Convicts," in *HRNSW, Vol. 1, pt. 2, 1783–1792*, edited by Alexander Britton and F. M. Bladen (Sydney: Charles Potter, 1892), 53.

46. David Igler, *The Great Ocean: Pacific Worlds from Captain Cook to the Gold Rush* (Oxford: Oxford University Press, 2013), 105.

47. Herries Beattie, *Our Southernmost Maoris* (Dunedin: Otago Daily Times and Witness Newspapers Co., 1954), 25.

48. Amasa Delano, *Narrative of Voyages and Travels, in the Northern and Southern Hemispheres: Comprising Three Voyages Round the World; Together with a Voyage of Survey and Discovery, in the Pacific Ocean and Oriental Islands* (New York: Praeger Publishers, 1970), 306; Beattie, *Our Southernmost Maoris*, 20. See also Charles Heaphy's description as quoted in Salmond, *Between Worlds*, 283.

49. McNab, *Murihiku and the Southern Islands*, 148–157.

50. *SG*, July 22, 1824, 4.

51. *SG*, April 22, 1815, supplement.

52. A. Charles Begg and Neil Colquhoun Begg, *The World of John Boultbee: Including an Account of Sealing in Australia and New Zealand* (Christchurch: Whitcoulls, 1979), 157n28.

53. Local historian Rhys Richards also comes to a similar conclusion. See *Murihiku Re-viewed*, 31.

54. Evison, *Te Wai Pounamu*, 30.

55. McNab, *Murihiku and the Southern Islands*, 163–166; Salmond, *Between Worlds*, 309–310; Begg and Begg, *The World of John Boultbee*, 275.

56. For an overview of the *General Gates*'s sealing voyage, see Briton C. Busch, *The War against the Seals: A History of the North American Seal Fishery* (Kingston: McGill-Queen's, 1985), 191–192; McNab, *Murihiku and the Southern Islands*, 180–189.

57. "New Zealand Cannibals," *Columbian Centinel* (Boston), August 18, 1824, 2. For a criticism of Anglo claims to Māori cannibalism, see Gananath Obeyesekere, *Cannibal Talk: The Man-Eating Myth and Human Sacrifice in the South Seas* (Berkeley: University of California Press, 2005). For a response, see Gillian Gillison, "From Cannibalism to Genocide: The Work of Denial," *Journal of Interdisciplinary History* 37, no. 3 (2007): 395–414.

58. Jules de Blosseville, "Voyage du Capitaine Edwardson," in *Nouvelles Annales des Voyages, de la Géographie et de L'Histoire, ou Recueil*, Tome XXIX (Paris: Gide Fils, 1826), 145–161, as translated in McNab, *Murihiku and the Southern Islands*, 200.

59. As told by Edwin Palmer to T. M. Hocken on July 12, 1879. See appendix C in Begg and Begg, *The World of John Boultbee*, 300.

60. Johann Friedrich Heinrich Wohlers, *Memories of the Life of J. F. H. Wohlers, Missionary at Ruapuke, New Zealand: An Autobiography*, trans. John Houghton (Dunedin: Otago Daily Times and Witness Newspapers Co., 1895), 142–143. For more on the Aboriginal woman, see Lynette Russell, *Roving Mariners: Australian Aboriginal Whalers and Sealers in the Southern Oceans, 1790–1870* (Albany: State University of New York Press, 2012), 43–44.

61. Phil Steinberg, *The Social Construction of the Ocean* (Cambridge: Cambridge University Press, 2001), 68–109.

62. Te Pai was Te Whakataupuka's cousin; Te Pahi, an ariki near Pahia Point in the Foveaux Strait, was the husband of one of Te Whakataupuka's cousins; and Te Wera, an ariki of the Bluff (a Māori village at the eastern end of the Foveaux Strait), was brother-in-law to Te Pahi. Begg and Begg, *The World of John Boultbee*, 274–278; Anderson, *The Welcome of Strangers*, 93; Evison, *Te Wai Pounamu*, 31–32.

63. John Boultbee, *Journal of a Rambler: The Journal of John Boultbee* (Auckland: Oxford University Press, 1986), 79–81.

64. Beattie, *Our Southernmost Maoris*, 17.

65. Beattie, *Our Southernmost Maoris*, 19.

66. One Māori sealer recalls this value, noting that he usually earned a shilling per gallon of oil, along with 2s 10d per skin. See Beattie, *Our Southernmost Maoris*, 23. However, the price for skins fluctuated greatly in Sydney, where they earned from three to forty shillings. Rhys Richards, *Sealing in the Southern Oceans, 1788–1833* (Wellington: Paremata Press, 2010), 237–239.

67. Boultbee, *Journal of a Rambler*, 81.

68. "Death of Mr. Benjamin Evans Turner," *Daily Southern Cross* (Auckland), October 6, 1876, 3.

69. Copy of deed in Robert McNab, *The Old Whaling Days: A History of Southern New Zealand from 1830 to 1840* (Christchurch: Whitcombe and Tombs Limited, 1913), 89–90. Although the deed is dated 1832, Williams claimed that he had purchased the land in 1829. For Te Whakataupuka's protection, see Williams's reminiscences excerpted in Richards, *Murihiku Re-Viewed*, 50–51.

70. Belich, *Making Peoples*, 156–178.

71. *Journal of the Rev. A. N. Brown at Matamata Tauranga and the Bay of Islands, Vol. 1: 1835–1838*, June 16, 1837, MSS and Archives A-179, Special Collections/ Kohikohinga Motuhake, Auckland University Library (AUL); Edward Jerningham Wakefield, *Adventure in New Zealand*, vol. 1 (London: J. Murray, 1845), 334–335; Edward Shortland, *The Southern Districts of New Zealand; a Journal, with Passing Notices of the Customs of the Aborigines* (London: Longman, Brown, Green, and Longmans, 1851), 301; Richards, *Murihiku Re-Viewed*, 61–69; Nigel Prickett, *The Archaeology of New Zealand Shore Whaling* (Wellington: Department of Conservation, 2002), 9.

72. Press clipping, "Voyage of the 'Novara,'" *Daily Southern Cross*, November 12, 1863, "Volume of Notes re: Treaty of Waitangi," MA 24/19, National Archives/Te Whare Tohu Tuhituhinga o Aotearoa, Wellington, New Zealand.

73. *"New Zealand Middle Island": Middle Island Journal, 16 January to 6 March 1844. Notes on Place and Tribal Names. Sketch Plans of East Coast of South Island and Banks Peninsula. Lists of Maori at Taumutu, Wairewa, Akaroa, Pigeon Bay, Port Cooper. "Extracts from Lyell's Geology," Greek Notes (Aristophanes)*, February 14, 1844, MS 23x, Shortland Papers, AUL, photocopy of original held by the Hocken Library.

74. Hazel Petrie, *Chiefs of Industry: Maori Tribal Enterprise in Early Colonial New Zealand* (Auckland: Auckland University Press, 2007).

75. Octavius Harwood, "Journal: 20 February to 26 November 1839," George Craig Thompson Papers, Hocken Library (as quoted in Waitangi Tribunal, *The Ngai Tahu Sea Fisheries Report*, 69); Thomas Arthur Pybus, *The Maoris of the South Island* (Wellington: A. H. and A. W. Reed, 1954), 62.

76. For more on the Treaty of Waitangi (1840), see Belich, *Making Peoples*, 179–211; Claudia Orange, *The Treaty of Waitangi* (Wellington: Allen and Unwin, 1987), specifically 77–80, for the extension of the treaty to the South Island. For the Treaty of Neah Bay (1855), see Reid, *The Sea Is My Country*, 124–163; Carole Seeman, "The Treaty and Non-Treaty Coastal Indians," in *Indians, Superintendents, and Councils: Northwestern Indian Policy, 1850–1855*, ed. Clifford E. Trafzer (Lanham, MD: University Press of America, 1986), 37–67.

77. Vincent O'Malley, Bruce Stirling, and Wally Penetito, *The Treaty of Waitangi Companion: Māori and Pākeha from Tasman to Today* (Auckland: Auckland University Press, 2010), 36–40.

78. For more on this interpretation and the complex layers of the Māori-language version of the treaty, see Dora Alves, *The Maori and the Crown: An Indigenous People's Struggle for Self-Determination* (Westport, CT: Greenwood Press, 1999), 67–91. For the Waitangi Tribunal decisions supporting this interpretation of *taonga*, see Waitangi

Tribunal, *Report of the Waitangi Tribunal on the Muriwhenua Fishing Claim (Wai 22)* (Wellington: Waitangi Tribunal, 1988), 179–181; *The Ngai Tahu Sea Fisheries Report*, 95–114, quotation on 106.

79. Kappler, *Indian Affairs*, 682.

80. “Ratified Treaty No. 286: Documents Relating to the Negotiation of the Treaty of January 31, 1855, with the Makah Indians,” 4, United States, Bureau of Indian Affairs, Documents Relating to the Negotiations of Ratified and Unratified Treaties, 1801–1869, RG 75, microfilm T-494, reel 5, National Archives and Records Administration, Pacific Northwest Region, Seattle.

CHAPTER TWELVE

Imperial Structures, Indigenous Aims

Connecting Native Engagement in Scotland, North America, and South Asia

JUSTIN BROOKS

When peoples native to the Scottish Highlands, North America, and Bengal faced empire between 1745 and 1775, they encountered a series of economic and military convulsions that would forever redefine each group's relationship to the expanding British state. For centuries, Crown officials had espoused a devolved mode of native governance in which they projected England's commercial, settler, and military presence into these regions by allying with select native heads-people and exchanging protections or patronage for concessions on the ground. From the middle of the eighteenth century, however, British imperial officials decentered allied and negotiated forms of rule across all three sites of expansion. For Highland, North American, and Bengali native communities alike, the result marked a new era for Anglo-Indigenous relations in which the government's former resort to diplomacy and patronage yielded to the use of military force and economic interventions by some of the highest institutional bodies of the imperial state.

The Highland clans first felt the sting of reform. Though Scotland was formally incorporated into Britain under the 1707 Act of Union, ministers had previously devolved governance to clan chieftains and left the Highlands a stronghold for clanship and for Indigenous Gaelic culture well into the eighteenth century. When disaffected clans rose against the British government in the 1745 Jacobite Rebellion, however, Crown ministers responded with what one scholar has justly described as "systematic state terrorism, characterized by a genocidal intent that verged on ethnic cleansing."[1] Ministers authorized the indiscriminate slaughter of Highland communities by the commanders of the British Armed Forces. Parliament passed legislation that disarmed the clans, disbanded their nonjuring Episcopal meetinghouses, prohibited Gaelic, banned Highland dress, and abolished the chiefs' customary jurisdictions to oversee civil and criminal cases of their dependents. Ministers next passed legislation annexing the rebels' estates to the Crown for new agricultural and industrial improvement schemes overseen by the British treasury. In these ways, Highland clans as diverse as the Camerons and Macleods faced an unprecedented degree of centralized state intervention aimed at obliterating clanship through violence and economic reform.

In North America, too, Britain's strained relations with powerful allies such as the Six Nations Iroquois and the Cherokee Nation led in 1755 to the creation of a centralized body to oversee Native American governance. All at once, the Indian Nations living in proximity to British settlements answered to Britain's new Indian Department and to its superintendent of Indian affairs. Because this body answered first to the military and then to the Board of Trade, this intervention, like in Scotland, yielded a regime "in which Indian submission replaced Indian alliance and in which access to the British market replaced customary exchange."[2] After 1760, the commander in chief of the British Armed Forces deployed genocidal force against Indian Nations and terminated Indigenous gift-giving protocols that had stood at the heart of the Anglo-Indigenous alliance for more than a century. From 1763, the Board of Trade's commercial reforms aimed to force Native Americans' "dependency" on the British Crown through new Indian trade regulations that standardized prices, limited saleable goods, and prevented settlement west of a boundary line determined by ministers in London. In North America, as in Scotland, then, these Indian Nations experienced crushing military force, new modes of governance that supplanted the traditional authority of chiefs, and interventionist schemes aimed at forcing their integration into the financial structures of the British imperial state.

The East India Company's (EIC) strategies for Indigenous governance in Bengal transformed in strikingly similar ways in the same space of time. As British ministerial involvement in Company affairs spiked after 1748, it dovetailed with new military and economic configurations by Company officials that decentered negotiation as their main strategy of engagement with Indigenous nawabs (regional Mughal princes). Between 1757 and 1765, the Company Army deposed and installed not one but *three* consecutive nawabs of Bengal. For most native Bengali people, however, the most palpable change accompanied Robert Clive's acquisition of the office of diwan (revenue collector) from Mughal emperor Shah Alam II in 1765. This stroke, which empowered the Company to extract Bengali capital through Indigenous Mughal taxation structures, inaugurated British colonialism in India by granting the

Company full territorial sovereignty over the region. For Bengal's Indigenous peoples, however, Clive's acceptance of diwan sealed a fate not dissimilar to those of Native Highland clans and American peoples: the subordination of allied systems of rule, the erosion of chieftains' traditional authority, and integration into the commercial and financial structures of the British empire.

Eighteenth-century Scottish, colonial North American, and Indian historians have universally derided these measures as having marked the emergence of more discernibly coercive or territorial forms of British governance over communities native to their regions of study.[3] Curiously, however, these writers have remained wary of bringing Highland Scots, Native Americans, and Indians into a single frame on the basis of their encounters with Britain's midcentury reforms. While native peoples' ways of facing these transformations have been documented in regional terms, the connective and comparative experiences of Indigenous peoples remain largely unexplored. This separation owes, in part, to the reticence of British imperial historians to explore Britain's midcentury reforms as connected in the first place.[4] The omission of Highland, Native American, and Bengali connections owes also to the vast differences between the Indigenous contexts in which Britain's reforms were enacted and understood. The most significant impediment to eighteenth-century comparative Highland, Native American, and Bengali studies, however, has been the radical separation of these imperial and Indigenous historiographies since the 1960s. By separating empire from their accounts of the Indigenous past, historians have neglected to analyze the linking features of Britain's imperial structures and thereby gravitated toward theoretical and scholarly models as the primary lens through which to connect Indigenous experiences with empire.

This chapter, by contrast, offers a preliminary reexamination of linking imperial contexts to tell a new, more interconnected story about native peoples' experiences facing the eighteenth-century British state. Rather than treating imperial and Indigenous historical narratives separately, it traces some of their key points of intersection to highlight the robustness of Indigenous engagement with empire and its role in reshaping the political choices available to ministers in Whitehall. The first half weaves an account of Britain's pre-1745 Indigenous alliance policies together with narratives of eighteenth-century political change. It finds that Native Highland, American, and Indian peoples entered into British alliances not to submit to the Crown but to contain the deleterious effects of expansion and forge new political or social formations in defiance of existing ones. The second half explores the causes of Britain's native reforms and examines Indigenous peoples' engagement with Britain's new modes of rule. Here, too, a more integrated reading of imperial and Indigenous narratives reveals that Britain's reforms arose not from ministerial confidence but from a collective core of frustration over the continued refusal of Britain's Highland, Native American, and Bengali allies to submit to their vision of negotiated rule. Across each site, native communities continued to adapt creatively to British reform. And as they did, many also reshaped both the policy choices and the categories of Indigenous comparison made by ministers in Whitehall.

Shaping British Alliance

To appreciate the linkages of experience that cut across eighteenth-century Highland, North American, and Indian native communities, it is worthwhile to recount that early modern English Crown officials lacked any unified or consistent term for bringing into one framework the sovereign and semi-sovereign peoples living at the frontiers of state expansion. "Native" came closest to the contemporary term "Indigenous," signifying a group's occupancy of a country. Even here, however, statesmen applied "Native" as freely to residents of Italy or France as they did to the colonized peoples of Britain's empire. Absent this term, Britain's imperial policymakers could frame native comparisons and intersect native policies along any number of axes, for any number of reasons. For even though Crown ministers well understood that Highland, Native American, and Bengali peoples sustained very different kinds of relations with England over time, they believed nonetheless that those communities shared in a certain relationship to the expansion of the English state that disposed their policies to overlap.

In certain respects, Indigenous peoples' cultural survival lay at the heart of this overlap. Scotland, North America, and South Asia had all been targets of English expansion since at least the seventeenth century, and communities native to these regions retained significant cultural and political autonomy well into the eighteenth century. Many retained languages, cultural markers, and modes of social and political organization altogether distinctive from those of the English. Most continued to hold spiritual and religious traditions that diverged significantly from those of England's established Church.[5] Individuals from all three regions therefore also became objects of English stereotypes, stressing what Britons believed to be their deviance from true religion—and increasingly during the Enlightenment, from the liberties of English commercial society. Highlanders were, for many, "of such a Nature, that the Barbarity of them would be abhorred even among Heathen Nations."[6] Accounts from India increasingly stressed the tyranny of the Mughal political system, the depravity of its natives, and conjectures on what Robert Clive called the "dark designs of these Mussulmen."[7] Though the distinctive religious and racial formations attached by Crown ministers to the empire's Indigenous peoples varied widely across each region, Britain's highest ministers of state also drew on these nebulous concepts to reimagine native "depravity" in comparable ways over time.[8]

Nonetheless, Crown ministers in London also took seriously the manifold considerations that prevented these views from translating consistently into state-sanctioned policies of violence on the ground. They were far too acquainted with the fiscal and infrastructural limitations of their empire to imagine that they could subjugate Indigenous populations at will. They were also too familiar with the ongoing political and military vitality of the empire's Indigenous peoples. Time and again, native leaders had forced England's highest ministers of state to acknowledge that expansion without aid from Indigenous communities posed an unthinkable prospect at best. The lessons took many forms: the slaughter of MacDonalds at Glencoe in 1692 became a rallying point behind massive Highland involvement in the Jacobite Rising of 1715, just as the intensification of settler violence precipitated Native American resistance in brutal conflicts such as Metacomet's War (1675–78), Bacon's Rebellion (1676–77), and the Yamasee War (1715–17). Coercive rule, ministers discovered, aggravated frontier conflicts, increased expenditures, and alienated native communities from the interests of the Crown. In policy terms, this drive for peace compelled Britain's highest ministers of state to advocate a *negotiated* mode of native governance, in which they projected England's presence by allying with select native heads-people and exchanging protections or patronage for concessions on the ground. Though this style of governance sometimes set the Crown at odds with colonial administrators and white settlers on the spot, ministers in London unswervingly returned to it as their primary form of resolution.

For British ministers, negotiated rule took on comparable functions and served compatible ends across the Highlands, North America, and Bengal. In all three cases, the central government aligned itself with powerful Indigenous groups and expected its allies to keep subsidiary or less influential Indigenous political units in line. They conceived of allied rule as "attaching" sovereign or semi-sovereign heads-people to the interests of the Crown and compelling them to carry out Britain's policies. In all three regions, moreover, ministers expected native leaders to align themselves as "friends" with Britain's foreign or domestic aims and to take on Britain's enemies as their own. Finally, negotiated rule increased in importance across all three sites during the early eighteenth century. This mode of governance acquired new importance following Britain's 1688 Revolution, which removed the Catholic King James II from the British throne and established the nation as Europe's foremost Protestant bulwark against the specter of French universal monarchy. When it did, French and British officials doubled down on alliance as their modus operandi and competed openly—in military or commercial terms—for the allegiance of Highland, North American, and Indian nations of indigeneity.

If one reads these ministerial views of negotiated rule against the history of Indigenous political change, however, it soon becomes clear that alliance rarely produced the universal compliance imagined by officials in Whitehall. In fact, native peoples played so central a role in reshaping the terms of alliance on the ground that negotiated rule operated in starkly different ways in each region by midcentury. In Scotland, where the clans shared a monarch with England after 1603 but remained members of a sovereign kingdom with its own parliaments, laws, and judiciaries until 1707, a group's status as allies depended increasingly on their political and religious alignments through the English Civil War (1642–51), the Stuart Restoration (1660–88), and the Revolution of 1688. Eighteenth-century Whig ministers projected their control into the Highlands by extending patronage and political favor above all to the House of Argyll, senior branch of clan Campbell. The Earls of Argyll, chiefs of clan Campbell, had proven their Whig credentials by reducing the power of enemy clans like the Donalds, cutting ties with the Stuart monarchy in the 1640s, lending military assistance to the 1688 Revolution, and actively supporting the Whig project of Union in 1707. In exchange for their "attachment" to the Whig government, the Dukes of Argyll yielded a power of patronage to secure the allegiance of select clan elites and to isolate their rivals.

This approach did produce a degree of Highland integration into the structures of British governance; the Campbells and other Whig clans fought in Highland military companies, received sheriffships, and in some cases even sat in the House of Lords. The Argylls also seized every opportunity created by seventeenth-century domestic strife to expand their territorial ambit and modernize their forms of land tenure, rendering themselves, by one account, "quite absolute in that Country."[9] Thus, while they emerged in the eighteenth century as the Whig government's leading power brokers in the Scottish Highlands, the House of Argyll had achieved this by pacifying enemy clans and incorporating those clans' mainland possessions into holdings claimed by clan Campbell.[10] The integration of Whig clans into the structures of British governance after 1688 thus rested not on a firsthand identification with the aims of the imperial state, per se, but on an uneasy marriage between ministerial views of alliance and the more long-standing native political contestations that both predated and endured English expansion.

Clan politics shaped the limits of that expansion in turn. The Crown's willingness to lavish rewards on its Whig clan allies produced a bloc of noncooperation in the southern Highlands—notably among groups such as the Donalds, the Camerons, the Macleans, and the Appin Stewarts—who resented the House of Argyll's power and associated the Revolution Settlement with territorial conquest by an enemy group. Moreover, because clan Campbell had achieved this through preferment and military force, many of its new tenants retained their ties to previous chiefs and resented submission to their foes. These tensions came to a head in 1715, when disaffected clans rose up against Britain's Protestant King George I and declared for the deposed James Francis Edward Stuart on the latter's arrival in Britain. The rising that ensued, known as the 1715 Jacobite Rebellion, revealed the tenuous nature of alliance and the immediacy of the threat posed by native disaffection. Within the localized contexts of clan contestation, alliance had failed to command the obedience of Scotland's native peoples.

Sharing neither a crowned monarch nor a history of domestic political strife, Britain's American Indigenous allies engaged with the British empire not as subjects of the same monarch but as sovereign nations reckoning with the full violence of colonial rule. Native American heads-people therefore engaged with early modern European empires not because they sympathized with colonialism but because it afforded them opportunities to assert renewed political pressure on colonial representatives, to increase their prestige within their respective nations, and to gain privileged trade access to the gifts and European wares that many believed necessary for their survival. By the eighteenth century, early accords with the Wampanoags and the Powhatan Confederacy had grown into a more extensive subsidiary alliance network, anchored by the Six Nations of Iroquois in the north and by the Creeks, Chickasaws, Catawbas, Choctaws, and Cherokees to the south. Like in Scotland, ministerial approaches to Indigenous governance entailed empowering some of its Indian partners and allies to mediate between or on behalf of those deemed less powerful native communities; the Okfuskees, for example, assumed a major role in brokering a British-sponsored peace between the Creeks and Cherokees in 1749, while the Six Nations Iroquois claimed to represent groups such as the Delaware, Lenape, and Susquehanna. These arrangements underscored imperial directives "that the several Governors of Your Majesty's Plantations should endeavour to make Treaties and Alliances of Friendship with as many Indian Nations as they can."[11] Doing so, metropolitan officials urged, would allow all "Indian Nations in Amity with Your Majesty's Subjects" to "be reconciled to each other" in the knowledge "that the English have but one King and one Interest."[12]

As in Scotland, however, alliance in North America operated inseparably from Indigenous political transformation. Many Native American headspeople leveraged alliance to reconsolidate their polities in the wake of British expansion. Most of those who fell prey to Britain's southern Indian slave trade between 1680 and 1715, for example, came from Indian Nations seeking to protect themselves and reconstitute their polities using access to goods such as firearms and gunpowder. Displaced Mascoutens, Kickapoos, Miamis, Wyandots, Shawnees, and Delawares resettled between the Great Lakes and the Ohio throughout the eighteenth century, seeking protection under the French alliance. Indeed, engagement with early modern European empires became so central to Native North American attempts to navigate the wake of invasion that some even leveraged the opportunities available through alliance to assert new influence over Indigenous political contests. The Iroquois in particular accrued such commercial, diplomatic, and military importance that they asserted suzerainty over nations such as the Shawnees and the Delaware by the eighteenth century. Eager to simplify imperial policy and to incorporate the Iroquois as subjects under the 1713 Treaty of Utrecht, Britain's statesmen supported the claim.

Once folded into North American Indigenous political contests, however, alliance often failed to achieve the compliance envisioned by Crown ministers in London. One central problem, like in Scotland, was that negotiated rule in British North America empowered some Indigenous nations while actively suppressing the opportunities available to others. The "Walking Purchase," undertaken in 1737, affords a crucial example. When the Delawares signed a document confirming an alleged 1686 transfer of the entire western shore of the Delaware River to William Penn, they unwittingly acceded to a fraudulent 1,200-mile land grab that deprived them of their home. Petitioning the powerful Iroquois for help, the Onondagas' speaker Canassatego argued that the Delawares had no right to sell the lands in the first place because the Iroquois Confederacy had conquered them. For these Delawares, then, Iroquois heads-people had come to cooperate with members of the proprietary government of Pennsylvania to deprive them of their homelands. Far from facilitating peace on the frontier, British endorsement of Iroquoian suzerainty had only exacerbated local Indigenous disputes and enfranchised select polities over others.

Set within localized contexts of Native American political change, then, alliance with Britain often only aggravated the conflicts that metropolitan officials aimed to quell. Many of the Indian Nations or villages who found themselves shut out from positions of influence within the British imperial system pursued alliances with Britain's rivals. The Delawares moved west into the Ohio valley to seek more advantageous terms with the French, embodying a broader move by other Native American nations to use French alliance as a political counterweight with which to leverage better terms from the British. Peter Chartier, a Shawnee metis who served as a trader to the British and joined the Shawnee migration across the Appalachians in the 1720s, reversed his loyalty and declared for the French after Britain discouraged Shawnees from undertaking diplomatic ventures independently of the Iroquois. Orontony of the Wyandots embodied the same shift but in the reverse direction; rising to influence as part of a French-allied group in the Great Lakes region, Orontony then became the head-person of an Indian republic in rebellion against the French and sought aid from the British in the 1740s.[13] Here, too, then, ministerial concepts of alliance failed to achieve the compliance envisioned by Crown ministers in London. In both cases, Native individuals used their privileged access to goods to forge new polities in defiance of the existing social and political order. In doing so, they deliberately leveraged European alliance to transform the very Indigenous diplomatic landscape that their allies sought to control.

Alliance in India also took shape around the formation of Indigenous Mughal imperial authority. The Company's royal charter, granted by Queen Elizabeth in 1600, sanctioned its servants to draw up treaties with local rulers for trading privileges and for the foundation of factories, or trading posts. Though large clusters of these factories came to be called settlements, and though larger settlements came to be administered by an agent with the title of governor, early English treaties in India did not operate in the same manner as early English treaties with American Indian nations. These accords did not aim at territorial sovereignty but were instead primarily commercial in nature: they granted small districts of land to Company servants to fortify and govern by their own laws, and after 1717, some began to convey phirmaunds, or royal grants, which empowered the Company to trade with Indian merchants duty-free. By the mid-eighteenth century, the Company had developed a sophisticated administrative structure on the Indian subcontinent, anchored by its three most important bases at Bengal, Madras, and Bombay. Still, the EIC depended entirely on the "attachment" of Mughal rulers to expand its commerce, and it acceded the autonomy of the Mughal Empire to set the terms.

Bengal's native peoples therefore also played crucial roles in shaping the limitations of Company alliance into the eighteenth century. In South Asia, Britain was the principal source of neither manufactured goods nor credit for its Asian trading partners, so the Company depended almost entirely on Bengal's robust Indigenous public finance system for its commercial operations. Furthermore, when the Mughal Empire slowly disintegrated after 1707, the British and French Companies alike dealt with Indian leaders committed to reshaping the structure of revenue rights in their provinces and to enhancing their position as independent successor states. In Bengal, a peculiarly robust successor state, nawabs eliminated subordinate chieftains who claimed rival authority over lands and peoples. They also reduced the number of *jagirs*, or imperial grants, to noblemen in return for their military service to the Mughal Empire. Here, too, then, the shifting landscape of Indigenous state formation defied any simple ministerial calculation of "attachment" to British imperial interests; in Bengal, as in other post-Mughal successor states, the commercial success of the East India Company depended on its ability to work along the grain of an Indian social order perpetually in flux—not the other way around.

Despite the similarities that appeared to cut across Britain's Indigenous alliances, then, native peoples played determinative roles in contesting or reshaping governance on the ground. In defiance of British terms like "attachment" and the subjection to European interests it entailed, Indigenous peoples in Scotland, North America, and Bengal consistently leveraged alliance to serve Indigenous ends. Most often, they entered into British alliances not to submit to the Crown but to contain the deleterious effects of expansion and preserve their autonomy vis-à-vis rival polities. Doing so offered a chance to preserve their language and culture, to maintain their prestige and influence among other native nations, and to perpetuate their positions as coveted allies and trading partners. Yet alliance also afforded opportunities for consolidating political power. For groups such as the Iroquois and the Campbells, this meant maintaining prestige and influence relative to rival Indigenous groups. For individuals such as Siraj-ud-Daula and Orontony, it meant a chance to forge successor polities unlike those that existed before. Indeed, some Indigenous peoples from within all three sites used their privileged access to European arms and commodities to assert new influence on Indigenous political contests and to emerge as autonomous regional power brokers. These views contrasted sharply with the ministerial view of alliance as an "attachment" to British Crown interests. They challenged the notion of alliance as collapsing Britain's enemies into the enemies of an Indigenous polity. Most significantly, they kept alive the idea that partnership with the British government depended on the continued ability of the Crown to serve Indigenous interests, rather than vice versa.

Transforming Imperial Rule

The renewal of war with France—first in the War of the Austrian Succession (1744–48), then in the Carnatic Wars of the East Indies (1749–54), and finally in the Seven Years' War (1756–63)—afforded the crucial contexts in which this negotiated system of governance came under British metropolitan reform. The cause, by many scholarly accounts, was the comprehensive breakdown of Anglo-Indigenous alliances at midcentury: a second Jacobite Rebellion in the Scottish Highlands (1745); the sacking of Calcutta by Britain's ally Siraj-ud-Daula, nawab of Bengal (1756); and the long-term deterioration of Britain's Native North American partnerships.[14] To view these events as failures of Anglo-Indigenous alliance, however, is to align oneself strictly with British imperial accounts of the purpose and nature of negotiated rule; for as this chapter has shown, native communities of the Scottish Highlands, North America, and Bengal had long used alliance as a means of reshaping rule on the ground, and many felt themselves entitled to assert their claims against breaches of treaties by Britain.

Disaffection ran deep in the Scottish Highlands, where the clans' staunch opposition to clan Campbell and the Anglo-Scottish Union of 1707 combined with their rejection of excessive malt and excise taxes under the government of Sir Robert Walpole. France provided them with an opportunity to challenge Union after 1744. On July 23, 1745, Charles Edward "Bonnie Prince Charlie" Stuart made landfall at Eriskay in Scotland with a handful of companions to regain the British throne for the exiled House of Stuart. By August 19, 1,300

Highland men had rallied to his standard at the Battle of Prestonpans.[15] Like in 1715, those who rallied to the Jacobite cause came disproportionately from those Highland clans most alienated by the policies of the Whig government. These included Episcopal clans frustrated by the Presbyterian-Whig alliance after 1688, individuals who suffered heavily under discriminatory excise and malt taxes, and, tellingly, those clans most excluded from the government's system of patronage. Also, like in 1715, clans in open rebellion aimed at nothing less than the reversal of the 1688 Revolution and the restoration of the Stuart monarchy to the throne of Great Britain.

The eruption of war in 1744 compelled France and Britain to mobilize their Indigenous allies as auxiliaries in North America as well. There, too, Britain received little support. In the Ohio Valley, most groups aligned at first with the French: Shawnee and Iroquois migrants living by the Cuyahoga River promised to plunder British traders, while Ottawas, Menominees, Winnebagos, Saulteurs, Mississaugas, Illinois, Huron-Petuns, and Potawatomis sent warriors to Montreal. When self-made Ohio chieftains such as Orontony and La Demoiselle rejected the French alliance and turned to the British for goods that would sustain and broaden the influence of their new successor states, this, too, placed new strain on Britain's other American Indigenous partners. The claims of Orontony and La Demoiselle conflicted with the claims of the Iroquois, for example, who sought above all to legitimize their claims to the Ohio region, to restore migrants from the east to the Covenant Chain, and to establish new ties to Algonquian groups. Britain's willingness to support the political claims of Ohio Indians abandoning French alliance caused members of the Iroquois council to fear that the British were guaranteeing the independence of Six Nations' client peoples and undermining the autonomy of Onondaga. These fears, coupled with a rise of fraudulent land grabs and the failure of New York to provide presents after 1748, caused Onondaga to press its own claim to the Ohio, deny any Europeans the right to establish posts there, and demand that British traders withdraw. They declared the Covenant Chain broken in 1752.[16]

The French and British East India Companies also sought Indigenous auxiliaries in South Asia, and here, too, the shifting terms of alliance pushed native leaders ever more gradually into opposition to the EIC. When central Mughal authority began to collapse, regional potentates reached out to the French and British East India Companies for military support as they re-forged their provinces into independent Mughal successor states against rival claimants. On the Coromandel Coast, the British Company allied with one contender for the newly created province of the Carnatic, supporting him against his French-backed Indian rivals and receiving in return grants of weaving villages and territory that would yield revenue to the Company. This heightened military presence of the EIC alarmed Siraj-ud-Daula, who succeeded his grandfather Alivardi Khan as nawab of Bengal in April 1756. Siraj-ud-Daula resented Company servants in Calcutta, who failed to contribute to his taxation and grossly abused the trading privileges granted to them by earlier Mughal rulers. He also expressed indignation at the heightened military fortification of Fort William in Calcutta, which he demanded the Company cease. When the Company refused their ally's request to "level the English fortifications" at Calcutta "on account of their great strength," Siraj-ud-Daula declared the alliance broken and sacked the city in 1756.[17]

In all three cases, Britain's highest ministers of state claimed that native leaders had failed to uphold the terms of alliance—by neglecting to align their constituents' interests with that of the Crown and by enabling circumstances to emerge in which France could drive a wedge between Britain and the Indigenous communities of the empire. These were, however, less moments of breakdown or failure than an adaptation of preexisting modes of Indigenous engagement with negotiated rule. In all three sites, Indigenous peoples had used alliance to reshape British rule long before midcentury. It was therefore not unreasonable that some leveraged the outbreak of Anglo-French war to reassert control over the terms of negotiated rule: in the Highlands to denounce the 1707 Union and the Hanoverian line of Kings, in North America to reconstitute or expand Indigenous polities that challenged the new social or political order as imagined by British policymakers, and in Bengal to forge robust post-Mughal successor states capable of dictating terms to the Company. From their perspective, it was Britain—not they—who broke from the terms of its treaties: by imposing discriminatory taxes on Scotland, for example, or by fortifying Britain's military presence in the Ohio Valley and Calcutta. Given their active role in contesting or reshaping alliance previously, many native communities in the Highlands, North America, and Bengal felt themselves once more entitled to assert their claims against any breach of alliance by Britain. Far from signaling the failures of alliance, then, the Indigenous resistance movements that incited British reform were, in fact, its most potent expression.

When British ministers reformed native governance from 1745 to 1775, then, they were responding not to the failure of alliance but to the failure of British *ideas* about alliance and the submission to Crown interests they entailed. This was why Britain's ministers deployed strikingly similar arguments across each case. In all three sets of reforms, officials aimed reforms explicitly at undermining the autonomy of Indigenous chieftains, whom, they argued, had acted independently of Britain's wartime interests and thereby failed to "attach" their constituents to those interests as well. In all three sets of reforms, moreover, imperial officials replaced native chieftains with British institutions as the primary means of "attaching" Indigenous peoples and securing their "dependency" on the Crown. "The great object," wrote one of the leading architects of Scottish reform, "will be to pass such laws, after the Rebellion is over, as may effectually reduce the Power of the Highlands; and thereby disable France from playing this game upon us . . . and so keep this country in their constant Dependence."[18] Robert Clive ejected Siraj-ud-Daula from power with the same aim: of "setting up another in his stead entirely attached to the English Interest."[19] The Board of Trade's commercial North American reforms aimed also to create Indian allies "who are absolutely dependant upon it and inseperably connected with its Interests."[20] Underlying these concerns about autonomy was a deeper ministerial distrust of Indigenous leaders; by making native communities "independent of their Chiefs, & Industrious," they believed, institutional reform would forge stronger bonds of attachment between the Crown and the native communities of its empire.[21]

Britain's Indigenous alliances had collapsed before, and ministers in London had always recognized power of the empire's native peoples to contest imperial rule. After 1744, however, ministerial fears about Indigenous autonomy translated into state-sanctioned policies of military and economic force for two interrelated reasons. First, the renewal of war with France threatened to destroy the Protestant succession at home and realize Bourbon universal monarchy abroad. Secondly, when Sir Robert Walpole resigned as First Lord of the Treasury in 1741, he ended twenty years of single-party Establishment Whig rule and catalyzed a tempestuous series of domestic political realignments in which members of Britain's parliamentary opposition threatened to derail successive ministries over questions of foreign policy and the national debt. For Walpole's successors, then, foreign policy and the reduction of debt became symbiotically linked to the fate of the Whig establishment in Britain—that is, if they reduced the nation's debt and acted aggressively to obtain a favorable peace, their opposition would lose ground in elections and imperial stability would resume. They therefore watched in horror as native uprisings in the Highlands, North America, and South Asia threatened to derail Britain's victory and increase the debt. As ministers grew desperate to command the war on their own terms against virulent domestic opposition, they increasingly linked the obstruction of native autonomy—that is, the reduction of their ability to act independently of Britain's interests—with success in the war abroad and the continuation of Whig governance at home.

Ultimately, then, it was a collective core of ministerial frustration over the continued refusal of Britain's Highland, Native American, and Bengali allies to submit to their vision for Britain's domestic and foreign affairs that compelled Britain's eighteenth-century ministers to implement more aggressive reform. The Scottish Highlands, British North America, and Bengal became the sites of reform precisely because they were the sites where Indigenous resistance to Britain's abrogation of the terms of alliance had been most concentrated. In consequence, many peoples native to Northern Britain, British North America, and South Asia faced new measures that shared key discursive and structural linkages. They withstood crushing—and in some cases, genocidal—acts of military force under British commanding officers. Native peoples from each region also endured forceful new economic interventions designed to foster their dependence on some of the highest institutional bodies in the British state. They faced new governing protocols designed to undercut the diplomatic prestige of native chieftains, tribal councils, and regional princes. And as they did, native peoples from Murshidabad to Detroit temporarily lost control of some of the channels through which they had formerly expressed their autonomy and leveraged their interests against those of the British state.

The marginalization of native potentates formed the central linking feature of this change. In Scotland, Highlanders endured an all-out assault on the social prestige of their chieftains and on the cultural vestiges of clanship.[22] Disaffected chieftains faced exile or death, while the abolition of heritable jurisdictions in 1747 further eroded the traditional basis of their sovereign authority. Native North American leaders expressed indignation at Britain's stoppage of Indian presents, which had stood as the cornerstone of Anglo-Indigenous diplomacy for more than a century. When this custom temporarily gave way to a new system in which access to European goods depended on one's access to the market, it also eroded one basis for American chieftains' influence within their respective nations.[23] Mughal potentates in Bengal also lost a significant degree of autonomy, becoming, in effect, puppets of a European Company that deposed and reinstalled three successive nawabs between 1757 and 1765. Bengal's large zamindars gradually lost their authority over military and administrative affairs as successive governors put the management of their lands under the control of less influential revenue farmers. These measures reflected ministerial concerns about the "perfidiousness" and "treachery" of native leaders outlined previously and caused tremendous social disruption across Northern British, North American, and South Asian Indigenous communities.

Even so, the implementation of Britain's new modes of native governance continued to depend on the engagement of native peoples themselves. The Crown, after all, relied on Highland factors to run rebels' forfeited estates, on Native Americans to consume British wares, and on zamindars to collect Bengal's revenue. Individuals from all three regions therefore continued to exert influence over British governance, even if the means by which they did so differed from before. A great many disaffected quietly or even disregarded the new measures altogether. Well into the 1750s, Crown officials continued to receive reports that Highlanders from disaffected families had illegally taken appointments as factors on forfeited estates and refused to provide "any Assistance, in letting them know the noted Thieves, or Those, who wear the Highland Dress; Nor have the Sheriffs taken up any Person for carrying Arms, or wearing the Dress, since the late Act."[24] Native North American nations continued to demand gifts from the Crown and held little regard for the 1763 Royal Proclamation, which, from their perspective, was not the King's prerogative to declare. In Bengal, where the coercive force of the new regime remained "pitted against the powers of concealment and evasion of those who held revenue rights," tenure holders and zamindars deducted far more considerable sums from the revenue paid to the Company than they had been authorized.[25] By 1769, this had grown so common that Company servants complained regularly of being kept in "ignorance of the real produce and capacity of the country . . . by a set of men who first deceive us from interest and afterwards continue the deception from fear."[26]

These and other moments, fleeting and disconnected though they were, pervade imperial records and thereby serve as stark reminders that native peoples did not passively accept Britain's new terms of rule. On the contrary, some continued to push for traditional channels of Anglo-Indigenous diplomacy, while others adapted new strategies for that end. In February 1764, the president of the Board of Trade, the Earl of Halifax, received requests from two Indians named Attakullakulla and Occunostota to travel to England.[27]

Unsurprisingly, Halifax urged Indian Superintendent John Stuart that he must "upon all occasions discourage such applications, which, when complied with, are attended with much Expence, and Trouble, and productive of little, or no, advantage."[28] Even so, voyages like these had a long historical precedent in London, and the appeals of Attakullakulla and Occunostota suggest their desire to continue working within traditional channels of governance. Bengal's native peoples also pushed for a return to Mughal forms of redress. Under the Mughal Empire, a ruler needed to be accessible to the complaints of his subjects in order to rectify their problems. Under Company rule, by contrast, one Indian observer remarked that "the gates of communication and intercourse" had been closed by the British, and that Company servants "constantly express an aversion to the society of Indians and a disdain against conversing with them."[29] Many therefore refined their petitioning techniques by translating them into English and recording them onto the Company's official proceedings, where they might catch the attention of senior officials and the Court of Directors in London. There is some evidence of their success. In the early 1770s, weavers from Dhaka deliberately withheld their complaints against Richard Barwell, head of the Dhaka factory, until his enemies joined the council. When they did, the weavers' grievances were taken up by Edmund Burke and were publicized in Britain by the Parliamentary Select Committee.[30]

In North America and South Asia, Indigenous resistance to Britain's new reforms escalated to the point of war. Pontiac's Rebellion, perhaps the most notorious Indian uprising in the history of British North America, erupted as a direct challenge to the failure of Britain to uphold the terms of its alliances—that is, the Crown's failure to curb the violence of white settler expansion, its reversal on questions of occupying the Ohio, and its abandonment of Indigenous diplomatic protocols. From 1763 to 1765, native peoples from the Senecas west to the Illinois and from the Chippewas down to the Delawares attacked colonial posts and settlers in an attempt to drive back British expansion. Though America's Indigenous nations did not know it, the British faced a native insurrection on the other side of the world at the exact same time. Mir Qasim, who ruled as Britain's allied nawab of Bengal from 1760 to 1763, grew upset with the Company's abuse of dastaks (imperial licenses to trade without tax) and famously allied with Indigenous powers Shuja-ud-Daula of Avadh and Mughal Emperor Shah Alam II in 1763 to eject the British Company from East India. Though their combined forces faced defeat at the Battle of Buxar (1764), Qasim's alliance with the Mughal

Emperor—like that of Indian nations under Pontiac—posed a formidable challenge to Britain's position in South Asia; in addition to facing an army with "artillery mounted in the English manner" and sepoys "armed, cloath'd, and accouter'd like our own," the Company's artillery was outnumbered by the guns of the nawab of Awadh.[31] The staggering costs of these wars posed an enormous challenge to a ministry already crushed with debt, and they were central to the emergence of policies such as the Stamp Act and Clive's acquisition of *diwani*, both of which followed in 1765.[32]

The Scottish clans, by contrast, did not rise up in the wake of Britain's post-1745 reforms. In fact, British ministers were so convinced that the clans would not support another French landing during the Seven Years' War that they refused to approve the preemptive seizure of chiefs of uncertain loyalty.[33] This was because many Highland clans actively supported their own integration into the British state after 1745—not as a subordinate people governed by alliance but as equal subjects of the Crown of Great Britain. Indeed, Highland Scots integrated themselves thoroughly into the structures of imperial rule after the 1745 Rebellion. Many of those who remained in the north actively petitioned the Treasury until the 1780s, seeking subsidies for roads, bridges, and other infrastructural or improvement projects. Many of these individuals served as colonial administrators in North America, India, South Africa, Australia, and the Caribbean. Others took on military posts and fought for Britain against its European and non-European enemies in the Seven Years' War (1756–63), the American Revolution (1776–83), and the French Revolutionary and Napoleonic Wars (1789–1815). To be sure, the transformation of Highland governance was no less brutal than that of Native North America or Bengal; in addition to proscribing aspects of their culture, landlords in the Scottish Highlands forcibly removed tenants from their land starting in the 1750s. The difference was instead one of status and the restoration of access to imperial institutions it entailed; for even though clan chieftains lost autonomy in the wake of the 1745 rebellion, they could still serve as members of Parliament and as ministers, driving Britain's colonial policies long after.

This divergence of Highland Scots away from Native American and Indian political trajectories after 1760 was indeed one of the most compelling legacies to emerge from this era. Most people today would not consider Highland Scots "Indigenous" or even include them in the connective story outlined in this chapter. Yet as Sir Christopher Bayly has remarked, "the very notion of 'indigenous people' within the British Isles was fundamentally reworked" after 1760, making the period "a critical one in the epistemological and economic creation of 'indigenous peoples' as a series of comparable categories across the globe."[34] Bayly's observation serves to remind us that indigeneity is not fixed in any group but historically reconditioned over time. Yet where Bayly centers intellectual history as integral to that process, this chapter centers the importance of political change. Between 1745 and 1775, the British imperial state devoted tremendous resources to "attaching" recalcitrant native communities of its empire more permanently to the Crown. In doing so, it brought to the fore difficult questions about the *nature* of that attachment and the imperial protections to which certain communities were entitled. As Highland Scots increasingly enjoyed the same protections and liberties granted to all British subjects, then, the nature of Native American and Indian peoples' "attachment" to the Crown became a subject of imperial inquiry. These questions, though first raised by Britain's midcentury native reforms, continued to defy easy resolution even after Parliament's 1834 Select Committee on Aboriginal Tribes considered them more closely.

Bridging Narratives

A chapter of this length cannot provide an exhaustive overview of every instance in which peoples native to Scotland, India, and North America resisted Britain's midcentury reforms. Nor does it aim to provide a comprehensive account of every native person's formal engagement with the newly reformed administrative structures of the eighteenth-century British empire. It offers instead a preliminary reexamination of the institutional contexts in which native peoples faced empire, casting new light on the connections that existed across the British government's native policies. In doing so, it unveils alternative linkages of experience that reached across those native communities most provoked by the heightened intervention of some of the highest institutional bodies in the British state. Native Highland, American, and Indian peoples entered into British alliances not to submit to the Crown but to contain the deleterious effects of expansion and increase their political influence vis-à-vis rival polities. Britain's reforms arose not from ministerial perceptions of native weakness but from a collective core of frustration over the continued resistance of Britain's Highland, Native American, and Bengali allies to submit to their vision of negotiated rule. Across each site, native communities continued to adapt creatively to British reform. And as they did, many also reshaped both the policy choices and the categories of Indigenous comparison available to ministers in Whitehall.

These findings suggest the importance of examining British political change and Indigenous political change not only side by side but also as intricately entwined. Just as British imperial contexts provide an alternative prism for linking Indigenous experiences with colonialism, Indigenous political contexts afford new ways of seeing the multitude of ways in which native peoples reformulated their modes of engagement with British structures and statesmen over time. At every stage in the evolution of Britain's native policies, Highland, Native American, and Indian peoples played determinative roles in contesting or reshaping the effects of Britain's directives on the ground. Even when Britain's midcentury imperial reforms aimed to crush native sovereignty by forcing their dependency on the state, many of these native peoples continued to create new ways of compelling imperial officials to respond to their interests. They did this not merely in reaction to imperial encroachment but as expressions of the localized political contexts in which they understood encroachment and, in some cases, forged polities of their own. The implications of this view pose a stark challenge to the separation of imperial and Indigenous historical narratives; by examining these narratives side by side, we see that imperial state-making and Indigenous state-making were, in fact, dialectically related and, at times, mutually reinforcing or limiting.

When read together, then, British and Indigenous political histories expose both the robustness of Indigenous engagement with the eighteenth-century British empire and the spectacular failure of that empire to achieve its vision for complete Indigenous dependency on the Crown. At every stage in the evolution of Britain's native policies, Highland, Native American, and Indian peoples played determinative roles in contesting or reshaping Britain's directives on the ground. Even when Britain's midcentury imperial reforms aimed to crush native sovereignty by forcing their dependency on the state, native peoples continued to create new ways of compelling imperial officials to respond to their interests. Thus, as British ministers responded with increasingly distinctive solutions for each site, the diversity of Indigenous peoples' engagement ensured that Scottish, North American, and Indian policies went off in vastly different directions the further they went out from Whitehall. In the process, these parties partook in a broader reformulation of indigeneities—one that separated the nebulous connections that previously existed between English conceptions of Highland, Native American, and Indian peoples. Ultimately, then, one can never comprehend the connective experiences of Indigenous peoples without the linking features of British empire, and one can never fully understand the political lives of empire without acknowledging the political lives of Indigenous peoples.

Notes

1. Allan Macinnes, *Clanship, Commerce, and the House of Stuart, 1603–1788* (East Linton: Tuckwell Press, 1996), 211.

2. Gregory Evans Dowd, *War under Heaven: Pontiac, the Indian Nations, and the British Empire* (Baltimore: Johns Hopkins University Press, 2002), 70.

3. Macinnes, *Clanship, Commerce, and the House of Stuart*; Dowd, *War under Heaven*; Richard White, *The Middle Ground: Indians, Empires, and Republics, 1650–1815* (Cambridge: Cambridge University Press, 1991); Seema Alavi, ed., *The Eighteenth Century in India* (New York: Oxford University Press, 2002), 70–71; Martin Daunton and Rick Halpern, eds., *Empire and Others: British Encounters with Indigenous Peoples, 1600–1850* (London: University College London Press, 1999).

4. Dowd, *War under Heaven*; White, *The Middle Ground*; Macinnes, *Clanship, Commerce, and the House of Stuart*; H. V. Bowen, *Revenue and Reform: The Indian Problem in British Politics, 1757–1773* (New York: Cambridge University Press, 2002). One notable exception is P. J. Marshall, *The Making and Unmaking of Empires: Britain, India, and America, c. 1750–1783* (New York: Oxford University Press, 2005).

5. For example, the Society for the Propagation of Christian Knowledge and the Society for the Propagation of the Gospel were active in the Scottish Highlands and North America, respectively.

6. John Willison, *A Letter to an English Member of Parliament, from a Gentleman in Scotland, concerning the Slavish Dependencies, which a Great Part of That Nation Is Still Kept under, by Superiorities, Wards, Reliefs, and Other Remains of the Feudal Law, and by Clanships and Tithes* (Edinburgh, 1721), 23.

7. Robert Clive to Warren Hastings, October 6, 1758, Sir John Malcolm, *Life of Robert, Lord Clive*, 3 vols. (London: J. Murray, 1836), I:381–82.

8. Peter James Marshall and Glyndwr Williams, *The Great Map of Mankind: Perceptions of New Worlds in the Age of Enlightenment* (Cambridge, MA: Harvard University Press, 1982); Edward Said, *Orientalism* (New York: Pantheon Books, 1978).

9. Duncan Forbes, "Memorial concerning the Present State of the Highlands of Scotland and What They Call the Clans There," 1745, National Library of Scotland, MS 81:1. See also T. M. Devine, *Scotland's Empire, 1600–1815* (London: Allen Lane, 2003), and Macinnes, *Clanship, Commerce, and the House of Stuart*.

10. Nicholas Phillipson and Rosalind Mitchison, eds., *Scotland in the Age of Improvement: Essays in Scottish History in the Eighteenth Century* (Edinburgh: Edinburgh University Press, 1970), 19.

11. Board of Trade to King George I, September 8, 1721, Cholmondeley (Houghton) Papers [hereafter CP], Cambridge University Library, 84:11.

12. Board of Trade to King George I, September 8, 1721, CP 84:11.

13. White, *The Middle Ground*, 196.

14. Bruce Lenman, *Integration, Enlightenment, and Industrialization: Scotland, 1746–1832* (Toronto: University of Toronto Press, 1981); Macinnes, *Clanship, Commerce, and the House of Stuart*; White, *The Middle Ground*; Dowd, *War under*

Heaven; Bowen, *Revenue and Reform*; Peter Silver, *Our Savage Neighbors: How Indian War Transformed Early America* (New York: Norton, 2008); Vincent Harlow, *The Founding of the Second British Empire, 1763–1793*, vol. 2 (London: Longmans, 1964).

15. Murray G. H. Pittock, *Jacobitism* (London: Macmillan, 1998), 98.

16. White, *Middle Ground*, chaps. 5–6.

17. P. J. Marshall, *Bengal: The British Bridgehead* (Cambridge: Cambridge University Press, 1987), 76.

18. Duke of Newcastle to Duke of Cumberland, March 5, 1746, *Official Correspondence of Thomas Pelham Holles, Duke of Newcastle, 1697–1768*, microfilm, Sterling Memorial Library, Yale University, reel 2315, vol. 119.

19. Robert Clive to Lord Barrington, August 21, 1757, *Original Correspondence of Robert Clive, 1752–1774: European Letter Book*, microfilm, British Online Archives, Yale University Library.

20. John Stuart to the Earl of Egremont, December 5, 1763, National Archives at Kew, CO 5/65/2:150–162.

21. Earl of Holderness, "Measures Taken by the Military, since the Rebellion, & the Effects Thereof" (1752), Holderness Papers (hereafter HP), British Library, Egerton MS 3433:15–17.

22. Holderness, "Measures Taken by the Military," HP 3433:16.

23. White, *The Middle Ground*, 267.

24. "Abuses, or Neglects, in the General Management in Scotland, since the Rebellion" (1752), HP 3433:1–4.

25. Marshall, *The Making and Unmaking of Empires*, 265.

26. Select Committee Proceedings, August 16, 1769, India Office Records (hereafter IOR), British Library, P/A/9:470.

27. Earl of Halifax to John Stuart, February 11, 1764, Colonial Records (hereafter CR), National Archives at Kew, CO5/65/2:196–197.

28. Earl of Halifax to John Stuart, February 11, 1764, CR, CO5/65/2:196–197.

29. Marshall, *The Making and Unmaking of Empires*, 267.

30. Marshall, *The Making and Unmaking of Empires*, 267.

31. Adams to Egremont, October 5, 1763, IOR, H/97:105.

32. "Third Report from the Committee of Secrecy," February 9, 1773, *List of Reports from the Committee of Secrecy Appointed to Enquire into the State of the East India Company* (London, 1776), 4:60.

33. Holdernesse to Lord G. Beauclerk, November 1, 1759, HP 3433.

34. Christopher A. Bayly, "The British and Indigenous Peoples, 1760–1860: Power, Perception and Identity," in *Empire and Others: British Encounters with Indigenous Peoples, 1600–1850*, ed. Martin Daunton and Rick Halpern (London: University College London Press, 1999), 20–21.

CHAPTER THIRTEEN

Shawundais and the Methodist Mission to Native North America

ELSPETH MARTINI

In March 1837, the Ojibwe chief and Methodist missionary Shawundais—also known by his baptismal name of John Sunday—gave evidence in London before the House of Commons Select Committee on Aborigines (the ASC). He began by characteristically downplaying his English language abilities. "I am so poor an Englishman," he told the committee, "that I am afraid you will not understand me." Shawundais nevertheless proceeded to speak lucidly about the need for his people, and indeed all First Peoples, to receive British-issued title deeds to their lands. Only with such (British) legal instruments, argued Shawundais, could they defend their property against the ongoing invasion of settler-colonists.[1] Shawundais's English expression never matched his mastery of Anishinaabemowin (the Ojibwe language). He nevertheless conversed fluently in another language he shared with the evangelical members of the ASC: the language of the civilizing mission. At a time when colonial policy aimed "to civilize" the Indigenous peoples within Britain's imperial reach, Shawundais emphasized his own commitment to these ideals.

Yet Shawundais never saw his Christian faith or his adoption of (so-called) civilized cultural traits as changing his Indigenous identity. Rather, his mission to Native North America and his subsequent 1836–37 stay in Britain seemingly increased his consciousness that his people shared a struggle similar to many others. Using the prestige he gained within the transatlantic Wesleyan-Methodist movement, Shawundais took this struggle to the Colonial Office in London—the nominal heart of imperial policymaking—where he petitioned as a "civilized" Christian to have the British colonial administration officially recognize his people's rights as original owners of their land.

Shawundais was a member of the Bay of Quinte Ojibwes or Anishinaabeg, whose homeland lies north of Lake Ontario.[2] The settler-colonial invasion of their homeland began after the American War for Independence, but then accelerated after the War of 1812. In addition to bringing disruptive agricultural practices and livestock, the settler-colonists introduced to eastern Anishinaabewaki (the Anishinaabe homeland) the Christian revivalism of the Second Great Awakening. Amid the hardships wrought by the invasion, Shawundais and a cohort of other eastern Ojibwes converted to Methodism in the late 1820s after hearing the exhortations of Peter Jones (Kahkewaquonaby), an Ojibwe from the Credit River.[3] Methodism held out the empowering promise that every person, no matter how sinful, could save their own soul by repenting and living by the grace of God. Its denominational structure also relied on sanctioning even the most recent converts to go forth and evangelize others.[4] But Jones also spoke to his fellow Anishinaabeg in their own language, thus providing the initial key to the spread of transatlantic Christian revivalism into Anishinaabewaki. The messenger and the message appealed to people such as Shawundais, who found themselves at a crossroads between European and Indian worlds.

Like Peter Jones, Shawundais embraced the evangelical message, and from 1829 to 1836 he dedicated himself to spreading Methodism to his "Indian brethren" in the Great Lakes region. He used his skills as an Ojibwe orator and his understanding of Anishinaabe customs to aid his missionary efforts. Through his travels, he made connections with a multitude of his fellow Anishinaabeg as well as other peoples of the region. He preached for the adoption of certain aspects of "civilized" culture but nevertheless emphasized the spread of Christianity in Anishinaabemowin—the lingua franca of the area—by Native missionaries. His envisioned a prosperous future for his "Indian brethren" in which they adopted Christianity and aspects of the colonizer's culture but retained their political autonomy.

Shawundais's winning personality, along with his missionary successes, also gained him considerable renown in wider Methodist networks. Above the average height for men of his time and possessing a muscular build, Shawundais cut an impressive figure.[5] In front of an audience, his fellow Methodist Ojibwe George Copway recalled, Shawundais's "keen black eyes flashing fire, and his large brawny arms extended, gave great effect to his speech."[6] Nonnatives were captivated by his manner of expressing himself in English and the originality of his exhortations and sermons. "The halls and churches were always crowded," recalled an Anglo-Canadian friend, "wherever it was known that John Sunday was to speak."[7] He appealed to these audiences partly because of his identity as a "converted Indian," and though he never consciously cultivated an image based on nonnative cultural expectations for Indianness, he did nevertheless stress his identity as both an Ojibwe and a Native North American. He used his popularity in transatlantic Wesleyan-Methodist circles to take his quest for Native land rights all the way to the corridors of power in the imperial metropole.

"I Had Trouble in My Heart": Shawundais's Conversion Experience

Shawundais joined the revivalist fervor of the Second Great Awakening when he was about thirty years old. Struggling to find peace and contentment amid the turmoil wrought by the settler-colonial invasion, he converted to Methodism in 1826. Shawundais would remember the day of his conversion as the first day in which he felt truly happy.[8] In joining the Methodists, he became part of a community that in many ways transcended ethnic or national boundaries. Yet Shawundais quickly channeled his postconversion energy and newly found beliefs into organizing a prosperous future for his people on the small area that they retained of their homeland.

Shawundais was born around 1795 into the Anishinaabe Zhaangweshi (Mink) clan. He grew up as a member of the Bay of Quinte Ojibwes in the eastern reaches of Anishinaabewaki (around present-day Belleville, Ontario).[9] His life spanned a period of turmoil for the Anishinaabeg along the northern and western shores of Lake Ontario. In the years immediately following the American War of Independence—about a decade before Shawundais's birth—the Bay of Quinte Ojibwes experienced significant pressure from their British military allies to cede large tracts of their homeland. By the mid-1780s, several thousand loyalist immigrants had taken up residence in the Kingston and Bay of Quinte area, on land the Ojibwes signed over in the "Crawford purchases" of 1783 and 1784.[10] Under further pressure from British officers, they then ceded lands west of the Bay of Quinte in 1787.[11]

British and Ojibwe versions of the Crawford purchases, in particular, differed significantly. The Ojibwes recalled that during the diplomatic councils of 1783 and 1784 they had retained title to their islands in the Bay of Quinte, as well as the right to hunt and fish on all the ceded territory. But according to the British, the Ojibwes had retained only a small reserve around the village of Asaukhknosk (renamed Belleville by the British in 1816).[12] The Bay of Quinte Ojibwes' efforts to demonstrate ongoing title to these reservations would prove especially difficult because the British negotiators failed to record the purchases in a written deed or indenture.[13]

Born after the settler-colonial invasion had begun, Shawundais grew up in a world of increasing instability and insecurity amid a people who had become a minority in their own homeland. As colonists flooded into eastern Anishinaabewaki, they began to transform the land by felling trees and fencing in crop fields.[14] They also brought destructive livestock onto Ojibwe hunting grounds and agricultural areas, and the increased threat of diseases such as measles, tuberculosis, and smallpox.[15] These upheavals had huge ramifications for people's ability to pursue their livelihoods. Men became increasingly unable to fulfill their roles as huntsmen and fishermen, and women were restricted in their capacities to grow the crops necessary for subsistence. These limitations affected more than the Ojibwes' material economy; they undermined the self-worth of the individual and the social and cultural cohesion of the community. Shawundais came of age in the midst of these changes.[16]

After the War of 1812, in which Shawundais had fought alongside the British, like many other First Nations peoples, Upper Canada became what historian James Belich has termed one of the "Exploding Wests" of the expansionist Anglophone world.[17] With a surge of postwar British immigrants, the colony's non-Indigenous population rose from 75,000 in 1815 to 150,000 by 1824.[18] For Shawundais and other Ojibwe warriors from the area, demobilization ended their chances to prove their manhood in battle only to usher in a period in which hunting and fishing—the other major activities through which they could affirm their sense of masculine self-worth—became further limited by this "second invasion of newcomers."[19] The postwar invasion also further militated against the Anishinaabeg's ability to resist British pressure to cede their remaining lands. In pressing need of a regular source of subsistence, Shawundais and other leaders from the Bay of Quinte and Kingston Ojibwes signed the "Rideau Treaty" in 1819, in which they ceded a huge tract of territory north of the Crawford purchases in return for yearly annuities from the British government.[20]

For many Anishinaabeg in the Lake Ontario region, this was a time of profound personal and collective despair, and population loss.[21] Recalling this period, Shawundais referred to himself as "one of the most miserable creatures on earth."[22] Sometime in the early 1820s, he married his wife, Mary, and like other Ojibwe men in the area, he tried to eke out a livelihood by hunting and fishing.[23] His efforts, however, were hampered by bouts of depression.[24] He spent many hours isolated in his wigwam or fasting for days in the forest with a blackened face, but he never managed to escape his "state of disquietude and unhappiness."[25] Failing to find relief, Shawundais lost faith in his existing beliefs and practices. Whiskey, instead, seems to have been his only means of effective escape. As with many of his contemporaries, it provided the most immediate relief—however temporary—from feelings of inadequacy and anguish. "After I took it—that fire water," Shawundais later recounted in English, "I feel very happy."[26]

Ultimately, however, Shawundais found a more lasting source of happiness in the beliefs and practices of Methodism. As noted, he first learned about Methodism from his fellow Ojibwe Peter Jones (Kahkewaquonaby). Born in 1802, Jones grew up among his mother's Ojibwe community on the Credit River (on the western shores of Lake Ontario) until—as teenagers—he and his older brother joined his British father's Mohawk family in (British-claimed) Haudenosaunee country. There they went to school, learned English, and were exposed to the Christian revivalism sweeping through the nearby "burnt over district" of US-claimed western Iroquoia (or New York State). Jones converted to Methodism in 1823 and quickly took advantage of its opportunities for lay involvement. With the sanctioning of the church hierarchy, who recognized the multilingual man's potential for reaching Native souls, Jones returned to the Credit River to convert his mother's community, then he began taking his Methodist message to other Anishinaabeg communities in the Lake Ontario area.[27]

Shawundais first met Jones in February 1826. While trying to procure whiskey, Shawundais had heard from a local trader that there were "Indians at Belleville" who had "something good to say to Indians."[28] With his curiosity piqued, Shawundais traveled the six or seven miles to Belleville with some friends. They spent the rest of the day waiting outside a meetinghouse until Jones emerged and stopped to make their acquaintance. This brief meeting convinced them to stay for the evening assembly, where they listened as Jones spoke in Ojibwe of the difference between "the broad road that leads to destruction, and the narrow road that leads to heaven."[29] Shawundais later recalled that Jones's words had a profound effect on him. He began "to feel bad in [his] heart" and worried he was on "that broad way" because of the "hard drink" he had consumed the previous night.[30]

This feeling of "trouble" in his "heart" initiated a period of even more intense turmoil and self-loathing, during which he had difficulty eating and sleeping, and feared that he was "so wicked" that he must be one of the devil's men.[31] In the spirit of repentance, he immediately gave up drinking and began working to convince his fellow Anishinaabeg about the evils of alcohol.

With his wife, his mother, and other members of the Bay of Quinte community, he tried to pray to the God Peter Jones had described, but all his attempts to find solace failed.[32] He finally found relief amid the collective fervor of a revivalist meeting that April. While listening to Jones exhort his fellow Ojibwes to lift up their "hearts to God," Shawundais knelt down and suddenly cried out, "O Keshamunedo, shahuanemeshim"—Ojibwe for "O Lord have mercy on me poor sinner"—then experienced a profound sense of joy. He interpreted this as "the good Lord" pouring "his spirit upon my poor wretched heart."[33]

Through his conversion, Shawundais connected himself to a community of settler-colonists and First Nations people, all of whom had (ostensibly) experienced the same spiritual awakening. Indeed, in retelling his conversion experience, Shawundais adhered to forms common to the vast majority of contemporaneous Methodist conversion narratives, Native and nonnative alike. As historian David Hempton writes, such narratives generally "stressed the drama of the second birth as a means of escaping a world of sin and licentiousness, and of entering a world of faith and godly discipline."[34] By following these conventions, Shawundais's accounts evoke a strong sense of experiential solidarity with all his fellow Methodists. The pathos with which he described his "sinful" preconversion life struck a particular chord with his later audiences. Like many others, his conversion took place in a community "experiencing rapid change or an unusual degree of social dislocation," and his retellings betray a "sense of deep psychological distress," to which many others could relate.[35] When he narrated these experiences and gave thanks to "the great spirit" for his salvation, he in many ways spoke to a community of fellow believers that transcended ethnic or national backgrounds.

Yet Shawundais's conversion also differed in important ways from those of the nonnative converts in his area. As Christopher Adamson argues, for colonists living on the "margins" of British and US settler-colonial expansion, part of Methodism's appeal "lay in its ability to foster a sense of community among widely dispersed people who faced common experiences and hungered for social contact."[36] For the colonists who immigrated to eastern Anishinaabewaki, experiences of social dislocation often stemmed from the realities of emigration. In contrast, many of Shawundais's hardships resulted from the fact that his homeland was, in fact, subject to this settler-colonial invasion. Unlike his nonnative neighbors, Shawundais therefore experienced the day-to-day dispossessions involved in having outsiders transform his homeland into the so-called margin of a foreign empire.

But perhaps most importantly, Shawundais seems to have been initially receptive to the Christian message because a fellow Ojibwe preached it in Anishinaabemowin. For Shawundais and most of the other eastern Ojibwes who converted in the late 1820s, Peter Jones's ability to speak to them in their own language held the initial key to their conversions.[37] Jones spoke of the same promise of redemption and happiness as English-speaking evangelicals. But by exhorting his fellow Ojibwes in their own language, he made these beliefs and practices fully accessible to them. In doing this, he also created space within the broader Methodist movement for worship in Ojibwe. In this linguistic space, the Anishinaabeg could focus their evangelizing on the specific concerns of their people. In declaring, for instance, the consumption of alcohol a sin, the Ojibwes adhered to one of the Methodist movement's fundamental tenets. Yet their emphasis on prohibition also addressed the specifically devastating impact alcohol dependency was having on their communities. Indeed, the Ojibwe converts' commitment to eschewing alcohol became a central statement not only of their individual faith but also of their belief that Methodism presented the best way to organize their communities and reclaim control of their lives.

Though part of the broader revivalism of the Second Great Awakening, Jones's exhortations therefore also held out the promise of a path through which the eastern Ojibwes could achieve a prosperous future within their colonized homeland. After his conversion, Shawundais actively worked toward this goal. In the late 1820s, two hundred Ojibwes from the Bay of Quinte and Kingston area moved to Grape Island to form the Methodists' second model Ojibwe community (after the Credit River mission).[38] The Grape Island community strategically adopted aspects of the colonists' (so-called) civilized culture. In particular, they transformed their gendered division of labor so that men now predominantly took responsibility for farming and women for running a household based on monogamous heterosexual domesticity.[39]

Shawundais made sure that neighboring colonists knew that the Grape Island Ojibwes adhered to this "civilized" understanding of gender. In an exhortation he delivered to a white congregation near Grape Island, Shawundais used the example of harvesting corn as a metaphor for the importance of living a sanctified life. Last spring, he told an audience in 1830, he had helped "the brothers divide the corn": "The brothers that hoed their corn and cut up the brush have very good corn; but the lazy ones have no corn, because they don't hoe it. My friends, just so it is with us, if we don't pray good deal and be faithful, we can't have but little religion."[40] Along with his religious message, Shawundais publicized how his community now adhered to notions of virtuous masculinity centered on industrious agricultural labor. Moreover, by focusing on corn—the crop so essential to eastern woodlands women's agriculture—he seemed pointedly to exempt his community from the derogatory attitudes, ubiquitous among Anglo-Americans in the early nineteenth century, about lazy Indian men and overworked Indian women.[41]

Shawundais wasted little time in highlighting these changes to bolster his people's land claims. At a council in 1828, he told the British agent that "since they had embraced Christianity" and moved to Grape Island, his people did not have "sufficient wood and pasture." He therefore asked—as his people had before the War of 1812—for acknowledgment from the British of their title to Big Island in the Bay of Quinte, which they had reserved during the Crawford purchases.[42] In Shawundais's vision, adopting Christianity and "civilization" offered a potential way to secure their land tenure against the still increasing flood of settler-colonists.

For Shawundais, though, religious change was more than a strategy. He credited Methodism with his personal salvation and remained a steadfast Methodist throughout the rest of his life, never again consuming alcohol. Though he never fully escaped his demons, his faith seems to have provided him with the strength to endure further challenges, especially the grief of losing many of his children.[43] In his words, his religious faith helped him "find peace to my soul."[44] Shawundais also saw Methodism as offering the means for communal salvation, believing that adherence to its beliefs and practices would end the collective suffering of the area's Anishinaabe communities and help them build a prosperous, autonomous future within their colonized homeland. With his ability to command an audience—both Native and nonnative—and to emphasize the drama of his "second birth," Shawundais became a licensed exhorter very soon after his conversion.[45] Like Peter Jones, he thus quickly found a place within a religious movement that encouraged even its newest converts to become involved in evangelizing.[46] At countless gatherings of colonists and Natives in the Lake Ontario region, he told the story of his conversion and—grafting together elements of his Ojibwe spirituality with Christianity—gave thanks for what "the great spirit" had done for him.[47]

Shawundais's Mission to His "Indian Brethren"

Shawundais believed that Methodism offered this same promise to the Anishinaabeg and other Native peoples further westward. From 1829 until he left for England in 1836, Shawundais—along with other members of his eastern Ojibwe Methodist cohort—made annual missionary trips through the Great Lakes region to spread a native-infused Methodism to the people he called his "Indian brethren."[48] Although they exhorted many of the cultural changes they had themselves adopted in eastern Anishinaabewaki, in many other ways the missionaries affirmed the ongoing importance of existing cultural traditions. Theirs was a Native mission, conducted in Anishinaabemowin, that affirmed both an Anishinaabe and a regional pan-Indian identity premised on people's ongoing political autonomy.

Most of the areas into which the Ojibwe Methodists traveled lay beyond the reaches of the North American settler-colonial invasion. They planned their tours to fit in with the existing diplomatic and economic routines of this Indigenous world. During summer, many people from the region visited British forts to receive the "presents" the British had promised them for their alliance during the War of 1812. In the early 1830s, thousands of people from the northern and western areas of the region traveled sometimes hundreds of miles to Penetanguishene, at the southeastern edge of Georgia Bay, to receive these goods and to parlay with their "British father." Many were American Indians whose homelands lay in US-claimed territory.[49] This location, in particular, gave the missionaries access to thousands of potential Anishinaabemowin-speaking converts.[50]

The Ojibwe missionaries tailored their proselytizing to the rhythms and protocols of people's visits. They inserted themselves into the already busy schedule of diplomatic councils and ceremonies, holding meetings in the bark council house or in their own wigwams. They smoked the calumet with other leaders to establish and affirm their place in the region's kinship politics, and they presented people with white strings of wampum through which they communicated their message and requested that it be circulated.[51] These councils and ceremonies occurred within a constant stream of arrivals and departures. By the 1830s, visits to British posts tended to last only a few days. In particular, those who had journeyed a long way, noted the Methodist press, "returned to their country as fast as they receive their goods," with others "daily arriving." John Sunday and "other native labourers" therefore reportedly continued "to visit and instruct" the travelers "as fast as they arrive[d]."[52]

Shawundais's Ojibwe oratory skills and his knowledge of regional mores gave him a particular advantage in this setting. When he addressed a group of Anishinaabeg from the Lake Superior region, for instance, he used the appropriate formal protocols and metaphors: "Brothers, you come a great way to see your father the agent, and to receive presents from him, that you and your children may be warm." He and his fellow missionaries, he explained, had "also come a great way" especially to see *them*, to speak to them of presents that "will never spoil." These presents, he continued, "are from our Great Father above, who has many good things to give to them that believe in him."[53] Shawundais thus assimilated his Methodist evangelizing to the regional political culture.

Shawundais and his companion's Ojibwe identity was very important in making these initial connections. In 1830, the same group of Anishinaabeg (who listened to Shawundais's speech about "our Great Father above") at first hesitated before accepting the Methodists' hospitality. Unable to identify these Ojibwe speakers from the east, the invitees sent a man named Koo-koo koo oo (Owl) to find out their credentials. Koo-koo koo oo told Shawundais, "Brother, I am sent on a message to ask what nation you belong. Are you of the *Mohawks*? Are you of the *Algonquins*?" Shawundais replied: "We are of the same nation to which you belong. Our grandfathers came from the country of the Chipeways in the west. They left their fathers, and came east in quest of good hunting." Now convinced they were not Mohawks, the other Ojibwes accepted the Methodists' invitation.[54] Then, once calumets were smoked, councils held, and wampum circulated, the Ojibwe Methodists became known and connected to many Anishinaabeg from the northern and western Great Lakes areas of Anishinaabewaki, as well as to other neighboring peoples such as the Menominees and Sauks.[55] Even when not successful in gaining converts, Shawundais's missionary travels therefore connected him deeper into Anishinaabewaki.

Among the cohort of eastern Ojibwes who undertook these missionary tours, Shawundais seems to have gained the greatest recognition and renown. His humor, warmth, and eloquence earned him the same popularity among communities in the Great Lakes as it did with his contemporaries back east. He had, what Peter Jones termed, a "peculiar satirical manner," and in Anishinaabemowin "spoke with much freedom and energy."[56] When he returned east from his missionary trips, Shawundais generally narrated his experiences to Jones, who transcribed them from Ojibwe into English and then circulated these written accounts in the Methodist press. In these and other Methodist reports, Shawundais appears as a popular figure whose success in converting people to Methodism had as much to do with his personal appeal as it did with the message he preached.

Shawundais's talent for gaining converts showed from his earliest missionary tours. Traveling in June 1829 with Peter Jones and other Native Methodists, Shawundais and fellow Grape Islander Thomas Biggs separated from the group in order to minister to communities on the eastern shore of Lake Huron.[57] The following summer, nearly fifty people, who the Methodist press described as "the fruits of the labour of John Sunday last summer and fall," traveled to Penetanguishene, where they took part in Methodist worship and were baptized by one of the ordained nonnative ministers.[58] Shawundais also had almost immediate success with a group of Anishinaabeg from Mackinaw in 1830. One of the nonnative missionaries described how two days after addressing the non-Christians among the group, Shawundais held another meeting, and while he "was speaking, the Holy Spirit came upon the hearers, when about fifteen mourners found peace, and experienced a change." Others members of the group then also expressed their wish to become Christian.[59]

His success in these missionary endeavors seems to have been due in large part to the positive impression he made on people.[60] Other missionaries reported that when they visited a place where Shawundais had been, people wanted to know when he would return. Such reports also described the joy with which people greeted Shawundais when they saw him at Penetanguishene during the summer.[61] A nonnative missionary who traveled to Sault Ste. Marie in 1832, for example, described how the "first inquiries made by the Indians were, if John Sunday and others were coming to teach them the good word. . . . All are desirous," he continued, "of the return of John Sunday."[62] Shawundais seems to have impressed during both his public orations and his more personal conversations. In addition to group proselytizing while on these tours, Shawundais dedicated himself to offering individual counsel and visiting the sick.[63]

Shawundais gained popularity in a world with long traditions of charismatic messengers traveling and disseminating religious ideas. The close association that people maintained between him and his religious message suggests that some people treated him as akin to prophets of previous generations.[64] Near Penetanguishene in 1831, Shawundais met Shingwaukonse—the principal chief of an Ojibwe village in the northern Great Lakes. After delivering a white string of wampum and addressing Shingwaukonse as "Father," Shawundais described himself as someone called on to tell his forefathers in the North of a pleasing message that he had received when "poor, wretched, and wallowing on the bare ground."[65] He told the northern chief of the happiness he would find if he became a Christian. Both Shawundais and his message stuck with Shingwaukonse, who was looking to incorporate a Christian religion in order to gain better access to Western technologies and forge an economic future for the Anishinaabeg of the western Great Lakes that avoided the (then present) threat of war with the Americans.[66]

Two years later, Shingwaukonse traveled to an Anishinaabeg council at the Narrows (on Lake Simcoe). There he rose with a white string of wampum—presumably the one through which Shawundais had delivered his message—to ask the Christian chiefs whether they were truly more happy in their hearts than when they had their father's religion. He asked, he said, because he had recently attempted to save the life of his much-beloved only child by using all the contents of his medicine bag, but to no avail. In disgust, he threw away his medicine, but then wondered what he would do without a God. He remembered "John Sunday speaking about a great God; and," he said, "I thought that I would come to this country, to see who knew about John Sunday's God."[67] For Shingwaukonse and others to whom Shawundais spoke on his missionary travels, the message about this Methodist "God" was closely associated with its messenger.

However, unlike most nativist prophets of previous generations, whose revivalism shunned nonnative cultural associations, Shawundais advocated not only for converting to "the white man's religion" but also for adopting particular aspects of their "civilized" culture. This required people to consciously repudiate specific aspects of their existing customs. In particular, the missionaries targeted medicine bags as signs of sinful practices; like giving up "fire water," the act of surrendering one's "medicine pouche" became a concrete statement of someone's intention to become a Christian.[68] Applying an epistemological distinction between Native medicine used in spiritual healing practices and the administration of physical substances to treat illness or injury, Shawundais told people that "all the medicine they used in their conjuring ceremonies was wicked," but they could keep "all the medicine that was good to heal a cut, or to drink when any one is sick."[69] And, in a prohibition that had a huge impact on existing rituals, the missionaries also asked people to replace ceremonies involving dancing with Methodist prayers and hymns. For Shawundais and his Methodist associates, living within God's grace meant abstaining absolutely from spiritual "superstition," alcohol consumption, and dancing.[70]

But perhaps the most profound change preached by the Methodists was the adoption of the colonizers' understandings of gender. On their missionary tours, the Methodist Ojibwes urged the same shift in the everyday meanings of masculinity and femininity that they themselves had adopted in their own communities. They therefore advocated for people to change their presumptions about masculine and feminine virtue. At Penetanguishene in 1832, one of Shawundais's fellow Christian chiefs attempted this by explicitly playing on these different cultural understandings of gender roles: "Brothers," he said, "I now look upon all men who refuse to take hold of the white man's religion and become Christians and farmers, to be as cowardly as old women." According to Peter Jones, "[t]his speech caused a great laugh among the pagan Indians." His hope that the audience would nevertheless "think more upon these things" showed his awareness that such changes would only be achieved through the missionaries' persistence.[71] Indeed, Jones, Shawundais, and their fellow missionaries did not insist on the adoption of such profound changes, which held much less pragmatic value in the fur trade–oriented political economies of the western Great Lakes than they did in the settler-colonist-swamped eastern areas.

Despite the cultural changes for which they advocated, Shawundais and his fellow Methodist Ojibwes never sought to undermine peoples' economic or political autonomy. Rather, theirs was also a mission that affirmed ongoing Indigenous identities. They worked within the political culture of the Great Lakes, and they communicated their message in the lingua franca of the region: Anishinaabemowin. Indeed, their ability to deliver their message in Ojibwe held the key to their success. They increased their popularity by disseminating books, printed in Ojibwe, containing gospel passages and hymns.[72] Recounting his stay in a village near Mackinaw, Shawundais stated that after people saw the hymn books and scripture written in Ojibwe, "they became very anxious to have us read and sing the hymns, and to read the scripture translations to them, which they were very fond to hear read."[73]

Indeed, many people were seemingly enticed toward Methodism after seeing their own language in print. When Shawundais gave his Mackinaw converts "two Chipeway hymn books and the translation of the first seven chapters in St. Matthew . . . [t]hey wrapped them up carefully as if they had been gold."[74] Subsequently, many chiefs who agreed to welcome Methodists to their villages emphasized that the missionaries must also send them books.[75] These texts, written in Ojibwe, became a sought-after commodity and made people more receptive to the missionaries' message. What they knew as "the white man's religion" now had the specific linguistic markings of Anishinaabe identity.

Shawundais and Peter Jones, in particular, emphasized to their nonnative associates the value of Ojibwes disseminating Christianity in Anishinaabemowin. They made sure to report that their "Indian brethren" especially loved the "good word" in Ojibwe, and that communities out west specifically requested visits from Native missionaries. When Shawundais returned from his travels in 1831, for instance, he told his nonnative superior, William Case, of "the strong wish expressed by the Indians in the north for religious instruction, and especially for native preachers."[76] Reports from both British and US Indian agents affirmed this mission. Henry Schoolcraft, the US agent at Sault Ste. Marie, entered into a correspondence with William Case to encourage the Canadian Methodists to continue sending "native speakers" to the Sault. "John Sunday and his companions," he wrote, enjoyed "extraordinary advantages in the use of their vernacular tongue in speaking to the Indians."[77] Agents such as Schoolcraft, who had spent years attempting to implement a "civilization" policy, no doubt welcomed the Ojibwe Methodists for the boost they might give their own career. For Jones and Shawundais, such acknowledgments strengthened their ability to mark out a space within the broader Methodist mission for the spread of their own Native-infused Methodism to Indian country.

Shawundais's Mission for Land Rights

Shawundais excelled in the missionary endeavors on which his Wesleyan-Methodist contemporaries placed preeminent importance. By the time of his ordination as a full minister in 1836, Shawundais was suffering from ill health due to the exertions of his previous seven years' travels. He accepted the invitation of a visiting Wesleyan to return with him to England, in order to restore his health.[78] Such an invitation was testament to the renown Shawundais had achieved in transatlantic Methodist circles, not only for his missionary work but also for the crowds he drew to fund-raising events and the donations he effected. As with his previous successful tours of the United

States, the Methodist press preemptively promoted Shawundais's fund-raising appearances by circulating news of his visit, making much of him being in England to recover his health.[79] Yet while in the British Isles, Shawundais also used his Methodist connections to pursue what had by that time become his overriding mission: to secure title deeds to his people's land.

By 1836, Shawundais had achieved a considerable level of prestige in transatlantic Wesleyan circles. Peter Jones contributed significantly to this by publicizing Native missionary endeavors in the Methodist press. In his English-language renderings of Shawundais's Great Lakes travels, Jones emphasized the hardships Shawundais had endured, thus strongly suggesting that his Ojibwe comrade had experienced "the genuine apostolic suffering expected" of Methodist itinerants.[80] He noted, for instance, how in the summer of 1829, Shawundais had survived mostly on a broth boiled from moss.[81] These depravations suggested Shawundais's Methodist credentials as much as the reported number of converted Native souls.

Given the Methodist movement's almost exclusive reliance on donations and subscriptions to fund their missions, Shawundais's talent for fund-raising also increased his renown. The Methodists' outreach to Native North America relied particularly on missionary contributions from the United States, and church leaders quickly discovered Native speakers raised more funds.[82] Shawundais showed his value during his first fund-raising tour of the United States in 1828. At a meeting in New York, for instance, he reportedly enraptured the audience with his open display of emotion; he ultimately had the entire hall crying out "Amen! Amen!" in response to his "loud exclamations" (in Ojibwe).[83] This first fund-raising tour was so successful that William Case—the Methodist cleric leading the tour—organized for Shawundais and Peter Jones to undertake a similar trip the following year.[84]

Partly it was Shawundais's stage presence that made him such a successful fund-raiser. As he became more comfortable speaking in English, he reportedly provided his audiences with a "thoroughly original" and "irresistible" mix of pathos and droll humor, making them laugh at his wit and gasp while he spoke with great seriousness and emotion of the dark days before his conversion.[85] But Shawundais's appeal to nonnative audiences lay not just in his creative mastery of the Methodist exhortation genre but also in the fact that he spoke these words as a Native man.

Shawundais's manner of expressing himself in English seems to have been particularly important to his draw as a speaker. While his fluency in English never equaled his mastery of Ojibwe oratory—and he often downplayed his ability to express himself in English—this gap in linguistic fluencies endeared him to people.[86] Anglo-Canadian contemporaries remembered with fondness the "broken quaintness of his utterances" and noted how they added to the effectiveness of his addresses.[87] This "broken English" reinforced his identity as someone who had grown up speaking his Native language, and even perhaps met with some of his audience's (essentialized) ideas about how a (supposedly) authentic "Indian" spoke English.

Shawundais himself seems not to have consciously affected his English expression to meet these expectations. But in other ways, he played on his audiences' ideas about Indianness. During his tours of the United States and the British Isles, Shawundais was seemingly well aware that his popularity reflected people's curiosity—particularly in Britain—to see and hear a "real converted Indian" from Canada.[88] Yet unlike Peter Jones, who wore his Ojibwe dress for strategic purposes, such as when he met Queen Victoria in 1838, Shawundais chose never to wear his "Indian dress" after conversion.[89] He nevertheless had a remarkable knack for playing to his audience's curiosities in order to communicate his message.

At Plymouth (England) in 1837, for instance, Shawundais told a congregation that he understood many of them were disappointed because he had not brought his "Indian dress" with him. He instead painted a tantalizing verbal picture of how he dressed when he "was a pagan Indian": "My face was covered with red paint," he said. "I stuck feathers in my hair. I wore a blanket and leggings . . . silver ornaments on my breast; a rifle on my shoulder; a tomahawk and scalping-knife in my belt." But when he became a Christian, he explained, he was born anew, like St. Paul in the second letter to the Corinthians. Thus, he proclaimed, "feathers and paint done away. I gave my silver ornaments to the Mission cause. Scalping-knife done away; tomahawk done away: that my tomahawk now," he said, holding up a copy of the Ten Commandments in Anishinaabemowin.[90]

In playing on his audiences' expectations and curiosities in this way, Shawundais also capitalized on his evangelical constituency's ardent desires—in the ubiquitous tropes of early nineteenth-century Anglo-American discourse—"to reclaim" or "redeem" all the world's "native" people from "savagery." His commitment to Christianity and his choice to eschew his "Indian dress" could be interpreted by white evangelicals as an affirmation that missionary labor—and the money they donated to support it—would ultimately not be in vain.

But while Shawundais's appeals on the fund-raising platform struck a tone of solidarity with his white audiences, their vision of the role Christianity and "civilization" held in the futures of the Anishinaabeg and other First Peoples likely differed from his. Many probably presumed that the civilizing mission held the promise of saving "native" peoples by absorbing them into so-called civilized settler society.[91] Shawundais, in contrast, clearly did not view his conversion to Christianity or his subsequent eschewing of "Indian dress" as giving up a separate Ojibwe or Indian identity. His commitment to the dissemination of Christianity in Ojibwe, in particular, reflected not just his goal of spreading the Methodist message; it also represented the strategy of his cohort of Native Methodists to promote a distinctively Native-controlled and Native-infused Christianity. Indeed, the copy of the Ten Commandments Shawundais held up to his English audience at Plymouth in 1837 was, notably, printed in Anishinaabemowin, not English.

Shawundais used the fund-raising stage to mark out space for this Native-controlled mission. To do this, he appealed beyond his Anishinaabe identity to a broader sense of pan-Indianism. When speaking at the Young Men's Missionary Society in Philadelphia in 1832, for example, he reportedly spoke of "the Indians at the northwest along the shores of lake Huron and Michigan, where he had travelled and preached," and stressed the need to send "more laborers into that new and large field." But he notably prefaced this apparently general call for missionaries by claiming missionary labor in this region as the rightful province of someone with an Indian identity. Cleverly combining an allusion to prevailing racial categories with a reference to the biblical account of Jesus "calling Peter and Andrew from their nets to become *fishers of men*," Shawundais pointed to a Wesleyan missionary who had recently returned from the West Indies and said: "He go back there to catch *black fish*; and as there be great many *white fish* here, these preachers must catch *white fish*; while I go way back in the woods to catch *red fish*, and so we *all catch 'em fish*."[92] With this appeal, Shawundais struck a tone of global Methodist solidarity while simultaneously claiming a specialist missionary role for "red" Methodists, such as himself, in "the woods" of Native North America.

The fact that the structure of the Methodist church offered Shawundais the chance to claim this space perhaps partly explains why he remained so committed to the denomination. During the late 1820s and 1830s, Shawundais, Jones, and their fellow Native converts resisted pressure from government officials and Anglican clerics—who distrusted the Canadian Methodists because of their mode of worship and their ties to the American Methodist church—to join the Church of England.[93] In early 1828, for instance, Anglican cleric Dr. John Strachan told Jones that the governor would only "assist the Indians" if they came "under the superintendence of the Established Church." And thinking it an added incentive, Strachan emphasized that such an association would free them from relying solely on subscriptions.[94] But for Jones as well as Shawundais, both the Methodists' independence from the colonial government in Canada and the fact that they relied on subscriptions seemingly represented a huge part of the organization's appeal. The ongoing need for the Methodists to raise funds, in particular, gave talented speakers such as Jones and Shawundais a transatlantic stage on which to advocate for the rights of both their own communities and their "Indian brethren" more broadly.

Like Jones, Shawundais's standing in the transatlantic Methodist movement ultimately gained him access to imperial policymakers in London. By the 1830s, the Wesleyans in Britain—in contrast to their counterparts in Canada—had gained the mainstream respectability they lacked in previous generations.[95] Their missionary commitments, in particular, accorded with those of the influential evangelical Anglicans of the Clapham Sect. During his 1836–37 stay in Britain, Shawundais used these connections to pursue what had, by this time, become his overriding priority: to secure title deeds to his people's land.

Shawundais's trip coincided with a crucial period for First Peoples in Canada and for British-Indigenous relations more broadly. While he was away, Shawundais's own community on Grape Island moved to a new, more expansive settlement on Rice Lake—an arrangement Shawundais had negotiated with the previous lieutenant-governor John Colborne.[96] While in England, he sought to gain a British deed of title to this new settlement of Alderville. This quest became even more urgent from the late summer of 1836, when First Peoples in Upper Canada came under markedly increased pressure to surrender their homelands as the new lieutenant-governor, Francis Bond Head, attempted to remove them to Manitoulin Island (on Lake Huron).[97] Shawundais's stay at the Wesleyan Mission House in London also coincided with the hearings of the House of Commons' Select Committee on Aborigines (the ASC)—a committee convened to inquire into the condition of the "Aborigines" in the British empire, prompted in particular by the war between the colonists and Xhosa in the Cape region of southern Africa.[98]

Shawundais used his March 1837 appearance before the ASC to emphasize the precariousness of his people's hold on their homelands amid the British settler-colonial invasion. He referred, for instance, to his people's earlier unsuccessful struggles to retain the islands in the Bay of Quinte they reserved during the Crawford treaties. But "the white people come and settle upon the Indian reserves," explained Shawundais, "and when they settle there, we cannot get them off." Only with secure title deeds, he argued, could they successfully defend their lands.[99]

In his advocacy, Shawundais emphasized his commitment to the civilizing mission, framing his quest for secure title deeds as consistent with the imperial government's civilization policy. At the ASC hearing, he appealed to the committee's evangelical members, insisting that the insecure legal status of his people's tenure held an impediment to their ability—and indeed all converted Native peoples' ability—to defend their lands against encroaching settler-colonists and thus sustain the evangelical ideal of a settled, industrious life.[100] He struck a similar tone of Christian solidarity with Lord Glenelg (the secretary of state for war and the colonies) in August 1837, when he wrote to him requesting a meeting. In this letter, Shawundais introduced himself to Glenelg as "a man in authority among the Chippoways" who worships "the Great Spirit by the same light of New Testament Revelation as you do: as Christians we are Brothers." He framed his case for land deeds in the language of the civilizing mission: "[U]ntil we get A Title Deed we shall not walk with Confidence along the Path of improvement . . . To you My Lord I look, to make a smooth road for our future Journey towards civilization."[101] Title deeds, Shawundais argued, were a necessary condition for Native peoples' ability to sustain the civilized life that these British evangelicals apparently so desired for them.

And yet Shawundais did not found his advocacy entirely on this argument. He also conveyed a strong sense of solidarity with his "Red Brothers" and other Indigenous peoples within Britain's imperial reach. By the lead-up to his meeting with Lord Glenelg in August 1837, Shawundais had begun to frame his people's specific quest for title deeds as a right inherent in their status as the land's Indigenous owners. Commenting on the upcoming meeting, the British press reported that Shawundais aimed to gain from the Colonial Office a formal recognition "*that the American Indian is the original proprietor of the soil.*"[102] In his appeal to Glenelg, he also conveyed a sense of fellowship with the Xhosa in southern Africa, who the British government had recently supported against invading settler-colonists. Commending

Glenelg, Shawundais wrote: "The uncivilized Caffer [Xhosa] was despoiled of his native Land by men of Your own Nation: it was told to you & you . . . restored the Caffer to his own."[103] Shawundais linked this situation to that of his "Red Brothers so often removed" in North America, asking Glenelg therefore to use the same power he had directed toward helping the Xhosa to secure his own people's land tenure amid the threat of removal.

During his British-based quest for title deeds, Shawundais ultimately articulated the principle on which he founded his people's right to British-recognized land title: that of original ownership. His immersion in imperial politics in London perhaps gave him a more global sense of other Indigenous peoples' similar struggles, though it likely also gave him the added impetus to delineate to metropole audiences those rights to land and political autonomy that he had always presumed his people retained. When discussing his Rice Lake community's land, he used the plural possessives "we" and "our," suggesting that he sought a confirmation of his community's collective title to their land and a continuation of their Indigenous communal holding practices. In his petition to the colonial office, for instance, he requested Glenelg "to Command that Sir Francis Bond Head do give unto us without delay the Deed of Settlement."[104] When he subsequently met with Glenelg in Downing Street, Shawundais no doubt advocated lucidly for his people's right to receive fee simple title to their land as both "civilized" Christians and original proprietors. That he was ultimately unsuccessful in gaining these deeds highlights the imperial government's reticence to grant the full recognition of Indigenous land rights and political autonomy that he sought. But his quest was nevertheless important. Though unquantifiable, his advocacy at that crucial time no doubt changed the way some policymakers understood Indigenous rights. In this struggle, he stated and affirmed a political sovereignty that the colonial administration sought to deny or diminish.

Conclusion

From the time of his conversion in 1826, Shawundais earnestly believed in the Methodist mission to create global human solidarity through (what he saw as) the work of God's saving grace. Throughout the rest of his life, he maintained strong ties of Christian fellowship that crossed ethnic, racial, and national boundaries. But he also clearly saw room within this global mission for ongoing Indigenous autonomy and independence. God's grace, he believed, had saved him from despair and given his people the tools to create a prosperous future for themselves amid the settler-colonial invasion of their homeland. And though they adopted aspects of the settler's "civilized" culture, these changes did not imply any renunciation of what we would now label their sovereign right of self-determination. Indeed, Shawundais's tireless quest to secure his people's tenure under British law shows his commitment to struggling within the colonial order to assert this political autonomy.

This presumption of Native autonomy infused Shawundais's religious organizing. In the late 1820s, he felt himself called westward into the Great Lakes region, where he would do his part for the global mission by sharing with his "Indian brethren" the religion he believed held the key to their happy, prosperous futures. Yet he and his fellow Ojibwe Methodists sought to spread a distinctively Native-infused Methodism, communicated in Ojibwe and fitting into the political landscape of the region. Through his commitment to this endeavor, Shawundais made connections that linked him westward into this Indigenous world, likely deepening his sense of identification with his fellow Anishinaabeg and other Native peoples of the region. Among his nonnative Methodist associates, and on the fund-raising stage in front of nonnative audiences, Shawundais—like Peter Jones—sought to mark out a space for ongoing Native control of the Methodist mission to Native North America.

The Methodist church, with its independence from the established church, gave Shawundais and his fellow Ojibwe Methodists the ability to retain institutional autonomy from the colonial government. The Methodists' reliance on donations and subscriptions to fund their missions also gave Native converts—with their greater fund-raising capacities—a valued place within the church's organizational structure. Indeed, Shawundais used his transatlantic renown as a missionary, preacher, and fund-raiser to travel to England. And there, in the metropole at a crucial time for British-Indigenous policymaking, Shawundais articulated his case for full British recognition of his people's rights to what they retained of their homeland. Though he was unsuccessful in receiving British title deeds, he had nevertheless faced empire in its political heartland and taken part in what would be an ongoing and global struggle to gain recognition of Indigenous sovereignty.

Notes

1. Aborigines Select Committee, *Final Report from the Select Committee on Aborigines (British Settlements)* (London: House of Commons, 1837), Minutes of Evidence, 28.

2. These and other eastern Anishinaabeg from the Lake Ontario region are often referred to in Canadian scholarship as "Mississaguas." See, for example, Donald B.

Smith, "The Dispossession of the Mississauga Indians: A Missing Chapter in the Early History of Upper Canada," *Ontario History* 73, no. 2 (1981): 67–82. However, for the purposes of this chapter I will refer to Shawundais and his people interchangeably as "Ojibwe" or "Anishinaabe" because these are the ethnic labels with which he identified himself. Note also that he occasionally also referred to himself as "Chippeway," the English world commonly used at the time for Ojibwe, especially in the United States.

3. On the life of Peter Jones, see Donald B. Smith, *Sacred Feathers: The Reverend Peter Jones (Kahkewaquonaby) and the Mississauga Indians* (Lincoln: University of Nebraska Press, 1987).

4. See, for example, Christopher Adamson, "God's Continent Divided: Politics and Religion in Upper Canada and the Northern and Western United States, 1775 to 1841," *Comparative Studies in Society and History* 36, no. 3 (1994): 417–46; James C. Deming and Michael S. Hamilton, "Methodist Revivalism in France, Canada, and the United States," in *Amazing Grace: Evangelicalism in Australia, Britain, Canada, and the United States*, ed. George A. Rawlyk and Mark A. Noll (Montreal: McGill-Queen's University Press, 1994); Michael Gauvreau, "Protestantism Transformed: Personal Piety and the Evangelical Social Vision, 1815–1867," in *The Canadian Protestant Experience, 1760 to 1990*, ed. George A. Rawlyk (Burlington: Welch Publishing, 1990); Elizabeth Graham, *Medicine Man to Missionary: Missionaries as Agents of Change among the Indians of Southern Ontario, 1784–1867* (Toronto: Peter Martin Associates, 1975); John H. Wigger, "Taking Heaven by Storm: Enthusiasm and Early American Methodism, 1770–1820," *Journal of the Early Republic* 14, no. 2 (1994): 167–94.

5. "Rev. John Sunday, alias Shah-Wund-Dais," WMNCC (April 1876): 107. Cited in Donald B. Smith, *Mississauga Portraits: Ojibwe Voices from Nineteenth-Century Canada* (Toronto: University of Toronto Press, 2013), 215.

6. George Copway, *The Life, Letters and Speeches of Kah-Ge-Ga-Gah-Bowh or G. Copway, Chief Ojibway Nation: A Missionary for Many Years in the Northwest* (New York: S. W. Benedict, 1850), 97; Smith, *Mississauga Portraits*, 215.

7. Egerton Ryerson Young, *The Apostle of the North: James Evans* (Toronto: William Briggs, 1900), 54.

8. See, for instance, George F. Playter, *The History of Methodism in Canada: With an Account of the Rise and Progress of the Work of God among the Canadian Indian Tribes, and Occasional Notices of the Civil Affairs of the Province* (Toronto: A. Green, 1862), 276–78, and Lucy Richards, *Memoirs of the Late Miss Lucy Richards, of Paris, Oneida County, N.Y.* (New York: G. Lane and P. P. Sandford, 1842), 206–07.

9. Smith, *Mississauga Portraits*, 215; Peter Jones, *History of the Ojebway Indians: With Especial Reference to Their Conversion to Christianity* (London: A. W. Bennett, 1861), 200.

10. During diplomatic councils in 1783 and 1784, Captain William Crawford, a Loyalist officer who had fought with them during the war, claimed to have made two binding agreements in which the Anishinaabeg ceded all their territory from the Toniata River on the northeastern shore of Lake Ontario to the western boundary of the Bay of Quinte, "including all the islands, extending back from the lake [Ontario] so far as a man can travel in a day": Robert J. Surtees, "Land Cessions, 1763–1830," in

Aboriginal Ontario: Historical Perspective on the First Nations, ed. Edward S. Rogers and Donald B. Smith (Toronto: Dundurn Press, 1994), 102.

11. Smith, *Mississauga Portraits*, 217. See also Smith, *Sacred Feathers*, 26. This agreement, made by Sir John Johnson and Colonel John Butler, was ruled invalid by the governor in 1794 because of irregularities in the treaty document. First Nation title to the land was not officially extinguished until the Williams treaties in 1923: Surtees, "Land Cessions," 107.

12. Smith, *Mississauga Portraits*, 217.

13. Smith, *Mississauga Portraits*, 216.

14. Smith, *Mississauga Portraits*, 217.

15. Smith, "Dispossession of the Mississauga Indians," 80–81; Smith, *Sacred Feathers*, 36. In contrast to reports of the smallpox pandemic that hit North America during the years of the War of Independence, subsequent outbreaks over the next decade do not seem to have been widely reported. However, it seems that smallpox hit the Lake Ontario region in 1793 and again three years later: Peter Schmalz, *The Ojibwa of Southern Ontario* (Toronto: University of Toronto Press, 1991), 104. Grant Karcich, *Scugog Carrying Place: A Frontier Pathway* (Toronto: Dundurn Press, 2013).

16. Meeting with the Missisagui Indians of the River Moira, at Smith's Creek, 24 July 1811, CO 42, 351:138. Quoted in Smith, *Mississauga Portraits*, 218.

17. James Belich, *Replenishing the Earth: The Settler Revolution and the Rise of the Anglo-World, 1783–1939* (Oxford: Oxford University Press, 2009), 94.

18. Surtees, "Land Cessions," 112; Smith, *Mississauga Portraits*, 218; Belich, *Replenishing the Earth*, 94. With the continuation of the boom through most of the 1830s, the colonial population reached nearly half a million by 1840: Surtees, "Land Cessions," 112.

19. Surtees, "Land Cessions," 112.

20. Smith, *Mississauga Portraits*, 219. For a map of First Nations land cessions in this area, see Surtees, "Land Cessions," 103.

21. Alvin Torry, *Autobiography of Rev. Alvin Torry, First Missionary to the Six Nations and the Northwestern Tribes of British North America* (Auburn: William J. Moses, 1861), 312.

22. Peter Jones, *Life and Journals of Kah-Ke-Wa-Quo-Nā-By: (Rev. Peter Jones) Wesleyan Missionary* (Toronto: A. Green, 1860), 175.

23. According to historian Donald Smith, Mary Sunday's Anishinaabe name along with many of the details of her life are unknown: Smith, *Mississauga Portraits*, 229.

24. Young, *Apostle of the North*, 55.

25. Young, *Apostle of the North*, 55–56.

26. For this English (written) account of his conversion, see Playter, *History of Methodism in Canada*, 276, and Young, *Apostle of the North*, 56. For a general discussion of the effects of alcohol consumption at this time among the Anishinaabeg in this region, see Smith, *Sacred Feathers*, 38.

27. Smith, *Sacred Feathers*, 38, 63–64. Such lay involvement was central to Methodism's organizational structure: see Adamson, "God's Continent Divided."

28. Playter, *History of Methodism in Canada*, 276. See also Richards, *Memoirs*, 206–07.

29. This quote is from Peter Jones's account of the two men's first meeting: Jones, *Life and Journals*, 59. For Shawundais's accounts, see Playter, *History of Methodism in Canada*, 277; Young, *Apostle of the North*, 55–56; Richards, *Memoirs*, 207.

30. Playter, *History of Methodism in Canada*, 277.

31. Playter, *History of Methodism in Canada*, 277.

32. Richards, *Memoirs*, 207.

33. Playter, *History of Methodism in Canada*, 278; Young, *Apostle of the North*, 59–60.

34. David Hempton, *Methodism: Empire of the Spirit* (New Haven, CT: Yale University Press, 2005), 60–62. See, for instance, the nineteenth-century Pequot Methodist minister William Apess's narrative of his conversion in Carl Benn, *Native Memoirs from the War of 1812: Black Hawk and William Apess* (Baltimore: Johns Hopkins Press, 2014), 98–102.

35. Hempton, *Methodism*, 63. For accounts of how successfully Shawundais conveyed the emotions of his conversion experiences to connect with his audience, see, for instance, Jones, *Life and Journals*, 174–76; Richards, *Memoirs*, 205–07; Young, *Apostle of the North*, 54–56.

36. Adamson, "God's Continent Divided," 425.

37. See Smith, *Sacred Feathers*, 92–97.

38. Smith, *Mississauga Portraits*, 212–14; Neil Semple, *The Lord's Dominion: The History of Canadian Methodism* (Montreal: McGill-Queen's University Press, 1996), 163.

39. See, for instance, Torry, *Autobiography*, 89–90. For a description of the households on Grape Island, see Jones, *Life and Journals*, 286.

40. *Christian Advocate and Journal and Zion's Herald*, 20 August 1830, 202.

41. See, for example, Torry, *Autobiography*, 89–90.

42. Jones, *Life and Journals*, 104. The Bay of Quinte Ojibwes had met British officials in July 1811 to discuss this issue: see Smith, *Mississauga Portraits*, 218.

43. At the time of his conversion, Shawundais was grieving the loss of a son from illness: Jones, *Life and Journals*, 175. In an 1846 letter, he mentioned that he and his wife had lost eight children: John Sunday to Richard Alder, 10 March 1846, in John Carroll, *Case and His Contemporaries: Or, the Canadian Itinerants' Memorial Constituting a Biographical History of Methodism in Canada, from Its Introduction into the Province, Till the Death of Rev. William Case in 1855* (Toronto: Wesleyan Conference Office, 1874), 4:468–69. Their daughter, Susan Sunday Rice, died in 1855, and their son, James Sunday, died in 1857: Smith, *Mississauga Portraits*, 229.

44. Jones, *Life and Journals*, 175.

45. Jones, *Life and Journals*, 229.

46. As Adamson argues, a major dynamic of Methodism's growth was that by bringing people together in this way, the itinerant clergy and their converts successfully fostered religious commitments at the local level, empowering even the newest and most uneducated converts to tell others of the happiness they had found through their conversion: Adamson, "God's Continent Divided," 433.

47. See, for example, Jones, *Life and Journals*, 174–75, 351.

48. Shawundais undertook his first mission westward with Peter Jones and a group of fellow Ojibwe converts and leaders among the eastern Anishinaabeg, including William Herkimer, David Sawyer, Thomas Magee (McKee), and the young Thomas Biggs: Jones, *Life and Journals*, 227. For more details on this cohort of Native

missionaries, see Semple, *Lord's Dominion*, 160; John Carroll, *Case and His Contemporaries: Or, the Canadian Itinerants' Memorial Constituting a Biographical History of Methodism in Canada, from Its Introduction into the Province, Till the Death of Rev. William Case in 1855* (Toronto: Wesleyan Conference Office, 1871), 3:20; Playter, *History of Methodism in Canada*, 276; and Torry, *Autobiography*, 311.

49. After the war, these people had traveled, whenever possible, to visit the more conveniently located Drummond Island, but after the British turned the island over to the United States in 1828, they had to travel further east to Penetanguishene: Helen Hornbeck Tanner, ed., *Atlas of Great Lakes Indian History* (Norman: Published for the Newberry Library by the University of Oklahoma Press, 1987), 126–27. For more on British policy toward "visiting" Indians from US-claimed territory, see Colin G. Calloway, *Crown and Calumet: British-Indian Relations, 1783–1815* (Norman: University of Oklahoma Press, 1987), 248–57.

50. See, for example, *Christian Advocate and Journal and Zion's Herald*, 8 June 1829 and 30 July 1830.

51. *Christian Advocate and Journal and Zion's Herald*, 13 August 1830; *Christian Advocate and Journal and Zion's Herald*, 25 November 1831; *The Wesleyan-Methodist Magazine*, no. 11, November 1832, 829–33.

52. *Christian Advocate and Journal and Zion's Herald*, 13 August 1830, 198. To be "clothed" by the British meant to have received their goods, not just clothing.

53. *Christian Advocate and Journal and Zion's Herald*, 27 August 1830, 205.

54. For Peter Jones's English transcription of Shawundais's oral report, see *Christian Advocate and Journal and Zion's Herald*, 27 August 1830, 205.

55. Peter Jones to Egerton Ryerson, 24 July 1832, in *The Wesleyan-Methodist Magazine*, no. 11, November 1832, 829–33.

56. Jones, *History of the Ojebway Indians*, 272; Jones, *Life and Journals*, 105.

57. *Christian Advocate and Journal and Zion's Herald*, 5 February 1830, 89.

58. *Christian Advocate and Journal and Zion's Herald*, 30 July 1830, 190. Presumably these people traveled to Penetanguishene especially to see the Methodists, as they would likely have received their British presents from the closer post at Amherstburg.

59. *Christian Advocate and Journal and Zion's Herald*, 27 August 1830, 205.

60. See, for instance, George Copway's recollections of being awestruck by the older Ojibwe leader in his youth, to which he attributed his own determination to become a Methodist missionary: Copway, *Life, Letters and Speeches*, 64; Smith, *Mississauga Portraits*, 171.

61. See, for example, Jones, *Life and Journals*, 350.

62. *Christian Advocate and Journal and Zion's Herald*, 3 August 1832, 194.

63. See, for example, Shawundais's reports of his summer travels to the Detroit and Mackinaw areas, after the Penetanguishene councils in 1830 (transcribed in English by Peter Jones): *Christian Advocate and Journal and Zion's Herald*, 19 November 1830, 45; 26 November 1830, 49; and his 1831 stay at Sault Ste. Marie: *Christian Advocate and Journal and Zion's Herald*, 2 December 1831, 54.

64. On these prophetic traditions, see Gregory Evans Dowd, *A Spirited Resistance: The North American Indian Struggle for Unity, 1745–1815* (Baltimore: Johns Hopkins University Press, 1992).

65. *Christian Advocate and Journal and Zion's Herald*, 3 August 1832, 194.

66. See Janet E. Chute, *The Legacy of Shingwaukonse: A Century of Native Leadership* (Toronto: University of Toronto Press, 1998), 39–71.

67. G. Marsden to the Editor, 23 December 1833, *The Wesleyan-Methodist Magazine*, no. 13, February 1834, 138. Shingwaukonse's speech at the 1833 council was recounted to Marsden by Pahtahsega (Peter Jacobs). See also Benjamin Slight, *Indian Researches, or, Facts concerning the North American Indians: Including Notices of Their Present State of Improvement, in Their Social, Civil, and Religious Condition; with Hints for Their Future Advancement* (Montreal: J. E. L. Miller, 1844), 76–77; Chute, *The Legacy of Shingwaukonse*, 47–48.

68. Peter Jones to Egerton Ryerson, 24 July 1832, in *The Wesleyan-Methodist Magazine*, no. 11, November 1832, 832.

69. *Christian Advocate and Journal and Zion's Herald*, 27 August 1830, 205; *Christian Advocate and Journal and Zion's Herald*, 26 November 1830, 49.

70. *Christian Advocate and Journal and Zion's Herald*, 2 December 1831, 54.

71. Peter Jones to Egerton Ryerson, 24 July 1832, in *The Wesleyan-Methodist Magazine*, no. 11, November 1832, 832.

72. The Canadian Methodist began printing the gospel of Matthew in Ojibwe during the early 1830s, while the British and foreign William Case reported: "The Gospel of Matthew in Chip-pe-way, is now printing in this town, and the Gospel of John in the same language is printing in London" (*Christian Advocate and Journal and Zion's Herald*, 20 January 1832, 82). Peter Jones read from the gospel of John, "from the translation lately printed by the British and Foreign Bible Society in London" 24 July 1832: *The Wesleyan-Methodist Magazine*, no. 11, November 1832, 829.

73. *Christian Advocate and Journal and Zion's Herald*, 26 November 1830, 49.

74. *Christian Advocate and Journal and Zion's Herald*, 27 August 1830, 205.

75. Marsden letter, 23 December 1833, in *The Wesleyan-Methodist Magazine*, no. 13, February 1834, 139; Peter Jones to Egerton Ryerson, 24 July 1832, in *The Wesleyan-Methodist Magazine*, no. 11, November 1832, 832.

76. *Christian Advocate and Journal and Zion's Herald*, 20 January 1832, 82.

77. Henry Schoolcraft to William Case, 1 March 1833, cited by Case in *The Christian Guardian*, 8 May 1833: Smith, *Mississauga Portraits*, 227. See also Case to the Missionary Society of the Methodist Episcopal Church, 9 July 1832, in *Christian Advocate and Journal and Zion's Herald*, 3 August 1832. Peter Jones noted in his journal of the sole success of "Native speakers" in achieving conversions at the Sault: Jones, *Life and Journals*, 363.

78. William Lord, "The Canadian Conference," *The Wesleyan-Methodist Magazine*, no. 15, October 1836, 784.

79. See, for example, *The Wesleyan-Methodist Magazine*, no. 15, September 1836, 688; no. 16, September 1836, 669, 705.

80. Adamson, "God's Continent Divided," 424.

81. Jones, *Life and Journals*, 258.

82. Smith, *Mississauga Portraits*, 224–26; Semple, *Lord's Dominion*, 160.

83. Playter, *History of Methodism in Canada*, 341. See also *The New-York Spectator*, 25 April 1828.

84. Smith, *Mississauga Portraits*, 225–26.

85. Young, *Apostle of the North*, 55, 60.

86. For descriptions of Shawundais's eloquence in Anishinaabemowin, see, for example, *Christian Advocate and Journal and Zion's Herald*, 20 August 1830, 202; Slight, *Indian Researches*, 40.

87. Young, *Apostle of the North*, 55; Carroll, *Case and His Contemporaries*, 4:186.

88. At Shawundais's appearance in New York in 1828, for instance, "many hundreds who wished to gain admittance were disappointed" (*New-York Spectator*, 25 April 1828). For other descriptions of the interest generated by his visits to the United States and Britain, see *New-York Spectator*, 11 April 1828; *Daily National Journal*, 24 April 1829; *Aris's Birmingham Gazette*, 1 August 1836; *Berrow's Worcester Journal*, 11 August 1836; *The Bristol Mercury*, 4 March 1837; *Hereford Journal*, 15 March 1837.

89. On Peter Jones's dress, see Smith, *Sacred Feathers*, 167. On this idea of nonnative expectations of "Indianness" and American Indians using this to carve out a space for their own agency, see Philip Joseph Deloria, *Indians in Unexpected Places* (Lawrence: University Press of Kansas, 2004).

90. Robert Alder, *Wesleyan Missions: Their Progress Stated and Their Claims Enforced, with Observations and Suggestions Applicable to Kindred Institutions* (London: Wesleyan Missionary Society, 1842), 23–24.

91. On the prevailing Anglo-American presumption that Indigenous people were dying out, see, for example, Steven Conn, *History's Shadow: Native Americans and Historical Consciousness in the Nineteenth Century* (Chicago: University of Chicago Press, 2004).

92. *Christian Advocate and Journal and Zion's Herald*, 25 May 1832, 155.

93. The Methodist missions to Upper Canada and Indian country were, until 1828, under the direction of the American Methodist Episcopal Church and funded largely by American subscribers, though unlike British officials' speculations, they were not involved in republican political intrigues: Semple, *Lord's Dominion*, 160–61; Adamson, "God's Continent Divided."

94. Jones, *Life and Journals*, 106–07.

95. See, for example, Hempton, *Methodism*.

96. The purchase of this 3,500 acres of land, immediately south of Rice Lake, had made with the sale of the Bay of Quinte Ojibwe's title to the Big Island, which was of no other value to them as the British would not evict the settler-colonists living there: Smith, *Mississauga Portraits*, 230.

97. See Theodore Binnema and Kevin Hutchings, "The Emigrant and the Noble Savage: Sir Francis Bond Head's Romantic Approach to Aboriginal Policy in Upper Canada, 1836–1838," *Journal of Canadian Studies* 39, no. 1 (2005): 115–38.

98. See Zoë Laidlaw, "'Aunt Anna's Report': The Buxton Women and the Aborigines Select Committee, 1835–37," *Journal of Imperial and Commonwealth History* 32, no. 2 (2004): 1–28.

99. Aborigines Select Committee, *1837 (Final) Report*, Minutes of Evidence, 30.

100. Aborigines Select Committee, *1837 (Final) Report*, Minutes of Evidence, 29–31.

101. Shawundais or John Sunday to Lord Glenelg, 4 August 1837, PRO CO 42/441.

102. *Reading Mercury, Oxford Gazette and Berkshire County Paper, etc.*, 19 August 1837, emphasis original; *The Belfast News-letter*, 25 August 1837; *The Bristol Mercury*, 26 August 1837.

103. Shawundais or John Sunday to Lord Glenelg, 4 August 1837, PRO CO 42/441.

104. Shawundais or John Sunday to Lord Glenelg, 4 August 1837, PRO CO 42/441.

Indigenous Politics after the End of Empire

SHINO KONISHI

In her 2013 article, "Imperial Literacy and Indigenous Rights: Tracing Transoceanic Circuits of a Modern Discourse," Tracey Banivanua Mar, the late historian to whom this collection is dedicated, noted three coinciding moments of Indigenous political assertion in Tahiti, Australia, and New Zealand. In 1838, under the threat of French imperial expansion, Queen Pomare of Tahiti wrote to Queen Victoria entreating the British government to provide her people with military protection. Pomare justified her demand by explaining that it was Britain that had originally brought her island into contact with Europeans by "open[ing] to us two new entrances to two new worlds," Christianity and civilization, but that the latter had begun "to embitter our lives, and will ultimately deprive us even of the dominion of the graves of our ancestors."[1]

Two years later in Port Phillip, Banivanua Mar explains, Billibellary, a Woiwurrung clansman and Wurundjeri elder, gave a lengthy and spirited address to his people, who had gathered at the Narre Narre Warren station. The station was located on a remote block of land deemed undesirable by the settlers who had flocked to Melbourne in the late 1830s. It was collaboratively selected by the Wurundjeri and the newly formed Aboriginal protectorate as a reserve for the Aboriginal people on whose lands Melbourne had been founded. Here, the protectorate expected that the Aboriginal people could be quarantined from settlers and introduced to Christianity and civilization, whereas the Wurundjeri anticipated that they would have "an undisturbed possession for hunting" augmented by government supplies.[2] Soon, however, the Aboriginal residents realized that the protectorate had not upheld its side of the bargain, as the negotiated rations had not eventuated, so many Wurundjeri returned to Melbourne in search of work. In his speech, Billibellary convinced the remaining residents to walk off the station and pointedly camp close enough for the assistant protector, William Thomas, to be able to see the smoke from their fires, in what Banivanua Mar suggests was an overt demonstration of their continual "autonomy of movement."[3]

That same year, at Waitangi in Aotearoa, New Zealand, Māori and British gathered to debate a treaty. Previously "a group of Maori chiefs from the North Island declared themselves an independent confederacy, emulating similar activity that had taken place in Tahiti and Hawai'i," but this had been rejected, and by 1840 the British demanded that Māori leaders sign a treaty ceding sovereignty and granting the British Crown the preemptive right to purchase land. These debates became heated and soon "every chief refused to sign."[4] Banivanua Mar acknowledges that while "some would eventually sign what became known as the Treaty of Waitangi, others permanently withdrew their consent and refused the British appropriation of full sovereignty over Maori land and its inseparable people."[5]

In drawing together an analysis of these three separate and "seemingly isolated moments of protest," Banivanua Mar sought to highlight a broader process that was under way in the 1830s and 1840s, in which Indigenous leaders adapted British imperial discourses about "protection," "sovereignty," and "land."[6] She argued that these three sites of colonization were "interlinked colonial 'nodes'" that connected imperial interests in Indigenous land and labor across the Pacific. While she acknowledged that these moments of protest ultimately failed to prevent the "waves of colonization" that swept over the region, Banivanua Mar showed that these three disparate case studies reveal the way in which Indigenous peoples "continued to adapt local forms of political management to meet the increasingly insatiable imperial hunger for land, labour, resources and territory."[7] Although these three examples of Indigenous protests were coincidental rather than conducted in concert, Banivanua Mar suggested that this period in time was significant, as Indigenous peoples in different colonial contexts confronted the British empire, and demanded that its imperial agents face up to their responsibilities, deliver on their promises, or treat them fairly.

In many ways the chapters in this fine collection, *Facing Empire*, build on and expand Banivanua Mar's illuminating article. The diverse case studies illustrate the ways in which Indigenous people, during the Revolutionary Age—a period of intense imperial expansion and revolutionary foment—faced imperial powers, melding Western and Indigenous political techniques in different ways to best suit local interests and imperatives. The chapters in *Facing Empire* amplify Banivanua Mar's transnational approach, extending well beyond the Pacific and Australia to North America, Asia, the Persian Gulf, West Africa, the Cape of Good Hope, and even Scotland. In his illuminating chapter, Justin Brooks reminds us that eighteenth-century Britain had no "unified or consistent term" for the "peoples living at the frontiers of state expansion," and despite the many differences between peoples and cultures across the empire, all "native" communities "shared in a certain relationship to the expansion of the English state." Thus this collection also expands our presentist notions of indigeneity, a "fraught and contested" term, as Kate Fullagar and Michael A. McDonnell observe in their introduction. It does this not only by including Highland Scots as natives but also by highlighting the fluidities of names used to identify different Indigenous clans and groups. It examines how the process of colonization and ensuing imperial mobilities led to the emergence of new Indigenous nationalities, such as the Griqua in the northern Cape, who included "ex-slaves, renegade Europeans, Korana San, Khoesan and mixed Khoesan, who," as Nicole Ulrich explains, "claimed a common ancestor on political grounds."

Facing Empire's transnational approach teases out the complexities of imperial encounters, interactions, and negotiations with Indigenous peoples throughout this period, revealing that Indigenous people were not passive bystanders, but active agents during this revolutionary time, and significantly contributed to the making of the modern world. Such contributions took myriad forms. Chapters by McDonnell, Rebecca Shumway, Colin G. Calloway, and Tony Ballantyne explore the different ways in which Indigenous peoples took advantage of competing imperial interests, be it French against British or the differing agenda of traders, settlers, missionaries, colonial militias, and governments in New Zealand and North America in particular. These chapters reveal the shifting alliances that some Indigenous people made with Europeans or neighboring Indigenous tribes, forcing imperial powers to endure processes of negotiation, accommodation, and appeasement for much longer than they originally anticipated, and for longer than is commonly acknowledged in colonial historiography. In a more unexpected take on how Indigenous people contributed to the making of the modern world, Bill Gammage explores the ecological environment that Australian Aboriginal people made in the millennia before the arrival of the British. Rather than "discovering" an untamed wilderness, the British colonists who arrived in 1788 encountered a seeming parkland congenial to agriculture, which had been carefully constructed and maintained by

Aboriginal fire-management techniques that kept wild scrub at bay, encouraged new growth, and produced tracts of grassland that enticed local game. Similarly, Joshua L. Reid challenges a myopic focus on land in settler-colonial histories by instead exploring Indigenous concerns over the marine space, reminding us that the ocean and seas provided rich economic, cultural, and spiritual sustenance to Indigenous peoples, as well as to the eighteenth- and nineteenth-century imperial powers that were built on maritime travel and trade.

Perhaps what this collection does most powerfully, and beautifully, is introduce us to the Indigenous worlds, peoples, and cultures that the British encountered. Gammage and Jenny Newell depict the new environments and ecologies that the British entered into. Fullagar, McDonnell, and Ballantyne provide detailed portraits of individuals—Cherokee warrior Ostenaco, Ra'iatean traveler Mai, Odawa *ogimaa* Nissowaquet, and the Māori *rangatira* Te Pahi—who recognized or resisted the opportunities and threats, including future threats, that engaging with the British empire entailed. They show how each responded in very different and distinctive ways. Finally, Robert Kenny reinterprets frontier violence in Port Phillip, in particular Aboriginal attacks on livestock, in terms of Taungurung ontologies, as a ritual to negate the power of the settlers' totems. Such an approach, from an Australian perspective at least, works to further unsettle the initial imperial and colonial fantasies that the Australian continent was *terra nullius*, a land owned by no one, and a *tabula rasa* ready to be inscribed as a new Britain in the wake of territorial losses stemming from the American Revolution.

This book not only writes Indigenous people back into a history that generations of historians had left them out of, but it also refrains from oversimplifying Indigenous responses to European expansion as uniformly heroic or tragic, or overly beholden to Indigenous protocols or traditions. Instead, it depicts individuals who were supple and responsive to the vicissitudes wrought by British expansion. Like the characters that populate Banivanua Mar's work, we find people who adapted new political techniques derived from Indigenous customs and British practices, and also honored and/or exploited old and new loyalties, be it toward fellow clansmen, neighboring tribes, itinerant traders, warring European governments, or local imperial agents. What makes the histories explored in *Facing Empire* particularly significant is that they reveal the relatively little-known pasts to the ongoing struggles Indigenous people face today as they continue to engage with the legacies of British empire, especially in the settler-colonial states that remained after the end of empire.

The revolutionary era that this book spans was followed in many respects by an even more turbulent period for Indigenous peoples who were not only now thoroughly entangled with imperial interests and agencies but increasingly ensnared by settler-colonial governments. Across the new settler states that were becoming increasingly autonomous, Indigenous peoples were corralled to distant and ever-shrinking reservations, missions, and Bantustans, and subjected to new assimilationist policies that curtailed their mobility, freedom to express their cultures and languages, and individuals' ability to define their own identities by imposing racialized nomenclature or registration. Families were also ruptured as children were removed and sent to government institutions and boarding schools in order to expedite the assimilationist agenda.

Yet, the periods following the revolutionary age also witnessed new forms of organized Indigenous protest, especially in the second half of the twentieth century as states in North Africa, South and Southeast Asia, and the Pacific decolonized and became independent. Indigenous rights groups were increasingly organized and pan-Indigenous in form as they responded to local and national concerns. For example, the American Indian Movement was first organized in 1968 to defend the Treaty of Fort Laramie (1868) and continued their protests at different sites throughout the 1970s to demand the return of ancestral and sacred lands, and to highlight the squalid living conditions of urban and rural Native Americans.[8] In 1971, the young Māori group Nga Tamatoa sparked an ongoing and enduring annual demonstration when they protested against national Waitangi Day celebrations by performing a haka and wearing funeral dress to highlight the government's failures in honoring the treaty. They asserted that the "treaty cannot provide a basis for future race relations."[9] The next year, Australian Aboriginal activists staged the 1972 Tent Embassy to demonstrate the ongoing poverty, segregation, and denial of self-determination that Indigenous Australian people faced, bringing the demand for land rights to a national level.[10] Finally, the Springbok rugby team's tours of 1971 and 1981 saw Aboriginal and Māori activists join international anti-apartheid protestors, as both Indigenous groups expressed their solidarity with Black South Africans and sought to highlight the ongoing racism they experienced at home.[11] And, most recently, 2016–17 saw prolonged protests over the laying of the Dakota Access Pipeline, as hundreds of Native American groups stood in solidarity with the Standing Rock Sioux to oppose the pipeline, which crosses sacred burial sites and threatens their water supply. Newspapers reported that these protests "sparked a resurgence of the indigenous rights movement."[12]

This book does not just introduce us to the other side of the revolutionary era better known through its European protagonists. It also reveals just how revolutionary Indigenous responses to the British empire were, and, like Banivanua Mar's work, it offers a deeper understanding of the imperial-Indigenous relationships forged during the earlier stages of British expansion, and why it was so heartbreaking when these historic treaties and promises were eventually broken. Such a history also provides rich insights into why Indigenous demands for the return of land, protection of sacred sites, and restitution and social justice are still so heartfelt today.

Notes

1. Queen Pomare and Chiefs of Tahiti to Her Majesty Queen Victoria, 8 November 1838, Enclosure 3, No. 67, Mr. Consul Pritchard to Viscount Palmerston, 9 November 1838, TNA, FO 534/1 Foreign Office: Confidential Print Pacific Islands: Society Islands: Correspondence, cited in Tracey Banivanua Mar, "Imperial Literacy and Indigenous Rights: Tracing Transoceanic Circuits of a Modern Discourse," *Aboriginal History* 37 (2013): 5.

2. William Thomas, assistant protector, Westernport District, Narre Narre Warren to G. A. Robinson, chief protector of Aborigines, 26 September 1840, PROV, VPRS 11 Item 330, cited in Banivanua Mar, "Imperial Literacy and Indigenous Rights," 13.

3. Banivanua Mar, "Imperial Literacy and Indigenous Rights," 13.

4. Charles Wilkes, *Narrative of the United States Exploring Expedition during the Years 1838, 1839, 1840, 1841, 1842*, 5 vols. (London: Wiley and Putnam, 1845), 2:375, cited in Banivanua Mar, "Imperial Literacy and Indigenous Rights," 18.

5. Banivanua Mar, "Imperial Literacy and Indigenous Rights," 1.

6. Banivanua Mar, "Imperial Literacy and Indigenous Rights," 1.

7. Banivanua Mar, "Imperial Literacy and Indigenous Rights," 2.

8. Mary Ellen Snodgrass, *Civil Disobedience: An Encyclopedic History of Dissidence in the United States*, 2 vols. (London: Routledge, 2009), 1:13–21, and Elizabeth Cook-Lynn, "Twentieth-Century American Indian Political Dissent and Russell Means," *Wicazo Sa Review* 29, no. 1 (2014): 14–18.

9. Sharon McKenzie Stevens and Lachlan Paterson, "Nga Tamatoa and the Rhetoric of Brown Power: Re-Situating Collective Rhetorics in Global Colonialism," in *Teaching Writing in Globalization: Remapping Disciplinary Works*, ed. D. Payne and D. Desser (Lanham, MD: Lexington Books, 2011), 25.

10. See Gary Foley, Andrew Schaap, and Edwina Howell, eds., *The Aboriginal Tent Embassy: Sovereignty, Black Power, Land Rights and the State* (London: Routledge, 2014).

11. Nick Scott, "Black-Bans and Black Eyes: Implications of the 1971 Springbok Rugby Tour," *Labour History: A Journal of Labour and Social History* 108

(May 2015): 149, and Elizabeth Rankins, "Banners, Batons and Barbed Wire: Anti-apartheid Images of the Springbok Rugby Tour Protests in New Zealand," *de arte* 42, no. 76 (2007): 21–32.

12. May Bulman, "Standing Rock Protesters to Lead Washington DC March Urging Donald Trump to Discuss Indigenous Rights," *The Independent*, March 8, 2017, available at: http://www.independent.co.uk/news/world/americas/standing-rock-washington-dc-march-donald-trump-dakota-access-oil-pipeline-indigenous-rights-tribes-a7617371.html.

CONTRIBUTORS

Tony Ballantyne is a professor of history, Pro-Vice-Chancellor, Humanities, and co-director of the Centre for Research on Colonial Culture at the University of Otago in Dunedin, New Zealand. He has published extensively on colonial knowledge production, on the networks and forms of mobility that shaped the British empire, and on the connections between religion and colonialism. His books include *Orientalism and Race: Aryanism in the British Empire* (2002), *Between Colonialism and Diaspora: Sikh Cultural Formations in an Imperial World* (2006), *Webs of Empire: Locating New Zealand's Colonial Past* (2012), *Empires and the Reach of the Global: 1870–1945* (with A. Burton, 2012), and *Entanglements of Empire: Missionaries, Māori, and the Question of the Body* (2014). He is an elected fellow of the Royal Society of New Zealand.

Justin Brooks is a PhD candidate in history at Yale University. His research considers the evolving relationship between Indigenous peoples and the early modern British Empire—an interest he developed while obtaining his bachelor's degree in history from College of the Holy Cross, serving as a Fulbright Scholar at the University of Melbourne, and pursuing a master's degree in world and international history from Columbia University and the London School of Economics. His dissertation, undertaken with the support of Yale's Fox International Fellowship, explores the entangled transformation of Britain's native policies across the eighteenth-century Scottish Highlands, North America, and Bengal.

Colin G. Calloway is the John Kimball Jr. 1943 Professor of History and Native American Studies at Dartmouth College. He received his PhD from Leeds University; taught in England, at a high school in Vermont, and at the University of Wyoming; and was assistant director of the D'Arcy McNickle Center at the Newberry Library. His books include: *The Indian World of George Washington* (2018); *The Victory with No Name: The Native American Defeat of the First American Army* (2015); *Pen and Ink Witchcraft: Treaties and Treaty Making in American Indian History* (2013); *"White People, Indians, and Highlanders": Tribal Peoples and Colonial*

Encounters in Scotland and North America (2008); *The Scratch of a Pen: 1763 and the Transformation of North America* (2006); *One Vast Winter Count: The Native American West before Lewis and Clark* (2003), which won six "best book" awards; *New Worlds for All: Indians, Europeans, and the Remaking of Early America* (1997, 2013); *The American Revolution in Indian Country* (1995); *The Western Abenakis of Vermont* (1990); *Crown and Calumet: British-Indian Relations, 1783–1815* (1987); and *First Peoples* (1999, 2004, 2008, 2012, 2016, 2019).

Kate Fullagar is a senior lecturer in modern history at Macquarie University, Sydney. Her most recent books include *The Savage Visit: New World Peoples and Popular Imperial Culture in Britain, 1710–1795* (2012) and (as editor) *The Atlantic World in the Antipodes: Effects and Transformations since the Eighteenth Century* (2012). She is currently completing a book on three different eighteenth-century lives—those of Ostenaco, Mai, and the artist who painted them both, Joshua Reynolds. She is also leading a project on the comparative nexus of portraiture and biography with both the National Portrait Gallery of Australia and the Smithsonian National Portrait Gallery.

Bill Gammage AO is emeritus professor in the Humanities Research Centre at the Australian National University (ANU). He was an ANU undergraduate and postgraduate before teaching history at the Universities of Papua New Guinea (1966, 1972–76) and Adelaide (1977–96). He wrote *The Broken Years: Australian Soldiers in the Great War* (1974), which went on to inspire the famous Peter Weir film *Gallipoli* (1981). He is also the author of *An Australian in the First World War* (1976), *Narrandera Shire* (1986), *Australians 1938* (1988), and *The Sky Travellers: Journeys in New Guinea 1938–1939* (1998). His most recent book, *The Biggest Estate on Earth: How Aborigines Made Australia* (2011), won several major awards, including the Prime Minister's Prize for Australian History in 2012. He was made a member of the Order of Australia in 2005.

Robert Kenny is currently associated with the Contemporary History Research group at Deakin University and is a research associate at the Centre for Inland Studies at La Trobe University. He has published widely on the histories of religion, of science, and of colonial encounters, often combining the fields. His most recent book, *Gardens of Fire* (2013), won the Victorian Community History Publication Award in 2014. *The Lamb Enters the Dreaming: Nathanael Pepper and the Ruptured World* (2007) won the 2008 Prime Minister's Prize for Australian History, the Australian Historical Association's W. K. Hancock Prize, the Victorian Premier's Award for History, and the Australia Centre's Peter Blazey Award. His current major research projects include a study of the relationship between psychology and anthropology in the late nineteenth and early twentieth centuries, and an investigation of the memory of the settlement of/in north-central Victoria.

Shino Konishi is an Australian Research Council research fellow in the School of Humanities at the University of Western Australia, where she is embarking on a new collaborative research project with the *Australian Dictionary of Biography* on Indigenous biography. Her publications include *The Aboriginal Male in the Enlightenment World* (2012), and the coedited collections *Representing Humanity in the Age of Enlightenment* (2013), *Indigenous Intermediaries: New Perspectives on Exploration Archives* (2015), and *Brokers and Boundaries: Colonial Exploration in Indigenous Territory* (2016). She is the former editor of *Aboriginal History* (2010–14) and a member of the National Indigenous Research and Knowledges Network. She is Aboriginal and descends from the Yawuru people of Broome, Western Australia.

Elspeth Martini is an assistant professor of history at Montclair State University. She received her PhD from the University of Michigan in 2013 and was a Kenneth P. Dietrich School of Arts and Sciences postdoctoral fellow in the Department of History at the University of Pittsburgh from 2013 to 2015. Her book manuscript in progress examines the influence of early nineteenth-century Anglo-American humanitarianism on Indigenous policy in the United States and British settler colonies. Originally from Australia, she received her undergraduate history and law degrees from the University of Melbourne. Her research interests include Native American and Indigenous sovereignty, US and British imperial cultures, and the nineteenth-century United States and world.

Michael A. McDonnell is a professor of history at the University of Sydney. He received his DPhil at Oxford University in 1996. He is the author of *The Politics of War: Race, Class, and Social Conflict in Revolutionary Virginia* (2007), which won the New South Wales Premier's History Prize in 2008, and (as coeditor) *Remembering the Revolution: Memory, History, and Nation Making from Independence to the Civil War* (2013). He has published numerous articles on the American Revolution and won the Lester Cappon Prize for the best article published in the *William and Mary Quarterly* in 2006. His work is featured in the Organization of American Historians' *Best American History Essays* (2008). His most recent, award-winning, book is titled *Masters of Empire: The Great Lakes Indians and the Making of America* (2015).

Jennifer Newell is comanager of the Pacific collection at the Australian Museum. Dr. Newell has previously worked at the American Museum of Natural History in New York and at the National Museum of Australia in Canberra, as a research fellow in the Centre for Historical Research (2008–12), and as an assistant curator in the Oceanic section of the British Museum in London (2001–08). Her first book, *Trading Nature: Tahitians, Europeans, and Ecological Exchange* (2010), explores the environmental and cultural implications of the exchange of plants and animals across Tahiti's shores in the eighteenth and nineteenth centuries. *Pacific Art in Detail* (2011), Newell's second book, is an introduction to the arts of the Pacific, presented through the contextualization of key objects in the British Museum's Pacific collection. She has a PhD in history from the Australian National University.

Joshua L. Reid (Snohomish) is an associate professor of history and American Indian studies at the University of Washington. He earned his doctorate in history at the University of California, Davis. His first monograph, *The Sea Is My Country: The Maritime World of the Makahs* (2015), has received awards and recognition from the Organization for American Historians, American Society for Ethnohistory, the Western History Association, and the North American Society for Oceanic History. Reid currently edits Yale's Henry Roe Cloud Series on American Indians and Modernity, serves on the editorial board of the *Pacific Northwest Quarterly*, and is a distinguished speaker for the WHA. Reid's next monograph project examines Indigenous explorers in the Pacific, from the late eighteenth century to the end of the nineteenth century. He is editing a volume of photographs of American Indian activist occupations and a volume about Indigenous communities and violence.

Daniel K. Richter is Roy F. and Jeannette P. Nichols Professor of American History and the Richard S. Dunn Director of the McNeil Center for Early American Studies at the University of Pennsylvania. His research and teaching focus on Colonial North America and on Native American history before 1800. He holds a PhD from Columbia University and taught previously at Dickinson College and the University of East Anglia. His most recent publication is *Before the Revolution: America's Ancient Pasts* (2011). His first book, *The Ordeal of the Longhouse: The Peoples of the Iroquois League in the Era of European Colonization* (1992), won the 1993 Frederick Jackson Turner Award and the 1993 Ray Allen Billington Prize, and was selected as a 1994 Choice Outstanding Academic Book. His *Facing East from Indian Country: A Native History of Early America* (2001) won the 2001–02 Louis Gottschalk Prize in Eighteenth-Century History and was a finalist for the Pulitzer Prize. Richter is also coeditor (with James Merrell) of *Beyond the Covenant Chain: The Iroquois and their Neighbors in Indian North America, 1600–1800* (2003) and (with William Pencak) *Friends and Enemies in Penn's Woods: Indians, Colonists, and the Racial Construction of Pennsylvania* (2004).

Rebecca Shumway is assistant professor in the Department of History at the College of Charleston and a specialist in the history of precolonial West Africa and the Atlantic world. Her publications include *The Fante and the Transatlantic Slave Trade* (2011), a study of the Fante society of coastal Ghana during the eighteenth century, and *Slavery and Its Legacy in Ghana and the Diaspora* (2017), a volume coedited with Trevor R. Getz that examines slavery, antislavery, and the lasting effects of slavery in Ghana and its diaspora. Dr. Shumway is currently working on a book project that examines the evolution of antiracist intellectual discourse and black identity on the Gold Coast in the nineteenth century.

Sujit Sivasundaram is reader in world history and fellow of Gonville and Caius College at the University of Cambridge. He is the author of *Nature and the Godly Empire: Science and Evangelical Mission in the Pacific* (2005), which opened a broader set of concerns regarding how to reshape the discipline of the history of science to encompass non-European voices, sources, and connections. His second book is *Islanded: Britain, Sri Lanka, and the Bounds of an Indian Ocean Colony* (2013). He is currently completing an account of the age of revolutions in the Indian and Pacific Oceans. This research has been supported by the award of a Philip Leverhulme Prize for world history. He is coeditor of *The Historical Journal.*

Nicole Ulrich is a senior lecturer in the History Department at Rhodes University, South Africa. She received her PhD from the Wits Institute of Social and Economic Research (WISER) at University of the Witwatersrand. Dr. Ulrich is a labor historian and has previously researched the Industrial Commercial Union (ICU) in the 1920s and trade unions in the 1970s. She is currently working on a book project dealing with popular insurgency in the Cape Colony during the Age of Revolution. Dr. Ulrich has contributed to the *International Encyclopedia of Revolution and Protest* and the *Palgrave Dictionary of Transnational History* and has published journal articles and book chapters on a range of topics. She has held a visiting scholar's fellowship at the University of Cambridge and is currently an associate of the History Workshop at University of the Witwatersrand and the Neil Aggett Labour Unit, Rhodes University.

INDEX